# Endless Forms

# Endless Forms

## The Secret World of Wasps

## Seirian Sumner

**WILLIAM
COLLINS**

William Collins
An imprint of HarperCollins*Publishers*
1 London Bridge Street
London SE1 9GF

WilliamCollinsBooks.com

HarperCollins*Publishers*
1st Floor, Watermarque Building, Ringsend Road
Dublin 4, Ireland

First published in Great Britain in 2022 by William Collins

1

A catalogue record for this book is
available from the British Library

HB ISBN 978-0-00-839447-9
TPB ISBN 978-0-00-839448-6

Typeset in Adobe Garamond Pro
Printed and bound in the UK using 100%
renewable electricity at CPI Group (UK) Ltd

To my parents, Frances and Graham,
for their endless love and support

# CONTENTS

Introduction                                                    1

Part One:     *The Problem with Wasps*                          9

Part Two:     *The Obsessions of Wasp Whisperers*             47

Part Three:   *How to Have a Social Life*                     105

Part Four:    *Playing the Game*                             143

Part Five:    *Dinner with Aristotle*                        195

Part Six:     *Nature's Pest Controllers*                    269

Part Seven:   *The Secret Pollinators*                       309

Last Word:    *A Future with Wasps*                          335

Notes                                                        347
Acknowledgements                                             367
List of Illustrations                                        373
Index                                                        375

# INTRODUCTION

... and books that told me everything about
the wasp, except why.

Dylan Thomas (1952)

When I was three years old, I lived in a tiny, forgotten village in West Wales called Cribyn. It's easily missed on the map. But at the time it was my whole world.

I remember the garden. A very damp garden. It was Wales. It may have been due to the dampness, or perhaps my father's home brew that bubbled away on the patio, but the garden had a lot of slugs. To be honest, my memories of it are hazy but I remember the slugs because one day I ate one. My mother was horrified. After all, slugs, she told me, are revolting creatures.

People pour salt on slugs when they leave their silvery trails on patios or lettuces, without considering how nature needs them or what they do for us behind the scenes. People throw other kinds of chemicals at other bits of nature they don't like. My toddler-self wondered why people didn't just eat the bits of nature they wanted to get rid of.

This book is not about slugs. I don't really have much time for slugs anymore. But maybe, deep down, the reason I am so fascinated with wasps is because of the slug, the one I ate in a lost village, in damp, beautiful Wales.

You see, people hate slugs, just as they hate spiders, worms, leeches, ticks. And wasps. Maybe my garden slug incident explains why I graduated so rapidly from an interest in slugs to birds, bypassing the other creepy-crawlies that the world had taught me not to like. This included wasps. I didn't like wasps at all. When wasps came near, I flapped. I screamed. I swatted. I ran. Just like you, perhaps. Ever since you were three.

Then one day I found myself lying flat on the jungle floor of a Malaysian rainforest with a wasp nest dangling above my nose. For my PhD, I had painted each wasp with a few spots so that I could distinguish one from another. I'd been watching my painted insects for several weeks: I saw them being born, I saw them fight for a place in society, I saw some rise to motherhood and others submit to a life of hard labour. Then it was done: in my wonder at their doings, I fell in love with the least-loved, most enigmatic of insects – the wasp.

Twenty-five years later, I am still asking questions about wasps, but (lamentably) mostly from my office at University College London, rather than a tropical jungle. The deeper I wonder, the more questions (and wasps) I find: why are there so many species? Why are wasps so diverse in form and function? How are they able to manipulate other insects so effectively? Why have wasps evolved societies so complex that they make ours look like childhood role play? Why are we not better harnessing the services of wasps as vital predators of pests?

When I explain to strangers what I do for a living, they ask a different set of questions: why should we care about wasps? What do they do for us? Why do you study them? Why don't you study something more useful … like bees? I explain that wasps are nature's pest controllers, that they are probably more diverse even than beetles, that a world without wasps would be just as devastating as a world without bees, or beetles, or butter-flies. My new friends shuffle with all the grace of a plastic bag at an organic food market. Yet on hearing the 'bee' word, they spot their chance of recovery and seize it to tell me how much they love bees. Safe territory. Wasps are forgotten, slipped into the recycling bin like unopened junk mail; my friends are relieved that the (wasp) conversation is over.

I can't blame them. Bees are good, and cute and useful. We love them, and rightly so. However, there are a mere 22,000 species of bees and there are over 100,000 species of wasps. Still, it is almost impossible to walk into a bookshop these days and *not* bump into a beautiful book about bees. Written by journalist, science writer or academic, there is a bee book to set any flavour of consumer buzzing. These tomes bounce off the media storms that have been generated by a burgeoning body of new science on the importance of bees, the plight of bee populations and the catastrophic effects that their decline is likely to have on our health, food security and happiness. It is not surprising that read-ers have an insatiable appetite for books about these adorable, *helpful* organisms.

In stark contrast to bees, wasps are depicted as the gangsters of the insect world; winged thugs; inspiration for horror movies; the 'sting' in the tale of thriller novels; conduits of biblical punishment. Shakespeare, Pope Francis, Aristotle, even Darwin struggled to speak favourably of wasps, and questioned the purpose of their existence. Scientists have been victims of this culture too, shunning wasps as research subjects despite the endless forms of these creatures that remain to be studied. It seems the root of this hatred is the wasp's sting,* its eagerness to

---

* Bees sting too!

keep on stinging,* and its apparent pointlessness in the natural world.

For most people, wasps are the yin (dark side) to the yang (sunny side) of the bee. This analogy from Chinese philosophy is appropriate on many levels: it describes our feelings about wasps (negative) and bees (positive). It articulates our perceptions of how useful wasps (not useful) and bees (very useful) are to us. It also describes the complementary roles in ecosystems of bees (as pollinators) and wasps (as predators). The importance of wasps as predators has gone largely unappreciated, and this is one of my reasons for writing this book. Wasps are important in ecological and economic terms; they have as many 'sunny sides' as bees do, with their fascinating social behaviour, their beauty and diversity, and their evolutionary importance as the ancestral root to all bees and ants.

Wasps hold hidden treasures of relevance to our own culture, survival, health and happiness. The 'bee story' was written by wasps before bees even evolved, and before wasps had shown humans how to make the paper on which the first bee book could be written. This book aims to balance the scales, to pull up a chair for wasps at the nature table of appreciation, and to transform the macabre repulsion that people have for wasps into the fascination and appreciation that wasps deserve.

If you love bees, this book may bring uncomfortable news: bees are simply wasps that have forgotten how to hunt. The 'original bee' was a solitary wasp who turned vegetarian, replacing the protein of meat with the protein of plants – pollen – and so kick-starting the bees' long co-evolutionary relationship with plants. This evolutionary shift in diet was not the birth of 'usefulness', though: the ancestor of the 'original bee' had proved

---

* Most bees also keep on stinging you too; it is only the highly barbed sting of the honeybee that gets stuck in your flesh, ripping out the innards of the insect when they try to detach themselves from you.

equally important in the environment as a master regulator of other insect and arthropod populations.

Wasps are also ancestors of ants: the first ant was a wasp that lost its wings. Today's solitary hunting wasps provide us with glimpses of what the original bee and original ant would have been like. Wasps are a time machine, ready to reveal the evolutionary secrets of one of the most diverse animal groups and some of the most complex societies on earth. While there are at least 100,000 known species of wasps, there are probably several million undescribed species waiting in the taxonomists' wings, and still their diversity has gone largely overlooked. The label of 'wasp' sits squarely under the shadow of the yellow-and-black-striped picnic-botherer of most people's imagination. New data and techniques in molecular biology (genome sequencing) that permit fine-scale dissection of evolutionary relationships (phylogenies) have revolutionised species detection. It is becoming clear that wasps rival beetles not just in the number of species, but also in diversity of form and function. This science is making us think again about which of the insect groups really do run the planet.

My view of wasps was changed on that damp forest floor of a Malaysian jungle by the drama of their societies. Despite their little brains, wasps live out soap-opera-style existences that sweep our television equivalents into the wings. Divisions of labour, rebellions and policing, monarchies, leadership contests, ASBOs, negotiators, social parasites, undertakers … wasp societies have it all. These citadels are products of evolution, and understanding why and how they evolved has been the driving force of my personal journey into the enigmatic world of wasps. Wasp social behaviour is genuinely fascinating, perhaps because of the parallels they share with our own social lives.

The most widely recognised bee is the western honeybee – *Apis mellifera*. Thanks to a millennia-long, close cultural relationship between human and honeybee, we know a lot about the behaviour and life history of this species, and how to harness its 'usefulness' as pollinator and supplier of nutrition. By contrast, wasps have been scholastically neglected, and consequently our understanding of these remarkable creatures is lamentable. A good example is the honeybee of the wasp world – the yellowjacket wasp, *Vespula vulgaris* – which is simultaneously the most recognised wasp and the most despised insect across the globe. Over 150 years ago, Sir John Lubbock (1st Baron Avebury, and Charles Darwin's neighbour) suggested that yellowjackets might be cleverer than honeybees. Astonishingly, we still know very little about the cognitive abilities of wasps but they are likely to be as impressive as those of bees, if not more so, as their prey is harder to catch. Insights into the remarkable social behaviours of the yellowjacket will surprise you.

Globally, bees are worth around $350 billion annually as crop pollinators. What's the economic value of wasps? We don't know. But we do know that wasps are voracious predators. They eat a wide range of insects (and a lot of them), many of which will be pest species in agricultural landscapes. Some wasps are already valued for this role, such as parasitoid wasps, which have been exploited as agents of biocontrol across the globe. You might even have bought some yourself, to rid your house of the dreaded clothes moth.

But the insects that most people identify as wasps – the hunting wasps, like the picnic-bothering yellowjacket *Vespula* – are not currently valued for their pest-controlling power. Scientists have not calculated how many tonnes of insect pests wasps remove from agricultural landscapes, nor the extent to which wasps may offer an economically viable alternative to chemicals as biocontrol agents. It is only now that we are beginning to appreciate the breadth of natural capital that is wrapped up in our planet's biodiversity. Unwrap the wasps, and you may be amazed by their potential as biocontrol agents within a sustainable global agriculture that relies less on chemicals.

Some of evolution's most mind-blowing stories are of wasps as pollinators. Take fig wasps, for example: without these minuscule insects there would be no figs (or figgy pudding!). Some orchids have evolved to mimic (chemically and physically) a rather sexy-looking female wasp. The orchid doesn't just look like a sexy female, it *smells* like one. Male wasps swoon helplessly from one flower to another, casually spreading orchid pollen along with their own fair seeds. Other orchids release a floral smell, mimicking that of a plant being attacked by juicy caterpillars. Greedy yellowjacket wasps detect these cues and come flocking in hope of picking off a tasty protein punch, only to be disappointed and inadvertently smothered with pollen. Apart from these extraordinary tales, wasp pollination is a much neglected subject. And this is despite there being an entire subfamily of wasps that feed *only* on pollen. Even their name – 'pollen wasps' – has failed to divert the interests of pollination biologists from the bee, fly and butterfly mainstays.

At the pearly gates of invertebrate heaven, how might the good deeds of wasps stack up against those of bees, beetles, butterflies or even slugs? Wasps are exquisitely endless in form and function, and (probably) more species-rich than any other animal group. Their behaviours are secretive, surprising and mysterious; their societies are equally as wondrous as those of the much-loved honeybee. Wasps are stewards of our ecosystems as pest controllers, pollinators, seed-dispersers and guardians of micro-organisms. They may bring sumptuous feasts to our tables, could be measuring sticks of planetary health, and they are medicine cabinets waiting to be discovered.

My hope is that this book will unravel the mysteries of wasps; that it will challenge your perceptions of them; that it will give you reasons to value them; and that it will stir new heraldry for these undiscovered gems of nature. In 1952, the poet Dylan Thomas recounted, with the confusing simplicity of childhood, his memories of Christmases in Wales. Among pointless presents of perceived importance were 'books that told me everything about the wasp, except why'.

This is the book that will tell you why wasps – the most enigmatic of insects – deserve a closer look.

# Part One

# *The Problem with Wasps*

If I be waspish, best beware my sting.

William Shakespeare,
*The Taming of the Shrew*

# Prelude

The problem with wasps is people. We are often rather ignorant. It's not our fault: there is a lot to take in and understand about this rich, bountiful planet. We are easily distracted; we make rash judgements based on limited experiences. We are simply trying to make sense of a complicated world. We are curious creatures, knowledge-thirsty. But a little knowledge is dangerous.

Take me and my slug. When I was three, society taught me that slugs are revolting; I extrapolated that negative, mucosal, social construct to all invertebrates.

Until I was rescued by wasps.

Part 1 of this book may surprise you. I hope it does. Please read it all to the end, otherwise you might find the rest of the book too unbelievable.

# I

'This is probably the weirdest phone call you'll ever have,' said Amit. 'I want the victim's sewn-up eyelids to *undulate, squirm* and *bulge*. And then big, gruesome wasps to burst out!' He continued, elated, 'Is this even possible? What wasp? How?'

Thriller writer Amit Dhand was surprised to hear that of course there was a wasp that could do this. With so many species, there was going to be something that evolution had cooked up to fit his script. Perhaps a spider-hunting wasp, something like a pompilid, and probably a tropical species, as they tend to be the biggest ones.

'But how will they breathe under the sealed eyelid?' he asked. 'What will they eat?' Amit was anxious. Sceptical.

The eye could be a source of nutrition for a developing wasp, I explained. As with its natural protein source – paralysed spider prey – the pompilid wasp could lay an egg on the eye; the egg would hatch into a larva, which would feed off the eye tissue, before pupating (like a caterpillar chrysalis) and finally emerging as an adult. If wasp biology was not quite sensational enough for Amit's readers, perhaps some of the colloquial names for pompilids might seal the bid – they've been called *throat locker*, *horse-killer*. Amit couldn't quite believe that such a solution for his gruesome storyline existed (albeit with a little artistic licence). What he had been asking for wasn't science fiction – it was evolution.

In fact, Amit could have chosen any one of some 5,000 species of pompilid wasps to star in his thriller. Some of the tropical species are the size of a small bird – you can hear them coming, their wings helicopter-humming. They have one of the most potent insect venoms and are able to paralyse the largest tarantulas. Their speed, life-freezing venom and skittish behaviour enable them to capture spiders several times their own size. A single sting renders their prey as putty in the mother wasp's mandibles; then she will drag the spider into a pre-prepared lair and lay a single egg on it. By the time the baby wasp is munching through its personal living larder, its mother has long since moved on to hunting and provisioning more offspring. It's a military operation, with no room for nurture.

Amit Dhand is not the first writer to have capitalised on our gruesome fascination with the behaviour of wasps. They feature in dozens of novels. Agatha Christie uses wasp poison as a murder weapon in her 1928 crime story, 'Wasps' Nest'. Eric Frank Russell's 1957 science fiction novel *Wasp* plays on the panic and damage that a wasp can cause in an enclosed space, to unfold a story about how a small, insignificant infiltrator from earth can destroy an alien civilisation. Russell's book has been described as a terrorists' handbook, and has disturbing parallels with the 9/11 attacks on America over 40 years later. Even Shakespeare teaches us to beware of waspish behaviour (mostly from women).

Expression of the fear, revulsion and horror we feel in the company of wasps goes back even earlier to some of the oldest literature. Almost 2,500 years ago, Aristophanes, the 'Father of Comedy', wrote *The Wasps* (422 BC), a work considered to be one of the greatest comedies of all time, named after the jurors in the play who cause trouble by inflicting a collective power over society. Wasps feature in religion too. God sends swarms of wasps to punish unbelievers in at least three books of the Bible. He was quite specific about the kind of wasp He summoned – it was always a hornet. Unfortunately, hornets don't often swarm. Maybe He got them confused with honeybees. Following in these biblical footsteps, Pope Paul IV was pope for just four years (between 1555 and 1559), but he squeezed in a holy hit at the wasp: 'Anger is as a stone cast at a wasps' nest.' This is indeed an accurate description of what happens if you throw stones at wasp nests (by accident or intentionally), but the same insect-fuelled anger would be elicited if you threw a stone at a bees' nest.

A Senegalese Creation story depicts wasps as the 'Eve' among animals. All the animals are asked to look away while God continues his work of creating the world, but the wasp can't resist taking a forbidden peek. To punish the creature, God pinches her around the waist: 'He squeezed the body at the waist so thin, so that it could neither hold a pregnancy nor pass an offspring … Henceforth the wasp was doomed to never know the joys of birth.'

The 'wasp waist' is indeed a signature trait of wasps, and one that distinguishes them from their cousins, the bees. This Creation story goes on to tell us that the wasp has 'divine know-how' and that it constructs a nest into which it places the worm-like larvae of other insects, and from these it rears its offspring. That is a pretty accurate description of the life cycle of many solitary wasps, who provision their nests with other insects, often 'worm-like' caterpillars. Potter wasps are especially fond of nesting on the mud-hut walls of rural Africa: this Creation story was clearly informed by the observations of early entomologists.

Such literary references – historic and contemporary – have capitalised on our generic, cultural fear of wasps and our stereo-typically (negative) emotional response to them. The wasp has long been a powerful metaphor for an evil, devious character who does no good. While reinforcing a negative image of wasps, this has also perpetuated many misunderstandings about their life history and behaviour. The same ingrained cultural senti-ment has spilled onto the silver screen too. The 1959 film *The Wasp Woman* topped the bill from a cultural and scientific perspective: a woman overdoses on an anti-ageing formula made from the royal jelly of a queen wasp, and at night she transforms into a murderous 'wasp-like' creature who devours (mostly) men.

*The Wasp Woman* is gloriously cardboard in appearance and plot. But its creators clearly had an idea of what type of wasp their lovely screen star should emulate (that is, a yellowjacket 'picnic' wasp) and they appear to have understood that the insect's appearance and behaviour can be manipulated through its secretions and nutrition. Royal jelly (often described less grandly as 'white snot') is produced from the glands of honeybee workers and fed to all of the brood when they are young, but it is only fed to those older larvae that are destined to be new queens. It is the honeybee's secret ingredient that catapults a

STARRING
**SUSAN CABOT · FRED EISLEY · BARBOURA MORRIS**
Produced and Directed by ROGER CORMAN · Written by LEO GORDON

larva down a queen's (not worker's) developmental pathway. What a great biology-inspired spin for a film about a Wasp Woman whose behaviour is altered by this magic jelly.

Unfortunately, wasps don't make royal jelly. In fact, we have very little idea how queen and worker castes are determined in wasps. There is probably some kind of cue that triggers the different developmental pathways and it is likely to be a nutritional one, as in the honeybee; but so far no one has looked at what this could be in yellowjacket wasps. The closest thing to royal jelly known in wasps is an abdominal substance produced by an unusual group found in Southeast Asia, the Stenogastrinae, or hover wasps. They are delightfully gentle, delicate creatures and you'd be excused for mistaking them for hoverflies, for that is what they do a lot: they hover. They also sport an exceedingly long and slender wasp waist, making them one of the wasp supermodels; and (like supermodels) they have a number of behavioural peculiarities, one of which is their egg-laying behaviour.

'Normal' wasps (like a yellowjacket or solitary hunting wasp) lay their egg directly onto the intended substrate (which could be a spider, caterpillar or the bottom of a cell). Not so for the hover wasp. When a hover wasp female is ready to lay an egg, she performs an enviable yoga move that unites her bottom with her mouth parts; a sticky gelatinous material is squeezed out of her abdomen, which she clasps in her mandibles. A second yoga move (that involves rotating her sting up at right angles) deposits an egg onto this blob. The 'egg and blob' unit is then carefully glued to the bottom of an empty cell.

We don't really know what is so special about this abdominal substance and why hover wasps do things differently to all the other wasps, but it probably has nutritional functions for the brood, as well as forming a secure base on which to anchor a precious egg. Sticking with the royal jelly theme, therefore, a film entitled *The Bee Woman* would have been scientifically sounder but lack that lustrous alliteration, and was incompatible with the lead role transforming into a man-eating woman (bees being strict vegetarians). With such divisive messages bestowed on wasps via literature, art and film, it is hardly surprising that they are perceived with great hostility by most people.

The most famous literary mention of wasps is probably Iain Banks's 1984 novel *The Wasp Factory*, which isn't about wasps except for a couple of passages about a disturbed teenager taunting captive wasps in the attic of his estranged family's home. Banks is one of my favourite authors, yet there are only so many copies of *The Wasp Factory* that I can keep on my bookshelf. It is one of those books that I keep being given by people who have not actually read it themselves, but they know I study wasps and assume that I need a copy.

*The Wasp Factory* was Banks's first novel and was designed to get him some attention. It did. The book's protagonist is a psychopathic multi-murderer, unknowingly transgender teenager called Frank Cauldhame who spends his time carrying out ritual killings of animals on a remote Scottish island, loosely based on the Isle of Islay. It is gruesomely compelling and a satisfying read if you're into full-spectrum societal depravity, but it's disappointing if you're hoping for insights into wasps. The novel's title refers to a kind of mini-beast torture chamber that Frank has built and hidden away in the attic. He uses it to subject yellowjacket wasps to unpleasant 'choice-chambers' of doom: a Russian roulette of options to choose from. How shall the wasp die today? Burned alive, crushed or drowned in urine? The wasps are just a sideshow to the storyline really – one of many heinous outlets for Frank's revenge on his anguished and disturbed life. Pitched alongside animal sacrifices, child murders and the maggot-riddled brains of a baby, the prolonged torture and untimely death of a few wasps is probably the least disturbing part of the book.

Imagine it wasn't wasps that Frank put in his torture factory, but bees: imagine Frank snatching poor hard-working honeybees from their daily labour of floral love and subjecting them to the same hideous ends that his wasps suffer. Ah-ha! Now the emotions tumble: 'That poor bee! What an evil, evil boy!' Why do you feel this way about bees but not wasps? It may be because you know how useful and important bees are for pollination, or perhaps it's the special relationship we humans have with the honeybee: our favourite domesticated insect, provider of honey and exhibitor of social pleasantries that we can relate to.

After over 20 years of studying wasps, I had grown weary of the universal opinions of people about how they loathe wasps. I felt sure that there were people out there like me, who appreciated wasps for what they do and who didn't see why wasps should be treated differently to bees. With two fellow wasp-fanatics, Alessandro Cini and Georgia Law, I concocted a plan to get to the bottom of why people felt such repugnance about wasps. We used the power of the internet to probe the emotions of the public towards wasps and bees, and to examine their understanding of what these insects do in ecosystems.

The results proved good news for bees: from a pool of 750 people, almost all respondents scored bees as highly positive on a scale of emotions, indicating that they were big fans. Our respondents used productive, positive words like 'honey', 'buzz' and 'flowers' to describe them. People also scored bees very highly on their 'value' to the environment as pollinators, but gave them very low scores for their contributions as predators. This was great news: the public have an excellent knowledge of what bees do (and don't do) in nature.

What about wasps? My worst fears were confirmed. The emotional responses to wasps were a mirror image to those for bees: almost everyone rated wasps with a negative 'emotion score'. Overwhelmingly, people used the same single word to describe wasps: STING! But, most concerning, people had no idea what wasps do in ecosystems. It was as if our respondents had plucked their scores from a lucky dip, blindfolded: the ratings they gave wasps for both 'predation' and 'pollination' were no different from random.

Everything made sense: people felt negatively about wasps because wasps sting *and* because wasps are perceived as serving no useful role in the environment. Of course, bees sting too, and this was acknowledged in the data: 'sting' was also among the commonest words used to describe bees. But people appreciate bees *despite their sting* because of their good services in the environment – as pollinators. A bit of pain is bearable if there's a hidden benefit. People also seemed to value bees, irrespective of their general interest in nature. Wasps, conversely, were more likely to be appreciated by people with a strong general interest in nature.

Could it be that people *only* know a lot about bees because they *hear* a lot about them, everywhere they go? Bees are in the media throughout the year, from appeals like 'Save the bees!' to 'Bee-bombs for your garden!' and 'Bee friendly, plant some flowers'. Perhaps this is also why people seek out information about bees more than they do for wasps: over the last five years, people have searched for 'bees' on the internet six times more often than they have for 'wasps'. Most of the searches for 'wasps' came from people wanting to get rid of them. Wasps get little coverage in the news. In the UK, they are lucky to make the headlines in the late summer if there's a shortage of 'real news' stories. Such stories are largely tabloid-hyped reports of 'killer wasps' and invasive species.

The arrival of the yellow-legged Asian hornet (*Vespa velutina*) in Europe in 2004, for example, refuelled the public's fear of wasps. This species is slightly smaller than the native European hornet (*Vespa crabro*), but it is a voracious predator. We have reasons to be concerned: it is spreading through Europe at around 100 kilometres per year, preying on native pollinators as well as domesticated honeybees. Media coverage of invasive species like the yellow-legged Asian hornet is extremely valuable in raising vigilance; having several million pairs of eyes and ears in citizens across a nation is priceless for the environment agencies trying to keep invaders under control.

Unfortunately, these news reports have often been coupled with scaremongering and misinformation: why pick a photo of an inconspicuous, smallish dark hornet (which happens to be what *Vespa velutina* is) to illustrate your tabloid article on killer wasps when you can pick a photo of *Vespa mandarinia* – the world's largest hornet with a wing span of 7.5 centimetres and a 6-millimetre sting which packs a venomous cocktail of compounds including several neurotoxins. This hornet flies at 40

Words used by the public to describe wasps (top) and bees (bottom).
The bigger the type, the more people who used that word.

kilometres per hour and dons a suitably scary bright-yellow face.
Even I would think twice about approaching *Vespa mandarinia*
(although apparently you would need around 58 stings at once
for the neurotoxins to kill you). But, dear tabloids, please get
your facts right: this is *not* the hornet that is invading Europe
(although it is invading the USA, but that's another story). The

media-fuelled juxtaposition of monster-wasp stories against industrious-bee stories is not helpful.

It's hard to believe now, but several decades ago a genuinely scary *bee* story dominated the headlines, after a hybrid of the western honeybee *Apis mellifera mellifera* and the East African lowlands subspecies *Apis mellifera scutellata* was produced and released to the wild by accident. Brazilian biologist Warwick Kerr had been attempting to breed a strain of honeybee that would produce more honey and be more resilient to tropical environments. Disaster struck when several colonies of his Africanised hybrids escaped from apiaries in São Paulo State. The bees quickly dispersed and crossbred with the local western honeybee colonies. These insects became known as African killer bees, or Africanised bees.

Over time this vigorous hybrid has spread throughout the Americas. Kerr's strain is indeed highly productive: good news for beekeeping economics. However, it outcompetes the mild-tempered western honeybee simply by being better at harvesting pollen, having a higher reproductive rate and a stronger work ethic (they forage in weather that see *Apis mellifera* hide in their hive). They are also more aggressive and are more liable to swarm, making them harder for beekeepers to work with and more likely to kill people. But that's old news now – beekeepers have adapted their management techniques and actively prefer to keep the Africanised bees over their western counterparts because of the higher productivity. The world has moved on since the 1970s. Scary bee stories no longer sell copy, while 'blessed bee' stories and 'evil wasp' stories do.

We have learned to detest wasps because we've been taught to do so by our families, educators, media, literature and entertainment. It's not our fault – we are products of our local cultures. Science must shoulder its share of responsibility for this. Over the last 30 years, there have been three times more scientific papers published on bees than on wasps, and conference talks on bees outnumber those on wasps four to one. The bee-bias in research has become more extreme over recent years, fuelled by large investments by governments into pollinator research, driven by our own self-servicing interests. In a world without pollinators, we go hungry.

But funding streams cannot shoulder the blame entirely for science's neglect of wasps. Some of our greatest minds have subtly sowed the seeds to promote scientific distance from them. It was parasitic Ichneumonid wasps that caused Charles Darwin to question the omnipotence of God and the story of Creation. In a letter to the botanist Asa Gray in 1860, Darwin wrote: 'I cannot persuade myself that a beneficent and omnipotent God would have designedly created the Ichneumonidae with the express intention of their feeding within the living bodies of caterpillars.'

Even contemporary wasp scientists concede the social stigma carried by wasps. American scientist Mary Jane West-Eberhard has devoted her life to studying wasps, but admits 'they terror-ize housewives, ruin picnics, and build large aerial nests that challenge fleet-footed stone-throwing boys the world over.' William D. Hamilton, a scientist who has had the most profound influence on our understanding of social evolution, acknowledged that 'Social wasps are amongst the least loved insects.' And Phil Lester, a New Zealand scientist who has been working hard to control invasive wasps (kindly introduced by the British) in his homeland, embraced the hype of public revulsion to wasps and called his book on them *The Vulgar Wasp*.

When scientific champions of wasps are struggling to describe these insects as anything but the gangsters of the insect world, what hope do wasps have? What happens in a world without wasps? We don't know for sure because we lack the basic science to tell us precisely what they do. But we know that wasps must be important for functioning ecosystems and a healthy planet. We know that they prey on the insects that would otherwise be a nuisance to us. In a world without wasps we would almost certainly need to use a lot of chemicals to keep other pests at bay. This, at least, is a good argument to forgive wasps for their sting just as we forgive bees.

It's time to solve the enigma of these beautiful, diverse and mysterious creatures. Let's give them a chance to prove themselves as worthy of our attention.

# II

'From so simple a beginning endless forms most beautiful and most wonderful have been, and are being, evolved.' I like to imagine that Darwin was admiring the beauty and wonder of wasps in his garden when he wrote these closing lines to his magnum opus *On the Origin of Species by Means of Natural Selection*, the book that revolutionised our understanding of life on earth. Many groups of organisms could be described as 'endless' in form, but natural selection has had an especially delicious time with wasps – teasing, testing, modelling and remodelling their forms and functions, spawning mind-blowing diversity. But this book is not a wasp encyclopedia; I simply cannot include them all. In fact, no one could, because for every wasp that has been named, there are likely to be around ten other species that *we've not yet discovered*.

I have to admit that Darwin was more likely thinking of beetles when he was writing his closing remarks for *On the Origin of Species*. Beetles are remarkable in their diversity: truly one of nature's wonders. Indeed, the second most famous quote of another evolutionary biologist, J.B.S. Haldane, is that any intelligent creator of life must have had 'an inordinate fondness for beetles'. His observation was pertinent at the time he said it

23

(the 1950s) as the debate between evolution and religion was tipping in favour of evolution.

If God really did create all beings on earth, He must have had a special penchant for beetles: they are the most numerous in terms of described species of any animal group, with 387,000 species. Accounting for cryptic species (those that look very similar to other species) and those yet to be discovered, scientists think that there could be around 1.5 million species of beetles. They are also among the most striking insects in appearance, from the flamboyant and exquisite to the ridiculous. In the absence of an intelligent creator, the diversity of beetles could have evolved through natural selection to attract members of the opposite sex, to repel salivating predators or to act as camouflage.

Because beetles look so extraordinary, we almost certainly suffer from a form of beetle-bias, making us more likely to find and describe new species of beetles than any other insect. People have noticed, collected and catalogued them for hundreds of years. In the nineteenth century, any respectable naturalist would have proudly shown off their personal collection of beetles and excitedly competed with friends for the largest, brightest or most outlandish specimens. In our admiration of beetles, we have inadvertently skewed our knowledge of insects in their favour.

Wasps belong to the order Hymenoptera, which includes bees and ants as well. There are around 150,000 described species of Hymenoptera. Of these, wasps make up over 80 per cent, with around 80,000–100,000 named species, almost five times more than there are bee species, and over 7 times more species than ants (which number about 13,000). Yet we notice and report wasps a lot less. In many parts of the world, wasp sightings are dominated by those of our friend the yellow-and-black-striped picnic wasp – the yellowjacket – that invades our personal space.

Of course, the number of species *described* does not reflect how many there *actually are*. Over a million insect species have been described, for example, but scientists estimate that there are likely to be 5.5 million species of insects on the planet. One of the big problems in counting species is geographical bias: the most intensively sampled parts of the world (for example, North America and Europe) are among the least biodiverse. Every insect order is likely to be several times more species-rich than current numbers suggest, and the Hymenoptera* especially so, with 60–88 per cent of its species thought to remain undescribed. Even the most conservative estimates suggest that there are between 600,000 and 2.5 million species of Hymenoptera. In areas that have been well sampled, such as temperate regions and some specific tropical ecosystems, hymenopteran species already outnumber beetles.

The vast majority of hymenopterans are hidden among the tiny and obscure parasitoid wasps. Parasitoids are insects that lay their eggs in (endoparasitoids) or on (ectoparasitoids) other organisms. When the egg hatches into a hungry larva, it proceeds to eat the living host alive as it grows. Parasitoids should not be confused with parasites, which spend their whole life living in or on a host, rather than just the larval stage. Some parasitoid wasps sport special severing structures on their heads which they use to tear their hosts open when they're ready to leave home. Eating living prey from the inside out may sound terrifying, but these wasps don't have the much-feared stings paraded by other wasps. In their place, parasitoids have an egg-laying tube called an ovipositor. Ovipositors are terribly useful: they reach places that other body parts could only dream of reaching. They can be inserted through tiny crevices into tree trunks, undergrowth or soil to deposit a precious egg, along with a cocktail of venom and cooperative viruses, into an oblivious caterpillar or beetle larva.

* Reporting the number of described species is harder than you'd think. This is because sometimes different names are given to the same species. Accounting for synonyms, the minimum estimate of described Hymenoptera is 117,000; the maximum estimate is around 150,000.

Wasps are not the only insect parasitoids, but they are by far the most diverse, numerous and species-rich. They are also incredibly important, as they perform a critical role in ecosystems by regulating populations of other insects. It is no surprise that they have been used extensively by humans in biocontrol. In some parts of the world these insects are farmed on a factory scale to be released into fields of maize and sugar cane, where they seek out caterpillars and other pests to lay their eggs in.

There are at least 80,000 described species of parasitoids. Most are diminutive in size: the tiniest are the fairyflies (Mymaridae – which are of course wasps, not flies), which can be as tiny as 0.14 millimetres, making them the world's smallest insects. Others, like the Ichneumonid wasps, can be several centimetres long, or twice that size if you take their ovipositor into account. Body size matters in species discovery. Take the 4,200 species of beetles found in the UK (arguably the best-studied group of beetles in the world): the mean body size of newly described British beetles decreased significantly between 1750 (when records began) and 1850 because entomologists had been much more likely to spot, collect and describe larger-bodied species before they noticed the smaller-bodied ones.

Given how tiny most parasitoid wasps are, discovery of their species starts at a disadvantage. To make matters more complicated, there are parasitoid wasps that lay their eggs on other parasitoid wasp larvae! These hyperparasitoids (parasitoids that live off other parasitoids) are often even smaller than their hosts – they are 'micro-wasps'. They represent a fourth layer of the food web: the hyperparasitoid wasp lives off the parasitoid wasp that lives off the caterpillar which lives off the host plant. Such multi-layered trophic chains can be unimaginably complex and are exhaustingly intricate examples of the endless forms of wasps and the plants and animals their lives are entwined with.

Finding parasitoids is just the first step; identifying them is exceedingly tricky too. Until recently only a handful of scientists around the world could do this as it required specialist knowledge of specific taxonomic traits, limiting the rate at which new species could be *described* even if they'd been *discovered*. But whenever scientists have taken a closer look at these creatures, they find *many* new species. This is especially so now with the use of DNA markers, which has made distinguishing similar-looking species less of a specialist skill and has exposed cryptic species that previous techniques had failed to identify. As a result, the number of named species of parasitoid wasps has exploded. It seems possible that wasps may in fact be the most species-rich of all insects, catapulting Haldane's fondness for beetles into a dusty corner of twentieth-century biodiversity science. We need only to visit a small area of a Central American rainforest and a 34-year-long study of caterpillars to understand why.

Área de Conservación de Guanacaste is a national park in north-western Costa Rica. It is around 1,200 square kilometres – a little smaller than Greater London – and is a protected area with diverse habitats and rich biodiversity. Over the last 34 years, scientists have reared thousands of caterpillars collected from this reserve, and from these caterpillars emerged many thousands of parasitoid wasps, most of which were undescribed. The researchers have their work cut out, sorting through all these wasps; but they've made a start by focusing on a single genus of a braconid micro-wasp, *Apanteles*, which are of economic interest because they have been used widely in biological control of caterpillar crop pests. In this part of Mesoamerica, only 19 species of *Apanteles* wasps had previously been described. From among 4,100 individual wasps, the scientists named no fewer than 186 new species: that's almost ten times more species of this genus than were previously known for this region. Remember, this is a *single* genus of wasps from a very small corner of the world.

Are we underestimating the number of species of parasitoid wasps by a factor of ten? If so, we'd be looking at there being in excess of 800,000 species of parasitoid wasps across the world. Of course, this may be an overestimate, as Área de Conservación de Guanacaste is known to be highly biodiverse. As an example, the region has five times more beetle species than are found in the whole of the UK. The UK is one of the least biodiverse nations on the planet, but even assuming that the species richness of this small area of Costa Rica is five times that of *any* other area in the world, this would still bring the predicted global number of species of parasitoid wasps to 160,000 – that's more than all the described hymenopterans put together.

If you aren't convinced by this, a foray into the ecology of parasitoids might persuade you. Beetles are up there with caterpillars as being the most favoured hosts for parasitoid wasp brood. Based on the known diversity of beetle hosts, and the fact that several different species of wasp can parasitise the same host beetle species (some parasitise larvae, others eggs), scientists have estimated that there are likely to be between two and three times more parasitoid wasp species *than there are beetles*. Before these studies, it was thought that parasitoids accounted for almost 80 per cent of described wasp species, but developments like these send diversity estimates for wasps into orbit.

If there is an intelligent creator of life on earth, almost certainly they had an inordinate fondness for parasitoid wasps.

My grandmother was a hoarder. She lived through two world wars and knew how important it was to value things, to look after them and keep them in order so that they could be found quickly and used when needed. She was especially careful with her buttons. Meaty wooden buttons for woollies, slippery cool buttons for shirts, modest brown buttons for trouser flies, lavish mother-of-pearl buttons for the Sunday frocks. When a garment died, she'd anxiously recover the buttons and secrete them away in her mysterious sewing cabinet, a labyrinth of furtive order. Each button was treated personally to this ritual, no matter how wild or simple its past, and laid with respect alongside its nearest buttony kin. Hundreds of them rattled with entitlement, precious playthings of my grandmother's discipline.

Their position and grouping in the cabinet was critical: each box was a protected enclave of buttons with shared beauty, form and function and which told common stories of past utility and future hope. Abutting boxes sheltered close relations: silky-green buttons stared out of their box at smooth-buttoned grey neighbours; floral-shaded buttons blushed alongside their baby-blue relatives. The arrival of a new button that did not match those of an existing box aroused uneasy excitement for both buttons and grandmother. On a bad day this would result in a large-scale reorganisation of buttons and boxes. As a child, I coveted my grandmother's button collection, but I wouldn't dare touch it; these were sacred places, laced with the order and precision of an evolutionary biologist's phylogenetic tree. Only she had the authority to order and reorder.

If my grandmother's buttons had been wasps, she would have been riddled with angst. Not because of them being wasps, but because of the difficulty she would have had in putting them in useful order. Granted, buttons can be endlessly beautiful and wonderful in form, but wasps are even more so and their traits and relationships are mysterious and complicated. Moreover, new species are being discovered and described faster than you can sew on a new button; some of these have unexpected qualities that upturn wasp relations with all the commotion of a rogue button in my grandmother's cabinet.

A button is just a button (my grandmother would disagree) and has a mere 2,000-year history, but wasps are 280 million years older than the oldest button and more eclectic and diverse than the world's combined haberdashery collection. In fact the term 'wasp' is a pitifully loose descriptor for such an assorted assemblage of insects. That there are so many species of wasps and of such diversity is both a headache and a joy for the evolutionary biologist: a headache because if we're missing data for too many species, any reconstruction of their family tree may be wrong; a joy because wasps have biological innovations that no other insect order has dared to evolve. This is why the wasp family tree matters to scientists and why they have argued over it for decades.

An evolutionary family tree helps us understand how, when and why a group of organisms, and their inner diversity, have evolved. The wasp phylogenetic tree reveals why some wasps are parasites, why some acquired that supermodel waist, and why some changed their egg-laying equipment into a poisoning device (the sting). It reveals how they have switched diet several times, and befriended and manipulated plants; and how a few became social, and others lost their wings to make ants, or turned vegetarian to become bees. To know these things, we need an accurate map of the evolutionary life of wasps.

Until recently, recovering such a tree of life for any organism relied on retracing the path left by shared traits – usually morphological ones – across species. Molecular sequencing methods are changing this because we can now look for differences and similarities in the DNA of different species. Those that had previously been grouped together based on physical appearance may have to be shuffled around to group with others, thanks to a combination of shared DNA and physical traits. Because of DNA sequencing technologies, our understanding of species' relationships is progressing at such a rate that the evolutionary history of the Hymenoptera has had to be rewritten many times over the last few years. But now is a good time to be getting to grips with the evolutionary history of wasps and their relations. While our understanding of the details will almost certainly need updating as more data for more species are uncovered, the broad-scale insights into the origins and the evolution of wasps and their relatives are unlikely to change radically.

Here's what the wasp tree of life has unveiled about the endless forms of wasps ...*

Current estimates put insects at around 479 million years old, making them the oldest land animals. One hundred and thirty million years later, holometabolous insects appeared: these are the insects that separate youth from adulthood with metamorphosis. Every child knows this as the process by which a worm-like, hungry caterpillar (the larval stage) spins a cocoon (the pupal stage), reorganises its body plan and emerges as a wing-clad, beautiful butterfly (the adult stage). Many familiar insects are holometabolous – the Diptera (flies), Lepidoptera (butterflies and moths), Coleoptera (beetles), Trichoptera (caddisflies) and the Hymenoptera (bees, wasps and ants). When the first hymenopteran came along a mere 280 million years ago, it was a wasp.

The prototype wasp was a vegetarian, and a rather inelegant-looking creature without a sting. We know this because this is what its ancestors – the sawflies – are like. In the absence of fossils, extant representatives of an extinct species give us a glimpse into the forms of the evolutionary past. The catch-all term for sawfly is 'Symphyta' (also known as wood wasps or horntails). Derived from the Greek *symphyton*, which means 'grown together', the name refers to the sawfly's lack of the wasp waist. They also lack the agile flight and hard-cuticle armour of their more waspish relatives. Sawflies are most certainly the broad-bellied maiden aunts of the wasp world: stumpy, fierce and functional, they trail a chunky ovipositor on their rear, corrugated like a saw to cut into the plants in which they lay their eggs.

Not that they've been left on the evolutionary shelf: these rotund wasps diversified rapidly and today are represented by at

---

* This may be out of date next week, next month, and almost certainly by the time you read this book. The main relationships will hold, it's just the details that may waver.

least 8,000 species and, unusually for an insect, sawflies are hyper-diverse in temperate regions. They include the emblematic giant horntail: a monstrous 20-millimetre-long beast that mimics the yellow and black stripes of a hornet, the female's ovipositor protruding rudely from her bottom, giving the appearance of a stinger. But sawflies cannot sting – the ovipositor only evolved into a sting in another bunch of wasps, 25 million years after the ancestral sawfly appeared. Adult females typically live only for a week or two, and they lay their eggs in plants, not prey. Their larvae are easily mistaken for the caterpillars of butterflies or moths, and are often brightly coloured, warning curious predators of their irritating secretions. The mobile caterpillar-like larvae chomp their way around a host plant for several months before entering metamorphosis.

The oldest living representative of the sawflies may be a xyelid, a relatively species-poor family but one which boasts the oldest hymenopteran fossil dating back to the era of the dinosaurs, around 245 million years ago. Today's xyelid sawflies are regarded as 'living fossils' because they appear to have changed very little since they first evolved. They can therefore provide us with a time-machine view of the original wasp's life history. Xyelids lay their eggs in pine cones and the larvae feed off leaves, buds or young shoots. When the larva has had its fill, it drops to the ground, where it builds a little cell in which to overwinter. Given their diversity and abundance, it's no surprise that these vegetarians sometimes cause economic and ecological damage to forests. The original wasp was (and still is) an enduring beast of ecological and evolutionary victory.

Around 240 million years ago, some wasps developed a taste for meat, sparking a huge speciation event and giving rise to the rest of the wasps. The last vegetarian wasp probably resembled today's turnip sawfly, *Athalia rosae* – a rather uninviting-looking orange insect with an ugly hunched back; anyone other than a sawfly expert would mistake it for a fly. From this Quasimodo-esque ancestor, wasps made two attempts at evolving flesh-eaters. One was a type of sawfly, the Orussidae. The Orussidae are exceedingly elusive: their blind, legless larva spend all their time inside dead wood, where their favourite prey — wood-boring beetles — live. As with all meat-loving wasps, it is only the larval stage that is carnivorous. The adult mother finds a beetle larva host under the bark of dead wood by detecting the vibrations it makes; she is effectively echolocating through a solid medium. She drills through the plant with her saw-like ovipositor and lays a long curly egg directly onto the beetle larva. On hatching, the sawfly larva feeds off its living meal before gnawing its way out of the plant as an adult.

These parasitic sawflies have remained rather understudied, buried with their silent victims in wooden nurseries. It is not difficult to imagine the conditions by which a switch from feeding on plants to feeding on insect prey might have arisen: any vegetarian sawfly larva could be forgiven for accidentally nibbling on an insect cohabiting their host plant. It would have been a small hop, skip and evolutionary jump to evolve ways to make use of this nitrogen-rich food source in place of plants.

In shedding their vegetarian ways, these parasitic sawflies also downgraded their sensory system. They lost a gene involved with vision; sight is overrated in dark, wooden nurseries where there is no sunlight to detect or respond to. The sawflies lost some of the genes involved in detecting chemicals and smells too: while vegetarian sawflies use smells to detect host plants, parasitic sawflies use vibrations to find their prey. Intriguingly, the nutritional switch from plant to prey didn't result in a reformation of their digestive system. This is surprising, because digesting nitrogen-rich prey instead of nitrogen-poor plants could be expected to require significant innovation at the level of the genes. Scientists think that the diverse diets of *adult* vegetarian sawflies – which include nectar, pollen and plant tissue – may have already required a complex repertoire of metabolic processes, which were then easily co-opted in the transition to carnivory.

The evolution of carnivory in the parasitic sawflies has been modest. They are the monks of the Hymenoptera and today represent only 1 per cent of sawfly species. A quiet life in a dark rotting cell, with a single host for company, may not be the place to inspire evolutionary thrills and innovations.

In a parallel evolutionary universe to the sawflies, another group of wasps – the parasitoid wasps – became flesh-eaters and they proved exceedingly successful. They are the descendants of a single plant-dwelling insect that lived in the Permian or Triassic periods, around 247 million years ago. The parasitoid wasps began to diversify only a few million years later, at a time when coincidentally their host lineages (Lepidoptera, Diptera) also started to proliferate. Today, every species of caterpillar, fly and beetle probably has at least one parasitoid wasp that exploits it. But acquiring a taste for a diversity of flesh cannot have been the only trigger for the mega-radiation of parasitoid wasps and their relatives, as otherwise parasitoid sawflies would surely have diversified in a similarly prolific way.

Something else has been going on.

The wasp waist is evolution's invention that best explains the success of parasitoid wasps. The much-envied corseted silhouette formed around 240 million years ago when the wasp's first abdominal segment fused with the thorax to form an elongated waist known as the propodeum. The wasp waist has functions beyond elegance. Shedding the clumsy, thick-waisted fashion so adored by sawflies afforded wasps manoeuvrability of their derrières. Ovipositor-clad abdomens could now be folded over and under the body, allowing the wasp to access the most hard-to-reach locations. Prey could no longer hide from this acrobatic and nimble apparatus. Articulated bodies paired with excessively long ovipositors became all the rage in the boom years of the parasitoid wasps. Along with whole-scale body miniaturisation and endoparasitoidism (laying eggs *inside* a host rather than on it), speciation events exploded as wasps adapted to exploit all manner of prey in any location.

All this was accompanied by a huge diversification in other insects, providing a smorgasbord of potential prey victims. Parasitoid wasps evolved a heightened sense of smell and a more acute ability to detect vibrations, enabling mothers to spot the presence of a wider diversity of prey in ever more locations. They also tweaked their ovipositor to deliver venom along with an egg, which helped numb prey into becoming more compliant living larders for wasp offspring. Many endoparasitoid wasps also evolved a special relationship with a virus that they inject along with the egg and venom into the host caterpillar. The virus suppresses the host's immune system, boosting the chances of survival and the quality of the developing wasp larva. So intimate is the relationship between wasp and virus that they have mingled their genomes to create a unique type of virus. As well as preventing the caterpillar's immune system from attacking the parasitoid larva, the virus alters the composition of the caterpillar's saliva, further suppressing the plant's immune system and allowing the caterpillar to grow faster and making a juicier meal for the baby wasp.

It has all the makings of a perfect love story of symbiosis. Except nature rarely spins such kind and simple just-so stories. The virus also inadvertently sends secret signals to another species of wasp – a hyperparasitoid, enticing it to exploit the virus's very own partner. By altering the caterpillar's saliva, the plant it feeds on is also stimulated to release airborne chemicals that hyperparasitoid wasps use to find parasitoid wasp larvae. A veritable Jekyll and Hyde, the virus helps our parasitoid wasp with one hand and stabs it in the back with the other. The complex interactions of such multi-layered relationships are matched only by the surprise and absurdity of a Shakespearean comedy, with a modern-day twist. The ecosystem that revolves around parasitoids is one of nature's most complex stories of interconnected adaptation, innovation, cooperation and exploitation: parasites evolve to be better exploiters, hosts evolve to avoid being victims, hyperparasites and viruses evolve to hitchhike with (and manipulate) whoever they can, in whatever way they can. If this doesn't blow your mind, I don't know what will.

Some of the most famous parasitoid wasps have reverted to the vegetarian life of their sawfly ancestors and evolved a special relationship with figs. All 900 species of fig wasps belong to the family Chalcidoidea. Their relationship evolved around 70–90 million years ago, and they remain important pollinators today. The fig provides a cosy nursery in which the young wasps develop (and mate); and when the female wasps burst from their pollen cradles as adults in search of another plant in which to lay their own eggs, the fig benefits by having its pollen carried to a nearby fig neighbour. Until recently, different species of fig wasp were thought to have faithful liaisons with specific fig species, forming fig-wasp matches made in reproductive heaven. However, scientists have discovered that due to a fair bit of wasp-fig infidelity, the figs have hybridised extensively, further driving the diversity of both plants and wasps.

Other parasitoid-turned-veggie wasps have become the strangest farmers on the planet. These are the gall wasps (Cynipidae). Like the eruptions on a teenager's acned chin, gall wasps cause nodules to grow on a wide range of trees, including oak, Southern Beech and rose plants. The wasps appear to induce the trees to grow protective casings around their eggs, which are laid on the undersides of leaves or stems. As if protection wasn't enough, the plant also provides the developing wasps with nourishment. Unlike the fig wasps, there doesn't appear to be any synergistic benefit between wasp and plant: the growth of the gall seems to be under the control of the wasp, not the plant. The plant is therefore providing a service to the wasp, without any benefit to itself. How these small insects (no more than 1–8 millimetres in length) are able to manipulate the growth of the tree remains elusive. Other gall wasp species don't bother making their own galls and instead lay their eggs inside those of 'honest' galling wasps. These parasites have evolved as a lineage embedded within the honest gallers.

Genomes of parasitoid wasps have revealed some of these evolutionary complexities, but they have also revealed how the genetic toolkit of life has been exploited, repurposed and redesigned to produce such variety in wasps. Parasitoid wasps have evolved new genes, duplicated genes and modified genes that are specialised for detecting an eclectic diversity of chemicals. A new toolkit for a new way of life. The arrival of the parasitoid wasp was to the Hymenoptera as was the invention of the electric sewing machine to my grandmother's generation: it marked a shift in diversity and complexity, away from the sedentary evolution of the sawflies.

And then came the innovation you've all been waiting for: the sting. It took a mere 100 million years after the first wasp appeared for them to get round to evolving this infamous weapon. As with the parasitoid's wasp waist, the evolution of the sting sparked a whole new mélange of biological diversity and speciation, producing that most emblematic group of stinging insects – the Aculeata. Evolving the sting was a pretty straightforward modification of the ancestral parasitoid ovipositor – that silent seeker which had delivered new life for 100 million years – and it happened just once (probably). The ovipositor became a hardened weapon designed purely to mark the beginning of the end for its victim. A life-giver became a life-taker, as no egg travels down this blade, only poison.* Our wasp became a hunter.

---

* Many parasitoids use their ovipositor to deliver venom as well as for egg-laying. And some ichneumonids (for example, *Ophion, Netelia*) readily sting in defence too. But the important point here is that for aculeates, the sting is entirely for delivery of venom, not eggs.

As a bow is to its arrow, the venom sac was an essential companion to the sting: the two interlocked to make a sweet killing machine. This weapon was a slow burner, designed to stun the victim into a state of suspended life until death, creating a living larder for baby wasps to feed on in the safety of a purpose-built nest. Indeed, the need to stun prey rather than simply lace it with an egg most likely preceded nest-building: placated prey could be easily transported to burrows and tunnels that had been dug into the earth, or to pots shaped from mud, or to homes sculpted from masticated plant material mixed with saliva and teased into papery nests as simple as a cup or as sophisticated as a space station. The nest became a place to store a mother's hunt and her baby; to keep them safe from predators, parasites, diseases and the elements when abandoned by the hunter mother.

The first stinging wasp appeared around 190 million years ago, and was probably something like a Chrysidoidea – a group of 6,500 species known as the peacocks of the hymenopteran world due to their delightfully cheerful appearance. Its life history was probably a muddy no man's land mix of parasitoidism (an evolutionary hangover of its parasitoid ancestors) and hunting (using the new apparatus in the wasp's toolkit), because that's what today's Chrysidoidea do. In total, the sting serves over 30,000 described species of wasps, most of which are solitary, as lonesome as their parasitoid ancestors were. But these hunters are a diverse company of characters: spider-chasers, beetle-worriers, caterpillar-masseuses, fly-catchers, canny scavengers. The sting is much more than a weapon: it is a prey-carrying kebab stick, a medicinal syringe; it delivers preservatives, anaesthetics, antibiotics, mind-altering drugs.

The sting took on a new function for social wasps – those that live together in groups. These include that picnic wasp, the yellowjacket and those uneasy media tarts, the hornets. They are the most emblematic and feared of wasps largely because of their sting. Social wasps do not use their stings to paralyse prey. They have no need to preserve their victims; fresh prey is delivered on-demand directly to the hungry mandibles of the colony's larvae. They might treat an especially feisty feast to a small prick of venom if it refuses to cooperate, but mostly a social wasp kills with her mandibles. The offensive sting of its solitary cousins has for the social wasp become defensive, poised to protect its fortress nest, as it is packed with brood and would make a nutritious feast for a mammal or bird, ant or reptile. At the first signs of attack, the wasp workers, in their hundreds or thousands, take little persuasion to defend their kingdom of kin, whether the threat comes from a genuine predator or a clumsy human.

After the sting, it is the evolution of sociality that wasps are best known for. Their societies can be as complex as our own (or more), and are home to many practising celibates – the workers, who divide among them the tasks required for a smooth-running colony – and one or a few dedicated mothers – the queens. These non-reproductive and reproductive units of the colony are mutually dependent and together they function as a single machine – the superorganism. Honeybees and ants are famous examples of superorganisms, and rarely are wasps praised for these same evolutionary powers. Yet it is the superorganismal wasps with their haughty reputation and characteristic paper-bag nests that we best recognise: the hornets and yellowjackets, their societies mirroring those of the honeybee as pinnacles of social evolution. Despite their infamy around the globe, these wasps number a mere 74 species. They are the Vespinae, and they evolved about the time the dinosaurs went extinct, around 65 million years ago. Most people can identify these insects as wasps, and yet they represent less than 1 per cent of all social wasp species.

There are at least 1,000 further species of social wasps that are neither hornets nor yellowjackets. These wasps deserve more attention. Around 750 of the 'other social wasps' live in societies that are as simple and endearing as that of a group of meerkats in the Kalahari Desert. They are the paper wasps (*Polistes, Belonogaster, Ropalidia*), and their simple way of living may be a precursor to superorganismality. Similarly adorable and even more socially simplistic are the hover wasps (Stenogastrinae) of Southeast Asia, which evolved sociality independently of all other social wasps. The societies of hover wasps and paper wasps may not be as sensational in complexity and size as those of the vespines, but they are nature's award-winning soap operas: on the stage of their open nest cartons they lay out their lives, their agreements and disagreements, their law and order, their deceit and cunning. These are the insects that have taught us about why social lives evolve and what it is that keeps a cooperative society on track. In fact, of all the social insects it is these simple-societied wasps that we humans have the most in common with.

The swarm-founding wasps of the Neotropics are the most enigmatic of the social wasps. Unless you live alongside them, you probably haven't heard of them, and you certainly wouldn't recognise their nests as being the constructions of wasps. They build colonies that look like air balloons, exotic fruits, gourds, cowpats, lumps of mud, Roman vases and even chamberpots. They invented origami, paper-making and sophisticated architecture 150 million years before humans existed. Inside their empires are hundreds of thousands of tiny but orderly and incredibly productive wasps. Little studied, their diversity provides glimpses of the stepping stones taken by evolution in the emergence of the superorganism: the journey from simple soap opera to an insect 'Internet of Things', with teeming bodies connecting, monitoring, responding, adjusting, communicating to produce a new level of organic automata.

There is one other type of social wasp that we need to mention: the one that lost its wings. You might call these ants. It happened around 100 million years ago. Ants today retain the developmental potential for wings, but use them only for sex and dispersal. When ants fly they are inferior pilots compared to wasps, with wings that make for clumsy domestic jumbo jets in comparison to the aerodynamic fighter-jet wings of the wasp. But that's OK, as ants don't need them for very long. For male ants (drones), wings are simply a means to an end: to find and mate with virgin females, spreading their seed in ungainly mating flights, after which they unceremoniously crawl away to die. The only female ants that have wings are the young sexuals; worker ants never fly. Sexual females use their wings for dispersal: better to set up a new nest a good distance away from your natal nest to avoid competing with your own gene-bearing relatives. Once a mated female ant finds a nesting site, she bites off her own wings and submits to a life on land.

Most ants retain the hunting drive of their ancestral wasp, although some have developed an appetite for seeds instead. Yet while less than 1 per cent of wasps are social, *all* ant species are social. They construct phenomenal underground cities, in which thousands (sometimes millions) of wingless female workers act as industrious bots toeing the factory line to propagate copies of gene variants shared by the colony. Thanks to their vast societies, ants dominate most terrestrial ecosystems. Famously, two of the world's most eminent ant biologists – the late Edward O. Wilson and Bert Hölldobler – claimed that the combined biomass of ants on the planet exceeds that of humans. Perhaps that was true before we got too numerous and too fat. But the general point still holds: there are an awful lot of ants and they have a tremendously big impact on our planet.

Present-day ecological dominance is not a new thing: of the insect fossils that date back to 20 million years ago, 20 per cent are those of ants. This amounts to a phenomenal 35 per cent of all insects in Dominican amber, dating from the Miocene period (20–5 million years ago). These wingless wasps are evolutionary giants of ecological success: they sculpt the surface, under-surface and canopies of the world as hunters, granivores and herbivores. They are agriculturists of underground fungi farms, extraordinary navigators, toilers of leaf litter and nutrients, migrators and mistresses of societal law and order.

There are about as many fossil ants as there are fossil dinosaurs: over 750 described species of preserved ants have been found from at least 70 locations across the planet. Everything we know about dinosaurs comes from their fossil record: 200 million-year-old rocks have revealed what they ate, their colour and size, and even their behaviour. The ant fossil record is an equally rich paleontological melting pot, bubbling with clues as to how wasps became ants. The earliest ant fossils coincide reassuringly with the date when molecular phylogenies have suggested the first wasp became an ant. It's a fair bet, therefore, that these oldest fossils are something approximating to the first ant. What they reveal could belong in a science-fiction movie: in the Cretaceous period, a huge diversity of crazy-looking ants evolved, and scientists have had *a lot* of fun naming them.

Take the 'hell ant', for example, with scythe-like mandibles that jutted menacingly upwards from the jawline. Hell-ant cranial morphology is unlike any modern ant group's, making them one of the most diverse forms of ants that ever evolved. There are also the 'iron-maiden ants', with ferocious mouth parts covered in spikes designed to immobilise prey. And the 'beast ants', so called because of their colossal forelimbs, enormous alien eyes and many-toothed mandibles that swivelled open to receive what must have been very large prey. These beasts are thought to be the lost intermediates between wasps and ants, and to date they are the most distant relatives of living ants. You might be relieved (or maybe disappointed) to hear that all of these fearsome creatures went extinct in the late Cretaceous mass-extinction event, over 50 million years ago.

Today ants sit within the evolutionary shadow of wasps. Their branch on the phylogenetic tree is easily missed as they are sunk deep between a quicksand of wasp beauties (like the delicate jewel wasps – the enigmatic Ampulicidae) and wasp beasts (like the stocky Scoliid wasps that hunt scarab beetle larvae). The first ant was probably something similar to the Sphecomyrminae, *Sphecomyrma freyi*, found in 92-million-year-old New Jersey amber, or beast ants that are now extinct. All evolutionary contenders for the first ant trophy certainly share a morphological mash-up of ant and wasp-like features – a kind of wasp-ant intermediary.

What, then, makes an ant an ant, and not a wingless wasp? Taxonomists love being asked this question, as there are some very clear physical features that distinguish them. Ants are the only stinging Hymenoptera that have a metapleural gland – a slit- or pustule-like opening found on the back end of the thorax in workers and queens. This is a rather clever invention as it exudes a range of antibiotics, which help combat diseases in the colony. It also produces chemicals used in communication. Ants also have 'elbowed' antennae ('geniculated' if you're an ant taxonomist), made possible thanks to an extra-long first antennal segment. Another ant giveaway is that the second abdominal segment is node-like, being constricted at front and back; in wasps, this segment is just a smooth and simple waist. It's true that the difference between an ant and a wasp is, in reality, not that exciting (unless you're a taxonomist), but it does make a fiendish tie-breaker question in a pub quiz.

Just remember this: ants are simply wasps that have been grounded by an evolutionary innovation. And with so much to say about the *real wasps*, I won't bother you with any more about these flightless mutants. Not in this book, anyway.

One hundred and twenty-four million years ago, all the bees were wasps. Then one day a wasp forgot how to hunt and developed a taste for pollen, and bees were born. Some of them even evolved special saddlebags on their back legs which helped them carry pollen back to their nests. Bees have become guardians of global ecosystems as pollinators, and a privileged few are honoured friends of humans as providers of honey, wax and other useful products, but the truth is that in evolutionary terms, there is nothing especially unique about bees: they are simply a specialised, vegetarian version of the largest group of wasps – the crabronids.

The bee fossil record remains scrappy and sparse compared to that of ants. Most of the bee fossils are solitary *species*, while most of the fossil *specimens* are social bee workers from species that lived in damp forests and fed on resins (like stingless bees). Since social bees didn't evolve until 60 million years after the first solitary bee, the vast majority of bee fossils are not especially useful for revealing how wasps became bees. Despite this, we have two fossilised contenders for the star role as the wasp-bee – a transitional state that links wasps to bees – and they come from Burmese amber that formed in tropical forests 100 million years ago. Fossils of *Melittosphex burmensis* and *Discoscapa apicula* both sport a mixture of wasp-like and bee-like features, suggesting that they could be missing links between crabronid wasps and bees. To the trained taxonomists' eyes, however, these two insects are so different from each other that they belong in different biological families. Moreover, there are no living representatives of their families, making them new to science.

The closest living wasp relative to bees is most certainly a wasp from the Crabronidae family, probably something like the aphid wasp, such as *Psenulus* – a global genus of around 160 species. As the name suggests, these solitary wasps hunt aphids, which they paralyse to provide as living prey to their larvae. Another candidate for the closest living relatives to bees are the Ammoplanidae, tiny wasps, barely 2–4 millimetres in length. These are compelling contenders, as the wasp-bee fossils (like *Melittosphex burmensis*) that have been found are also extremely small (around 3 millimetres). Since the flowers of the early Cretaceous would have been very small, it would make sense if the first bees were sized to fit. Intriguingly, Ammoplanidae hunt tiny pollen-eating insects called thrips. In the late 1960s, the Russian entomologist Sergei Ivanovich Malyshev suggested that wasps which hunted flower-visiting insects could have experienced the conditions needed for a diet hop from hunting meat to pollen-foraging. Fifty years later, his theory finally appears to have received some evidence.

These thrip-hunters would already have had a sensory system well tuned to locating flowers: a perfect starter toolkit for the proto-bee. It is easy to imagine these wasps carrying home a few pollen grains as a side-dish to the crunchy thrips. All that would have been needed was some genetic mutation that enabled the brood to make nutritional use of pollen, and the evolutionary seeds for the original bee would have been sown.

In 2019, another piece of 100-million-year-old Burmese amber provided definitive evidence of a pollinating wasp: it revealed a stinging wasp with plumes of pollen wafting from its mouth, and a pollen ball stored *inside* its body – direct evidence that this was a pollen-feeder. The wasp looked unlike anything seen before, with somewhat ancestral or primitive features, and it didn't fit into any of the main lineages of modern stinging wasps. The researchers called it *Prosphex anthophilos*, forming a new genus *Prosphex* (*pro-* meaning 'first'/'before' and -*sphex* meaning 'wasp').

The scientists proclaimed it to be an unprecedented discovery because it was the earliest direct evidence of an insect pollinating a flowering plant. Given the beautiful story of co-evolution between flowering plants and their insect pollinators, this was indeed a landmark discovery. But equally important is that it provided evidence of wasps evolving pollen-foraging at least as early as the origin of bees and around the time that flowering plants started diversifying. This is indisputable direct evidence that dependence on pollen can evolve from a predatory ancestor.

Perhaps we shouldn't be so surprised that stinging wasps gave rise to some of the pollinating giants. Wasps have many traits and behaviours that could have been pre-adaptations for becoming effective pollinators. They are aeronautical champions with good memories: their strong, coordinated flight and ability to learn landmarks (from building and provisioning many new nests over many months) would have provided a physical and cognitive toolkit for finding good pollen sources and returning to the same food source until it was depleted. And their sting: what better way to protect yourself when foraging on exposed flowers? It is small wonder that so many hundreds of flower-visiting flies, beetles and moths have mimicked the wasp's signature yellow and black outfit. Equipped with speed, intelligence and defence, the wasp that became a bee was well set up for a lifetime's devotion to flowers.

Wasps are old. Wasps are varied, bizarre and beautiful. There are probably more species of them on this planet than any other insect (or animals, for that matter). Without wasps, we would have no ants or bees. Their evolutionary history is more mysterious and tantalising than a grandmother's button box to a small child. Let's open that box now and explore the endless forms of wasps in a bit more detail.

# Part Two

# *The Obsessions of Wasp Whisperers*

This is to be a story of a tribe of troglodytes who lead a curious life, in some ways the most remarkable of all who inherit the land of Hexapod. A true story it will be … a tale of skilled hunters and adept home-builders, of hard-working mothers and shiftless fathers, of clever crafts and strange customs, of peace and of war.

Edward G. Reinhard,
*The Witchery of Wasps* (1929)

# Prelude

The more we intrude on nature, the angrier we get with it for bothering us. Nature is an unwanted house guest, a flaw in our perfect gardens, an uprooter of our concrete deserts. We are so busy complaining about how nature disrupts our sterile order that we miss most of the beauty that is under our noses. Perhaps this is why most people today recognise wasps as only the social wasps – those picnic-botherers, loft loiterers, 'murder hornets' – for it is these particular wasps that we notice when they cross our paths. It's an awful shame that we don't take more care to notice the 32,000 other species of hunting wasps – the solitary ones – which comprise 97 per cent of all the world's stinging wasp species. You might have seen these lonesome insects in the summer, digging into sand banks or excavating crevices in stone walls or patios. You probably mistook them for bees.

Our blinkered and vexed view of what wasps are appears to be recent. The writings of early naturalists are littered with impassioned accounts of the ways of solitary wasps. They were a favourite of the gentleman and gentlewoman naturalist in the nineteenth and early twentieth centuries. Their out-of-print books hide gems that show we were not always quite so ignorant and blinkered in our view of wasps. These naturalists started to uncover the endless forms of solitary wasps almost 200 years ago. Their careful obsessions have provided the natural history needed to guide modern scientists, as few have the patience these days to spend time with a solitary wasp.

The life of a solitary wasp is predictable and cyclical: she digs a burrow with one or more brood cells, provisions it with prey she has caught, lays an egg and seals it up before abandoning it forever. Without a whiff of nostalgia for her abandoned babe, she moves swiftly on to digging her next burrow. Then repeat. And repeat. She doesn't have much opportunity to work on her social skills. She never meets her own offspring because they emerge long after she has disappeared. She rarely interacts with fellow mothers except when reprimanding an interloper intent on stealing her prey. She does have sex, probably only once though, stockpiling enough sperm in her sperm-storage sac to last the rest of her short life.

As well as being unsociable, she's deadly if you happen to be an arthropod. Solitary wasps are some of the planet's most ingenious executioners. A silent assassin. The stinging apparatus of a female delivers a chemical cocktail of toxins, enzymes and amines which simultaneously paralyse prey and inoculate it with antimicrobials. The venom is a hunting tool and a preservative, keeping her victims alive, a helpless but healthy sack of living nutrients that can be easily transported and stored in the burrow. Her blossoming babes eat the still-living prey over several weeks.

Honed for success by natural selection, our solitary slayer is unhurried, skilful, punctilious. Evolution does not tolerate a clumsy, careless solitary wasp, especially when it has worked so hard to provide her with the perfect hunting toolkit to deliver a chemical cocktail fit for a long, clean and final sleep. Evolution has also had fun generating an eclectic array of execution styles and strategies through these multifaceted chameleons. Solitary wasps are mistresses of many guises, each with her own macabre theatre of tricks and personalities in her quest to be the best single mum a baby could wish for.

It is not difficult to understand why those early naturalists – I'll call them the Wasp Whisperers – were obsessed with finding out how wasps hunt, how they kill and what they do with their victims. The Whisperers' florid and entertaining texts describe how these insects hunt with elegance, kill with compassion and store with style. Watching solitary wasps was the ultimate action thriller entertainment in a pre-movie era. They offer some uncomfortable parallels with assassins in our own world, but unlike the typical human assassin, the solitary wasp cares about her kill: she has a vested interest in being tender, benevolent, and attentive to its comfort and health. The slow, controlled death of her victim delivers life to her own offspring.

The Wasp Whisperers make no apologies for giving personality to their insect playthings but they don't intend to imply any logical thinking on the part of the insects.* In their defence, I can personally attest that unconscious anthropomorphism is irresistible when watching solitary wasps. It is hard not to relate to them as you would to a friend or even a foe.

Abandoned books, forgotten tales, dusty truths and observations; it's time to give a whisper from the grave to those early naturalists and their obsessions with solitary wasps. What have we learned from these Wasp Whisperers of the past and have we done them scientific justice with the gems they bequeathed us?

---

* This sentiment is spelled out explicitly on page iii of Phil Rau and Nellie Rau's 1918 book, *Wasp Studies Afield*: 'We have no apology to make for the frequent use of anthropomorphic ideas, terms and interpretations. However, one must not read into these terms any subtle metaphysical meaning. They are used as apt descriptive expressions and not for the purpose of predicating logical thinking to these creatures.'

# I

Jean-Henri Fabre is perhaps the most famous of the Wasp Whisperers. The Frenchman broke the mould of nineteenth-century naturalists in *not* being a privileged gentleman of means. Fabre grew up in poverty in the 1820s and 1830s but, driven by his passion and tenacity, he taught himself entomology. He qualified as a teacher, although he is best known for his observations and experiments on insects, which he published in ten books. Fabre's work was noticed by Charles Darwin and is thought to have influenced Darwin's own writings, despite Fabre's staunch objections to the theory of evolution by natural selection. *Souvenirs Entomologiques* formed the original collection of Fabre's writings on insects, and multiple editions were published between 1879 and 1909. The book has 31 chapters on wasps, yet these only really made it into the public eye after being translated into English and republished by Alexander Teixeira de Mattos in 1915 and 1920 respectively as *The Hunting Wasps* and its imaginatively titled sequel *More Hunting Wasps*.

These books are a tsunami of science, obsession and comedy. Although Fabre's rhyme is eccentric and excitable, each morsel is underpinned by observation and thanks to his bell-glass observation chamber, he was able to replicate his findings with a level of integrity. I make no apology for preferentially picking out gems of intrigue and delight from the works of Fabre, for it is he who whispers most prominently from the graves of the Wasp Whisperers.

Fabre was obsessed with the sting. And quite rightly too, for a solitary wasp is not a hunter without her sting – it is the tool by which she conjures her assassin's magic. It delivers the venom – the essential cocktail of chemicals that renders prey as helpless, paralysed but perfectly preserved larders containing all the nutrients needed for baby wasps. Fabre called the sting 'mother's stiletto', perhaps in reference to the offensive stabbing weapon of the medieval assassin.

Anyone who has been stung by a wasp (or bee for that matter) will appreciate why it's called a 'sting'. There is no denying, it really *does* sting. Pain surges from the focal point of venom entry

Jean-Henri Fabre, observing insects in his bell-chamber observation dome.

(being stung on the finger is particularly bad for this – such a high concentration of nerve endings) and seeps up the body like the darkness of Sauron. Later, the itching starts and (sometimes) it stays with you for days. This is a best-case scenario – for some people the venom sends the body into immunity override, which ends in a rapid trip to hospital, and sometimes (sadly) even death. But it is typically only the stings of social wasps that cause this much inconvenience.

One of the most frequent questions I'm asked is 'How do you get the sting out?' I will say this just once: only honeybees leave their sting in you when they sting. Most of the other 22,000 species of bees and the 32,000 species of solitary and social hunting wasps are sensible enough to keep their stings intact for future use.* Why honeybee workers have evolved the self-destructive behaviour of having their innards ripped out when they sting you remains an unanswered question.† Whether an insect leaves its sting in you is down to sting morphology. I realise stings are an uncomfortable topic for everyone. However, as the sting is the critical tool in the hunting wasp's portfolio, evolution has paid very careful attention to making it bespoke for the many different ways that these wasps slice their hunting pie.

Remember that the origins of the sting lie in the egg-laying sheaths of the parasitoid wasp, which didn't have a proper sting, only a long, elegant ovipositor that it used to deposit eggs (and a little bit of venom) onto or into prey. The egg-laying apparatus needed to be long and malleable for delivery of her babies to

---

* An exception is the social wasp *Synoeca* which has a barbed stinger that becomes lodged in the skin of their attacker.

† Honeybees may have evolved a barbed sting in response to predation by vertebrates. Embedding the stinger (and the venom gland) in the flesh increases the amount of venom delivered. Tearing out the venom gland may also increase the amount of alarm pheromone released by the attacking bee and thus the potency of the alarm signal, calling more worker bees to defence.

hard-to-reach prey. How did a tool of maternal love transform into a killing implement?

The weaponised ovipositor is short compared to its gentler ancestral forebear: the willowy egg-laying tube can be up to eight times the length of the wasp's body, but the weaponised version of today is rarely longer than the abdomen. At least part of the answer, then, is down to physics: the force needed to pierce the prey's skin would buckle even a moderately long sting, especially when the quarry is wiggly and intent on escape.

A typical wasp sting is made of stiff cuticle plates down which the venom can be administered, surrounded by flexible membranes. The stiff 'stingy bit' is called the shaft and it's far from being a simple pin. It comprises two rod-like structures connected via a clever sliding interlocking mechanism and it is attached to cuticular basal plates. The shaft can be a curved scythe, a straight dagger or a spring-loaded arrow. It can have barbs, big or small, or be smooth. Ancestrally it is gently curved, but some species (like velvet ants, which incidentally are wasps, not ants) have shafts that coil up inside them.

When not in use, the shaft sits politely inside its sheath. Shaft and sheath vary enormously in shape, size and mobility across species. It is the interaction between sheath (and specifically a hardened flap called the third valvula) and shaft that is the engineering marvel of the sting and the success of the hunter. The flap has evolved many functions: it cleans the sting shaft and protects it from damage, and in some species provides strength and rigidity to the shaft, important for defence. But most critically it provides the clever biomechanics needed to guide the shaft to penetrate its victim in precisely the right place, close to the nervous system, to deliver the juicy surprise. This precision is helped by sensory receptors that the hunting wasps inherited from their parasitic ancestors – these same receptors help identify the spot for an ovipositing wasp to drill into. Remarkably, the flap is not controlled by any muscles. Instead, proteins are thought to help it return to its resting position after stinging: it is truly a feat of engineering innovation and ingenuity, an area of wasp biology waiting to be noticed.*

The sting of the fly-hunter *Oxybelus* deserves a special mention. Most hunting wasps carry their prey to a lair using their legs or mandibles. *Oxybelus* uses her sting, impaling her paralysed victim to transport it to her burrow: it is the ultimate assassin's backpack, provided obligingly by evolution. She preys on small flies that she catches in flight. After stinging the fly, she folds her abdomen under her body, inserting her sting through the squishy membrane at the base of the fly's forelegs.

What sparked the first *Oxybelus* to have the ingenious idea of using her sting to carry her prey? Did an over-zealous paralysing sting result in an accidentally impaled prey? Behaviours that make hunting more efficient will be favoured by evolution. But the use of a sting as a backpack has only been observed in a handful of species, all belonging to this single genus of crabronid wasp *Oxybelus*; the assassin's backpack method for prey transport appears to be hard to evolve. It's not just a behavioural innovation: it also required some careful re-crafting of the sting morphology. The secret to fly-carrying lies not in having stronger stings but in having a sting that is better designed to bear mechanical loading. Fly-impalers have a slightly (but significantly) more curved sting than their non-fly-impaler relatives. The trick lies at the end of the sting – the bit that hooks into the fly. It also has a few barbs on the sting shaft which probably help via traction. Both these modifications may alter how the stress of mechanical loading is distributed – another biomechanical solution provided by wasps.

Perhaps the assassin's stiletto weapon is a good simile for the

* The machinery that mediates sting precision is quite specific to the solitary hunting wasps. For social wasps who primarily use their sting for defence, the precision, the ability to identify the right substrate, the careful cleaning of the sting are all less important than for a solitary hunting wasp.

wasp sting, after all. Stings are modelled as diverse variations on a theme, to suit the personal style of the wasp who chooses to wield it. But the mechanics and external appearance of the sting are only the start of the story. The secrets of solitary wasps lie hidden inside their stings.

# II

Even the most devoted entomologist struggles to get a grip on the huge diversity of life histories, behaviour and ecology of solitary wasps: with 32,000 species, there is no shortage of delights. But how to make sense of them? Naturalists of the late nineteenth and early twentieth centuries would have benefited from *On the Origin of Species* (published in 1859) in which Darwin's insights led him to use a genealogical tree in order to consider evolutionary relationships. Indeed, in 1866 they would have seen the first Darwinian phylogenies published by the German zoologist Ernst Haeckel in his book *Generelle Morphologie der Organismen*. In this landmark of evolutionary biology, Haeckel proposed his biogenic law, famously stating that 'ontogeny recapitulates phylogeny'. By this he meant that organisms should be grouped together based on genealogical (heritable) development, not typological classification based on common characteristics that shows no regard for shared inheritance.

Haeckel's evolutionary family trees were elegant and stylised: the pedigree of man depicts a sturdy baobab-esque tree, with a thick trunk indicating the crucial importance of man at the canopy. Trees for other organisms resembled willowy seaweed being buffeted by the waves. Sadly, in the late 1800s and early 1900s there was not even a basic evolutionary tree of the Hymenoptera, and certainly nothing for the specific cluster of hunting wasps. Early naturalists, therefore, had to take matters into their own hands and work out how to make sense of these eclectically diverse insects. Guided by the natural history they'd observed, what better way to make sense of the solitary wasps than to group them according to their prey?

Collectively, solitary wasps prey on a huge diversity of creatures, including caterpillars, crickets, roaches, flies, spiders and even weevils. But scrape the surface of taxonomy and a remarkable pattern of prey fidelity emerges. At the family, sub-family, genus or even species level, solitary wasps are specialist assassins. The profound importance of prey-type to the early Wasp Whisperers as a way to impose order on the myriad of hunting wasps is evident from their books. Many chapters were devoted to specific wasps based on what they hunt, from 'The Bee-eating *Philanthus*' (Fabre, 1879), 'The Spider-Hunters' (Peckham and Peckham, 1905) and 'The Bug-Hunters' (Peckham and Peckham, 1899) to numerous chapters with titles devoted to other wasp enemies such as the caterpillar, grasshopper, beetle and fly – not least entomologist Howard Evans's 1963 'Thirteen Ways to Carry a Dead Fly'. The Wasp Whisperers framed their stories around the taxonomy of the prey rather than that of the wasp.

It was this prey fidelity that sparked Fabre's obsession with solitary wasps. We see it begin with an unexpected moan in the first chapter of *Souvenirs Entomologiques* about how poorly paid he is, for one so highly educated. Happily, Fabre is distracted from this injustice when reading about a yellow-faced crabronid wasp that hunts the beautiful emerald and gold *Buprestis* jewel beetle: 'And so I was forgetting the poverty and anxieties of a professor's life.' The essay Fabre was reading was written by the father of entomology Léon Dufour (1780–1865)* who described

---

* Léon Dufour was the first to describe the spermatheca (the sack in a hymenopteran female's abdomen that stores the sperm of her mate(s)), the poison gland and also another gland – named after Dufour himself – involved in the sting apparatus that secretes chemicals used in communication by social insects. Dufour's gland also produces the abdominal secretion that hover wasps use to place their egg in a cell of their nest.

the unearthing of hundreds of jewel beetles from the burrows of the wasp *Cerceris*. In 20 years, Dufour had managed to spot only one of these beetles above ground and yet here he wrote of the buried treasure under his feet – more gems than he could count. Even more remarkable, no matter which corner of the country he went hunting *Cerceris* treasure, the beetles he found all belonged to the same single genus, *Buprestis*: 'Not even the very smallest mistake had been made by the wise wasp,' said Dufour of this remarkable discovery.

Fabre's interest in insects stretched back to his early childhood, when he had delighted in collecting bees, beetles and butterflies, yet reading Dufour's account of the beetle-hoarding *Cerceris* proved to be Fabre's wasp-eureka moment, and it's worth quoting in full:

New lights burst forth: I received a sort of mental revelation. So there was more in science than the arranging of pretty beetles in a cork box and giving them names and classifying them; there was something much finer: a close and loving study of insect life, the examination of the structure and especially the faculties of each species.

Is this picture of prey fidelity by these early naturalists too convenient? It makes for a good story. Or are these solitary wasps truly so faithful to their meals? My curiosity piqued by these old books, I decided along with two colleagues, Alessandro Cini and Ryan Brock, to scour the literature to identify the prey for as many solitary wasp species as we could find; 25,000 records from 15 wasp families* and a lot of backache later, we assembled a predator-prey network for the solitary wasps. The Wasp

* There are 22 families of solitary wasps. We could find no data in the literature on the predator-prey relationships of the Bradynobaenidae, Chyphotidae, Mutillidae, Myrmosidae, Plumariidae, Sierolomorphidae or Thynnidae.

Whisperers were right: the majority of these wasp families (10 of the 15 for which we found data) hunted prey from a single taxonomic group. Some were partial to a specific genus or species; others were a little more eclectic in their taste, but still limited themselves to quarry from the same family or order. The prey loyalty of solitary wasps is *not* entomological mythology.

The secret to being a successful hunter, and a specialist at that, lies in the wasp's method and the active ingredients of its venom. A solitary wasp may need to paralyse prey that is 15 times her own body weight, and so it is perhaps unsurprising that the venoms' active molecules are of significant pharmacological interest to us humans. Venom therapy was practised in ancient Greece, China and Egypt, but apart from a flurry of interest in 'apitherapy' during the nineteenth century, its benefits for human health have been remarkably unstudied until recently. The early naturalists clearly recognised that wasp venom was pretty special stuff, but they knew little about its composition and mode of action.

By the 1950s, biochemists had started to play around with wasp venom, identifying some of its key ingredients as histamines and polypeptides called kinins. Modern scientific techniques have helped to move venom research from the alchemy of the biochemistry lab to the domain of the geneticist, revealing how the insect synthesises the venom and how this varies among species, and giving us its active ingredients – the proteins. Venom components are now used widely to treat inflammatory diseases like rheumatoid arthritis and tendonitis, and interest is growing in their use as treatments for immune-related diseases and even tumour therapies. Unsurprisingly, the best-studied venom is that of the most aggressive social wasps, which has provided vital information for treating people with highly allergic reactions.

Bee and wasp venom appear to share many chemical and biological properties: they include proteins and neurotransmitters like serotonin, histamine, dopamine, noradrenaline and adrenaline. Bees are just vegetarian wasps, after all, who owe the basis of their venom cocktail to their evolutionary waspy roots. Useful bee-specific venom constituents include peptides like melittin and apamin, which have anti-inflammatory properties. But from an ecological perspective, bee venom is less interesting than wasp venom as bees only use venom in defence, while wasps use their venom for both hunting and defence. So despite the interesting beneficial ingredients of bee venom, there are likely to be more interesting and useful biochemical properties in the venom of wasps, especially solitary wasps who need to paralyse and preserve their prey so carefully.

Biochemically, is what you need to perfectly paralyse a grass-hopper the same as you need to knock out a spider? What subtle alchemy is it that makes one wasp an effective assassin of caterpillars and another the mistress of flies? Why does the venom of some species result in complete and permanent paralysis of not just the preferred prey but other invertebrates too (for example, *Philanthus* beewolves), while different species' venom succeeds only in temporary paralysis (such as *Homonotus* spider-hunters)? Venom potency might also influence which part of the prey is stung: a weak venom must be inserted in or near nerve centres; a powerful one, or one that retains its potency over time, might not need to be delivered quite so precisely. At least that's the idea.

The possibility of harnessing the pharmacological power of solitary wasp venom was first suggested by researchers in the 1980s when they began to access the technology needed to interrogate the active ingredients of venom. Yet solitary wasp venom, and how it influences behaviour and ecology, remains poorly studied. This is a shame, as unravelling its chemistry could reveal insights into the co-evolution of this predator's toolkit (her venom) and the prey's physiology. Could this knowledge even have the potential to unlock such biochemical secrets as the design of pesticides for particular species of arthropod pests?

Imagine labs dedicated to synthesising the prey-paralysing ingredient of wasp venom. You could order a biomimetic pesticide specifically for paralysing garden aphids or cabbage-white caterpillars, or if you're a bit of an arachnophobe, you might choose one that targets house-spiders.

There are two components of wasp venom that scientists think are of medical importance. The first are the bradykinins. These are peptides (chains of peptides make proteins) that promote inflammation. This can be a good thing: it makes them a useful tool in medicine. For example, bradykinins cause vasodilation (opening of the arteries) and drugs that stimulate these peptides can be used to treat high blood pressure. Bradykinins are also used in intensive care patients to help the blood system deliver drugs around their bodies, quickly. But they have a dark side: bradykinins can induce pain because blood vessels are liable to expand and become leaky, leading to inflammation of surrounding tissues.

Bradykinins were discovered in 1949 when a team led by Brazilian pharmacologist Maurício Rocha e Silva hit upon them by accident while studying snake venom. At the time pit vipers were presenting enormous clinical problems among workers in the sugar and coffee plantations of Rocha e Silva's state of São Paulo. One day a pit viper was brought to his lab for the team to observe how its venom induced vascular shock in dogs. Rocha e Silva was expecting to find that the dog's muscle contractions were due to histamine or acetylcholine, which was the understanding of venom action in the 1940s. However, when the venom was added to defibrinated blood it sparked huge amounts of activity, which could not be explained by these chemicals. Moreover, the activity was rather delayed in its onset, with slow contraction of the muscles. Rocha e Silva named the factor responsible for this activity 'bradykinin'.

A few years later, in 1954, a pair of chemists plucked the venom sac from the nether regions of a living (but chilled) social wasp, *Vespula vulgaris.* Just like Rocha e Silva, the researchers were on a quest to determine whether the liberation of histamines could explain venom action, but they also had a hunch that something else was going on – 'an extremely potent, unidentified constituent' which produced delayed, slow muscle contraction. Sounding familiar? They concluded that it was a bradykinin-like chemical, with similar properties to that described by Roche e Silva and colleagues a few years earlier. These became known as 'wasp kinins', but would later be given the more generic description of bradykinin.

Today, it is well known that bradykinins are the key neurotoxin component of wasp venom. They give the hunter the power to ensure that its prey victim is properly paralysed. Immediately after injection, bradykinins trigger the relaxation of smooth muscle in the victim, causing its muscles to contract more slowly and disrupting the neurotransmitters in the insect's central nervous system. The result is an effective numbing of the victim's nerve activity. Ants also have 'wasp kinins', inherited from their wasp ancestors and retained for hunting. Bees, however, appear to have lost them. This is excusable, since synthesising a nerve agent that paralyses living tissue could not be considered an essential tool for pollen-foraging. Intriguingly, though, not all wasps have these magic peptides. Apoid wasps (Crabronidae and the Sphecidae digger wasps), Eumeninae (such as potter wasps) and Pompilidae (the spider-hunters) all appear to lack bradykinins in their venom, but they still manage to paralyse their prey effectively. The jury is out on which ingredients they use.

The 'mammoth wasp' is a European species of scoliid wasp, and it happens to be the largest wasp in Europe. Fabre described it as a monster 'sucking at the breast' of her prey. He wasn't being melodramatic: they are impressively vulgar-looking insects that sometimes cause great commotion as they are often mistaken for being large social wasps like the *Vespa* hornets. Stocky, with large abdomens – they lack the supermodel-extended slender waists of their more elegant relatives – these scoliids spend their time digging around in the dirt, looking for scarab beetle larvae.

In the 1980s, the mammoth wasp became a leading lady in a series of landmark papers that used cockroaches to show how wasp kinins can irreversibly block synaptic transmission across nerve cells. Interestingly, the neurone pathways that are disrupted by bradykinins are the same as those targeted by the group of widely used pesticides (known as neonicotinoids) that have been contributing to the declining populations of pollinating insects around the world. There is now overwhelming evidence that these pesticides have detrimental effects on the cognitive functioning of insects. Wasp kinins and pesticides act on the same insect neuronal machinery. It seems that the pharmaceutical industry has been mimicking the pharmacological secrets of solitary wasp venom without even realising it.

The importance of understanding bradykinins goes far beyond wasp venom. They are thought to play some role in explaining the more severe symptoms presented by COVID-19 patients during the 2020–21 pandemic. The virus SARS-CoV-2 that causes COVID-19 upsets the balance of two enzymes in the body that regulate blood pressure (ACE and ACE2). When it invades, SARS-CoV-2 triggers a decrease in ACE levels. These ACE enzymes degrade bradykinins, and as a result of this imbalance bradykinins start to build up, causing inflammation in virus-infected cells and their neighbours. This has been termed a 'bradykinin storm' because of a positive feedback loop: inflamed cells trigger changes in bradykinin levels and receptors, leading to even greater inflammation.

An analysis of sequence data collected from critically ill COVID-19 patients in Wuhan, China found that the gene expression of cells in their airways showed reduced levels of ACE and increased levels of ACE2. The same study also detected increased production of hyaluronic acid in lung cells. Hyaluronic acid is an important 'goo' produced by your body – it's in your cartilage, eyes, skin, and is a highly hydrophilic component that can absorb more than 1,000 times its weight in water, forming a jelly-like 'hydrogel'. In the right place, it's useful. But put it in the eye of the bradykinin storm, and the leakage of this fluid into the lungs may explain why COVID-19 patients struggle to breathe.

Bradykinins are not the only chemical of note in the cauldron of wasp venom. The toxic peptide mastoparan is one of the best-studied components of wasp venom because of its anti-microbial, anti-viral properties and its potential role in cancer treatment. Mastoparan is more toxic to cancer cells than it is to normal cells. Exactly how it messes with those cells depends on the cell type, but typically it adheres to the cell wall, forming transient pores. By effectively causing cell walls to haemorrhage, cell death follows. *In vitro* trials with mice have shown it to be successful in killing cancer cells. But using venom is challenging: it's highly toxic, not just to cancer cells. It also rapidly degrades in the blood, making it hard to harness for the purpose of tackling specific cells.

Scientists have begun to solve this problem by providing it with a carrier – a polymer or liposome – that can circulate for longer in the body and that preferentially accumulates at the tumour site. Researchers have developed Mitoparan – an analogue of mastoparan – to target breast cancer cells, just like its wasp-made cousin. Mitoparan remains inactive when attached to a polymer carrier, but becomes active once released at the tumour site, infiltrating cell walls and causing tumour cells to die.

Not all solitary wasps completely paralyse their prey. Perhaps the most famous example of this is the zombification of the American cockroach *Periplaneta americana* by the Emerald jewel wasp, *Ampulex compressa*. Several times smaller than its prey, the wasp can't carry, or even drag, the victim to her burrow. Instead, she has evolved a clever way of manipulating the cockroach such that it will walk itself to its own underground tomb.

She delivers just two stings. The first is a rather crude stab at the thorax, designed to disable the prey by temporarily paralysing its front legs. With the cockroach immobilised, the second, more toxic sting can be administered directly into its brain, and the behaviour-changing zombifying magic starts to work. A neurotoxic cocktail blocks the receptors of the neurotransmitter involved in complex movements like walking, which transforms the roach into a zombie slave who can just about walk but cannot resist the commands of its mistress. Using its antennae as a leash, the mistress wasp leads the roach like a well-trained poodle to an underground nursery for baby wasps. The chemical cocktail of the jewel wasp's venom is among the most remarkable of all the venoms of hunting wasps, a delicate balancing act rendering the prey helpless enough to be led to its own tomb yet alive enough to remain fresh and juicy for the baby wasps to consume, organ by organ.

If Léon Dufour and his jewel-hoarding *Cerceris* wasps had not persuaded Jean-Henri Fabre to become a wasp whisperer, undoubtedly the chemical magic of solitary wasp venom would surely have done the trick. In fact, I think I can hear a little more than a whisper coming from his grave.

# III

The female beewolf (not to be confused with the male protagonist hero of the Old English poem *Beowulf*) is aptly named, as many species of its genus *Philanthus* wolfishly hunt bees. Since so many of us are fond of bees and appreciate the important jobs they do, you are forgiven for feeling a little uncomfortable at the prospect of hearing about these specialist bee-killers.

The European beewolf *Philanthus triangulum* hunts honey-bees.* Jean-Henri Fabre was enthralled by the 'bee-slayer', as he called her, taking great scientific pleasure in placing her in his signature bell-glass observation chamber along with a handful of honeybees, whereupon he would sit back to watch the show. Wasp and bee wrestle like gladiators, tumbling around the bell chamber, belly to belly, the wasp tussling 'with the rough clumsiness of a child handing its doll', until she stands 'magnificent' with the bee straddled beneath her, and folds her abdomen upwards to sting it 'under the chin'.

Fabre claimed her method was unique among the hunting wasps, and he took great pains to find the exact incision point on the bee's chin, 'a defect in the armour'. But what was even more remarkable, thought Fabre, was that unlike the other hunting wasps the beewolf was 'a butcher not a paralyser', as her sting delivers the venom directly to the cervical nerves, rendering the victim immediately dead: 'She wants a corpse, not a paralytic patient.' The full compliance of death is needed, Fabre reasoned, in order to 'milk' the honey from the bee's crop and lap up the sugary meal from its mandibles. A paralysed insect may be inert, but there are 'internal energies and organic forces' that mean it will not yield. 'Things are different with a corpse.'

Fabre watched wasp after wasp squeeze, bleed and milk her victim until there was no syrup left inside, before delivering it to her burrow for her baby to feed on. But why should the mother murderess rob the bee of its honey before serving the corpse to her young? If it is for her own delectation, it would surely be easier to visit a flower, as the bee did. Fabre conducted an impressive array of experiments, in which he offered beewolf larvae (and indeed other larvae) bees whose crops had not been emptied, bees emptied of honey experimentally and bees he had

---

* There are at least 50 species of *Philanthus* beewolves. But it is only the species *Philanthus triangulum* that specialises in hunting honeybees.

refilled with honey. So many died – Fabre was flummoxed. He had proven abilities as a 'foster-father' of wasp babies – 'How many pupils have not passed through my hands and reached maturity in my old sardine-boxes as comfortably as in their natural burrows?' He concluded that the crop must be emptied otherwise the larvae would be poisoned by the syrup.

After pages of musing about the unfathomable efforts of the mother slayer, he 'withdraws [his] epithets in order to admire the insect's maternal logic'. But how does the mother know that the syrup is poisonous for her offspring? How has the situation arisen in which a mother feasts only on sugar and her babies only on flesh? Fabre ranted feverishly about how, if he 'were a believer in evolution', he might imagine that in the ancestors of the beewolf both adults and larvae may have lived off prey, but that 'the costly habit of living off prey, which does not favour large populations, was maintained for the feeble larva'. Yet Fabre was a steadfast critic of Darwin's, and he delivered this explanation mockingly, like a child's playground taunt, eventually dismissing it very simply: 'I don't believe a word of them [the evolutionists].' He'd rather claim that 'science offers no reply' to the question of why the split diets exist than to accept the 'chain of very logical deductions' from an evolutionist.

Fabre's experiments with *Philanthus* were impressive, but his conclusions were not entirely correct. He was wrong about the beewolf mother killing her prey; she is merely paralysing them, just like the other solitary wasps. He would also be horrified to learn that occasionally female beewolves provision their cells with the parasitised males of their own species. He was so close to discovering the pharmacological magic that lay buried in the mother beewolf. The wasp removes the honey from her victim's crop probably to minimise the chances of microorganisms devouring the prey before her baby has feasted fully. But this is only the beginning of a beewolf's repertoire in her marvellous medicine cabinet; the real magic lies in the antibiotics she produces.

It wasn't until ten years after Fabre's death that Alexander Fleming accidentally discovered antibiotics. But Fabre was no stranger to the concept of the importance of controlling micro-organisms. By the time he first wrote about wasps in the 1880s, Louis Pasteur's germ theory had become widely known (if not accepted) and Joseph Lister had just demonstrated the importance of using carbolic acid as the first antiseptic to kill bacteria in the operating theatre.

It may have been a letter from Léon Dufour that introduced Fabre to the question of a role for antiseptics in wasp venom. In their correspondence, Dufour suggested that these wasps might use some form of preservative, an 'antiseptic', to ensure the paralysed beetle prey stay fresh. Dufour was a trained medical doctor and so understood the general importance of antiseptics. He was also a microscope enthusiast and he'd examined the beetle victims of *Cerceris*, only to be astounded that beetles which had been buried with a wasp larva for a week or more would be in pristine condition. 'There is some special circumstance about the *Buprestis* [beetle] killed by *Cerceris* that saves them from desiccation and putrefaction for a week and perhaps two,' he wrote.

Dufour experimented by exhuming beetle victims from the lairs of wasps, keeping them for a few days before dissecting them, only to find they were 'as perfectly preserved as if I had used my scalpel on the insects' live entrails'. Dufour concluded that the wasp must inject some antiseptic of some sort into the beetle prey. 'How immensely superior to our own pickling-processes is that of the wasp!' he remarked. 'What lessons can we not learn from her transcendental chemistry!'

Fabre did not share Dufour's enthusiasm. In fact, throughout his writings he remained scathing of the idea that wasps create their own form of antiseptic. Perhaps he misunderstood antiseptics, for he appeared to think their presence was incompatible with the fact that prey were paralysed and unable to move. After a few pages of ranting in *More Hunting Wasps*, Fabre concluded: 'There will be no more talk of antiseptics, unless and until tinned Herrings begin to frolic in their brine.'

Over a century later we have some answers for both Dufour and Fabre.

I have discovered that having teenage children in the house limits the opportunity for kitchen microbiology experiments. This is because teenagers move in on leftover food faster than microorganisms do. But on the rare occasion that I am home alone for a while, I am all too readily reminded of how quickly leftover food can become a playground for opportunistic bacteria and fungi. Early humans learned to preserve food by burying it in ice or drying it in the sun. Today we pickle, cure and can it, but we also rely on expensive chemicals and chilling equipment. If our preservatives don't work, we simply throw out the offending items.

Solitary wasps don't have this luxury: once they've sealed their living larder, their babies are at the mercy of a plethora of underground microbes that are as eager to suck life from the prey as the hungry wasp larva itself. Luckily, tucked inside the bodily fluids of solitary wasps is a smorgasbord of antiseptic and antifungal tricks.

The beewolf has a large and varied medicine cabinet, yet its chemical secrets lie not in the wasp's venom but in its head, and it is all because of the problem that bees have with fungi. Here is an experiment that you could try at home: find yourself a bee and a beetle and (for purely scientific purposes) treat them to a couple of hours in your kitchen freezer for a quick and uniform euthanasia. Then take them out and bury them both in separate pots of soil. After a week or so, dig them up and you'll find that the bee is a fuzzy ball of diverse life forms, most of which is not bee. Conversely the beetle will be largely intact. This is because the surface of a beetle is much harder than that of a bee and when buried in moist soil it takes fungi much longer to set up residence. Fungi are the Achilles heel for personal hygiene among Hymenoptera in general: fungi and microorganisms love them. So if you're a bee-hunter (and especially if you're burying a bee with your beloved babies), you need a kick-ass microbe-management plan if you want to keep your prey from becoming a breeding ground for fungi and bacteria. Evolution has dealt beewolves several trump cards in this respect.

A mother beewolf's first trick is to construct a disease-repelling death chamber for the prey by embalming it in her spit. The mother wasp licks her victim all over before laying an egg on it. The embalming process encases baby and prey in a water-repellent casing. Many insects similarly produce their own waterproofing, which serves as a protective cloak against desiccation and disease. The beewolf's prey-embalming waterproofing stops water accumulating on the outside of the death chamber, making it less favourable for fungi growth. It's akin to wrapping a waterproof jacket around your child to keep them dry on a damp day – pretty average parenting.

But the beewolf-mama is not your average parent. Her second trick involves antibiotics. You have most likely benefited from a dose of these to help you fight off an infection. Before antibiotics were discovered, something like a minor scratch could have landed you with blood poisoning, which was often fatal. Antibiotics – or bacteria-killers – are in fact bioactive secondary metabolites that are produced by bacteria. Their discovery by Alexander Fleming, in the form of penicillin in 1928, marked a revolution in our ability to combat infectious diseases. A professor of bacteriology at St Mary's Hospital in London, Fleming discovered the antibiotic properties of the fungus *Penicillium chrysogenum* by accident after returning from holiday to find that his plates of *Staphylococcus* (a bacteria that causes boils, sore throats and abscesses) had been invaded by mould. He spotted a strange *Staph*-free zone around the invading mould, as though a forcefield were preventing the *Staphylococcus* from growing beyond.

The forcefield had been generated by secretions from the fungus *Penicillium chrysogenum*, which turned out to have the same effect on a wide range of harmful bacteria, including *Streptococcus*, *Meningococcus* and the diphtheria bacillus. It would be a further 13 years before another set of scientists at Oxford University – Howard Florey, Ernst Chain, Norman Heatley and a team of 'penicillin girls'* – transformed Fleming's accidental discovery into something that was clinically useful, saving millions of lives in the process, especially during the Second World War, and making it one of the greatest advances in therapeutic medicine.

Today, over 100,000 tonnes of antibiotics are produced annually for use in agriculture, food and health, and society faces the challenge of bacteria having evolved resistance to the most commonly used antibiotics. We tend to forget that the antibiotic products of microbes and fungi are a natural phenomena: organisms produce them, along with other useful bioactive agents like anti-fungals, anti-virals and immunosuppressants, to combat other microorganisms they come into contact with. Just like any other living organism, bacteria microbes evolve in response to changes in their environment to maximise their fitness. Chance genetic mutations afford new strains of the bacteria the ability to resist the toxicity of antibiotics. These mutant variants survive and become the dominant genotype in a population. We would be better equipped to predict and manage antibiotic resistance if we understood more about the ecology and evolution of antibiotics.

---

* The penicillin girls were real. A team of six women were recruited by Howard Florey to 'farm' the penicillin. Their names were Ruth Callow, Betty Cooke, Peggy Gardner, Claire Inayat, Megan Lancaster and Patricia McKegney. They were paid £2 a week, and their tasks were to inoculate and oversee fermentation.

Beewolves have made a surprising contribution to our understanding of this area. The mother wasps inject their swaddled babes with antibiotics from their antennae. Beewolf mums are hosts to *Streptomyces* bacteria, which under a microscope look like the threads of a chaotic long-pile carpet. Importantly, it is a species of *Streptomyces* (*Streptomyces griseus*) that produces the antibiotic Streptomycin, the second most medically useful antibiotic to be discovered after penicillin, in 1942. Today, 80 per cent of medicinal antibiotics are sourced from *Streptomyces*.

What can the beewolf teach us about these medically important microbes? The beewolf mum excretes *Streptomyces* bacteria from gland openings between her antennal segments and deposits it as whiteish masses onto the walls of the baby's cocoon. Originally these deposits were thought to serve as orientation marks for the emerging adult wasp, helping it to find its way out of its nursery. But their role is much more impressive: these helpful bacteria kill any fungi inside the cocoon. Once deposited by mother beewolf, the wasp larva spreads the bacteria around its nursery (like any diligent toddler). If the larva happens to be female, it adopts these bacteria as a lifelong companion so that, just like her mother, she is equipped to keep her own offspring fungi-free.

This clever evolutionary mechanism (known as vertical transmission) ensures the bacteria stays closely hooked up with its host across generations. It's worked like this for 68 million years: evolution holds on to good innovations. The bacteria benefit too – they get exclusive bacterial rights to their house (the brood cell) in which they can propagate and hitch a free ride to the next generation of wasps via the larva, and they may even benefit nutritionally from the beewolf. Male beewolves lack the gland reservoirs that house the bacteria, and so say goodbye to their mum's friendly bacteria when they leave the cocoon as adults. This is a good example of how evolution invests in sex-specific parental care: mums need the bacteria as they do all the brood care; dads are just flying sperm – once mated, their lives are useless so they have no need to invest in apparatus for parental care.

Since the discovery of this relationship in 2005, researchers have found the same co-evolutionary relationships in all 25 studied species of *Philanthus*, but not in close relatives of beewolves (such as *Clypeadon* and some *Cerceris*) that do not hunt bees. Bees, tasty to both wasps and fungi, appear to have driven its evolution. Bacteria-insect relationships have been widely reported in a range of insects, but until this wild leap into the beewolf's cocoon, the only Hymenoptera known to have such remarkable relationships were the superorganisms of the leafcutter ants. This lowly solitary wasp has slowly begun stealing the stage as a model organism for understanding the ecology and evolution of antibiotics.

The pharmacological cabinet of the beewolf has further depths. The baby wasp can't spread the antibiotics around its nursery unless it hatches into a larva, and to do that the egg must first survive. This stage is a vulnerable one, since disease could strike. Anyone who's spent time with human babies will know that they are capable of producing the most horrifying smells, unbefitting one so small. Beewolf eggs also emit a highly toxic and volatile gas into their nursery: nitric oxide. This is the chemical used to fumigate fruit against fungal contamination. It infiltrates all the spaces in the brood cell where fungi could hide and kill it. But don't worry, the wasps' friendly *Streptomyces* bacteria appear to be immune.

The nitric oxide also condenses on the surface of the bee, gaining an oxygen molecule and producing globules of highly concentrated nitrogen dioxide – another antimicrobial agent. Because of the embalming, the amount of condensation is very small, meaning these droplets are highly concentrated, which makes them extra powerful fungicides. The magic combination of fumigation and embalming provides the beewolf babies with the cleanest nursery nature can buy.

Fabre's writing woke us up to the astonishing world of the beewolf, and his careful observations must surely have helped pave the way for the incredible discoveries of this insect's medicinal cabinet. Thanks to his medical knowledge, Léon Dufour was ahead of his time in suggesting wasps might produce their own antiseptics. But I think both Fabre and Dufour would have been truly flabbergasted to learn about the biological wonders of the solitary beewolf. The embalming chemistry, antibiotic-oozing antennae and toxic-fart eggs of this insect have certainly knocked me sideways. It's the stuff of science fiction, a barely imaginable evolutionary cocktail of chemistry, bacteria and behaviour that hides the complex secrets to one of nature's most remarkable pharmacists.

# IV

It's all very well having a sting that can deliver a cauldron of chemicals to asphyxiate a prey. But, Jean-Henri Fabre wondered, how should the victim be processed? Once it has been caught, how and where should it be stung? Recall the great pains he took to discover that the beewolf stung its quarry under the chin, where the armour was faulty. He was obsessed with the location and sequence of the stinging, which he believed would tell him how the prey was eased into a painless eternity of living sleep.

Fabre was not crazy to think this was an important question. Prey-handling involves effort; the energy invested in 'processing' a particular prey type needs to be weighed against the nutritional gains from that specific victim. Scientists have devoted whole careers to understanding how predators manage to balance the scales of energetics to ensure their hunting strategy is optimal. Prey profitability depends on the energy gain versus the hunting effort. Prey-handling is only part of the equation; searching for it and transporting it to the right place (usually a burrow, in the case of a solitary wasp) are also important.

How the solitary digger wasps, *Ammophila*, deal with their prey occupied a large part of Fabre's essays on wasps. It takes an especially curious type of person to want to figure out *how* a wasp manages to paralyse a writhing 'dragony thing' – a caterpillar 15 times her size. Fabre could not interrogate the content of the venom as we can today, but he could *watch* a female wasp grapple with her victim and *observe* the choreography of the first act of her prolonged execution dance. He deduced that the caterpillar's body has 13 segments, each of which has its own nerve centre. You know this too: if you were to chop the end segment off a caterpillar (please don't) or to damage a middle segment (no advocation intended), it can still crawl away.

Fabre realised that such anatomical independence presents our solitary wasp with a problem in the job of rendering its victim lifelessly living. Small caterpillars are easily tackled with one or two stabs, but dragony 'Grey Worms' (Fabre's favourite term) require more artistry. In order to transport the super-sized victim to her prepared burrow, our huntress needs to be sure that the prey has been properly anaesthetised, in order to curb its writhing and lashing as it attempts to escape. But the wasp also needs to be sure not to kill her victim. Because the nervous system of the caterpillar is compartmentalised into segments, a single sting will not do the job for a larger beast: the caterpillar will put up a valiant fight, flailing around with the segments it can still use, baring its leaf-mincing mandibles at its hunter and limp-looping away if it can. Fabre grasped that the wasp has to sting her prey several times to paralyse it properly. Remarkably, methodically, she administers a sting to most (if not all) of the caterpillar's segments.

This is where the elegant wasp waist really comes in handy. Via enviable acrobatic contortions, the wasp manoeuvres her sting to deliver shots in exactly the right places along the caterpillar's body. Her precise surgery stirred the 'innermost being' of Fabre and his companion as they lay prostrate on their tummies in the undergrowth, witnessing this vivisection for the very first time. He described their 'tears of undefinable emotion'. Do not mistake these for tears of empathy with the victim. These were the tears of scientists who had stumbled upon a moment of truth. Fabre believed that the processing of prey by a solitary wasp was a behavioural sequence that was fixed as a way to ensure that each wasp species excelled in handling its preferred quarry.

Fabre was not the only Wasp Whisperer to obsess over how *Ammophila* digger wasps deal with their victims. George and Elizabeth Peckham were trailblazers in the naturalist communities of the United States in the early 1900s, publishing joint papers on spider biology and behaviours, and leading the Wisconsin Natural History Society. The Peckhams were fans of Fabre and disciples of Darwin. They spent a good deal of their time in physical pursuit of wasps on their Wisconsin estate, which they documented in the books *On the Instincts and Habits of the Solitary Wasps* of 1899 and *Wasps: Solitary and Social* of 1905.

Their accounts ramble charmingly with relatable narratives of their (notably controversial) observations of the digger wasps that they chased through the cornfields, potato plantations and grasslands surrounding their Midwestern homeland. As a lion stalks her deer, as Indiana Jones pursues his treasure, the Peckhams hunted scores of wasps with enormous energy: 'We ran, we threw ourselves upon the ground, we scrambled along on our hands and knees in our desperate endeavours to keep them in view, sometimes with our eyes upon the wasps themselves and sometimes in pursuing their shadows ... and yet they escaped us.'

My fantasy Hollywood-esque image is of Elizabeth leaping fences in a hooped, ankle-length skirt and bloomers, with George at her heels in his shirt and neck-tie, under the blasting

Midwest sun. They told of weeks where they 'lived in the bean patch, scorching fatigue', lamenting how the wasps' prime hunting period coincided with the hottest time of day. Their tenacity was inspired by their hero Jean-Henri Fabre's account of his daughter Claire who followed an *Odynerus* wasp with 'unfaltering zeal until a sunstroke laid her low'.

The fine detail of the hunt held the Peckhams captive: why did the wasps show such diversity in their hunting strategies? The unpredictability of the behaviour of different individuals ground them down, their addictive desperation running close to madness. The Peckhams shared Fabre's feverish passion and drive to know *how*: how far did wasps have to fly to find their prey? How and where should the wasp sting the quarry to be sure of paralysing it effectively? How did the wasps get their elephantine victims home in one piece? What determined if they were successful or not? The Peckhams were asking the same questions that today's scientist would ask under the premise of optimal foraging theory, and they pursued their beloved wasps with the dogged resolve of a twenty-first-century urban commuter, leaping fences, elbowing commando-style through grasslands, zigzagging through giant corn stands, desperate not to lose sight of their wasp with her freshly hunted victim.

Reading the Peckhams' accounts, you can't help but leap these obstacles with them as they take you on their frantic adventures. We share their dismay when, after hours of chasing, they lose their wasp or the wasp inexplicably drops her prey so close to home and flies away. After the initial relief – the Peckhams 'were very glad of the chance to rest our tired eyes and nerves from the strain of following her' – their brilliant questions continue: why should she quit after carrying her quarry for so long? They had followed her for over two hours. Had she lost her burrow? Surely not, as 'at every return she proceeded on her journey in one general direction without any hesitation'. They settled on the conclusion that 'she had hunted too far afield': in modern-day behavioural ecology, this would be an example of optimal forag-ing theory – the energetic *costs* of getting the prey to the burrow weighed against the nutritional *benefits* of the booty to her larva, and coming up short. The concept that such trade-offs could explain animal behaviour would not appear in the scientific liter-ature until the mid-twentieth century, a good 50 years after the Peckhams' antics.

Just like Fabre, the Peckhams worried greatly about the order in which the segments of a prey caterpillar were paralysed, and they were vexed by the variations they observed in the hunting strategy of different wasps and different prey. But most of all they fretted about how some of their own observations did not agree with those of Fabre. The Frenchman had been sure that the middle segment of the caterpillar (on which the egg is usually laid) was invariably paralysed the most heavily, so that the baby larva's first meal would be sedated such that the larva would not be dislodged by the discomforted contortions of a dinner being eaten alive. There was much wringing of hands over this, as the Peckhams did not see the same thing. Where Fabre tended to focus on the bigger picture of biological processes and behav-iours, in search of a perfect single solution bestowed upon nature by God, the Peckhams embraced the importance of natural vari-ation as the fodder on which natural selection can act.

These early wasp luminaries brought collective unity to our understanding of how solitary wasps hunt, but they sat on opposing sides of Darwin's theory of natural selection. Fabre saw the careful choreography performed by *Ammophila* in subduing her prey as evidence for an omnipotent rule-making creator: the wasp's operation was far too incredible and effective to be the product of any natural process of selection or chance variation. In stark contrast, the Peckhams interpreted the same behaviour as evidence of natural selection through variation and survival of the fittest: the Peckhams were true disciples of Darwin, and the hunting precision of *Ammophila* (together with the wasps' many failures and strategies) no doubt inspired their efforts to introduce Darwinian concepts into secondary school education in the US.

If I were a steadily numbing caterpillar, I would think about defence. My mandibles are my only hope. I may look like a tranquil vegetarian but, if needed, my jaws are ferocious chompers of anything that upsets me and can be quickly redeployed from leaf-munching to wasp-munching. It would be too risky for my hunter to sting my head, as that would paralyse my brain (yes, we caterpillars do have brains) and ruin the whole 'living larder' plan. Instead, the wasp repeatedly squeezes my head with her own mandibles, which serves to put just enough pressure on my brain to sedate me. In between each squeeze she lifts her head to check on me: like the most skilled torturer, she wants to cause enough damage to tip me into a blissful and suppliant coma, but not so much that I die.

Our Wasp Whisperers were right about the importance of the stinging pattern and stinging effort. Where the venom is injected is indeed critical: most solitary wasps partially paralyse the central nervous system of their prey, immobilising but not killing it. The location determines how effective this is. The Whisperers were also right that the number of stings is important, for this ensures that the correct amount of venom is delivered for that particular target. Too much and the victim might die, rendering it useless for the wasp's purposes; too little and paralysis might be incomplete or temporary, risking the baby wasp's prey becoming its predator. But is this processing best described as the rigid behavioural programming championed by Fabre or a more flexible strategy as suggested by the Peckhams?

Rest easy in your graves, Elizabeth, George and Jean-Henri. You're all a little bit right. And all a little bit wrong.

Strict sting protocols exist, but the exact protocol varies depending on the type of wasp. The ancestral solitary wasps (like Scoliidae, Tiphiidae, Pompilidae, Ampulicidae) appear to paralyse their prey with just one or two precisely aimed stings. Crabronidae appear to exhibit a 'complete four-sting pattern': one to the throat and one to each of three thoracic segments; although with over 9,000 species in this group there may be variation in this pattern, yet to be discovered. The Eumeninae have two strategies: some apply a 'complete two-sting pattern', while others sting the throat, followed by the thorax and one or more to the abdomen. The number of stings ultimately depends on the size of the quarry.

This might explain why the Peckhams observed variation in the stinging behaviour of their *Ammophila*, and it shows how flexible predatory wasp behaviour can be. There are limits to this flexibility, though: a minimum number of stings is needed in order to hit those sweet nervous system spots which assure that ever-important lifeless living. The rest comes down to size. The fussier wasp species tend to favour the precise sting schedule much coveted by Fabre, while wasp species that are a little more eclectic in prey choice tend to be a bit more slapdash, causing more damage to their victim and adjusting their sting-invest-ment depending on its heft. Clever wasps. Mathematicians, as well as chemists.

Around the fire in my imaginary sitting room are assembled my three favourite Wasp Whisperers. I've brought them up to speed on our twenty-first-century understanding of how solitary wasps process prey. We've not made a huge amount of progress on their collective careful observations over the last century. There is an awkward silence. Elizabeth's hooped skirt and prim-trimmed blouse are rustling in synchrony, betraying her anticipation. George's head is bowed deep in thought. Even Jean-Henri Fabre is too polite to express his dismay, or perhaps he just wants another of those nice cakes I'm serving.

'Jean-Henri,' I say, 'you were absolutely right about the impor-tance of behavioural sequence.'

Fabre flashes a glee-filled grin around the room, galloping inwardly with the glory of a genius.

'But ...'

He dims a fraction.

'Elizabeth and George, your observations of divergent strategies show such incredible attention to detail; and how brave you were to question what you saw, what you'd read. That wasps deviate from the protocol is fascinating and important. Perhaps your prey were more variable in size than those that Jean-Henri observed?'

They nod like under-performing students, desperate for explanation.

All three luminaries fix their eyes on me. I am burning. I stare at the fire, wondering how to melt the tension that is growing in the room.

'Wasps play with the innate templates they inherit,' I say. 'These give them boundaries, rules. But without the ability to tweak that template and adapt to the prey they encounter, templates limit their options. Like the best chefs, evolution fiddles with its recipes when needed. If your recipe asks for a white onion and you only have a red one, do you go without dinner? Of course not: you adapt, adjust your recipe. If you don't, you go hungry. Maybe even die. That means no offspring for you.'

I look at Jean-Henri, the evolutionary sceptic in the room. He's not blinked yet.

'Predatory wasps need the discipline of that recipe – just as you, Jean-Henri, described,' I explain. 'But if the recipe doesn't have the flexibility observed by Elizabeth and George, the costs of processing prey may end up outweighing the benefits of the feast to their offspring.'

Jean-Henri nods slowly. Maybe he's coming round to the idea that evolution by natural selection is not so ridiculous after all.

'More tea, anyone?'

# V

Caterpillars are a bit like buses, or rain at a summer picnic: they arrive at unwanted places in unwanted numbers at unwanted times. Except when you want to *find* caterpillars; then they are never where you'd expect them to be. You'd be looking for caterpillars if you wanted to study how wasps find their prey, as Fabre did. His solution to the caterpillar hunt was to round up his entire family and get them searching while he lay belly-down keeping his eye on an *Ammophila* digger wasp: three hours, one sunstroke and a lot of very grumpy family members later, there were still no 'Grey Worms' to be seen.

Once Fabre stopped shouting at his incompetent family, he noticed that the wasp he'd been watching was lashing the ground with her antennae. Flicking his pocket-knife into action, he scraped at the spot in the earth that she was drumming on. She prodded a little more at the newly exposed soil. And then begins an unbelievable sequence of 'wasp-prods, man-digs' until ... 'Well done, my canny *Ammophila*!' Together they uncovered a Grey Worm. They repeated the sequence. And again. Eventually, after a mere five hours of wasp-leads-man teamwork, they had together dug up a bounty of five caterpillars! It is hard to believe such a story until you have spent a little time sitting with these elegant (and clearly clever) wasps. They quickly habituate to the presence of an observer, and you can happily sit beside them as they go about their important business. They become so fixated on their task that you can tickle their tarsi* while they dig a burrow, bury a caterpillar or disguise the entrance to a freshly laid brood chamber.

---

* Tarsi is plural for the 'tarsus', which is the 'toe' of the insect – the terminal segment of the leg.

What Fabre had witnessed is how gifted digger wasps are in detecting prey that live below ground. Hunting subterranean victims, as this digger wasp was doing, is a lot more challenging than hunting something above ground because visual cues are no use. If you have ever worried about the size of your nose, please just be thankful it is attached firmly with a broad base to the middle of your face and that you only have one (at least the two nostrils are stuck together to make a single compact unit). Your nose may be a little pointier or lumpier than you might like, but it is in no danger of running adrift. Not so for a wasp: her nose (or noses to be correct) is often longer than her body, ungainly, wispy and prone to getting caught in sticky crevices. These lustrous antennae have evolved to be expert detectors of both odour and rhythm: they are the insect's equivalent to a metal detector, revealing hidden secrets of the underworld.

Fabre's teamwork with *Ammophila* taught him that the wasp's antennae must be able to sense the caterpillar underground, but for the life of him he could not work out *how*. He decided that the Grey Worms had no odour, after testing this out on the 'young nostrils' of his children (being more sensitive than his own) and finding that none could detect a smell. He also excluded the possibility that the wasp was sensing underground vibrations made by the worms: after unearthing some and finding nothing underground for them to nibble on, he concluded that the worms could not be alerting the wasp to their presence by bumping around. He gave up trying to find out more: 'I despair of ever knowing.'

We can now relieve some of Fabre's despair. Chemicals are the internet of insect life, mediated via their own personal mobile device – the antennae. Chemicals connect an insect with every part of its life cycle – sex, prey, predators, food, living quarters. Their importance in insect communication was brought into sharp focus in 1959 with the discovery of bombykol – the first pheromone to be synthesised, and the sex pheromone used by females of the silkworm moth (*Bombyx mori*) to attract males across long distances. Male *Bombyx mori* have evolved preposterously feathery, double-Mohican antennae that can detect a molecule of a female's sexy perfume several hundred metres away. Despite this elaborate apparatus, chemically speaking the male's equipment is as simple as it gets: one type of odorant receptor in the bombykol receptor neurones of his antennae is all he needs to find his mate.

The chemical sensing mechanisms of moths have been well studied because they are an economically important group of insects, and this is especially so for *Bombyx mori* because it gives us silk, hence the name 'silkworm moth'. In fact *Bombyx mori* only exists in this form because we domesticated it (like we did cows, sheep, chickens, honeybees) over 5,000 years ago. Since being domesticated, male moths have lost the ability to fly and so rely entirely on the helping hand of humans: they are farmed as silk-pumping machines. The economics of the silk trade have helped fund research into their biology (what's left of it) in order to breed them effectively. *Bombyx mori* was the first lepidopteran (butterflies and moths) to have its genome sequenced (in 2008), and this was quickly followed by studies on the genes and receptors active in the antennae. This research has provided us with one of the most comprehensive tools for understanding the chemosensory mechanisms of insects.

Our knowledge of how wasps detect chemicals comes almost entirely from the parasitoid wasps, who have evolved to sense the cues of hidden prey.* In Part 1 we learned a bit about how some wasps respond to chemical cues sent into the air by plants that

---

* Recall from Part 1 that parasitoids are different to hunting wasps: they haven't evolved stings but instead have an ovipositor that they use to lay their eggs in or on their victims wherever they might find them. Hunting wasps, on the other hand, have evolved a sting – which is a modified form of the ovipositor – and they lay their egg on the prey after transporting it to a ready-made burrow.

are being eaten by caterpillars, bugs or beetle larvae. Plant volatiles produced in response to herbivory are widely used to draw
in natural enemies, like wasps, flies and beetles, to rid the plant
of its own predator, and such cues are easily detectable over long
ranges.

Cues produced by hosts may be more reliable than cues
produced by the plant, but are sometimes harder to detect. One
such cue is the smell of the host's excretory products. Few organisms can help their poos being a little smelly; it's the nature of
waste products, unfortunately. If you are hunting a specific type
of prey, what better way to find it than to grow highly attuned to
the smell of its poo? It's a form of chemical eavesdropping and
one that parasitoids have become well known for (insect poo
even has its own name, frass, which may not sound any less
silly). There is even a technical term for a chemical that is emitted by one organism and detected by other species which then
benefit from it – this is called a kairomone. Whether it's long-
range eavesdropping on the sweet stench of poo or on a plant's
call for help, the parasitoid wasp is able to narrow down its
search to a specific plant, and then it can use other cues like
vibrations to actually find the prey.

Less is known about how hunting wasps, like *Ammophila*, use
chemicals to locate quarry. But it is likely that they use kairo-
mones too as they would have inherited the same chemosensory
machinery from the common ancestor they shared with parasitoids. One such example comes from the tiphiid wasps, which
hunt scarab beetle larvae feeding on grasses. These wasps can
detect the chemicals that the grass releases when it is being eaten
by the larvae. In fact, these wasps are so effective at hunting beetles
that they have been used as biocontrol agents to control invasive
populations of beetles like the Japanese *Popillia japonica* and
oriental *Anomala orientalis*, which are major pests of turfgrass.

For prey that live underground, however, cues like vibrations
and chemicals are only useful for the hunter at very short range

since these don't travel far through soil. For example, the tiphiid wasps also hunt beetle larvae that burrow underground, locating these underground feasts by detecting the chemicals of body odour or frass emitted by the grubs and their trails – but they can only detect these chemical cues up to a depth of two centimetres below the surface. Anything beyond will likely be too deep to pinpoint.

The olfactory skills of wasps have made them patentable property, thanks to the creation of the 'Wasp Hound', a hand-held odour detector that uses the sensory powers of parasitoid wasps to indicate the presence of explosive materials like TNT, Semtex and gunpowder, or illicit substances like cocaine. The work engines of the Wasp Hound are the tiny parasitoid wasps *Microplitis croceipes*, which respond to chemical cues in the frass of their host, the moth *Heliothis zea*, in order to locate it. In the 1980s, scientists discovered that females of this wasp could be taught to associate a specific type of molecule with a reward through associative learning and so could be trained to detect very specific odours, even very closely related chemicals.

Wasps make better odour detectors than sniffer dogs for several reasons. First, they don't get tired like dogs and so can work longer hours. Second, unlike dogs, wasps are not likely to be influenced by the behaviour of their handler, or someone nearby. In dogs it's called handler bias, when an animal appears to be responding to a test stimulus when in fact it is reacting to the human close by. Clearly, if you're using an animal to tell you whether there's an explosive or dangerous chemical within reach, you want that animal to respond only to the presence or absence of the offending chemical and not to the anxious behaviour of a nearby human.

The most famous example of handler bias comes from a horse and his owner who gained fame in the early 1900s. Clever Hans the horse has since become a textbook story in any psychology tome. This is not a pantomime wind-up: Clever Hans was famous for his mathematical skills – he could count, he could add, subtract, divide, multiply, do fractions, tell the time, spell and even understand German. Incredible. His owner, Herr Wilhelm von Osten, could not be more proud: he'd say to Hans, 'What is six plus six?' and the horse would tap his hoof 12 times. Herr von Osten toured Germany with Hans, amazing crowds wherever he and Hans went. Such intelligence in a non-primate (for chimps can count) soon attracted the attention of scientists. They ascertained that this was not some cheap trickery on the part of von Osten: Hans would also get the answers right when other people chose questions and even when von Osten was not around.

But the scientists also realised that Hans only got the answer right when he could see the person asking the questions, and (importantly) only when that person also knew the answer. The scientists figured out that a raised eyebrow, an excited jiggle of a foot, a little intake of breath – any small signal from the handler – could trigger Hans to give any answer they wanted. So Hans was pretty clever: he was responding to cues given to him (unknowingly) by the human in front of him, cues so subtle that even the poor human didn't know they were doing it. But Hans was far from the mathematical genius that von Osten made him out to be: his maths prowess was simply an excellent example of handler bias. Dogs are equally vulnerable to handler bias. That is one reason why a sniffer wasp is better than a sniffer dog.

The third reason why parasitoid wasps make good odour detectors is because they are easily trained. Training an animal – be it a sniffer dog or a Wasp Hound – to respond to a stimulus is known as Pavlovian (or classical) conditioning. This kind of learning was discovered by a Russian physiologist, Ivan Pavlov, in the 1890s when he realised that he could get dogs to salivate at the ring of a bell. There is no evolutionary reason for a dog to salivate at the sound of a bell (unless their wolfy ancestors hunted circus bears). The dog had learned to associate the ringing with the arrival of food, because Pavlov had taken to ringing a little bell just before giving the animal its dinner. He had paired the innate response of the dog to food (release of saliva from the salivary glands, which help digest food) with a learned response to an inanimate object that was absolutely no use to the dog (a bell).

Every new parent learns to use Pavlovian conditioning to get their newborn baby to sleep: they pair a stimulus (such as a lullaby or rocking motion) with a physiological response (sleeping). Any parent will also know (through trial and error) that if they slip up and accidentally start singing the conditioned lullaby during playtime, the spell will be broken: baby does not want to sleep! This is a learning 'extinction': the association between that lullaby and sleep is broken. You might even have conditioned yourself to associate sleep with a nice cup of herbal tea before bed, or even a lavender-scented pillow spray.

The parasitoid wasps and the sniffer dog can both be trained to associate odours with a reward. Evolution has equipped parasitoid wasps to be excellent associative learners in order that they can update and modify the cues they use to detect the presence of prey, and even assess its quality. Scientists have found that these wasps are able to discern changes in the chemical cues released by plants that have been infested with caterpillars and also subterranean root-feeding flies. Why should this matter? Well, if a plant's roots are being eaten, this could affect the quality of the plant and possibly the quality of the caterpillars that are feeding on it. Some species of wasp have learned to tell whether a plant has infested roots or not and are therefore *attracted* to that plant. Other, closely related wasps are *deterred* by the same cue. It's not yet clear why this is so: such above- and below-ground interactions have not been so well studied. But the point here is that parasitoid wasps don't just have an incredibly well-developed chemosensory system, they can also adjust how they respond to these cues depending on the circumstances. Such associative learning is a more complex form of Pavlovian conditioning and makes them extremely useful insect versions of sniffer dogs.

The Wasp Hound takes advantage of these traits. Parasitoid wasps can be trained to detect methyl benzoate – the volatile component of cocaine – at concentrations as low as three parts per billion. They can even do this when the drugs are packed inside tea, but not when they are inside coffee. Who doesn't get distracted by the smell of a good brew of coffee! The Wasp Hound is an incredibly low-tech biosensor: a bunch of trained wasps are placed in a tube with a pinhole at one end. Air is pumped into the hole, and if the chemical that the wasps have been trained to respond to is present, they will flock to the pinhole. You can make it a bit fancier if you add in a little video camera connected to a computer, which can measure the density of wasps around the pinhole, and so give you an idea of how much of the chemical is present. Wasp Hounds caused quite a stir about 15 years ago, and they are now used to detect drugs, dead bodies, explosives and even 'boar taint' – the unsavoury smell, taste and flavour that pork has if it is produced from uncastrated pigs.

One hundred years ago, a little digger wasp taught Jean-Henri Fabre how to find a hidden caterpillar. Since then, we've learned a lot about the incredible abilities of parasitoid wasps as detectorists. We've even learned to exploit their amazing super-senses for purposes as diverse as controlling pest populations and combatting terrorism and drug-smuggling. I regret to say that, yet again, we may have disappointed Jean-Henri as we still have much to learn about how solitary hunting wasps, like *Ammophila*, use smell and vibrations to detect their prey.

# VI

The mud-dauber wasp *Sceliphron* is among the largest and most elegant of the solitary wasps.* You cannot fail to notice and be awed by her striking beauty, with her 5-centimetre-long body, supermodel wasp waist, yellow-and-black-striped abdomen and colour-coordinated long, dangling legs. She is a sphecid wasp, just like *Ammophila*, and is one of the six genera of sphecid wasps that hunt spiders exclusively. The Wasp Whisperers adored her. She earned herself an entire book, *The Ways of a Mud Dauber*, from the American entomologist George D. Shafer, who in 1949 wrote with endearment of hand-rearing these wasps, training them to lick honey from his finger. Shafer built special gelatin capsules that mimicked their mud cells, and studied their development, with a particular curiosity about their digestive tract and excretory products. In his 1963 book *Wasp Farm*, Howard Evans described how their unsightly nests, clustered like rusty pipes of slapdash clay, were as unpopular in people's houses as the elegant, black and yellow adult occupants. The husband and wife teams of Phil and Nellie Rau (1918) and the Peckhams (1905) both devoted a chapter each in their books to *Sceliphron* and her hunting of spiders.

The Peckhams were so enthralled with *Sceliphron* they wished they 'could get inside of that little head! If only we could be wasps for a day, and then come back and tell about it.' They watched the hunt with great excitement, as each wasp disturbed two or three spiders until she was satisfied with one as her prey. She would sting it once, perhaps to disable it (as with the jewel wasp and her cockroach), and then play with the quarry, rolling it into a ball this way and that before stinging again. A mother

---

* There are around 35 species of *Sceliphron*. All are equally impressive-looking.

wasp crams up to 20 spiders into a single brood cell, before sealing it up and bidding her spider-larder offspring farewell. She is pretty unfussy about her prey and fills her brood cells with a diverse range of spider species, reflecting her opportunistic attitude to stockpiling.

She builds her brood chambers side by side, like clusters of cocktail sausages, from mud masticated and moulded with some secret *Sceliphron* saliva. Chipping open her nests requires some effort but reveals the ugly side to her elegance. Her offspring go crazy for cruddy-brown, Jabberwocky-esque, pot-bellied, hairy-legged spiders. The larvae are naked, pasty sacks, puckered at one end with monstrous mandibles. They chomp their way through their hairy larder, to emerge several weeks later as beautiful as the mother. It's a journey of metamorphosis from naked beast to stripy beauty via hairy spider.

Phil and Nellie Rau played a mean game with their baby *Sceliphron*: they supposed that the larvae were somewhat sparingly fed by their mother and so added three extra spiders into a cell. The wasp larva promptly gobbled them up and so they added one more. By the following evening this too was gone and so they fed the larva another four more fat spiders. Gluttony got the better of the baby, for the next day two of the spiders had been eaten but the wasp baby was dead. It is rather hard to believe that the wasp larva should die of overeating, but sadly neither the Raus nor anyone else appears to have repeated this death-by-gluttony experiment on *Sceliphron*. What we do know about *Sceliphron* is a little bit more about how she catches her prey.

If there is a creepy-crawly that people fear more than wasps, it's spiders. If you are one of these people then one reason to appreciate wasps is their efforts as spider-killers. That a wasp should hunt any spider is quite amazing as spiders are no walkover as prey for an insect: they have ghoulish fangs that can administer a poisonous punch, and for those that live in webs, these are effective sticky traps for any insect predator. Moreover, spiders have an impressive array of abilities to outwit even the shrewdest of predators, from a direct spider-on-predator mandible wrestle to playing sitting duck, to skydiving from their webs by a thread to the ground and scampering off into the undergrowth, or just drag-lining to hang on a tantalising, hard-to-reach thread away from their web. Fleeing the web is a behaviour that many spiders have evolved to avoid ant predators, and it serves to confuse many wasp predators, but not all.

The strategies of wasps who hunt spiders are honed by natural selection to match well to their prey of choice in a co-evolving battle of wits: mistakes can be lethal for either party. Paralyser versus slaughterer: which will become the other's prey? Befitting the risks of the spider-hunter's trade, evolution has tweaked the sting apparatus of these wasps to ensure they minimise the risk of themselves becoming their victim's prey. The pinpointing and mobility of the sting is thought to be more advanced than in other hunting wasps: as keenly observed by the Peckhams, having a short and accurate capture-to-paralyse handling time must be under strong selection, and their ability to administer multiple jabs to any single victim certainly suggests evolution's risk assessment of their welfare has been thorough.

Madame *Sceliphron* is not just a pretty face: she hunts with the skill of a circus acrobat, plucking her prey straight from its web. Long legs and sticky webs do not sound like a great combination, especially when poisonous fangs are poised to take advantage of any mistakes that she may make. The secret to a successful hunt appears to be choosing the right kind of web. Over 3,000 species of spiders build two-dimensional webs: these orb webs are quick to build, and the proud spinner can sit at one end of the web or in the centre to await her prey. Another 8,000-plus species spin more complex webs, making a three-dimensional matrix of silk: these take several days to build, and the happy spinner sits deep inside her 'funnel'. 3D spinners are a bit younger, in evolutionary terms, than the 2D spinners.

*Sceliphron* hunt only the spiders that make the 'primitive' 2D webs. Spiders build webs to catch prey, of course, but they also serve to protect the spider from predators (like wasps). Which evolved first: waspy hunting ways or the spider web structure? It may be easier for a wasp to snare a spider sitting on a primitive web than one inside a funnel web: if so, the evolution of fancy 3D architecture may have been driven by the risk of predation from threats like wasps. Does the web prevent wasp attacks? Predator-prey interactions are shaped by natural selection, giving rise to a constantly evolving arms race in the strategies of hunter and defender. The spiders-evolved-3D-webs-to-deter-predators story is compelling, but the actual story (at least with wasps) is more of a conceptual tangled web.

Thanks to *Sceliphron* and our curiosity about how she hunts, we know that primitive web-spinners smell different to funnel web-spinners. This is because, depending on their web preferences, the spiders come laced with different chemicals on their cuticles. Cuticular hydrocarbons – producing and detecting them – are part of the perfumery toolkit of most arthropods, and have also been exploited by social wasps as identity badges, signatures of status and nest membership. The body surfaces of 2D spinners have more of these hydrocarbons than their 3D-spinning relatives, and thanks to an intricate array of choice experiments we know that the wasps use spider smell, not web design, to choose their prey. *Sceliphron* prefer 2D spiders over 3D spiders on or off their webs. They are also more attracted to a freshly laid primitive web than they are to a funnel web, suggesting that the web itself may also hold a chemical cue.

Frustratingly, the question of whether wasp predation has driven the evolution of complex spider webs remains outstanding. Wasps have evolved to associate specific chemical cues with 'safe' prey. Wasp individuals that have the chemoreceptor mutation that allows them to distinguish primitive spinners from funnel-spinners survive better and pass that useful mutation on to their offspring. The spider-smelling mutant would have spread through the wasp population, and their hunting habits would have become exclusive to 2D spiders. Imagine what this does to the 3D-spinning spiders: no wasp predators mean they do very well indeed. We are still waiting for the definitive experiment: present *Sceliphron* with a choice of 2D spiders on funnel webs and 3D spiders on primitive webs. Which one would *Sceliphron* go for? Such an experiment might tell us how useful 3D webs are as predator deterrents and the original drivers of predator-prey interactions. The wasps may associate chemical cues with web architecture, but it is equally possible that funnel-web spiders are more dangerous to wasps, not because of their web but because of some behavioural difference between spinners, which makes wasps more likely to be caught.

A final suggestion is that sphecid wasps simply have not evolved the chemoreceptors required to detect (and thus hunt) 3D spinners. According to the fossil record, 2D spinners were the only (main) spiders around when sphecid wasps evolved (in the early Cretaceous). 3D spinners do not appear in the fossil records until 2 million years later, after which the chemical toolkit needed by the wasps to hunt spiders had already evolved as a tight predator-prey interaction. I find this a hard explanation to swallow: there are almost three times as many species of 3D spinners as there are 2D spinners. Evolution is not static once it has solved a problem: if it were advantageous for the sphecid wasps to evolve the chemical machinery to hunt 3D spinners they would have done so. I'm still placing my bets on (but not in!) the funnel webs as the ultimate wasp deterrent.

The Peckhams were bewitched by the way *Sceliphron* goes about her work, 'briskly and gaily' gathering her clay and building her pots. It's as if the wasp takes pleasure in the tasks, and I defy anyone who spends even a little time watching *Sceliphron* not to be swept up into her world.

# VII

Sphecid spider-wrangling tactics are impressive, but the real spider-hunting champions are the playful pompilids, another group of arachnid connoisseurs found all around the world. They are such experts that arachnologists often use their nests as sampling pots for the local spider population: an especially clever trick for finding rare species too. There are many reasons to admire pompilids, above and beyond finding uncommon spiders. They are easy to identify, with their elaborate, often comically curly antennae. They are also behaviourally distinct: they remind me of a hyperactive toddler as they skip and skate along the ground haphazardly and apparently without direction or reason.

This playful behaviour must afford some benefits in detecting and/or catching their prey. It also makes them notoriously difficult to catch, as they perform Houdini-style disappearing acts within your insect net. It can be amusing to watch an engrossed entomologist, net in hand, skipping determinedly around a heathland in pursuit of a pompilid. It is less amusing to be stung by one: to paralyse a spider several times your size, you need a hefty venom cocktail and a meaty stinging apparatus. They are impressive stingers.

The success rate of the pompilid wasp's spider-hunt can be as low as zero per cent over dozens of attempts. Is the function of this game really to hunt or is it simply playtime? Play is rare in the animal kingdom and appears to be largely limited to mammals and birds, and the juveniles of those species at that. It is thought to help in cognitive development, improving the animal's ability to engage in cooperative behaviours such as sharing resources or access to mates. Play in insects is undescribed, possibly because many don't have a 'juvenile' life stage in which they are mobile and free to play, being holometabolous (whereby immature and mature life phases are separated by metamorphosis). Playful though our pompilid appears, and inefficient as it may seem, her 'play' is to confuse and tire her prey, not to cavort with it. Such cat-and-mouse confusion tactics are common among pompilids and worth the playtime as these wasps typically provision their brood with a single monstrous spider.

This behaviour extends to the hunt itself. Some species can walk Jesus-style across a web without getting stuck. Others use their incredible acrobatic flying skills to pluck individual spiders directly from webs. *Poecilpompilus mixtus* uses her body as ammunition, erratically dive-bombing the periphery of orb-web spider webs in the hope of dislodging an especially juicy eight-legged victim. As the harassed quarry skydive to the ground in a bid for freedom, our canny huntress gets to snap up the best of the bunch for her brood on a substrate more amenable to her hunt, apparently following an olfactory trail if the spider scuttles out of sight. These wasps have been clever enough to exploit the spiders' web-fleeing anti-predator behaviour to get them away from the sticky webs for an easier hunt.

Other pompilids specialise in hunting web-less spiders that nest in burrows. Any plucky young naturalist will know that the best way to get a spider out of her burrow is to poke a stick in and lure it out. The wasps play a game of peek-a-boo with their prey. Dozens of species of pompilids and sphecid wasps appear to play out these most energetic games and performances with little chance of reward. Tarantula spiders, for example, build nests out of furled leaves, providing an entrance at each end. From the spider's perspective, having a front and back door provides two lures for unassuming prey who might poke their curious heads in.

There appears to be a carefree childishness in the pompilus wasp, which takes advantage of this: she teases the spider by dashing between the front and back doors, taunting it with the idea that she (the wasp) might be an easy dinner, as the arachnid chases back and forth from door to door in a frantic attempt to capture this overly curious quarry. With any luck, an exasperated spider might finally make the mistake of stepping outside her burrow to sort things out once and for all: with a quick flick of the wasp waist, the spider is pierced (just once) on its abdomen and slips into a suppliant coma as the wasp's living larder.

Although intended as traps, webs also act as visual cues to predators like wasps that a juicy meal is waiting inside. How, then, does the spider-hunter find a spider that does not make a web? It is only recently that we have gained insights into how pompilid wasps pinpoint their webless prey. The secret lies, of course, in chemical cues. Just as digger wasps and tiphiid wasps are able to detect caterpillars several centimetres below the surface of the earth, and parasitoids can locate their host deep within the whorl of a plant, pompilid wasps use chemical signals to find their spider as it lurks deep in the sticky depths of its burrow.

Jean-Henri Fabre was perplexed by the apparent immunity of pompilid wasps to spiders: why did so few of the wasps he watched succumb to the murderous fangs of the arachnid? Ingenious as ever, he created a fight club for spider-on-wasp-on-spider action. In his bell-glass amphitheatre, he presented his *Segestria* (tube-dwelling) spider with a range of insects and observed the inevitable arthropod-wrestling that commenced. As he suspected, there was apparently something distasteful to the spider about the pompilid wasp: the *Segestria* was perfectly capable of pouncing on the wasp, overcoming it and piercing it with its mandibles, but for some inexplicable reason it would soon discard its prey like a mouldy egg.

Conversely, the spider would have no trouble in gobbling up a honeybee or fly. The magic of the pompilid remains elusive, but based on what we now know about the cuticles of other insects it is most likely that these wasps have evolved some sort of chemical component produced on their exoskeleton that is mildly repellent to spiders. It is most probably a non-volatile cuticular hydrocarbon, as the last thing a hunting wasp would want is to advertise her arrival at a spider's burrow with a waspy stench. Yet again, one is left bemused that the chemical composition of spider-hunting wasps has not been extracted and bottled as a household deterrent to spiders.

Other pompilids lurk around *Segestria*'s homestead, flitting imperiously across the funnel-web nest entrances, seemingly impervious to the trip-wire traps that would ensnare most other insects. Our huntress dips her antennae in and out of the entrances, checking who's home and which funnels are empty. She'd never be so careless as to enter an occupied burrow. If the owner is in, she might taunt them into protruding an exploratory leg, which she grabs in order to throw the spider to the ground for an easier hunt. Once it is paralysed, she must hide the prey away (usually hanging on some vegetation like a lost pair of pants) until she is ready for it. This is because pompilids hunt before they build their nest. It is the ancestral state for solitary wasps but it carries the obvious flaw that a hard-won prey item can be pilfered by another hunter while the mother is busy excavating a burrow.

There is a furtive market in stealing among the pompilids: why chance a high-risk, low-return spider hunt when you can steal a ready meal from the bushes? Equally, why dig a burrow if you can make use of a ready-made one? Solitary wasps are mistresses of theft: stealing prey from other wasps and a burrow from prey are low-cost strategies that compensate to some degree for a high-cost hunt. Natural selection ensures there is a balance among these two strategies within a population: if the propensity to steal becomes too common, the return for doing so diminishes and the pay-offs of doing your own hunting grow. It is evolutionarily stable for a mixture of strategies to persist.

It gets even more bizarre. Spiders parasitised by *Homonotus* wasps soon recover their faculties and go about their business, oblivious to the fact that they have a wasp egg attached to their abdomen. The spider remains ignorant even when that egg hatches and the wasp larva begins to chomp its way through the less essential body parts, ensuring that the spiders' vital organs remain intact until the larva is ready to pupate. Only then, when the spider larder has served its full nutritional purpose, does it finally keel over and perish. Spider claws and mouth parts are all that remain. The idea that an animal is happily wandering around with a part-chewed bottom might be a little stomach-churning, but this gruesome event is painless to the spider and all over within a few hours!

What is even more remarkable about *Homonotus* is that she appears to only select gravid female spiders to parasitise. She positions her egg in exactly the right place so that the hatching baby wasp larva can dive straight into the spider abdomen and feast deliciously on the developing spider eggs.* *Pompilus* is even cleverer, as she also manipulates the weaving skills of the spider to provide safety for her offspring. The spider spends her days in the terminal cell of her burrow, ever decreasing in form thanks to the fattening wasp larva. But during this time she inadvertently spins a protective envelope among the sand, making the burrow a safe haven for wasp pupation.

\*    \*    \*

* The insight that *Homonotus* selects only gravid spiders comes from a personal communication with entomologist Stuart Roberts, who reports having observed over 30 female *Cheiracathium erraticum* spiders with *Homonotus* larvae attached. All but one were gravid. The one that was not had already laid its eggs and the wasp larva died soon afterwards. This is truly remarkable: *Homonotus* females don't only find a specific spider prey, they can also somehow tell if it is a pregnant one or not.

The wasp-tarantula fights continue with the Peruvian *Pepsis heros*. If ever there was a group of wasps more responsible for the negative press than the vespines, it is this insect, known as the tarantula hawk wasp. These pompilids are the largest of the genus and specialist hunters of tarantulas. She is the darling of the nature docu-dramas, usually seen on screen in intimate contact with her hairy beast co-star, a stupidly fearless tarantula. *Pepsis* boasts a pair of beautiful danger-signalling orange wings and the second most painful sting of all insects (beaten only by the South American bullet ant, *Paraponera clavate*). But she gains her screen time thanks to her fearless success in hunting down tarantulas several times her size. Fangs on mandibles, it's a clash of the arthropods as the spider fights for its life. But a pair of palpitating arachnid pincers is no match for that wasp waist, which permits the acrobatic delivery of a killer shot into the spider's ample derrière. Unceremoniously, the stunned carcass is hauled to an underground lair, where the wasp has prepared it to be wet-nurse to a single egg.

You have to be lucky to witness this wasp-on-spider action first-hand and have the good fortune of living in (or visiting) South America. Before the technicolor glory of modern cinematography that now streams *Pepsis*-style horrors and wonders of the natural world to our living rooms on demand, we relied on the painstaking observations of our Wasp Whisperers. The last we will meet in this chapter is the great Russian arachnologist Alexander Petrunkevitch, whose delightfully descriptive prose conjures a picture of the action just as well as any film can. Petrunkevitch's 1926 30-page account of his experiments brings into sharp focus the nuances of the lengthy stake-out between these poorly matched boxers that we miss in filmed versions, including the nonchalant taunting of the spider by the wasp. It is a carefree wasp who skips around the spider as if she is wearing an invisibility cloak and pokes her head out just for fun every so often. This will be the chemical cloak of immunity that Fabre stumbled upon in his glass amphitheatre in France many years before. Twenty-seven encounters later, Petrunkevitch described a critical moment with a crushing of wasp wing in the spider's jaws. *Pepsis* has surely met her match. But with the panache of the best boxers, she brushes her wings down and appears unscathed.

Petrunkevitch noticed that she produced a rather nasty odour, which he later deduced was her 'anger' smell. And yet the fight goes on. Four days and fifty encounters later, we wonder how Petrunkevitch, let alone the spider or wasp, could possibly keep going. On day five, he decided that the spider species must be not to the wasp's taste, so he swapped it for another species and resumed the watch with victim no. 2. Half a day and 11 encounters go by. If you are losing the will to live, this is the time to start paying attention: sod's law states that the more effort you put into watching insects, the more likely you are to blink and miss the action. Petrunkevitch turned to have a conversation with a colleague, but a sixth sense caused him to turn back to the cage: 'The "deed" has been committed and I have not seen it!'

Ever determined, he repeated the experiment the next day and did not make the same mistake: glued to his cage, he finally witnessed the terrible kill.* With the comfort of more cameras and technology than we know what to do with these days, it is perhaps difficult to appreciate the tenacity and patience required of the naturalists of the past. The dedication, persistence and attention to *every* detail shown by our Wasp Whisperers was utterly remarkable. Without their committed vigils, the secret lives of solitary wasps would be even more mysterious than they are today.

\* \* \*

* If you manage to get through Petrunkevitch's 30-page tome describing the hunt, you will also learn that hawk tarantulas have a weakness for orange marmalade as a pre-hunt refreshment. Sweet!

We are indebted to the legacies left to us by the Wasp Whisperers of the nineteenth and early twentieth centuries for their entertaining, educational and thought-provoking accounts of the lives of so many solitary wasps. Progress has been made since then, but the overwhelming reality is that the science of these insects holds many more secrets. Some may have direct benefits for our own health and wellbeing, while others will offer great evolutionary stories of surprise, shock and splendour, the very best in arthropod entertainment. Have we done our Wasp Whisperers justice? In the words of today's Insect Whisperers: 'Fabre's books are probably [still, today] the most insightful.'*

If we listen carefully, we might hear a murmur of approval from the graves of the Wasp Whisperers. But there is so much more to learn about solitary, predatory wasps. That's what makes them the greatest enigma among all wasps.

---

* While writing this chapter, I solicited opinions from entomologists on Twitter about the books of the Wasp Whisperers of the nineteenth and early twentieth centuries. There was agreement that the Peckhams and Fabre were hard to beat. On wasps, the consensus was that Fabre's accounts are unmatched by any modern biology.

# Part Three

# How to Have a Social Life

Evidently the higher Hymenoptera are somehow
pre-adapted for social life, and since ants and
bees are believed to have been derived from
wasplike ancestors, it is possible that the
wasps hold the key to an understanding
of this problem.

Howard E. Evans & Mary Jane West-Eberhard,
*The Wasps* (1970)

# Prelude

What do you have in common with a genome, a cell, a worm or a wasp colony? This might sound like a pub quiz question, but the answer is simple: you are all societies. Each is made up of citizens who are specialist operators, who are mutually dependent, who cannot exist alone and who have to cooperate for the society to function. Genes are the citizens of genomes; organelles are the citizens of cells; individual wasps are the citizens of the colony. You are like the worm: your multicellular body is a society. The cooperative units are your tissues: your liver specialists cannot function without your heart specialists; your lung specialists are obsolete without your kidney or brain specialists. The society of your body functions well because all your cells and tissues work together, committed automatons, fuelling a higher level of individuality: you.

This makes you much more like a wasp nest than you might think.

Genes were not always strung together like beads in a genomic chain. Cells didn't always have organelles to carry out the tasks needed to make them work, and neither have they always snuggled up with other cells to make a multicellular organism. Evolving the societies of genomes, cells and multicellular organisms were some of nature's biggest achievements, and are collectively known as major evolutionary transitions: genes transitioned to become genomes, prokaryotes (single-celled organisms) evolved into eukaryotes (multi-celled organisms), and solitary wasps transitioned to wasp societies. Each of these biological conglomerates represented a new level of complexity, a new type of individual: a society, an empire. Understanding how and why these transitions happened is one of science's holy grails in the piecing together of the ingredients that make up the complexity of biological life.

In this part of the book, I'm going to explain what wasps have to offer, in this holy grail.

Along with mice in the rafters and spiders in the bath tub, a yellowjacket wasp nest in your loft probably makes for one of nature's most unwelcome guests, intruding into your personal space. That unwanted loft dweller is, however, one of the most impressive examples of a major evolutionary transition. The nest is a superorganism made up of a few thousand 'units' – the individual insects – which function together as a coordinated, committed, synergistic gene-replication machine. Each individual insect is dependent on her nestmates; without them she cannot perform life's essential purpose – to pass on genes to the next generation. There is a single queen: she is an authoritarian egg-layer who is useless and lost without her worker force. Some of the workers might be dedicated foragers – hunters of the protein required by the colony's hungry brood. Others guard the entrance to the nest, checking who is coming in, poised to launch a front-line defence should a plucky predator attempt an ambush. Inside are the nurses who tend and feed the brood, and who keep things clean. Without foragers, there would be no food for nurses to distribute; without nurses, there would be a backlog of food arriving at the nest; without guards, the nest would be exposed to infiltrators (who may try to dump a few eggs, cuckoo-style) or predators (who would feast on the defenceless, naked babies). It is this society – and the intricate structure of their nests – for which wasps are most famous.

The wasp nest in your loft is a lot like your own multicellular body: it is a tightly regulated civilisation of expert specialists who work together like cogs in a machine. The wasp society is the outermost shell of evolution's complex Russian-doll hierarchy of life: step inside, and the next layer is made of the individual wasps – multicellular beings in their own right (like us). Each cell in each wasp is a society; and each cell contains a full copy of the wasp's genome, which is a society of genes.

This hierarchy is complex and multi-layered. At each layer there are conflicts to be resolved, cooperative deals to be struck and behaviours to be coerced and coordinated. Natural selection acts at each of the layers, and traits that are favourable at one may not be so at another. The more levels of selection there are for evolution to tinker with, the more complex life becomes. The superorganism itself therefore has added another level of intricacy to an already multifarious structure: it sounds like a difficult thing for evolution to have stumbled upon, and even more challenging for it to work out ways to regulate and maintain.

It is remarkable, therefore, that superorganisms have evolved multiple times across the tree of life: at least 25 times in multicellular organisms and at least six times among the social insects as sociality. It is no wonder that the phenomenon of sociality has captured the interests of scientists, from theoreticians and modellers to experimental empiricists, behavioural ecologists and molecular biologists. Superorganisms didn't appear overnight: they evolved over millions of years. How? Why? We need to unpick the actions of evolution on the path of this major transition. We can tinker with the components of a wasp's nest in a way that we can't with a genome or a group of cells. It is hard to disassemble a genome and work out the contributions of each gene, and just as hard to know how and why it evolved to cooperate with another. But it *is* possible to deconstruct the wasp society to find out how and why an individual becomes a worker rather than a queen.

Not all wasp societies are 'super' like the yellowjacket nest lurking in your loft: in fact, most species of social wasps exhibit much smaller, more modest societies. Take the *Polistes* paper wasp, for example: there might only be half a dozen members in a group, and they lack the dogmatic commitment to their roles that your yellowjacket wasps have. But they still function as a society, with jobs divided up among them; they are just a simpler form of sociality. These species are evolutionary wonders of their own. They may have simpler societies, but they do not 'aspire' to be any more (or less) super or complex, because they are evolutionarily stable, happy and successful, as they have been for millions of years. Such wasps may not be as impressive in size, structure or function as the yellowjackets and their relatives, yet they are equally (if not more) precious and special: they are windows into evolution's covert journey from a solitary life to being full-blown socialites.

It was the mysteries of how and why the simplest of wasp societies knitted their lives together that first drew me in to the enigmatic world of wasps. Once they'd hooked their social tarsi into me, I needed little tempting to submit to the astonishing diversity buried in the clandestine chambers of the social wasp. Clambering through the waspish paths left by evolution, I've joined others in a voyage of discovery, unfolding the plot in the story of sociality.

Evolution's insect sociality portfolio is, of course, also shared with social bees, ants and termites, which are equally marvellous. Together the social insects account for 75 per cent of the world's insect biomass. But wasps tell the story of sociality better than do ants and bees. There are no solitary ants and all ant species are superorganisms; they've left nothing in their evolutionary wake to tell us how they got there. Honeybees, bumblebees and stingless bees are socially diverse and exciting; however (as we learned in Part 1) bees are just wasps that forgot how to hunt. Social bees and ants evolved from wasps: so why opt for second best, when the motherlode of secrets is there in all its resplendent glory? The evolutionary gravitas, prodigious diversity and staggering abundance of wasps lays out the evolutionary roadmap as to how and why sociality arose.

Let's unravel the lessons of social living, schooled by wasps, to understand why life history, family, games and commitment matter in becoming social. We will learn how evolution toyed with a soulful solitary wasp and moulded her evolutionary descendants into a social animal; about the social contracts, turmoil and taunts faced by wasps and how they solved them. The journey to sociality written by evolution and played out by wasps is undoubtedly one of nature's most marvellous feats.

# I

During the UK's first national lockdown of the 2020–21 coronavirus pandemic, I spent an indecent amount of my time on the internet lusting over images of potter wasps. One species in particular caught my eye – the heath potter wasp, *Eumenes coarctatus*, whose UK population is limited to precious patches of pristine heathland in southern England. By mid-lockdown I had devoured every YouTube video I could find on how the females of this species constructed and tended their bulbous clay pot nests. The species is so interesting because it's a solitary vespid wasp, a eumenid – and likely to be something close to what the solitary ancestor of the social wasps would have looked like. There are over 3,000 extant species of eumenid wasps, but I had good reasons to take a closer look at this particular one.

As the name suggests, solitary potter wasps build exquisite clay pots, each resembling a roman vase with a globular base that narrows to a restricted entrance, laced with a delicate opening lip that serves as a landing platform. The wasp collects clay from a designated 'quarry' (aka a patch of exposed sandy clay soil) and carries it to her construction site, where she will set about designing her pot. She uses exactly the same method as you might have done when making a coil pot at school, perhaps out of plasticine: each ball of clay is distributed evenly around the circumference of the developing pot.

Remarkably, once the wasp has found herself a good quarry spot she will use it for her entire two-to-three month potting career, during which time she will construct around 20–25 pots, each about a centimetre across. She gradually populates the surrounding heathland with her exquisite pots, at ever-increasing distances from the quarry site. Each is a cradle for a precious baby, made with a silken lining (surely rich in antibacterial compounds). Once complete, she will fill her pot with tiny, paralysed caterpillars (up to 38 of them), and then lay her precious egg. Each *Eumenes* female is a role model for the self-sufficient, single mum: she sources and carries her own building materials. She designs and builds her own disease-free house. She gives birth alone and stocks the cradle with everything her baby needs to thrive. Her parental care ends here. Once a pot is properly provisioned and sealed, she abandons it in order to divert her attention to the next pot and egg. Pot, lay, provision: she repeats this up to 25 times during her short life.

The repetitive life cycle of a potter wasp is not special. Each of the solitary wasps we met in Part 2 is tied to a similar cycle of reproductive and caring tasks, regulated by strict chronology, repeated over and over again on the treadmill of gene propagation. What is remarkable is that these very same tasks are also performed collectively by individuals in a *social* wasp colony, except this time by different colony members, known as queens (who do the egg-laying tasks) and workers (who build the nest and provision the brood). Remember also that social wasps (and bees and ants) evolved from a solitary wasp ancestor.

Put these two facts together and we arrive at an exciting proposition: perhaps the alternative behavioural roles of queens and workers in social wasp colonies were 'made' by evolution simply decoupling the reproductive and provisioning phases found throughout the nesting cycle of the solitary ancestor. Such a simple idea. We saw glimpses of these concepts in the classic wasp texts of our Wasp Whisperers, like Jean-Henri Fabre and the Peckhams, but it was the American biologist Mary Jane West-Eberhard who would first articulate the idea in a form that caught the interest of scientists.

# II

I first met Mary Jane when I was a young postdoctoral researcher at the Smithsonian Tropical Research Institute in Panama, during a brief flirtation with ants. Her earliest work was on the social paper wasp *Polistes* (which we'll learn more about later), but while pondering the behaviour of social wasps, a solitary wasp called *Zethus miniatus* caught Mary Jane's attention. *Zethus* is a genus of tropical eumenid wasps, and this particular wasp would shake up our understanding of the mechanics of how sociality might have evolved.

Mary Jane's story begins with her staring at a wasp on a bougainvillea at her daughter's nursery school in 1970s Colombia, where she was living at the time. Her daily visits to the school gave her an excuse to linger around the bougainvillea and she became curious about the many different ways in which the wasps on it spent their time. Just like the potter wasps of southern England, the life of *Zethus miniatus* revolves around predictable cycles of reproductive and provisioning behaviours. In the reproductive phase of the cycle, the wasps had ovaries bursting with ripe eggs, desperate to be laid, and during this time the wasps would be devoted to egg-laying (just like a social wasp queen); but during the provisioning phase when they were foraging (just like a social wasp worker), their ovaries were modestly diminished. Was there a mechanistic connection between ovarian ripeness and these different behaviours?

Certainly, such links have been found in other insects; for example, in mosquitoes and black flies, reproductive hormones change foraging behaviour by altering how the insects perceive their environment. If ovarian development somehow also controlled the expression of worker-like and queen-like behaviours in a solitary wasp, perhaps this same regulatory machinery could be used – co-opted, adopted and adapted – to evolve the separate castes found in social species. Evolving queen and worker castes from a solitary wasp ancestor could therefore have been a relatively straightforward step: the ancestral regulatory machinery could have been exploited simply by dissociating the reproductive and provisioning components from their nesting cycle into two different, but complementary, types of *wasp* rather than two types of *activity*. Like uncoupled carriages of a cargo train destined for opposing sides of the country, the machinery, rules and tools needed for provisioning could be redeployed to make a worker and those for reproduction to make a queen.

This is a simple conceptual idea. But at the time scientists could not explain *how* (in mechanistic terms, at the level of the genes) such phenotypic flexibility (where the phenotype describes both behaviour and physiology) could be exploited by evolution. A critical part of Mary Jane's hypothesis was that the different phenotypes must be expressed in response to prevailing conditions, such that the insect could perceive changes in her immediate environment and change her phenotype in a flexible, sometimes unexpected way. Different phenotypes exhibited at different times by the same individual? How could this be achieved by a single genome?

In the 1970s scientists viewed the genome as they would the indelible pages of a rather inflexible instruction book – the DNA sequence. DNA is a twisted double-stranded string of organic molecules. As a rule, a genome sequence doesn't change during an individual's lifetime (apart from mutations, some of which can cause diseases such as cancer). Different types of behaviour were thought to be determined by the type of genetic variant of a gene (known as an 'allele') that an individual carried, which often consisted of just a single nucleotide difference. There was already evidence for how genetic variants provide the means for phenotypic variation: for example, scientists had been able to trace the different foraging strategies of fruit flies to a simple difference in the genetic variants of the *foraging* gene. Flies that tended to sit around and forage on resources at a nearby patch – 'sitter flies' – had a different variant of this gene to flies that tended to roam around looking for food – 'rover flies'.

Piecing together how variants of genes provide the instructions for different behaviours and other traits, such as eye-span or thorax width, dominated the field of evolutionary genetics in the 1980s and 1990s. Yet there on that bougainvillea plant, individual wasps had been happily oscillating between a range of different phenotypes without any changes in their DNA. They had even been breaking their clockwork cycle of build, lay, provision. A secret I kept from you in Part 2 is that solitary wasps don't always lead a life of complete solitude. *Zethus miniatus*, for example, often builds her brood cells in a group with other females: sometimes she is neighbourly, defending or adopting orphaned nests, but at other times she is a nasty neighbour usurping another female from their cell and replacing the brood with her own. She might even raid a neighbour's cell, stealing their hard-earned prey.

These wasps weren't juggling genes or variants of genes because these don't change during their lifetimes. They were expressing different behaviours in response to both their internal environment (whether they had a mature egg or not) and their external environment (whether there was a neighbouring cell to rob). In other words, different behaviours were being produced in a context-dependent fashion, by a single genome.

Today, context-dependent gene expression is an increasingly well-understood process. The secret lies in the RNA (ribonucleic acid), which can be thought of as the personality that hides behind DNA. Just as your mood can quickly change if something in your environment changes, RNA is also highly dynamic and can respond rapidly to what is happening around it. RNA determines how the genetic information carried by the DNA sequence is expressed at any one time, which it does by copying the DNA code and translating into a product, like a protein. If the activity of the gene is changed,* the amount of protein produced changes too.

In recent years, scientists have identified different components of the genome which influence how genes are expressed. One of these includes chemical modifications made to genes – like a Post-it note being added to a page of a book, marking it out for amendment. Adding or removing specific chemicals can have profound effects on a gene. The term used to describe this process is 'epigenetics': *epi* in Latin means 'above' or 'upon' and this is exactly what the term epigenetics means here: it is referring to things that are added (or removed) 'above' the genome.

In the 1970s, scientists knew little about epigenetics and how these chemicals could permit the genome to adopt different

---

* Gene activity is measured in terms of its expression: this is simply the number of copies it is instructed to make of itself, and which ultimately determines how much of a specific protein is produced. Gene expression can be measured experimentally by counting the number of RNA transcripts in a tissue at a specific time point (for example, in response to change in day length or temperature).

guises rapidly and dynamically. In fact, it was only in 2017 that the molecular mechanisms, permitting the expression of sitter and rover behaviours in the fruit fly, were found to involve an interaction between epigenetic marks and the genetic variants that had been identified 20 years previously. And so perhaps it's not surprising that Mary Jane sat on her *Zethus*-inspired thoughts on social evolution for over a decade. It wasn't until the late 1980s that she used her observations on the natural history of this little-known Neotropical wasp to illustrate how flexible behaviours must be conditionally expressed and how cycles of ovarian development inherited from solitary wasps may provide a mechanistic 'ground plan' from which queen and worker castes evolve.*

Such a ground plan can be thought of as a blueprint – a guide for making something, a design or pattern that can be easily followed, replicated and if necessary adapted. You make a copy of a blueprint every time you use a photocopier. Evolution uses the concept of blueprints for many purposes: the original copy might hold instructions for making a symmetrical body shape in a worm or a particular arrangement of colour patterning on a butterfly wing. A blueprint that links ovarian development with behaviour could be tweaked by evolution, redeploying its different components to make social castes.

Wasps on bougainvillea, however, were merely the tip of Mary Jane's intellectual iceberg: in 2003 she published an 800-page tome of evidence on the subject in her landmark book *Developmental Plasticity and Evolution*, which marked a pivotal point in reshaping our understanding of the interplay between

---

* It is not intended to suggest that there is some kind of directional 'destiny' or 'journey' in evolution's remit. To ensure no one gets into sticky soup, I will spell this out explicitly: there is no assumption here that solitary wasps are 'on their way' to evolving castes. The relevant point is that solitary wasps may possess traits likely represented in the solitary ancestor which *did* become social.

genes, environment and behavioural plasticity. And all because Mary Jane got distracted from school-gate gossip by a wasp that no one had bothered to inspect before.

The idea that existing regulatory processes can be co-opted to generate behavioural innovations explains a lot about the evolution of life more generally. In simple terms, a lazy way to evolve novel traits is to recruit them from existing machinery. Reorder and/or reschedule developmental processes by tweaking existing genes or gene networks that regulate physiology, behaviour or morphology, and if you're lucky the new product will be something that gives its owner a fitness benefit, resulting in more genes being passed on to the next generation. In other words, the solitary wasp provided the toolkit – from the regulatory machinery to the physiological and behavioural product – that was exploited by evolution to make queen and worker castes.

If all this talk of genes, machinery and co-option is leaving you cold, let's huddle round a nice bowl of *al dente* pasta and I'll explain, because the story of pasta provides a compelling analogy for the concept of how conserved evolutionary toolkits can give rise to biological innovations. Pasta is one of the oldest processed foods, dating back to around 1100 BC. It is made from the unleavened dough of wheat flour with some eggs and water thrown in. The 'ancestral' state of pasta is hotly contested (especially as it probably came from China, not Italy), but the least contentious idea is that the first pasta was sheet-like, similar to today's lasagne. A few streaks of a sharp knife, though, and ribbon- or noodle-shaped pasta evolved, which held an accompanying sauce very differently to the lasagne-like sheets, improving the taste of certain dishes.

This innovation happened due to a novel reuse of the basic (ancestral) sheet-pasta 'toolkit'. Over the next 500 years, pasta evolved few innovations because it was so labour-intensive to make: in other words, its evolution was constrained by the regulatory processes that determined its construction. However, in the fifteenth century a significant 'mutation' in mechanical engineering occurred, with the invention of the extrusion press. This allowed the basic pasta toolkit to be easily and quickly reorganised in different ways to produce pasta of diverse shapes and textures: such innovations sparked a huge pasta diversification event and all because of a single but profound change in the regulatory process – the extrusion press.

What does this pasta analogy have to do with explaining how ovaries might provide a blueprint for caste evolution? Our solitary ancestral vespid (*Zethus*-like) wasp represents the sheet-like pasta before it is divided up ('uncoupled') into the component parts of queen and worker castes of an insect with simple societies (*Polistes*-like), just like the ribbony-noodle pasta. The pasta innovations made possible by the extrusion press represent what can happen if a species commits to a life of sociality and becomes a superorganism (like the yellowjacket loft dweller). At that point the fitness interests of a group's members are so intertwined and mutually dependent that it is difficult (probably impossible) for them to revert to a non-social existence. This is the insects' major transition to a committed life as a superorganism. Evolution's equivalent to pasta's mechanical revolution lies in the genomes: genes are modified, and gene families are expanded and diversified, generating a regulatory machinery that reads like a very different instruction book from the original blueprint that was written by the solitary wasp.

Ideas are great, but until you can test them, they are just stories. Does the secret to evolving sociality really lie in the ovaries of a solitary wasp, or is it just a story? It's been 40 years since Mary Jane West-Eberhard first articulated this hypothesis, and we've made rather modest progress in testing it. This is because her ideas required the ability to interrogate the relationship between the genome and the phenotype. Things only properly gathered speed at the turn of the century when new methods in molecular biology meant that any organism (not just fruit flies, worms and mice) could be studied at the level of the genes.

In the early 2000s I was a young postdoctoral researcher with a fondness for wasps, and I was keen to jump aboard the socio-genomics train, a high-speed vehicle of molecular analyses that allowed scientists to study social life in molecular terms. I won an independent research fellowship to return to Panama to work on *Polistes* wasps, with Mary Jane as my advisor, and to my amazement she joined me regularly on fieldwork. Aside from keeping me calm while we were drifting down the Panama Canal in broken boats, or easing the way with her impeccable Spanish when our (apparently abandoned) field site became occupied by a dozen workmen in hammocks, we talked lots about wasps and ovaries and behaviour. My aim was to test whether queen and worker behaviours in *Polistes* societies were produced by express-ing shared genes differently.

*Polistes* wasps are one of those species that provide a precious glimpse into the process of social evolution: they live as a group with specialist queens and workers, but these roles are highly plastic, enabling individual wasps to change their behaviour from provisioner to egg-layer opportunistically if circumstances shift within or outside the group. This plasticity in behaviour reminds us of *Zethus* on that bougainvillea, where Mary Jane saw wasps quickly change their strategy depending on local conditions, and which might provide a recipe of ingredients from which sociality evolves. In short, my quest was to find the genomic machinery that could explain how Mary Jane's ideas might work.

Looking back on it, I realise that this was a naively ambitious project as the methodologies for looking at gene expression in wasps were still not well established. At the time, no one had sequenced the genome of any hunting wasp, and an obscure tropical wasp was certainly not high on anyone's agenda. But I was inspired by recent work that had been done on the honeybee using 'arrays' of genes spotted onto microscope slides ('micro-

NEST of a WASP.
POLISTES hebræus.
*India.*                                    *C. Marten, Esq.*
BMNH(E) 650079

NEST of CHARTERGUS chartarius
*British Guiana.*        [34-6]        *Lord J.H. Archer.*
BMNH(E) 650100

NEST of
CHARTERGUS amicalis

NEST of CARD MAKING WASP. [CHARTERGUS chartarius]
*Amazons.*        [Fig. 4]        *R. Spruce, Esq.*
BMNH(E) 650102

NEST of a WASP.
[POLYBIA rejecta]
*Brazil.*        [92]
BMNH(E) 650128

Wasps are supreme architects
of paper. Their nests resemble
footballs, string, tennis rackets
and designer dresses.

NESTS of a WASP.
POLYBIA occidentalis.
*Brazil.*
BMNH(E) 650118

The evolution of the 'wasp waist' gave parasitoid wasps like this Sabre wasp (*Rhyssa persuasoria*), extra manoeuvrability in egg-laying, opening up opportunities to parasitise a wider range of prey.

Sawflies are the ancestors to parasitoid and stinging wasps. They are a highly diverse group of wasps, with over 8,000 species, and a characteristic tail, which is not a sting, but an egg-laying device, called an ovipositor.

The giant Asian hornet *Vespa mandarinia* is often mistakenly used in media stories about the invasion of Europe by the yellow-legged Asian hornet *Vespa velutina*.

Gall wasps lay their eggs on the underside of leaves of trees like oaks, beech and rose. They induce the plant to grow a protective casing around the egg – the gall. The plant also provides the wasp larva with nourishment, but the plant does not appear to benefit at all.

The beewolf, *Philanthus triangulum*, hunts honeybees. It produces a cocktail of antibiotics and anti-fungal chemicals to keep its brood free of disease.

Solitary wasps, of the genus *Oxybelus*, have evolved a clever way of carrying flies to their burrow: impale the prey on their sting.

An American cockroach being zombified by the jewel wasp, *Ampulex compressa*. She uses her venom to turn her cockroach prey into a zombie which she leads, like an obedient dog, back to her burrow.

The sand wasp, *Ammophila*, was a favourite of both Jean-Henri Fabre and the Peckhams. They marvelled at her hunting skills, watched her paralyse caterpillars and wept when she thwarted their many hours of observation with an unexpected move.

A spider-hunting pompilid wasp with a wandering spider victim.

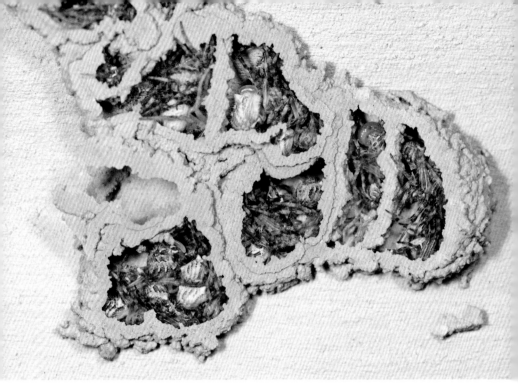

The mud nests of solitary wasps are packed with paralysed prey on which the baby wasp will feast.

The mud-daubing wasp, *Sceliphron jamaicense*.

The mammoth wasp, *Megascolia maculata*, is a European species of Scoliid wasp – the largest wasp in Europe. It played a key role in research into the medical benefits of wasp venom.

Wasps love human-modified habitats. Hover wasps (*Stenogastrinae*) nest in their hundreds on bridges and drainage tunnels in Southeast Asia.

Watching the behaviours of individual wasps on nests of species like *Polistes canadensis* has helped scientists understand how and why sociality evolved.

Radio-frequency identification tags attached to the bodies of *Polistes* wasps allow researchers to monitor their movements between nests.

*Polistes* paper wasps show enormous variation in their facial patterns. Some species use this variation in appearance to distinguish one nestmate from another.

arrays') which revealed that queens and workers differed in their expression of hundreds of genes. The honeybee is a superorganism, far removed from a solitary wasp and the root of sociality, and so while these findings were encouraging, tantalising even, they told us little about how the simplest (and putatively first) forms of insect societies evolved. *Polistes* isn't perfect (as we'll find out later), but if we could find evidence of conditional expression of caste-biased genes in these simple societies, we would be a lot closer to turning a story into fact.

After many months of fun in tropical rainforests, messing around with wasps and boats on the Panama Canal, learning to dance salsa (badly) and speak Spanish (very badly), the cold realities of the molecular lab hit hard. In the early 2000s, microarrays were a fantastic 'designer' technology for savvy molecular biologists but only if you had the right genomic resources and support. Neither my wasps nor my resources were up to this game. I conceded: this was not going to be the scientific party I would wear a designer lab outfit to. With a deep sigh of scientific defeat, I buried the microarrays with their ideas in the back of my lab cupboard and turned to a tried-and-tested splash of radioactivity. Clones of genes have been happily (and messily) labelled with the radioisotope Phosphorus-32 (32P) since the 1970s in a method known as Northern blotting: a crackle of the Geiger counter and a flurry of photographic film can quickly reveal which genes are differentially expressed between samples.

After months of poring over radioactive autoradiographs, I finally found what I was looking for. The plastic roles of queens and workers in *Polistes* were indeed associated with different levels of expression among the genes they shared: this was the very machinery of conditional expression that evolution needed to co-opt from a solitary life cycle and use to make a social life. In the grand scheme of evolutionary genomics, my discovery wasn't especially ground-breaking as the genomics train was running at high speed all over the world by this point. But for wasps and our understanding of the mechanisms for social evolution, I'd done my bit. My contribution was the first of its kind for wasps and for a simple social insect with plastic castes. It proved that the flexible machinery required for an insect to respond plastically to her environment did indeed lie in the genes.

# III

While I was chasing wasps in Panama, genomics hysteria was sweeping through labs across the globe. Researchers had cottoned on to the way these new molecular methods could be used to test longstanding hypotheses, not just the ovarian blueprint for social evolution. The quest to find 'the gene for X' had suddenly become feasible and very fashionable. Molecular labs everywhere filled with scientists delirious with the excitement of small children in a newly opened, sugar-fogged sweet shop. For social insects, the torchbearer proved to be the honeybee, whose genome was sequenced in 2000, opening up a box of delights for researchers.

Recall from Part 1 that (just like social wasps) social bees (such as the honeybee) evolved from a solitary bee ancestor. In fact solitary bees inherited that same chronological nesting cycle – build, lay, provision, repeat – from their solitary wasp ancestors. And so the idea that the egg-laying and provisioning cycles of a solitary insect could provide a mechanistic blueprint for evolving castes applies just as well to social bees as it does to wasps. Moreover, working with the honeybee brings collateral benefits because we know so much about what makes it buzz, including the diversity of behaviours *within* the worker caste and how these are regulated. The natural next step was to work out how genomes manage to regulate these different facets of social behaviour while also permitting flexibility. The treat from the honeybee's box that I'd like to tell you about here concerns a 'gene of importance' – a master regulator and facilitator of social behaviour in the honeybee, and perhaps beyond.

Honeybee workers can't possibly become queens: they are each doomed from birth to be a working cog in the machine of the colony, helping generate more copies of their genes by raising sibling brood. But life as a worker isn't quite as tedious and static as this might sound. Even if you've never actually watched a honeybee colony, you might know that there are two types of workers: 'nurses', who tend to stay at home to help with housework and brood care, and 'foragers', who leave the hive to gather pollen and nectar. What determines who's a nurse and who's a forager?

The answer is age. Simply age. Young bees start off their working life as nurses. As they get older, they graduate to out-of-hive work as foragers. Age is a steadfast regulator of behaviour in many social insects, not just honeybees, so much so that the process has its own name: 'age polyethism'. Does it also remind you of our solitary wasp, with her clock-like nesting cycle? Build, lay, provision, repeat. Chronology determines *when* she behaves in a particular way. The question is: what is the gene (or genes) that controls this clock?

Biological clocks are a regulatory rock onto which frills and deviations can be added. The honeybee worker's behavioural clock can be accelerated if a sudden demand arises for more foragers and fewer nurses – workers whose lives are fast-forwarded in this way are called 'precocious foragers'. And no matter how old they are, foragers can retreat to in-hive jobs should they be needed. Scientists can coerce bees into roles atypical for their age by manipulating the conditions of the colony – removing nurses or foragers, taking away or adding brood. The bees cope marvellously with these changes.

Such behavioural flexibility is reminiscent of the plasticity we saw in the behaviour of the solitary wasp, and also our simple-societied *Polistes*. So now we are pinning plasticity – the ability to respond to change – onto on our chronological rock. This plasticity determines *how* you change your behaviour. This adds a second question: how can the gene(s) that regulate behaviour also be responsive so that it permits this *plasticity*, within the constraints of the clock?

A time-bending genetic clock sounds complicated enough. But the plot thickens. Sets of seemingly unrelated behaviours can be co-regulated. Some foraging honeybees specialise as nectar-foragers, while others are pollen-collectors. Having a balance of preferences means the colony's needs are met. Pollen-foragers tend to switch from nursing to foraging at a younger age than nectar-foraging workers. Entwined with these preferences is a difference in sensitivity to sucrose, *and* a subtle plumping of the ovaries: pollen-foragers have slightly bigger ovaries and are especially sensitive to sucrose, while nectar-foragers have more slimline ovaries and are not so fussed about sucrose. This means that how a honeybee worker behaves is not a binary choice between nursing or foraging.

What they do, when and why is determined by a co-regulated set of *four* connected traits that *all* matter: ovaries, forage type, sugar cravings and age. This concurrent behavioural cocktail is not a special gift bestowed only upon honeybees. These same co-regulated traits can be traced to their solitary ancestors: solitary reproductive insects forage on pollen and feed it to their brood, while they forage on nectar for personal delectation (a non-reproductive's foraging option). Honeybee worker behaviour can therefore be traced to the blueprint of their solitary ancestors, just as Mary Jane suggested for that wasp on her Colombian bougainvillea.

Even more astonishing, this suite of linked behaviours appears to respond to the instructions of a master regulator gene: a one-stop gene shop for social behaviour. Vitellogenin* is a

---

* The name 'vitellogenin' is used synonymously to refer to either the gene or the protein.

precursor to egg yolk, and fundamental for reproduction in all egg-making animals, including the solitary ancestors of social insects. It conducts the symphony of worker behaviours by altering its expression in concert with the age and type of worker. Pollen-foragers and nectar-foragers are the complementary musicians in the solitary ancestor's orchestra. Vitellogenin conducts them separately to meet the demands of the colony. An up-flick of vitellogenin's baton and the sugar-crazed pollen-collectors with their slightly swollen ovaries switch from nursing to foraging at a younger age than do nectar-foraging workers. By regulating the expression of vitellogenin in a chronological manner, workers play the music of the colony in the right key with the right time signature.

Of course, the orchestra of the genome doesn't really have a single conductor, even for a single sonata: vitellogenin acts within a whole network of genes, producing molecules like hormones that carry instructions for the endocrine system. One of vitellogenin's most important relationships is with juvenile hormone, a primary regulator of physiology, especially reproduction, in insects. Juvenile hormone has the experimental advantage that it is easier (and cheaper) to measure and manipulate than a gene like vitellogenin. You can buy a synthetic analogue of this hormone and simply swab it onto an insect. Experiments like this have revealed how in solitary insects the production of juvenile hormone is associated with increased levels of vitellogenin expression and active reproduction.

The hormone appears to have diversified its role in social insects: honeybees, bumblebees, ants and wasps all show evidence that juvenile hormone has different roles in workers compared to queens. Typically, juvenile hormone retains its ancestral function as the mistress of egg development in queens, but in workers it has gone functionally off-piste, and has become the provocative puppeteer of nursing and foraging behaviours, having lost its role as a regulator of reproduction. Indeed, a perfect way to tinker with a *Polistes* worker's behaviour is to swab her with juvenile hormone's synthetic analogue and watch as she irresistibly succumbs to precocious foraging. Meanwhile, *Polistes* queens exhibit the highest levels of the hormone, demonstrating its role as the mechanistic monarch of reproductive regulation. The fact that juvenile hormone has both old and new functions in social insects is evidence of how evolution can exploit the ancestral blueprint inherited from the solitary ancestor. Uncoupling the reproductive and non-reproductive machinery opens the door to a fairground of innovation. And for social insect castes, this innovation is to refashion an old gene (or hormone) to simultaneously regulate behaviour and physiology in two very different phenotypes: queens and workers.

It's not so unusual for a single gene (or hormone) to have multiple effects on behaviour. It's a classic example of pleiotropy, a rather technical scientific term that can be better explained with potatoes. In the beginning, a potato is always a potato – like a gene is always a gene, determined by the string of nucleic acids that make up its personal DNA sequence identity. But what that potato (the proxy for 'a gene') becomes (how it is 'expressed') depends on its individual experience. For example, do you like to steam or bake your potatoes? The environment it experiences (the oven, the steamer) produces different outcomes.

Potatoes can also change expression over time in response to changes in their environment, and can end up serving different functions. Take your humble boiled potato: its function might be to accompany grilled fish. But that same boiled potato can end up mashed, changing its function to being a creamy cushion for some quality sausages. Expressions of potatoes that are still recognisable as potatoes (like boiling and mashing) are akin to the conserved (ancestral) role of a gene, like vitellogenin and the yolk it goes on to help make, or juvenile hormone, which controls the expression of vitellogenin: it's all neatly within the expected remit of being a potato (or reproduction, for vitellogenin).

But let's say you take your potato, mix it into a dough and thrown it in a pan of boiling water: you end up with gnocchi, which looks more like pasta than potato. Ancestrally, gnocchi is still potato, but now it has an entirely different culinary function. Vitellogenin (and juvenile hormone) remains important for its ancestral function of regulating ovarian development in reproductive castes of social insects (akin to the humble boiled potato), but vitellogenin (and its associated juvenile hormone pathway) has also been co-opted by evolution to perform additional functions in regulating worker behaviours (akin to the gnocchi innovation). Vitellogenin and its conspirators are to insects as the humble potato is to the people of the world: vital.

# IV

Given the excitement among scientists to establish the links between juvenile hormone, vitellogenin, behaviour and reproduction in ants and social bees and social wasps, it is astonishing that the most *fundamental* test of the ovarian blueprint hypothesis has been almost ignored. We need a test in the insect that matters most: a solitary one (a solitary wasp, to be specific) that is likely to represent the ancestral state of the social insects. The best model we have for this is a solitary eumenid wasp – the last common solitary ancestor to the social wasps: the root of sociality. If a solitary wasp like this really was a cooking pot of ingredients for castes in social insects, the same molecular machinery must surely be regulating the queen-like and worker-like behaviours in these lonesome insects as it is in social insects.

A first test of this came to light in 2018, with a solitary eumenid wasp from South Africa, *Synagris cornuta*. As expected for such a wasp, changes in queen-like and worker-like behaviours correlated with cycles of ovarian development. Worker-like behaviours (foraging) were associated with smaller (or slower-growing) eggs, while queen-like behaviours (cell-building – that is, getting ready to lay) were linked with mature (or fast-growing) eggs. In other words, caste-like behaviours were expressed in sequence over a period of time and were mirrored by differences in egg status, just as the ovarian blueprint hypothesis had predicted. Today, we still lack the killer experiment to determine whether the regulatory molecular pathways of the solitary ancestor were harnessed and repackaged to make societies. This is why I'm (still) chasing potter wasps in England's finest heathlands.

The heath potter wasp – *Eumenes coarctatus* – is the only species of potter wasp in the UK, but there are over 100 species of *Eumenes* around the world, all of which construct pots. In warmer climes you can find them littering soft furnishings, the walls of your house, clothes lines, anything near a suitable quarry that stays still long enough to be 'potted' onto. Their stately pots are thought to have inspired the pottery designs of Indigenous Americans, who some 4,500 years ago were sculpting vessels that mirror the curvaceous birth-cells of the potter wasp. Potter wasps have an 85-million-year head start on these human mimics, and so it is hardly surprising that the wasps win in sophistication and quality. Their pottery concoctions are not a simple mix of clay and water. The wasps perform some insect chemical wizardry while coiling the pots, enriching their walls with essential minerals such as magnesium, zinc and iron. Undoubtedly these garnishes contribute antibiotic properties to the nests, ensuring the brood is kept free of disease while it completes its lonely childhood, sealed in a pot.

The alchemy skills of potter wasps are so potent that people in remote tropical parts of the world rely on these nests to distil essential minerals, processing the nutritionally enriched earth into an irresistible bite-sized pot-shaped medicine cabinet. The eating of insect-transformed earths (geophagy) is a traditional practice in parts of Africa, Asia and South America, culturally transmitted down the generations. It provides women and children with the very same mineral supplements that you might buy in your local pharmacy. Anthropologists think these insects play a critical role in fertility and reproduction in West African culture, in which pregnant women and children regularly pluck the clay nests of *Synagris* wasps from the sides of their mud-walled homes, leaving the walls obviously scarred. Where I come from, if a woman of childbearing age develops a sudden craving for ginger biscuits, you quietly nudge a pregnancy testing kit her way. In rural West Africa pregnancy kits are not so available, but if an appropriately aged woman starts scratching the earth in search of a termite mound or wasp nest, it is taken as evidence that she is pregnant. These women have described how they 'felt need' or 'strong desire' to eat insect earths, just as I did for crackers and ginger biscuits when I was pregnant (except ginger biscuits were not as good for me and my growing baby as a wasp nest would have been).

The medicinal importance of potter wasp nests first came to light by accident, after a 2013 outbreak of Ebola virus in a remote village in south-east Guinea. An infectious viral disease whose natural reservoir host is most likely to be a fruit bat, Ebola jumps into humans every so often, with devastating consequences. It is highly contagious, with mortality rates ranging from 22–88 per cent, exceeding those of other high-mortality viruses such as HIV, Smallpox, SARS, MERS. Patient zero was an 18-month-old toddler called Emole Ouamouno who lived in the village of Meliandou. The domino effect of Ebola's disease transmission resulted in the 2014–16 epidemic, claiming over 11,000 lives across three West African countries (Sierra Leone, Liberia and Guinea).

The remarkable insights into the importance of wasp earths came about because Emole Ouamouno's mother had developed an insatiable appetite for the nests of *Synagris* wasps. She also happened to be pregnant with another child at precisely the time when Emole was incubating the disease. In an attempt to understand the routes of the disease's spillover into surrounding communities, these extreme wasp nest cravings became a topic of investigation because mothers are known to share their geophagy feasts with their children.

At the time of the outbreak a British anthroplogist, James Fairhead, was studying geophagy among the village's people. Despite spending a year in the Kissi village, Fairhead admitted he had overlooked the holes in the interior walls of their houses as wear and tear. They were only brought to his attention during the Ebola investigation: the holes were the locations of wasp nests. Mineral content analyses of the wasp earths revealed that they were enriched with magnesium, phosphorous, potassium, iron, cobalt and zinc. Pregnant women typically snack on up to 20–80 grams of wasp earths a day, and Emole's mum was thought to be at the top end of this range, warranting investigation. We still do not know how Emole contracted Ebola, but it's more likely to have been from a fruit bat than a potter wasp nest.

Back to our more recent pandemic and the potter wasps on England's heathlands, where I was resisting the urge to nibble a pot or two. After the 2020 UK lockdown eased, I had dashed down here in the hope of collecting samples of these solitary wasps. The Twitter-entomology paparazzi's mobile phone photography had teased me into thinking this to be a Lilliputian-sized potter, delicately coiling a tiny porcelain cradle for her pin-head baby. I was therefore somewhat suspicious at my first sighting because the wasp was much more substantial than I'd expected (also because I'd only been staring at the bare bank of sandy clay for a mere ten minutes: finding wasps is rarely so easy).

Yet this was most pleasing since it already had me thinking about what might be going on at the molecular level, inside her brain, the epicentre of behavioural regulation. Big wasp heads mean big wasp brains, which means lots of genetic material to interrogate Mary Jane Eberhard's hypothesis.

On that sunny day, I found myself belly down on a sandy bank surrounded by a sea of heather: my mission was to catch the heath potter wasp *while* she was performing her 'worker-like' jobs (catching caterpillars) and her 'queen-like' tasks (laying eggs) in order to capture gene expression in action. Pleased to have found some clay-collecting females and admiring their good-sized heads, I thought the hard bit was over. I was already greedily anticipating the oodles of RNA that each wasp brain would yield for our project. I'd studied the YouTube videos of these wasps and was confident that I'd have my samples of foraging and egg-laying wasps all tubed-up before the sun went down. Oh, how naive I was. It's all very well finding a clay-collecting wasp, it is quite another matter to find her pot nest.

Oblivious to the concerned looks of passing walkers, I found myself leaping clumsily across swathes of heather as I attempted to chase the wasp back to her pot from her quarry site. Bee-lining is a tried-and-tested method for tracking an insect back to its nest. If you have tried keeping your eyes on a tiny flying insect while galloping across uneven ground, you will sympathise with the scrapes and sore ankles I came away with. After a few more embarrassing attempts at 'wasp-lining', and another hour or so desperately scouring the heather for pots (fat-eyed needles-in-haystacks), I realised I needed more people to hold stations along the wasp's flightpath.

Reinforcements arrived on a convoy of bikes, with varying levels of enthusiasm. The benefits of having several children spanning a range of ages (and heights) is that they can occupy different sampling points on the vertical trajectory of a wasp flightpath. The four-year-old could man the ground post, ready to alert the next-in-line when the wasp was leaving her quarry. The 12-year-old stood a few metres further along, ready to relay the trajectory of travel to the 14-year-old, who was most keen to traverse the heathland at speed in pursuit of the wasp. My husband meanwhile took himself off on a needle-in-haystack forage for pots in a completely different direction (probably so he could listen to the cricket in peace). Surely, we could track down at least one pot.

Maybe we would have, if the four-year-old hadn't got distracted by an enormous bag of potato crisps, or the 14-year-old hadn't instead decided to practise artistic shots of his bike on his new camera, or the 12-year-old hadn't found herself testing out her newly mastered 'aerial' cartwheels across the heathland. There is only so far that one's family will go in humouring a mother with crazy wasp fetishes. The threshold for tolerance is strictly determined by how long the snacks last. We slunk off home, without a single wasp.

Given their beauty, potting skills and observable behaviours, it is remarkable that these ancient potters have been so little studied. There is a smattering of research from the mid-twentieth century on the population dynamics of potter wasps in nice holiday locations, like the Seychelles, but there has been little else to satisfy general curiosity. Pushing the peer-reviewed literature aside, the world of potter wasps was opened to me by the remarkable naturalist and wasp-tracker John Walters. A freelance ecologist who has created his own dream job, John gets paid to track down random species and find what is interesting to film or talk about. The heath potter wasp was one such random species that he was commissioned to 'track down and figure out' a few years ago. Little did he know how captivating these wasps would be. Such is his fascination with them that he has recreated his own bespoke potter wasp quarry 30 minutes' drive from his house in the Devonshire heathlands, so that he can observe them in comfort.

To my great delight, John took little persuasion to give me some first-hand training on how to track a potter wasp. We met on the Dorset heathlands and I soon learned what I was doing wrong: I needed to lie down *flatter* on the ground beside the wasp. In fact, you really need to lie on your back, so you can see the wasp's silhouette against the sky. I needed to leap up *faster* when the wasp takes off – keeping my eyes fixed on that small blob flying into the sky. I needed to run like a gazelle – rather than a middle-aged mother-of-three. But above all: *do not, at ANY point, take your eyes off the wasp!* It was quite remarkable watching John at work: he had eyes only for the wasps.

Traversing the heather like a Jesus lizard that barely seemed to break its surface, he tracked wasps hundreds of metres from their quarry. But the wasps were against us, and again we didn't manage to track a single one back to its nest. I felt somewhat vindicated: if even John-Chase-a-Wasp-Walters failed to track a wasp to her pot that day, I couldn't be too hard on myself. John blamed the terrain – it wasn't flat enough to get a good clear view of the wasp against the horizon, and he recommended I try a less undulating part of the heath.

John pottered back to Devon to his bespoke wasp farm, while I planned Wasp-Chase Part III. Dorset is not only a hotspot for potter wasps, I learned, it's a hotspot for potter-wasp fanatics. While I was scouring John's recommended sandbank, a heavily tanned man appeared, holding the biggest camera lens I'd ever seen. After a few minutes' conversation (and some surreptitious Googling), I learned that this was none other than Dr Bob Gibbons, ecologist, wildlife photographer, naturalist, nature tour guide, and author/illustrator of more than 40 books and nature guides.

Bob was looking for potter wasps too. We happily traversed the bank together, but the wasps were not playing ball, so Bob called up two of his fellow naturalist friends, Sue and Chris, who were also out looking for potter wasps on the Dorset heathlands.

In fact, they'd been counting these wasps and hunting their pots all summer for the National Trust. Little did the wasps know that they had such a big fan club. And so we stood: Bob, Sue, Chris and me transfixed by miniature potters as they went about their end-of-season business.

It was a delight to stumble across such a guild* of potter wasp fans in one day. I had to pinch myself to check it was real. In fact, the only people I recall seeing that day were potter fans, and very lovely people they were too. Together with their incredible knowledge of natural history (not just on potter wasps), I admired their unwavering love and dedication to these little creatures. But herein lay a problem. I was there (with permission from the National Trust) to sample potter wasps so that I could analyse the gene expression in their brains and test the reproductive blueprint hypothesis. This involved catching a wasp in the act (of a behaviour), plunging her into a tube of fluid that would preserve her RNA, while simultaneously chopping off her head (to ensure the fluid penetrated the precious brain tissue). Gene expression changes quickly: beheading must be done as fast as possible, on site, where the wasp was doing her stuff – not in secret, back at the lab.

My scientific aim was noble, but I simply could not bring myself to behead the potters in front of Bob, Sue and Chris: these were the very wasps they'd been lovingly watching all summer. Even though the wasps were in the twilight of their lives (autumn was advancing), I just couldn't do it.

I waited until I had gracefully waved goodbye to my new

* I am not sure anyone has previously tried to find the collective noun for a bunch of potter-wasp fanatics. Inspired by the popular use of the collective noun 'Potters' Guild' to describe a group of artists who enjoy making pottery, I've gone with 'guild', which has a dictionary definition of 'an association of people in pursuit of a common goal'. Here my friends on the Dorset heathland were united in the common goal to bestow love and admiration on the potter wasp.

friends before running back onto the heath in the hope of grabbing a few wasps out of their sight. But such had been the enthusiasm of the Potter Wasp Guild that the day was now very late, the sun was setting and the wasping day was almost at its natural end. I managed to collect a small number of wasps, but not in the numbers needed for our analyses.

There is not yet a satisfying finale for my part in the story of the potter wasp and the insights it may give us into the blueprint of social behaviour. You may wonder why I bother to include it here. I do so because I think it's important that people understand how not all scientific endeavours work out, at least not on the first (or even second or third) attempt. For me, this had been a success, albeit not quite in the way I expected. The pandemic had 'grounded' me (in many ways) to UK species, forcing me to learn a bit about what was on my doorstep, rather than jumping on a plane to a tropical country in pursuit of more exotic species. I had learned that we have very special wildlife in the UK, and there is still much more to learn.

I met some fantastic people who were not professors in insect behaviour, nor did they hold PhDs in entomology, but they have precious knowledge that would never find space in an academic journal. It is the same detailed understanding of natural history that had enabled Mary Jane to formulate her influential work on the nature of alternative behaviours. Thanks to John Walters, we are now in the process of sequencing the genome of the heath potter wasp, and we are halfway through the sampling needed to test the reproductive theory for how social insects became that way. We may not manage to be the first to do this on a solitary eumenid wasp, but I'd trade a scientific first for a few hours out on the heath with the Potter Wasp Guild any day.

# V

Ovarian cycles are not the only blueprint in evolution's portfolio. In the early 2000s, wasp biologist Jim Hunt suggested how winter diapause in solitary insects could be exploited by evolution as a blueprint for making queen and worker castes. Diapause is a core insect life-history trait, a state of seasonal dormancy that insects use to sit out unfavourable environmental conditions like winter. The insect slows down its metabolism, ceases to 'behave' in any perceptible way, and both development and reproductive function shuts down, slowing growth almost to a standstill. The ability of insects to shut down their biological functions and survive extreme environmental conditions has fascinated biologists for hundreds of years.

The first to describe this in detail was the French naturalist René de Réaumur who, in his 1734 treatise on insect winter behaviour and physiology, remarked how the cold 'puts bees into a state in which food ceases to be necessary to them; it holds them in a sort of numbness'. But it was not until the last couple of decades that scientists have really started to understand diapause: why it happens, what the cue is and what the mechanisms are that regulate it to ensure it happens at the right time. Triggers for winter diapause include temperature, humidity, diet and hours of day or night.

Diapause is just one example of the biological rhythms that have fascinated humans for thousands of years, probably since we became agriculturists who had to understand and master the natural cycles of animals and plants in order to exploit them effectively. Could the mechanisms regulating diapause in solitary insects be remodelled to build queens and workers in a social insect?

Let's head back to the heath and our potter wasp to understand a bit more about how the diapause hypothesis might work.

A couple of days after the mother potter wasp lays her egg, the baby larva hatches and it tucks straight into its personal caterpillar larder. If it's early in the summer the larva will pupate and soon emerge as a first-generation potter (if female) or a potential mate of potter (if male). However, if it's later in the summer, the baby wasp (male or female) will go into diapause as a second-generation wasp in its pot and emerge as an adult the following spring. Insects in temperate regions have no option but to enter diapause to survive the winter. But diapause is a risky process and so if early-season offspring can forgo dormancy it cuts the risk of overwintering for at least some of them.

Delaying diapause for early-season brood is common among temperate insects and our heath potter wasp is no exception. What is quite extraordinary is that a single potter wasp mother can produce a same-season-generation offspring one week and switch seamlessly to an overwintering offspring the next. This might sound trivial until you consider the fundamental differences between same-season and diapause brood: a same-season brood needs to develop quickly into an adult so it has time to find a mate and construct and provision 20-odd pots before the onset of autumn. Conversely, a diapausing brood needs to suspend development during pupation, slowing down its metabolic activity and growth until spring. The cue for a potter wasp on whether to enter diapause or not could be day length since pots made *after* the last week of June are almost invariably diapausing brood, while those made *before* this point tend to be same-season brood. Equally, the decision might be made in response to the type of food there is, since the types of caterpillars available to the provisioning potter will change during the season. No one has bothered to explore this question yet.

Irrespective of the specific cue, the potter wasp – like many solitary insects which exhibit diapause – produces two types of offspring (same-season or diapausing): they enjoy two very different physiological states and are programmed following specific mechanistic blueprints, triggered by specific environmental cues.

Jim Hunt suggested that the ancestral blueprint for diapause could have been repurposed during social evolution to produce queen and worker castes. The control circuits that produce the first-generation brood of a solitary eumenid could be used to make a worker (the same-season brood), while those of the second-generation brood (which overwinter) could be co-opted to make a queen. His ideas were specifically shaped by *Polistes* wasps, and particularly those living in temperate regions. There certainly are compelling similarities between diapausing solitary insects and *Polistes* brood destined to be the following year's queens: such traits include faster larval development, slower pupation time and high levels of storage proteins (known as hexamerins) than found in non-diapausing individuals.

The behaviours of diapausing and non-diapausing *Polistes* wasps also differ: females that do not enter dormancy are capable of reproducing but instead they tend to forage for protein, care for brood, contribute to nest-building and have a short lifespan – this sounds a lot like a worker. Conversely, females destined for diapause don't forage for protein, or engage in nest-building or brood-care duties, and they have a long lifespan – this is sounding a lot like a queen.

Research suggests that, at least in *Polistes*, the trigger for the two different types of development may be nutrition: what these wasps are fed as larvae determines whether they diapause or not. Feed your brood highly nutritious food and they are likely to grow up to be adults predisposed to diapause; feed them low-nutrient food and they are likely to give diapause a miss. The different diets of *Polistes* larvae appear to affect the expression of genes known to be involved with insect diapause in solitary insects, like pea aphids and parasitoid wasps. These are genes associated with the production of storage proteins (hexamerin) and stress response (heat shock proteins): they are expressed differently among early (worker-destined) and late (queen-destined) broods of the temperate wasp *Polistes metricus* as well as the adult queen and worker castes of this species.

The idea of a diapause blueprint for sociality has also caught the interest of bee researchers. Bumblebees are only found in temperate regions and they all exhibit diapause. In the autumn, the future year's queens go into hibernation, emerging the following spring to found their own nest alone and provisioning the brood until the first workers hatch. Diapause in bumblebees appears to use the same machinery as that found in other insects, including the pea aphid, parasitoid wasps and *Polistes*. These similarities extend to changes in physiology, gene transcription, and protein production related to nutrient storage, stress resistance and metabolism. And, just as with the temperate *Polistes*, some of the genes involved in regulating bumblebee dormancy are also differentially expressed by adult bumblebee queens and workers. This could be more evidence for a diapause toolkit being co-opted for the evolution of castes. The machinery is certainly there.

Having the right kit, however, is not always enough. You've got to know how to use it and when. In order for the diapause toolkit to be exploited to make castes, the life stage at which diapause occurs needs to shift: solitary ancestors of social insects are likely to have diapaused as larvae (as in our potter wasp), but social insects diapause as mated adults (as in our *Polistes* and bumblebees). If adult dormancy is important in the evolution of castes, we would expect the evolution of sociality and adult-stage diapause to coincide. This is exactly what was found in an analysis of 155 species of bees across all seven bee families, representing six independent origins of sociality.

Among the solitary species, over 70 per cent had larval diapause, while in the social species none showed larval diapause and instead 80 per cent of species exhibited some form of adult-stage dormancy (the remaining 20 per cent had no diapause).

Even after taking into account phylogenetic relationships and shared evolutionary history, the evidence remained: the most recent common ancestor of all bees (the wasp that became a bee) had larval diapause. The shift from larval diapause to adult-stage diapause appears to have coincided with some sort of caste evolution. Diapause may indeed be a prerequisite for the evolution of sociality in bees.

The evidence is stacking up in favour of the diapause idea. But there remain unanswered questions, especially concerning the wasps. All the evidence to date is correlative and has only been tested in temperate species of *Polistes*. There are two problems with this. First, late-season brood wasps in a temperate *Polistes* nest, which are destined to be queens, may be exhibiting the signatures of diapause simply because they need these traits in order to survive the winter and so there has been strong evolutionary selection for them to do so. The difference between early (worker-destined) and late (queen-destined) season broods therefore may be nothing to do with the co-option of a diapause toolkit to make castes. Instead it could simply be natural selection for dormancy traits (or not), depending on when they emerge.

Second, the prevailing consensus is that *Polistes* evolved in the tropics, where there is no winter diapause and no evidence that early- or late-colony-stage brood differ in any way. The tropics are not without seasonality of course, and even those species with colony cycles that build nests, rear brood and have sex all year round certainly experience 'quiet times', often during a prolonged dry season or at a slightly cooler time of the year. These seasonal changes are not enough for colony functioning to cease, but activity is reduced. Perhaps these seasonal variations are enough to generate some form of subtle diapause-like blueprint from which castes can evolve.

It's not just the tropics that present this problem: even in temperate regions, dormancy requires a sufficiently mild climate such that there is time for both worker and reproductive brood to be produced. A good example of this is the bee *Halictus rubicundus*: when nesting in warmer latitudes a female is able to fit two broods into a season, and the first stays at the nest as her helpers (workers), becoming a society of a mum and her daughters. However, if these same bees are nesting in colder latitudes, they have only one brood in a season and so remain solitary. In other words, the environmental conditions under which dormancy could be co-opted to make castes are pretty narrow. For me at least, the jury is out on how important the diapause toolkit has been in providing the machinery for the foundations of a social life.

The mechanics needed to evolve a social life could be derived from the ovaries, a long winter's sleep, something we've not yet measured or a combination of any (or none) of them. What is clear is that basic blueprints of solitary insect life have provided an assortment of raw materials from which to build a social life. My final word on this: mechanistic blueprints are useful for understanding sociality, but they only describe the nuts and bolts of *how* social life might arise, and they don't explain *why* sociality evolves. What causes sociality to evolve in the first place is the question for our next section.

# Part Four

# *Playing the Game*

Every schoolchild … ought to sit watching
a *Polistes* wasp nest for just one hour …
I think that few will be unaffected by
what they see.

William Hamilton (1996)

# Prelude

The abandoned building in a forgotten corner of secondary forest by the Panama Canal felt a little like a recently evacuated war zone. However, I would grow to love this place as it was my introduction to the magical world of *Polistes* wasps. I'd landed in Panama a week previously, excited to be starting life as an independent researcher on my own fellowship. From the (dis)comforts of my damp flat in north London, I had devoured a 316-page thesis on *Polistes canadensis* studied in Panama by John Pickering – an unpublished treasure trove of delights on the life history and behaviour of this little-studied tropical wasp, teasing me with morsels that promised to reveal the secrets of a social life in insect terms.

I had idealistic dreams of what lay ahead. But in the 20 years since Pickering had conducted his research in Panama's Canal Zone, the place had changed a lot: there were new buildings, less forest, and the canal was no longer owned by the Americans. The railway running the width of the isthmus was now active with tourist and cargo trains. Wasps seem pretty robust in the face of anthropogenic change, but none of Pickering's sites had wasps in 2002. Wasp populations move. Suddenly. Unpredictably. A lot. (I now build at least three weeks 'wasp-hunting' into my tropical field trips before I expect to start working.)

Luckily, the ever helpful Dr Bill Wcislo, an expert on bees and social evolution at the Smithsonian Tropical Research Institute in Panama, was certain he knew places where these wasps might be. Before long we were a few miles outside Panama City, hacking through scrub that grew deeper, into the wastelands of a country with a history of corruption, drug-lords, war and worse. We traversed vegetation and barbed-wire fences, until Bill stopped and gestured proudly at an abandoned military base: the two ex-US Army buildings were crumbling wrecks, still standing thanks only to their military-gauge reinforced concrete and corrugated iron. I was confused. I wondered if Bill had had too much sun (or gin). Oblivious, he thwacked at the vegetation to clear our way into the first building. And then I understood.

It was wasp mecca. From every beam and doorway hung what at first glance looked like the soles of many much-loved shoes. Grey and papery. A closer look revealed the teeming bodies of chestnut-coloured insects, sleek and elegant. These were nests of *Polistes canadensis*, just as John Pickering had described. But this was a citadel of nests – over 30 in the first room, and countless more beyond. These tropical wasps are almost two centimetres in length with monster stings to match. They are wasps who raise their wings in synchrony, poised to attack if you move too suddenly; wasps who dive bomb if you get disrespectfully close to their brood; whose stings extract the liveliest of vocabulary from the politest of people. But, most importantly, they are wasps who brazenly lay out their personal lives, interactions, tussles, ambitions and personalities for the evolutionary biologist to admire and record.

*Polistes* wasps live in simple societies. They lack the celibate worker-bots of honeybee or yellowjacket wasps who carry out their tasks with little regard for what the alternative options might be. Each *Polistes* wasp enjoys autonomy and relative freedom in her life-choice, because when she emerges from her pupal cell she is not necessarily committed to the proletariat existence of the honeybee or yellowjacket wasp worker. Granted, she typically starts her life foraging, toiling to help raise siblings. But if the opportunity arises she could end up straddling the social strata of colony life, turning her back on a high-risk life of work and becoming the sole matriarch (the 'queen') of the colony. Alternatively, she might choose instead to strike out alone (or with some siblings) to set up house nearby. In some circumstances, she may insinuate herself into a neighbouring nest, where she tries her luck as a cuckoo, slipping in an alien egg for others to rear, or even attempting to overthrow the matriarch.

I like the egalitarian message issued to every *Polistes* wasp at birth – all wasps are equal: you can be a proletarian today, but a royal tomorrow. Rising in the ranks is every wasp's prerogative. But only under the right conditions. For a *Polistes* wasp, the conditions are shaped by those around her – her family and her enemies, her neighbours and her neighbourhood. For the scientist, understanding these conditions may unlock some of the elusive secrets of social evolution, because the simple group living displayed by *Polistes* is likely to represent something akin to the first stages of sociality. *Polistes* display the best domestic melodrama that nature has to offer, but they also take us closer than any organism can to understanding the first steps in playing the social game.

Studying wasp behaviour demands daily commitment and long hours of watching. Watching. Watching. The discovery of a Panamanian wasp mecca that day with Bill Wcislo brought on a medley of emotions for me, from elation (lots of wasps meant lots of experiments) to trepidation (they were *very* big wasps), and then anxiety over the daily jungle scramble to get to the wasps (I didn't sign up to be a Panamanian Indiana Jones). I laughed with amusement and relief when I saw there was in fact a road that came right up to the buildings. To this day I still believe that Bill knew this, and that jungle scramble had been a form of initiation – a Smithsonian Institute version of artificial selection for fresh-faced new research fellows.

Sitting at my bullet-littered new field site, I quickly learned that the wasps would become accustomed to my presence, and would no longer show alarm unless I moved too suddenly or clumsily. These wasps lack the cover ('envelope') around their nest that is found in those of yellowjacket wasps, and they rarely nest in the ground or inside tree trunks. Their brood combs are open to the elements, predators, parasites and the entomologist. Once an egg is laid in a cell, it stays there until it hatches as an adult wasp.

Forceps held in a steady hand (clad in a protective Marigold glove), I could entice a newly hatched wasp from her nest without her dozens of family members noticing. A dollop of superglue and number tag later, she would be branded for life as one of my study subjects, individually identified – named. I would know her age, whom she bullied, who she was beaten up by, how much work she did. Ultimately, I was able to predict how likely it was that she would defect to start her own nest, reproduce in her home nest or stick to being a dedicated maiden sister. I was embarking on the start of my own journey in understanding the soap opera of these wasps.

The social behaviour of *Polistes* wasps has enthralled entomologists like me for over a century. The scientist who first put these wasps on the research map was an Italian named Leo Pardi. In the first half of the twentieth century Pardi described how each individual in a family group behaved in a way that suggested she had her own agenda. The *Polistes* society is an orderly one, but is swathed with the implicit expectation that anyone might thwart the rules if they can get away with it. Sound familiar? One of the endearing qualities of these wasps is the uncanny parallels they share with our own human societies, from divisions of labour, rebellions and policing to monarchies, leadership fights, undertakers, police, ASBOs, negotiators and social parasites.

Every attribute of the human soap opera can be found in the social wasps – only wasps found their stage millions of years before we did. On the surface, a social wasp colony may look cooperative and harmonious. But lift the lid and you'll see a veritable Game of Thrones in full swing. It is no surprise that these wasps have revealed some of nature's best-kept secrets about how and why organisms play the social games of life.

# I

'I would gladly give up my life for two brothers or eight cousins.' Historical records differ over the details, but we can be pretty certain that the evolutionary biologist J.B.S. Haldane made this argument on several occasions. It is simple maths: two siblings equal eight cousins or one Haldane. The currency of his calculation are gene variants – the building blocks of life that package up the genetic code (DNA) into meaningful chunks.

Haldane (just like you and most other multi-celled creatures) was a diploid organism: he had two copies (variants called alleles) of all his genes arranged on pairs of chromosomes. One copy was inherited from his father and the other from his mother, who might have different variants of any one gene. For each gene, therefore, there is a 50 per cent chance that his sibling shared the same version: this means that on average he shared half of his DNA with each of his siblings, but only 12.5 per cent of his genes with each cousin. Hence, in genetic terms two siblings equal one Haldane, just as eight cousins equal one Haldane. Haldane's genes don't care if they are carried in the packaging of two siblings or eight cousins or even the great biologist himself, so long as they survive to the next generation. Personal grudges and favourites aside, in evolutionary terms the choice is not a dilemma: what matters is that the representation of his gene variants in the population is not depleted, and for that either option will do just fine.

What Haldane was trying to explain was an evolutionary argument for altruism – the expression of selfless behaviour to benefit others. Altruism has furrowed the brow of philosophers, naturalists and evolutionary biologists for millennia. The martyrdom of worker honeybees caused Aristotle to marvel, while in *On the Origin of Species* Darwin mused for several pages over the worker bee's commitment to celibacy. If evolution selects organismal traits that are reliable vehicles for gene propagation, what explains the existence of a sterile worker who will not pass on her genes by reproducing? The honeybee workers, with their famously heroic acts of altruism and self-sacrifice, represent the pinnacle of social evolution. Yellowjacket wasps and hornets, and most of the ants, also share this accolade.

Haldane's story of sacrifice goes a long way in explaining why: workers forgo the chance of raising their own offspring in order to help raise relatives. Usually, these relatives are siblings. Workers belong to their own super-society, in which family life has been taken to extremes with a single matriarch who is usually the mother of the many (often hundreds of) others in the society. A hornet worker, for example, is committed to a life of work and celibacy from a very early stage in development as a young larva, with no say in the matter. A few days after she emerges as an adult from her pupal cell, she will embark upon a dangerous and risky life as a hunter. Fly, caterpillar, butterfly, spider, dead pigeon or your ham sandwich, all carry risks to her – disorientation, disease, death. Life for a hornet worker is usually short – three weeks at best. Although she will never mate and be a fully-fledged mother herself, her short life will be fulfilled if she has helped part-rear enough sibling brood to replace herself, in genetic terms.

A worker wasp and Haldane therefore have a lot in common: they will both sacrifice themselves to promote the survival of their relatives. The currency of genes guides their decisions. However, it took a further nine years after Haldane's profession of hypothetical self-sacrifice before William D. Hamilton came along and expanded on *exactly* why altruism could evolve. His theory (known as 'Hamilton's Rule', 'kin selection' or 'inclusive fitness theory') draws its evidence from a plethora of social insects. But there is no doubt that Hamilton's ideas were especially influenced by *Polistes* wasps, perhaps because they parade to the observer both conflict and cooperation, with unashamed brashness. He'd marvelled at the industrious zeal of their reproductive sacrifice, played audience to their physical quarrels in the amphitheatre of their nest, pondered at the juxtaposition of covert infidelity with familial commitment. Hamilton's insight was that the benefits of an altruistic act must outweigh the costs to the altruist. A simple fictional role play will help explain this.

You'd love to set up a home and start a family, but you're not head-over-heels in love with your current partner, and anyway there's a housing shortage. You decide to stay at home and help your mum out. Your help is invaluable, and your mum and dad decide that with your help they could have another child. Before you know it, you are largely responsible for feeding and looking after a delightful younger sibling. Luckily, you've read William Hamilton's 1964 paper on his theory of kin selection explaining why altruism can evolve.

Hamilton's Rule explains that an altruistic act (like you helping to raise a sibling) is evolutionarily advantageous when the genetic fitness gain from helping raise your siblings (known as 'indirect fitness', or the copies of your own gene variants ('alleles') that you pass on 'indirectly' via the vehicles of your relatives) exceeds the genetic fitness you have sacrificed (that's your 'direct fitness', in other words the copies of your own genetic variants that would be passed on via your own offspring – you are forfeiting this in order to help rather than reproduce). Some simple maths explains this:

$$\mathbf{r\ B\ >\ C}$$

| | | |
|:---:|:---:|:---:|
| 'r' is your **Relatedness** to your sibling. It is the chance that a given allele is shared between you and your sibling, relative to the chance that two random people in the population share this allele. | 'B' is the **Benefit** – that is, the extra offspring your parents produce thanks to your help. | 'C' is **Cost** to you, in choosing to help your parents rather than reproducing yourself. |

After a quick calculation you realise that, as far as your genes are concerned, your current strategy of staying at home to help your parents is just fine: you share 50 per cent of your genetic material with your sibling (so r = 0.5). Your help results in one extra offspring for your parents (B = 1), which is the equivalent to 50 per cent of your gene variants being propagated. This is your 'indirect' fitness, the genes you pass on *indirectly* by helping relatives (in this case, your parents). In the currency of genes, helping raise one sibling is in fact exactly the same as if you had your own child (C = 0.5) – you still only share 50 per cent of your gene variants with your child as the other 50 per cent come from your partner. Slot these values into Hamilton's equation and you get: 0.5 x 1 = 0.5. In other words, the genetic pay-off from your altruistic behaviour is in perfect balance with that of being a parent yourself.

Then circumstances change: a huge government housing initiative kicks off, making the idea of setting up your own home entirely feasible. Coincidentally you also meet someone with whom you'd *definitely* like to mingle your life (and genes). You now have the option to have your own house and your own children. But there's some bad news too: tragically your dad dies and your mum remarries; before you know it she's expecting a third child – your half-sibling. This tips the scales of altruism away from staying at home and in favour of having a family of your own, because the benefits of raising a half-sibling are outweighed by the costs. For any allele picked at random in your half-sibling, there is only a 25 per cent chance that you have the same gene variant, because 50 per cent of their gene variants come from your stepdad, with whom you are no more likely to share gene variants than any random punters from the wider population (that is, you and your stepdad are unrelated). The genetic pay-off of helping (0.25) no longer outweighs the costs you pay (0.5). It is time to up sticks and leave home, to invest in *direct* reproduction of your own.

Your best reproductive strategy changed because of the conditions, and you were able to detect these changes and respond in a way that served you best. Wasps play the same game, constantly assessing the pros and cons of being a worker versus flexing their oviducts and striking out alone. *Polistes* had been a model organism for studying behaviour since Leo Pardi's founding work in the first half of the twentieth century. Yet Hamilton's simple explanation for the evolution of altruism suddenly brought *Polistes* (and other wasps and bees with simple societies) into the spotlight for evolutionary biologists. These insects were observable, autonomous units who respond to fluctuations (or experimental manipulation) in the pay-offs for helping, and whose societies are likely to represent the first stages in the evolution of one of the longest-standing puzzles in the natural sciences – altruism.

# II

Hamilton's Rule may be a simple concept, but testing it is quite another matter. The most tangible term of the rule is 'relatedness' – the 'r' in the equation on the previous pages – because it is a quantitative measure of the probability that any given allele (gene variant) in one individual is also carried by another individual, relative to the probability of that allele being shared among two randomly selected members of the population. If we could somehow sample the gene variants from the altruist (the worker), the beneficiary (the queen) and some other 'random punters' from the population, estimating this probability would be trivial. Unfortunately, it would be a few decades after Hamilton's conceptual eureka moment before methods in molecular biology made this possible. There was (at the time) no way to assess relatedness other than by observing who laid the egg, who emerged from that cell, and hoping that the egg hadn't been replaced by some interloper when you weren't looking.

In the absence of experimental evidence, Hamilton and his proponents pondered the conceptual options. The altruists needed to be at least more related to the brood they helped raise than they were to a random individual drawn from the wider population. If not, it could spell doom for Hamilton's idea, as helping behaviour can only evolve if helpers (altruists) pass on their genes indirectly, contained in the bodies of relatives. The best-case scenario would be if altruists were the offspring of the breeder: this would mean that the altruists were raising siblings, which is (usually) as good in genetic terms as being a mum yourself.

Or perhaps altruists were sisters of the mother, or cousins? The genetic outcome of this would not be as bad for a wasp (or indeed a bee or an ant) as it would be for you. This is because bees, wasps and ants have a quirky genetic system of reproduction called 'haplodiploidy'. The 'ploidy' of an organism tells us how many copies of each gene are present in each of their cells. You and I are the diploids: all our genes are present in pairs, with a copy of each one nestled on *each* of the two arms of our body's 23 pairs of chromosomes – the structures that bundle up your genes inside your cells. At least, this is how it is for our non-reproductive cells (known as somatic cells).

However, our reproductive (sex) cells (also known as gametes) are haploid (the word is derived from the Greek root of *haploos* meaning 'single') – they have only one arm from each chromosome pair. So your sex cells contain half the amount of DNA of all your other cells and only one copy of each gene. They need to be haploid so that your offspring end up being diploids, not tetraploids: one 'arm' from each of your 23 chromosome pairs comes from your mum's sex cells (the proto-you egg) and the other comes from your dad's sex cells (the sperm that fertilised the proto-you egg). In this way sexual reproduction does a great job of mingling the genes from the parents. Hymenopteran females are diploid (just like your somatic cells), but males are haploid (just like your sex cells). This means male wasps have half the complement of DNA of their female counterparts, and that they are simply clones of half their mum's DNA.*

The quirks of the haplodiploid genetic system give rise to several intriguing implications for wasps (and bees and ants). First, it means that males have no dads, as they develop from unfertilised eggs. This is brilliant for unmated workers who might want to squeeze out a sneaky male egg when their queen (or fellow worker) is not looking.

The second implication of haplodiploidy was thought to be the key in explaining why altruism had evolved more times in

---

* Haplodiploidy is quite mad. It's also fascinating: we still don't really understand how or why haplodiploidy evolved (but that's another book).

the Hymenoptera than in any other group. Workers are invariably female in the social Hymenoptera (unlike the diploid termites, where both males and females work). Due to the jiggery-pokery of haplodiploidy, females share 75 per cent of their alleles with their own sisters (recall that you share a mere 50 per cent with your sibling), because while they inherit only half of their mother's DNA, they all inherit the same 100 per cent of their father's alleles. As a result, an allele randomly selected from a female has (on average) a 75 per cent chance of being identical in her sister. This means a female could pass on *more* genes by altruistically raising sisters than she could by reproducing herself. Could the quirky genetics of the Hymenoptera predispose them to evolve sociality? Hamilton appeared to have simultaneously solved the problem of evolving altruism and explaining why it had evolved so many times in the Hymenoptera.

A few years after Hamilton's Rule shook the ivory towers of evolutionary biology, a couple of his admirers, Robert Trivers and Hope Hare, uncovered a bittersweet flaw in his otherwise brilliant work. The genetic benefits of altruism due to haplodiploidy hold only if workers raise more sisters than brothers, because workers pass on only 25 per cent of their genes (on average) by raising brothers. A quick back-of-the-envelope calculation reveals that a worker rearing an equal ratio of sisters to brothers would in fact be passing on 50 per cent of her genes ((75 per cent + 25 per cent)/2 = 50 per cent), which is exactly the same return as if she had reproduced herself. Haplodiploidy genetics could therefore not explain the evolution of altruism in Hymenoptera, because the reduced relatedness to haploid brothers cancelled out the benefit of enhanced relatedness to diploid sisters.

It is a devastating compliment to have your academic peers find a flaw in your work. However, Hamilton came out of it better than most, as Trivers and Hare simultaneously offered a solution: what if workers could preferentially rear more sisters than brothers? By skewing the sex ratio of the brood to be female-biased, they could minimise genetic investment in low-rewarding males and maximise it in high-rewarding females. Trivers and Hare worked out that if a worker could raise three sisters for every brother, she'd break even, compensating for her altruism in genetic terms. This was a brilliant solution to the perfect flaw of the haplodiploid hypothesis, and one that they found evidence for in the literature, to the tune of 20 species of ants.

Except, yet again, biology is never that simple. Any retailer knows that the rarer a commodity becomes, the more desirable and valuable it grows. Conversely, wares in excessive abundance can devalue a product such that it becomes next to worthless. A canny retailer will work hard to stock their shop with more of the rare product in order to boost profits. This explains why most natural populations balance a 1:1 sex ratio (equal numbers of males and females). In a population with an unequal sex ratio, the value of the rarer sex exceeds that of the more widespread sex. Any gene variant that causes parents to skew their offspring production towards the rarer sex will spread rapidly through the population. The result would be a population tending back to the 1:1 sex ratio.

This is an example of an evolutionary stable strategy and it explains another problem with the haplodiploidy hypothesis. Take a putative population of wasps in which workers preferentially rear three sexual sisters for every brother: on average each male will mate with three sexual females, while each sexual female will (typically) only mate with one male. This makes males much more profitable, in reproductive terms (three times more valuable to be exact), as they pass on their genes via three different vehicles (females). The genetic gains of raising a sexual-female-biased sibling brood are exactly cancelled out by their diminished reproductive value.

Why, then, did Trivers and Hare find sex biases in so many ant species? Later researchers found that within a population over a given area, some colonies often produce a male-biased sex ratio while others produce a female-biased sex ratio. These are known as split-sex ratios. But at the population level everything usually levels out to an even 1:1 sex ratio. Helping behaviour would only be favoured in those colonies with female-biased ratios. In the colonies with male bias, there would be selection *against* helping behaviour because workers are more closely related to their own offspring (sharing 50 per cent of their genes with both their daughters and sons) than they are to brothers (sharing only 25 per cent of their genes).

In other words, haplodiploidy might even predispose groups *not* to be social! The rise and fall of the haplodiploidy hypothesis makes for great undergraduate teaching material on the bittersweet nature of the scientific game and how explanations that seem plausible at the level of the individual can rapidly unravel when population-level dynamics are considered. Among the convoluted story of altruism and haplodiploidy, it's easy to lose sight of what's important: the concept and predictions of Hamilton's Rule as an explanation for altruism remain unaffected by the fall of the haplodiploidy hypothesis. For altruism to evolve, the benefits of the altruistic act must outweigh the costs. The secret to balancing this equation is to direct your help at your relatives.

In the mid-1990s, a molecular revolution shook genetics labs across the globe. Scientists had worked out a way to quantify accurately the relationships between individuals of any organism. The magic bullet was the microsatellite, short fragments of repetitive DNA that resembled a kind of genetic 'stutter' which mutate very easily, to give alleles with different numbers of repeats. The hyperdynamic nature of microsatellites makes them brilliant genetic markers for quantifying relatedness. Close relatives are more likely to share the same number of repeats for a given microsatellite than are more distant relatives, because the more generations or lines of pedigree that stand between any two individuals, the more chance there is that the repeat sequence has slipped while being replicated and become expanded, or that it has dropped repeats and contracted. By analysing repeat-sharing across many different microsatellites scattered through the genome, we can obtain a very accurate measure of the probability that an allele in one individual is shared by another – that is, relatedness.

Microsatellites revolutionised forensic medicine (they are the go-to tool used for DNA fingerprinting), paternity testing and disease identification. But they also changed the level of resolution with which ecologists and evolutionary biologists could interrogate population structure and kinship in pretty much any organism. Today's high-throughput genome sequencing makes it extremely simple to find microsatellites, but at the dawn of the microsatellite era it was less trivial. I can personally attest to this, as I spent two years of my PhD life trying to find microsatellites in hover wasps. I did find some eventually, but many tears of frustration were shed in the process. Tears aside, it was an exceedingly exciting time to be working on the evolution of altruism in social insects because suddenly *everyone* was quantifying relatedness in colonies of their favourite species.

William Hamilton would have been pleased with the results. In *Polistes* alone, relatedness data now exist for over 20 species from around the world, and the overall pattern is clear: family matters. Foundresses (the group of females who found a new colony together) are usually sisters, meaning that a foundress who ends up as a non-reproductive subordinate doesn't do too badly since the odds are that the reproductive female will carry 75 per cent of her genes. A similarly pleasing family structure persists in established colonies: the queen (who would usually be the foundress dominating reproduction in the early stages of a colony's life) is typically the sole mother of the colony's members – that includes the worker force as well as the sexuals of the future. As Hamilton predicted, workers help raise relatives and so pass on their genes indirectly by being altruistic.

It's not just wasps that have helped explain the evolution of altruism. Altruism pervades societies of ants, bees, termites, shrimps, thrips, aphids and cooperatively breeding vertebrates like long-tailed tits, pied babblers, meerkats, mongooses and mole rats. In almost all cases, altruists raise relatives.

Since Hamilton's day, scientists have realised the importance of understanding the breeder's behaviour as this affects relatedness. It all boils down to sex and infidelity: the sexual behaviour of the breeder has a huge impact in the meaning of the word 'relative'. Altruism is much more likely to evolve if the breeder is a faithful female committed to a lifetime of monogamy, having mated with only one male. The 'lifetime' bit means that she remains faithful to that partner throughout her life, and that she lives long enough that the conditions of monogamy remain so for the tenure of a helper's life. In this 'nuclear family', the genetic incentives for offspring to stay home and help are maximised because helpers raise full siblings; in fact, helpers are (in genetic terms) indifferent between raising siblings or offspring because the genetic pay-offs are the same. This means that a tiny ecological difference in the efficiency of either option can tip the decision from help to leave, and vice versa.

The importance of monogamy as a condition for altruism sounds so obvious, yet it was only articulated clearly as a hypothesis for explaining the origins of social evolution within the last decade. The most basic, far-reaching condition for altruism is the family group. The so-called 'monogamy hypothesis' has since won countless empirical awards across the natural world, from the social Hymenoptera to the cooperatively breeding birds and even social bacteria. In all these groups, the evolutionary ancestors of the lineages that evolved altruism have invariably been monogamous.* Lineages with more promiscuous mating and breeding systems are statistically less likely to have evolved sociality.

Hold your hymenopteran horses!

So far we've been obsessing over a *single* term in Hamilton's Rule: relatedness. What about the other terms in his equation? Relatedness alone cannot explain why a youngster stays home to help rather than jumping ship to be mistress of her own reproductive empire. Recall that even with the quirky genetics of the haplodiploid hymenopterans, the genetic returns of producing your own offspring are equivalent to helping raise a full-sibling brood: so why would you stay home and help rather than exercise your independence and strike out alone if you have the ability, as does a *Polistes* wasp?

Altruism in the nuclear family can only work if the benefits outweigh the costs. In other words, the benefit (or B) term in Hamilton's Rule – which can be measured in terms of the extra offspring your mum produces thanks to your help – outweighs the cost (or C) term in Hamilton's Rule, which can be measured as the number of offspring you would otherwise rear on your own. The benefits of group living are very clear for a *Polistes* wasp: her brood are vulnerable to parasites, predators or even 'cuckoo' interlopers if she has no comrade to help defend the nest while she is off hunting for food. The odds are similar for

---

* In the social insects there are in fact lots of species that are not monogamous – they have multiple queens and/or queens who've mated with several (sometimes dozens) of males. But these have nothing to do with the *origins* of altruism. Deviations from monogamy only arise once the major evolutionary transition to superorganismality has *happened*; at this point, each individual is committed to a life of dependence on her colony members – a worker no longer has the option to explore reproductive opportunities outside the colony. Only at this point can the rules of monogamy be relaxed. Multiple mating (and multiple queens) generates genetic diversity that can then be used to diversify colony division of labour and resistance against interlopers like parasites and pathogens.

cooperatively breeding birds. Young blue tits often stay to help at their home nest for a season before spreading their reproductive wings and heading out for some procreation. Nests with helpers often do better than those without. They are better protected from predators, parasites and cuckolds, and the chicks are less likely to go hungry. Help means more chicks and healthier chicks.

But helpers only help if there are no better options available. If there are good nesting sites nearby, it is hard to persuade a helper to stick around. Limited nesting sites alter the *cost* term in Hamilton's Rule. A shortage of nesting sites means there are higher risks associated with leaving home – and probably a lower cost to being a helper; in fact the housing shortage that a hypothetical you experienced in the above example, where we first met Hamilton's Rule, will certainly have reduced the C term. But flood the neighbourhood with artificial nests (or new housing developments) and they are rapidly adopted, by ex-helpers. Local ecology affects the pay-offs of being an altruist.

The equation of group living is a numbers game: if you can transmit more copies of your alleles to future generations indirectly, by boosting the number of offspring your mum can have (B), than you would by having your own offspring alone (C), then helping behaviour will be favoured by natural selection, and altruistic behaviour evolves. So it's not just relatedness (or even monogamy) that determines whether altruism evolves. The ecological conditions and the variability of the environment matter too.

Across the tree of life, group living has been made possible because of seemingly selfless altruists. But apparent selflessness is deceptive: every altruist is in it for her own gain, quietly packaging up her gene variants in the bodies of non-offspring relatives in order to post her genetic material safely off to the next generation, without flexing a single reproductive organ in her body. Altruists from birds, bees, wasps and bacteria may be united by the way they transmit their genes, but they are not born of the same, single evolutionary quirk. Altruism has evolved independently more than 12 times in the insects and dozens of times in the vertebrates. But few organisms have taken us quite as far in the quest to understand the origins of altruism as has *Polistes*.

# III

One of the irritating things about science is that once you've answered one question, it prompts new questions that sometimes cause you to doubt the very one you think you've answered. Knowing that altruists (usually) manage to end up helping in family groups raises the question of how they find family to live with in the first place. This is not such a problem for a wasp born in early summer as the odds are that the current queen is indeed her mother. But for a wasp born in late summer in a temperate environment, things are a little bit tricky, as her opportunity to be altruistic really only kicks in *after* a winter of hibernation, when she emerges into an optimistic spring air and starts on her quest to found a new nest. How do these bleary-eyed foundresses manage to find relatives to nest with? Once ensconced in a group, how do they recognise who is who in the nest? And can they then tell if their nestmates are kin or not? If so, how?

These questions have sparked a large literature on the kin- and individual-level recognition skills of *Polistes* wasps. Like most social insects, *Polistes* live in a very smelly world – a veritable cocktail of chemical cues, serving diverse functions, one being recognition. Wasps are clothed in a chainmail suit of linear carbon atoms linked to hydrogen molecules. Known as cuticular hydrocarbons, these are synthesised and carried on the exoskeleton cuticle of the insect. Cuticular hydrocarbons are ubiquitous among insects, serving as waterproof jackets and diverse communication-signalling devices.

Thanks to these hydrocarbons, each nest of *Polistes* has its own odour, shared by the family members and the paper carton of their home. This chemical signature is used by the wasps to distinguish nestmates from non-nestmates. At most the queen may smell a little different to her workers, but this doesn't mean the odour carries information about kinship – it is simply a nest-level signature and it can be acquired by any wasp who spends enough time there. If a newly hatched wasp finds its way onto another (unrelated) nest (either by accident or at the hands of an experimental entomologist), she will soon acquire the signature perfume of her adoptive nest. Indeed, social parasites are known to exploit the flightiness of nest odour, gaining a chemical cloak of invisibility to insinuate themselves into a nest of their host and exploit the worker force for their own personal gain.

Perhaps foundresses use visual cues to recognise each other. In some American populations of *Polistes*, wasps do seem to be able to recognise individuals by their facial markings, and they can also learn new facial patterns, updating their information. This remarkable skill of individual-level recognition and specialised face learning is shared with primates and other mammals, but *Polistes* are the only insects known to exhibit it – not even honey-bees can learn to recognise fellow bee faces.

To be fair, being able to recognise and update information on group membership is not that useful for a honeybee, as every worker is (largely) equal and there is no benefit to knowing who's who. For a small foundress group of *Polistes* females, however, knowing who's who and being able to update that information is critical to societal law and order and, crucially, to the establishment and maintenance of the social hierarchy. A pecking order of wasps is the calibrator of societal lawfulness, with the reproductive (dominant) foundress at the top and her subordinates forming an orderly queue below her.

The orderly queue is maintained by dominance interactions among group members: if A is the dominant, she will typically focus her domination efforts on the next most important wasp in the group – let's call her 'B'. B is equally single-minded, directing her autocracy at 'C', C at 'D', and so on down the pecking order. This linear hierarchy dictates how food, work and reproduction are distributed among the colony. On the rare occasion of social unrest (for example, if the dominant dies, or is rudely removed by a curious entomologist), a wasp may direct her dominance 'up' the hierarchy (that is, C kicks B, or D nudges C). After a bit of a scuffle though, a new dominance hierarchy is established and interactions revert to a line of tolerance. Their politeness outstrips that of obliging Brits waiting their turn in an orderly queue at the supermarket. The predictability of dominance hierarchies in *Polistes* has been admired ever since Leo Pardi first described them in the first half of the twentieth century. It is only in the last ten years that scientists have worked out *how* they do this.

American cognitive biologist Liz Tibbetts manipulated the facial markings in the American paper wasp – *Polistes fuscatus* – to see if it affected their interactions. These wasps have very distinctive, but variable, yellow markings on their otherwise dark chestnut heads. Some flaunt yellow eyebrows or moustaches, or perhaps sport a subtle flick of yellow eyeliner, while others may lack any yellow at all. Liz Tibbetts is the first person to have documented this variability in a systematic way, and she found that a few judiciously applied splashes of yellow face paint could upset the social pecking order. Nestmates whose facial markings had been altered were attacked more often than their untreated 'control' counterparts (who were painted, but not in a way that altered their markings). She deduced that the wasps were attacked because they had suddenly become unfamiliar-looking. After an hour or so, however, social order would be re-established, suggesting that the wasps had learned the new look of their nestmates. Better still, these wasps seem to be especially good at learning *faces*, not just any random shapes or other body parts. They are veritable cognitive queens of the insect world.

Diving into the genome of *Polistes fuscatus* has revealed the genetic basis of their cognitive superpowers, and pinpointed them to several novel mutations in genes involved in learning, memory, brain development and visual processing. These mutations appeared only in the last 2,000–8,000 years, but have clearly been advantageous for this species as they seem to have spread very rapidly through the population, reducing variation in the surrounding nucleotides until the favourable mutation has reached 'fixation' and become the dominant genetic variant – what geneticists call a 'selective sweep'. This happens when a mutation is especially good at increasing the fitness of the carrier.

Having the ability to recognise individuals and to update information on who everyone is should clearly be of enormous benefit in achieving a cooperative social group. So far, individual-level recognition has been found only in *Polistes fuscatus*. Does that make this wasp the supreme socialite of *Polistes*? Well, we don't know that *no* other *Polistes* species has this ability as there are over 300 of them to check out, and it remains a strange coincidence that this very one lives on the doorstep of the world's expert in *Polistes* cognition. It's not trivial to evolve a suite of the right mutations over thousands of years, but my hunch is that if we looked hard enough, we'd uncover more remarkable cognitive superpowers in other *Polistes* species, and indeed in other organisms for whom a cohesive social life among relatives is important.

Liz's experiments have since gone on to reveal that the brokenness of black facial markings provides an indication of social status among foundresses in US populations of the European paper wasp species *Polistes dominula*, which is an invasive species in America. In this species, larger wasps tend to wear a bigger, blacker, but more broken-up bandana across the centre of their face than do smaller wasps. Liz suggested this could be a badge of social status: the bigger, blacker wasps tended to be the more dominant in a colony. Moreover, the facial markings are an honest signal of their worth: when the wasps' bandanas were manipulated (painted) to be *more* broken (falsely indicating a higher status than they deserved), they received more aggression than their sham-control counterparts (painted without altering their markings). But never did these facial manipulations result in a reversal of dominance. In other words, cheating did them no good. Rather, false displays of an inflated social status were punished.

Perhaps, then, these facial markings are used by the wasps as an honest indicator of how socially important they are. Evolving honest signals can be very costly. But it's not the production of fragmented wasp bandanas that is costly here, it's the social cost of having a dishonest signal. If a low-quality wasp can get away with deceiving her nestmates (relatives) into believing she's of higher quality (fertility) than she can deliver, this affects the inclusive fitness of *all* relatives – it's a social cost that affects individual fitness. Moreover, it will make it harder to evolve Hamiltonian altruism.

How on earth can such a complex linkage between face-markings, size, quality and dominance evolve into a reliable, honest signal? Liz has argued that hymenopteran visual systems have evolved to be especially sensitive to perceiving disrupted patterns, for example for finding prey or flowers. Team this with a highly variable trait (brokenness), and therein lies the evolutionary fodder to be co-opted into an honest signal. Wasps with broken bandanas are broadcasting a more obvious signal, which comes with higher social costs. At least they do in some populations. Attempts to replicate these experiments in native European populations of the same wasps have failed to find any evidence of such an honest signal. And so, on goes the rollercoaster of science: one turn reveals another twist, sometimes ugly, sometimes sweet.

\* \* \*

Impressive though it is, *individual* recognition is not the same thing as *kin* recognition, and so the evidence that *Polistes* wasps can calculate the *r* term in Hamilton's Rule is still lacking. Perhaps they don't need such a metric. Is there a 'rule of thumb' that helps them maximise the likelihood that who they end up with is a close(ish) relative? For a tropical species, such a rule could be: 'Build a new nest with others from the same "mother-ship".' And this is in fact exactly what many tropical *Polistes* do. Typically, a group of females from the same nest will 'fission' away together from the motherland and build a new home, often nearby.

Even if they cannot distinguish kin from non-kin, the odds that a female from their own nest is a sister are likely to be in their favour because a queen tends to reign for many months: even a wasp that is a month older than you could well be your sister. Where you find one tropical *Polistes* nest, you often find another or more nearby – some populations persist for years, producing aggregations of many nests, just like the Panamanian war-zone wasp mecca that Bill Wcislo revealed to me. We now know that the nests in these sorts of aggregations are often related, 'sisterhoods' set up as satellites to their mothership. Such extended family networks take Hamilton's original explanation of altruism to a whole new level.

How females of temperate species manage to find relatives to nest with is more troubling, as the winter shutdown of the colony cycle means that the family group dissolves and the newly mated sexual females (next season's foundresses) go into a form of hibernation – the diapause we heard about in Part 3. It takes some strong evolutionary selection to ensure that foundresses end up nesting with relatives the following spring, especially when you remember that, to our knowledge, *Polistes* can't tell a sister from a stranger. Another convention is needed.

The world's hotbed for *Polistes* research is undoubtedly Italy, thanks to the legacy of Leo Pardi. One of Pardi's students,

Stefano Turrillazzi, went on to attract a hive of wasp-crazed researchers to his lab in Florence, and he and his collaborators uncovered what *Polistes* get up to in the winter-wasp wonderland of diapause. In the stately cool of the Italian autumn, young, freshly deflowered sexual females cluster in their hundreds at hibernation sites known as 'hibernacula'. Like any good den, the same sites are used year after year, with each winter playing host to a new suite of wasps.

The team found that the hibernacula are chemically marked by the bodies and venom of the previous year's occupants. By separating out the components of venom and cuticular peptides and giving wasps a choice of the different chemicals, the researchers worked out that *Polistes* look for a specific part of this chemical cue – a peptide named *dominulin* (after the wasp it was discovered in, *Polistes dominula*) – to choose a haven for hibernation. A hydrophilic molecule such as this would only survive if the hibernacula were waterproof, making these chemicals good indicators of well-sheltered hibernation sites. Using chemicals to mark good places to hang out is not unusual or new: barnacles and mussels release chemicals to signal a good place to gather.

A family vault for hibernation would be a brilliant way to keep the family together so they can find relatives to nest with the following spring. Unfortunately, hibernating wasps are typically a mixed bag of relatives and strangers, lured to the same cosy hideaway. Moreover, unlike a diapausing butterfly, hibernating wasps don't wind up their metabolic clocks completely over the winter, at least not in the mild Italian ones. Hibernacula are certainly no respite from the complexities of a social life. Granted, the wasps are dopey during this period, but they are awake enough to interact with each other. It is thought the social play that helps them while away the long winter months could have a role in determining with whom these wasps end up starting a nest with in the spring, and ultimately help shape the outcome of negotiations over reproductive conflicts that take place on the nest.

When the first rays of Italian sunshine kiss the hibernacula, sleepy wasps will stir and venture out into the spring air. If they choose to nest near to their winter hideaway, they have a better chance of ending up with a relative or two. Indeed, most co-foundresses in nests of the European paper wasp *Polistes dominula* are related. In fact, similarly to my Panamanian wasp mecca, these wasps will form aggregations of loosely related nests in the same area if there is enough suitable nesting substrate. The same rule of thumb for finding kin may therefore work for temperate species, as it does for tropical species, despite winter's rude interruption of the colony cycle.

*Polistes* and I are a bit like an old married couple, at least from my perspective. We've been together so many years, and yet I still gaze at her with admiration and awe. She and her societies are packages of scientific wonder that just keep on giving. Altruism may have remained a paradox of nature with only a theoretical solution if it weren't for *Polistes*. In probing their lives to better understand it, scientists have discovered the unexpected and the curious.

The simple theory of altruism is spun together by a complex web of evolutionary inventions and designs, many of them unimagined by scientists. Our thirst to discover the secrets of altruism has exposed *Polistes* as cognitive queens in the insect world. Their remarkable recognition systems secure social order and function, but the conditions for altruism don't seem to rely on this. Instead, simple ecological rules of thumb ensure that the genes of altruists are packaged up safely within parcels of their relatives. But finding relatives to be postie for your genes is only one prize in the lucky dip of reproductive strategies for *Polistes* wasps. Rummage deeper in her sack and secrets spill on how *Polistes* ensures she gets the best genetic deal she can find.

# IV

*The Apprentice* is a reality TV game show that offers life-changing opportunities for a single lucky wannabe-business magnate. A group of young, hopeful people plough through a collection of high-stress challenges that require them to coordinate, communicate, cooperate, but also to compete with their fellow candidates. They are watching one another, learning to anticipate each other's moves, interpreting behaviours, assessing relative abilities of teammates, all so that they can act in a way that manipulates their standing within the ever-changing group dynamics.

It's a social game of negotiation and competition, and one person is expelled in each round. Contestants interact in a series of tasks over several weeks and so have the chance to build (or break) relationships through reciprocal interactions, to make judgements on the abilities, behaviour and competitiveness of others and to determine the best line of negotiation, depending on their teammates and competitors. It makes for compelling viewing, largely because it's almost impossible to predict who will win in the end. People are complicated. Social networks of interacting people are even more complicated.

Personally, I prefer to watch the real-life battles and negotiations that are played out by *Polistes* wasps. During the nest-founding phase of their colony cycle, when they start out building a nest as a group of (usually) sisters, they form an insectopolis version of *The Apprentice*. Just like the show's contestants, each wasp is capable of winning – becoming a queen – but there will only be one winner. Those who fail will be kicked out of the direct reproduction market and become the queen's subordinates, helping to raise her brood.

Hamilton's Rule explains why this is not a terrible outcome so long as the foundresses are sisters: by raising nieces and nephews, subordinates still pass on a good whack of their genetic material to the next generation without actually reproducing themselves. But there is no denying the fact that it's always better to be the egg-layer than a subordinate on a foundress's nest. As a non-reproductive subordinate, the best you can hope for from helping to raise your sister's offspring is that on average 37.5 per cent* of your gene variants (over and above those you share with the average punter from the wider population) will be passed on to the next generation. This is a far cry from the 50 per cent you'd package up in your own offspring, if you were the reproducer.

A second problem is that life as a subordinate is much riskier than being the queen. Once she has won the negotiations over who becomes the egg-layer, a foundress queen lives a life of relative luxury within the safety of the colony, where she benefits from the collective defence of her fellow nestmates. She gets all the nourishment she needs from her companions, via the mysterious 'social fluid' that is transferred readily among adults and brood.† Most importantly, she has a relatively low chance of dying, as she leaves the nest only rarely to collect building materials. Departing the safety of the colony is one of the riskiest things a wasp can do: you might be eaten by a hungry bird, get lost in a rainstorm or be injured in a grapple with unaccommo-

---

* You share on average 37.5 per cent of your gene variants (alleles) with your nieces and nephews. This is calculated as your relatedness to your sister, with whom you share on average 75 per cent of your alleles (due to haplodiploidy), divided by two (because only half of her alleles are passed on to her own offspring): 75/2 = 37.5.

† The exchange of fluids (or food) between members of a community is known as 'trophallaxis'. It is ubiquitous in social insect societies, where adults and brood exchange fluids with each other via their mouth parts. The content of the fluids and their purpose are not well studied. They are certainly of nutritional importance, but they also carry information in the form of pheromones, are important in the formation of social bonds, and in some insects they confer the transfer of beneficial microorganisms.

dating prey. Subordinates have little choice but to go out hunting for food to feed the growing brood. If they don't pull their weight, they get bullied by the queen or more dominant subordinates, forcing them to go out foraging. Every day a worker goes out it has a substantial 7 per cent chance of dying.*

Who ultimately gets to be the queen is determined by games of negotiation and competitive events played out among the foundresses. The outcome will be shaped by social and ecological factors like kinship (foundresses are not always sisters), competitiveness and how productive the group is, as well as outside influences such as opportunities to set up camp elsewhere and become a breeder.

Working out how wasps deal with the debate over queenliness was one of the topics that lured me into the world of wasps over 20 years ago. At that time a plethora of theoretical models flooded the academic literature, each adopting nuanced variations on what the underlying assumptions of negotiations might be, and how these might be influenced by the messy diversity of social and ecological factors. Theoretical models based on cherry-picked terms and assumptions are much easier to produce than are empirical tests of them. As a scientist at the empirical end of the scientific spectrum, I recall the relentless cascade of new models on the so-called 'reproductive skew theory' that were published back then. The phrase 'reproductive skew' refers to the inequalities in reproductive shares that different group members enjoyed: a high skew meant a single female ruled a reproductive monopoly as the single egg-layer; a low skew described a society where many (or most) females had a share of the egg-laying pie. By now there have been over 1,000 papers proposing, adapting or critiquing reproductive skew models, or presenting tests of them.

The skew models are all based on the same premise: how do genetic, ecological and social factors explain the distribution of

---

* This estimate is for the tropical wasp *Polistes canadensis*.

reproduction among group members? What factors shape the negotiations between a dominant and her subordinates in ensuring that subordinates 'agree' to work with the least fuss? The 'currency' of negotiation is, of course, a share of the group's reproduction. These models apply as equally to the charismatic vertebrate cooperative breeders, like meerkats and long-tailed tits, as they do to societies of bees and wasps. But being such agreeable study creatures, *Polistes* took centre stage in empirical tests of reproductive skew models, partly because of those new-found molecular methods to quantify relatedness that we mentioned earlier. The foundress colonies of temperate species were especially popular, as typically groups would consist of only two to five wasps, all potential wannabe-mammas.

Any single skew model has tended to be a variation on one of two themes, which differ only in the assumptions made about who is in control of reproduction. Concession models assume that the dominant has complete control over who her group members are and what they do, but in order to keep the peace she needs to offer her companions a bribe in the form of a share of the reproductive pie. Such models are based on the concept of a 'transaction' taking place between the dominant and subordinate(s): if the subordinates do not comply, they risk being ousted from the group, losing all the genetic, social and ecological benefits it provides.

Predictions in concessions models arise directly from a Hamiltonian-style of reasoning, with inclusive fitness at its heart. If the chance of a lone female's nest being attacked by predators or parasites is high while they are off foraging, or if there are few good nesting sites available, the dominant would perhaps not need to offer much of a concession to subordinates to retain them as amenable helpers. Compliant subordinates may pass on more of their genes (indirectly) than does a subordinate who is kicked out of the group, and gets to be breeder on her own solitary nest, but also shoulders the high risks of solo living. This argument only works, however, if the subordinate and dominant are close relatives, as in *Polistes*. If subordinates are distant relatives of (or unrelated to) the dominant, the queen would need to concede a larger portion of reproduction if she wanted to lure the subordinate to remain in the group as a peaceful helper. It's a negotiation between the subordinate and the dominant, influenced by internal and external factors, the outcome of which is supposed to be a fitness-enhancing solution for each player.

The second theme of skew models assumes that no individual in the group has complete control over who is in it and who reproduces. The reproductive shares are determined as a game theory-style evolutionary stable strategy in which there is no direct influence of kinship. It becomes a 'tug of war' among potential breeders, the outcome of which is a compromise determined by their ability to fight or otherwise impose their own selfish interests. Importantly, the threat of the group dissolving does not matter in these models, and neither do outside options for leaving and setting up camp alone. All that matters is your ability to stand your ground – your so-called 'resource-holding potential' – relative to the others in your group.

The benefit is *being* in a group, and the sharing of reproduction is the outcome of the battle for reproduction. If you can fight your corner, you get the lion's share of the reproductive pie. How reproduction is divided up depends entirely on the extent to which resource-holding potential varies among the group members. In *The Apprentice*, this might be represented by an individual's ability to make a convincing argument or the efficiency with which they can assemble or sell a product. In our wasp example, resource-holding potential typically comes down to their ability to win a physical fight: larger wasps or those with relatively large mouth parts (for biting) might have an advantage.

Tug-of-war models and concessions models therefore emphasise different things: concession models suggest that how reproduction is shared depends mostly on variation in related-ness and alternative options outside the group, while tug-of-war models depend mostly on competitiveness, or ability to impose an agenda of selfishness.

Two decades of theoretical and empirical studies have left us somewhat dissatisfied. There have been hundreds of attempts to test these models empirically (not all of them on *Polistes*) and we still don't really know *how* social groups negotiate reproduction among themselves. The results are, as a whole, a bit of a muddle, with little consensus on how variation in relatedness or compet-itive ability influences negotiations.

Perhaps there is no unifying rule: maybe different species settle reproductive disputes using different sets of rules because they are limited by different factors – physiology, lifespan or life history. If pushed, we might tentatively conclude that concession models do slightly worse than tug-of-war models: attempts to manipulate relatedness don't seem to influence bias in species of *Polistes* or indeed other species of cooperatively breeding wasps, bees, fish or mammals. If we squint at the data, perhaps there is a tiny bit more support for tug-of-war models, but the evidence is still somewhat flimsy.

The news is a little better if we take a broader view across populations or species. Comparative studies across a diversity of bird, mammal and insect (including wasp) populations found overwhelming support for the concession model's relationship between reproductive sharing and relatedness, suggesting that the benefits achieved through altruistic behaviour may indeed be shaping negotiations over reproduction, at least at the popula-tion level. However, attempts to test this experimentally (by manipulating relatedness between subordinates and dominants) resulted in either no significant effect on skew or support for the tug-of-war model predictions instead. Even more perplexing are studies that found that individuals sometimes choose the subop-timal strategy, losing fitness by joining a group or not leaving it.

Overall, none of the current reproductive skew models has explained the dynamics of negotiations over reproduction in groups.

Is this so surprising? We know that in *Polistes*, individuals can distinguish nestmates but there is no evidence that they can assess how related they are to each other. How could we expect to find a relationship between relatedness and reproductive bias if the study subjects lack the mechanisms to detect and measure the very variable that we think is important? Furthermore, in *Polistes* (and other bees and wasps) age or order of arrival at the nest appears to be a better predictor of reproductive share than size. Is it therefore any surprise that there appears to be little relationship between competitive ability and bias?

Perhaps we're not measuring competitive ability in a way that is biologically relevant to the question. Are group members fighting furiously *in order* to secure a slice of the reproductive pie or are they fighting *because* they need to retain the share they've got? Discerning between cause and effect is always the elephant in the corner of the empiricist's field site, and experimental manipulations of potential variables rather than observed correlations are critical here. What else might be going on under the hood of negotiations over reproduction that we haven't observed?

Until quite recently, the options available to a subordinate were thought to be binary: stay with the group and help, possibly with a small slice of the reproductive pie, or strike out alone and be in control of your own destiny as a solo breeder. Are there other options? Perhaps subordinates have more choice than we thought, especially if their help is such a valuable commodity for a dominant breeder. The value of helping may, then, be affected by the supply of and the demand for help. Do dominants decide on how much they are willing to pay for help, depending on the abundance of available helpers?

This is classic market theory and you will no doubt have experienced this yourself. An example is the price that people were prepared to pay for essential building materials in the UK between 2020 and 2021. Dwindling supplies caused by the coronavirus pandemic pushed up the prices by 20–50 per cent. People would pay whatever they had to to get their hands on the bricks, roof tiles, cement, or timber needed for their building project. Remarkably, foundresses in *Polistes dominula* colonies appear to do exactly this. When there is a shortage of helpers in the population, dominants will concede a larger share of the reproduction to their subordinate foundresses in order to secure the help they need.

This puts the power of choice into the tarsi of the subordinates: the outside options suddenly become rather splendid. A canny subordinate will tout her commodity around to different nests to find the highest-bidding cooperative partner, and the quality of those outside options (what another bidder will offer her) will also affect the trade value of her help. Skew models have clearly been too simple. Social contracts run like markets: consumer choice, commodity-switching and a changing landscape of competition make for a dynamic market floor, not dissimilar to our own stock markets. The negotiations that take place in these simple animal societies may be more like those in human societies: we work hard to explore all the options before settling for the best of a bad job. Why shouldn't wasps do the same?

# V

I'd like to take you back to that frosty hibernaculum in Italy, where dozens of sleepy European paper wasps jostle together like expectant tourists in an airport departure lounge. Recall how these wasps appear to use rules of thumb to find a relative to nest with. Let's unpack the data a bit here. Although most foundresses *do* end up nesting with relatives, the uncomfortable truth is that in a typical population 15–35 per cent of subordinates are in fact unrelated to the dominant wasp. That means a significant number of wasps are gaining zero indirect fitness from being an altruist in a group. The brood they raise as helpers are no more likely to transmit their genes to the next generation than would be any random punter in the population. If helping were your only option, this could be excused, but these wasps are all potential breeders. Why forgo independent nesting to help raise unrelated brood?

The secret of the perplexing case of unrelated subordinate wasps may lie in their fur-coated doppelgängers. I don't mean bees. Remember that *Polistes* wasps are basically arthropod versions of meerkats, or any other cooperatively breeding vertebrate for that matter. Often, vertebrate societies contain at least some helpers who are unrelated to breeders; the reason they cooperate is because there's a good chance that they will inherit the opportunity to reproduce. Inheritance of the reproductive throne is also a great incentive for a wasp: wait your turn to pump up your ovaries, it will come – unless you die before you get there. Inheritance is the missing piece of the jigsaw in explaining why unrelated co-foundress subordinates help rather than nest alone.

We have the hard work of evolutionary biologist Elli Leadbeater to thank for this insight, and a few thousand *Polistes dominula* wasps who lived along the south coast of Spain. Elli painted 4,185 wasps to give each its own unique name tag. After spying on their private lives for several weeks, she discovered that females who settled as subordinate foundresses produced more offspring than did the average female who nested alone. Subordinates, it seems, play the waiting game: 13 per cent of them struck gold by inheriting the throne when their dominant died or disappeared. Thirteen per cent might not sound like much, but the pay-offs from inheriting an established nest are high; so high that for the average wasp, it's better to gamble a subordinate's life, even if you're unrelated to the egg-layer, than it is to nest alone.

Queuing for reproduction is a common theme in the social games played by wasps. *Polistes* are good at it; but the queens of queuing are the hover wasps (Stenogastrinae) of Southeast Asia, the insects with which I began my wasp journey. They live in small groups of around three to eight individuals on nests that are easily mistaken for knobbly roots hanging from a bank or clumps of congealed mud clinging to the underside of damp bridges. During my PhD I spent a lot of time watching them queue under bridges like these in Malaysia. Hover wasps are the subtlest form of a wasp you can find – their fragrant sting is a tickle, and rarely even pierces your skin. Their defence response to anything that comes close to their nest (be it predator or friendly entomologist) is to drop off like dead flies, leaving the nest undefended. As wasps they are quite pathetic, making them an excellent entry-level wasp for naive researchers. But they rub shoulders with *Polistes* as textbook examples for understanding social behaviour, providing eye-popping glimpses into how the simplest forms of group living evolve.

The hover wasp's family pedigree is perfection: always a single egg-laying queen, with a small but perfectly ordered worker force of daughters who form a flawless queue to the throne. Their queue is strictly governed by order of appearance on the nest, which happens to be age. With a queen mum who is faithfully monogamous, each nest is formed of a tight-knit group of close relatives providing just the right genetic conditions to reward helping behaviour. Should the queen die or disappear (perhaps aided by the experimental hand of the entomologist), the oldest maiden daughter will quietly slip off to a nearby group of dozy males to gather some sperm, and then calmly step into her mother's shoes.

Her sisters are equally graceful in stepping into line behind her. The queue simply shifts along, and with the entitlement of a high-class debutante the oldest wasp seamlessly flips her fitness investment from indirect reproduction (raising siblings) to direct reproduction as the egg-layer. There is rarely any contest or dispute: they have age as the calibrator of convention, avoiding any costly contests. Like opposing escalators, as wasps ascend the queue to be queen they descend the staircase of hunting, spending less time foraging and more time on the nest, where they help with brood care and nest maintenance. Tipping the scales of investment in this way makes perfect sense because hunting is risky, and a wasp that is soon to inherit the throne should be less inclined to engage with such danger. Their perfect order is a little stifling. As domestic (insect) melodrama goes, these wasps win last place in the daytime TV awards. But for the evolutionary biologist wanting to understand the importance of queuing for inheritance, they are Emmy Award-winners.

When it comes to inheritance, most small-colonied wasps appear to have read the same rulebook: gerontocracy matters. Take the old faithful *Polistes dominula*, for example: if misfortune befalls the queen, the subordinate foundress inherits because she happens to be the oldest and, by default, at the front of the queue. Their process of appointing the new royal is not quite as unassuming as that of the hover wasps, but nonetheless it is largely calm and dignified, with little contest. The same seems to be the case for other temperate species of *Polistes*, although sometimes size plays a secondary role in helping a wasp over the royal line if there is any indecision. This is all sounding a bit too perfect: surely there should be some sort of scrap to be queen? Remember that all wasps in these societies are potential egg-layers and a precocious worker can never be sure that the oldest wasp on her nest is indeed a close relative, especially if that wasp is a foundress. Even if the new queen is her sister, every wasp would still do better by being the queen and laying her own offspring ($r = 0.5$) than by helping raise nieces and nephews ($r = 0.375$).

The pacifist gerontocratic rule of thumb seems as if it should be vulnerable to cheats, whose genes would prefer they risked a fight rather than raising a brood of uncertain kinship. However, thanks to the work of my PhD student Ben Taylor, who invested hundreds of gripping hours watching slow-motion videos of *Polistes dominula* workers contesting to be queen, we know the reality. We hoped that the slo-mo resolution might reveal the more elusive signs of blood-curdling competitiveness, some devious cruelty executed by hopeful future queens on their nestmate competitors to win the throne.

The Game of Thrones for wasps can be likened to (and analysed with) the scoring system used in chess tournaments. Every wasp begins with the same arbitrary starting score (let's say 1,000), just as it would in a chess tournament. After each pairwise interaction, there is a winner and a loser; the score they get depends on how unexpected the outcome was. Unexpected outcomes win high scores. I am a dependably mediocre chess player. My daughter, however, is irritatingly good. In fact, she beats me in most two-player games, not just chess. I would gain a disproportionately high score if I were to win a game against her, because the expected outcome is that she will win. Conversely, when she wins (which is often), she gets only a small gain in score because, well, we expect her to win based on her previous performance. Wasps don't move pawns around a chequered board; instead they duel each other using their antennae. Ben's video marathon revealed that only the oldest wasps engage in antennal duels; the younger wasps carry on business as usual, keeping the colony going and their indirect genetic fitness flowing. Simple conventions (like gerontocracy), along with a few low-cost antennal flurries to clarify fuzzy boundaries, are enough for groups to avoid the costs of conflict, costs that ultimately all gene-variant-sharing individuals would bear.

Not all wasps are so reasonable.

Nestled cosily among the forgotten walls of my Panamanian wasp mecca, the domestic dynamics of *Polistes canadensis* told quite a different story. In tropical species of *Polistes* like these, aggression appears to be part of family life. Conflict can carry serious consequences. Nestmates who attempt (and fail) to get above their station are punished – by biting and stinging; limbs are amputated, antennae are battered, in grappling and falling fights that often prove lethal. If you're not being bitten or chased yourself, you are probably the perpetrator.

The zeal of tropical *Polistes* was first described by Mary Jane West-Eberhard (of *Zethus* fame). In the 1960s she described vicious fights that ensued after the loss of the egg-layer, fights that resulted in successors to the throne who were not the oldest wasp. What, no gerontocracy? Had these wasps not read the rulebook for social etiquette, so closely observed by their temperate cousins or their Southeast Asian hover wasp counterparts? Why did they opt for conflict over convention, especially when the conflict is so overtly costly?

I was determined to understand more about the battle for queenhood in *Polistes canadensis*, which is why I had front-row seats for the biggest insect fight-club in Panama City. I wondered if workers were already pumped up, ready for a fight if the queen showed any signs of weakness. You can set the queen up to fail, duping her workers into *thinking* she is subprime by cheekily stealing her eggs from the nest. Within minutes, the inquisitive antennae of an ambitious worker will detect the missing egg, and the power of the matriarch is thrown into suspicion.

A one-off egg loss is forgiven, but repeated offences do not go unnoticed. Social harmony is shaken, and the nest swells with activity as bodies jostle together, escalating to a sea of motion. The stylised displays of a (relatively) calm and ordered society give way to anarchy and aggression, revealing the Jekyll and Hyde dual personas of nestmates as they switch from submissive wallflowers to belligerent gladiators. Antennae dance, mandibles nibble and nip, abdomens pump. If there is a chance to take the throne, it is worth being ready. Even in the presence of the queen, her workers – her daughters – are primed to respond to the slightest whiff of weakness.

The real fun starts when the queen disappears. Within an hour, workers start twitching, foraging slows, there's a change in mood. The jostling starts. Pulsating abdomens thump. The nest is their war-drum, the enemy is within. Yesterday's comrades are today's competitors. They break all the rules set by temperate *Polistes*; they take the 'hood' out of sisterhood and smash it against the nest. Previous submissives fight back; there are reciprocal bites. Stings are administered relentlessly, lodged between body plates. The gladiators are entangled, writhing. Embraced bodies are falling, with slipping, stabbing stings; where's the sweet spot to sweep this sister out of the game?

Yet not everyone is in the fight. There are passive sisters who sit by. Are they blind to it? They might turn their bodies away a little, acknowledging the inconvenience of the disturbance with subtle disdain. Others retire behind the nest; they see no place for themselves in this battle. The juxtaposition of slaughter alongside indifference among sisters is disturbing; condoned anarchy.

This is *The Hunger Games* and *Game of Thrones* rolled into one. And the show goes on for days. I am perplexed by their desire for audience participation. (As I sit and watch, wasps propel themselves at me like cannonballs on a battlefield, befitting their bullet-marked habitat.) Are the actors lost in fury or do they really consider me part of the contest? Bee-hat-clad, I sit motionless as they sting my hat, my pencil, my notebook. I disappoint them with my lack of response and they soon learn I am not worth the effort. I can get back to scribbling down the stage directions they leave for me in their paper theatre.

10.35 a.m. Nest 105. No. 46 enters stage left; bites No. 23; No. 23 retreats stage right; No. 46 runs around stage, abdomen beating a blaze.

Uprising breaks the rules of convention. Mutiny unsettles the laws of hierarchy. The rules of gerontocracy are jumbled. Older wasps have no urge to be queen. They are the cowards who shun the fight, who look on with disregard, who cower behind the nest, who carry on their industry to keep the young well fed and protected from the anarchy that surrounds them. The uprising is the game of the youth, and it is impossible to predict who will win before the contest starts. It can be a week or more before the new monarch is securely mounted on the throne. Social order is resumed. There appears to be little convention to succession. If there are secret messages encoded in their behaviour, age or size, we are yet to break them. Our clumsy analysis reveals only that it is one of the younger wasps who will become the new queen, but what determines who it is remains a secret of their societies.

Why are these tropical wasps so different to their temperate counterparts? To be honest, we lack the data to be sure that this is typical behaviour of *all* tropical *Polistes*. The right experiments have been conducted on too few species. But pushing this caveat aside, the explanation may lie in the relative longevity of wasps and their colonies. A worker in a temperate zone who succeeds to be the queen will never reign for longer than her mother would have because the colony will always dissolve at the start of winter. For a worker in a tropical species, however, the social group can be long-lived – many months to a year or more – and so there is much direct fitness to gain from contesting the position of queen, and relatively little indirect fitness to lose by overthrowing their mother or older sibling.

But I think there is more at play here. Even when an old wasp is experimentally gifted queenhood on a nest by the removal of all her nestmates, she prefers to wait for a younger sibling to emerge from a pupal cell and for *her* to be queen. Perhaps older wasps lose some fertility. Is this the cost they pay for being a hard-working hunter? If so, why does the same cost not apply to temperate species? Another possible explanation may be to do with group size. *Polistes canadensis* live in large groups of 50–200 wasps. Imagine how disruptive queen succession would be if all wasps took part in this fight? Perhaps there has been selection for older wasps (who haven't already become egg-layers) to lose some (all?) fertility, taking them out of the contest and reducing the number of competitors: an insect version of menopause? We haven't got answers to these questions. We don't even know how widespread this phenomenon is among tropical *Polistes*. What we do know is that these wasps make damn fine evolutionary theatre.

Convention or conflict, tropical or temperate, it is clear that propagating your gene variants by nurturing relatives does a good job in explaining altruism in *Polistes* societies. That tight-knit family group provides the right conditions for altruists to propagate copies of their gene variants via the bodies of close relatives and to resist the seductive lure of lone nesting. When the matriarch wavers, her legacy continues, headed by a successor of kin. With or without a period of conflict, the investment of family in family is preserved and thus assures genetic rewards for all family members even when one dies. They cooperate not for the good of the group, but for the good of their own selfish genes, secluded within the vehicle of the wasp.

# VI

It would be quite boring if the puzzle of altruism had been solved back in the 1960s through a simple equation, if not least because scientists like me would have fewer excuses to study wasps. Having argued that *Polistes* are the textbook darlings of social evolution, despite a bit of disorder and law-breaking, I am going to rock the boat with some disturbing news. These disputatious wasps sometimes flout the rules of altruism with bravado, provoking us to puzzle, doubt and then probe the boundaries of what we understand.

Back in my crumbling Panamanian wasp palace, daily nest censuses would reveal who belonged to which nest, how much effort they invested in foraging, and provide some idea of the dominance hierarchy. Censuses involved a bee-hatted, gloved person perching on a ladder – usually propped jauntily against a withering, bullet-pocked wall – eyes fixed on the teeming bodies of painted wasps on the nest in front of them. The ladder dweller yelled out the paint marks on each individual wasp.

LADDER DWELLER: 'Red-Green-Yellow-Blue.'

A second person at the bottom of the ladder would tick off the wasp on the census sheet:

TICKER: 'OK!'
LADDER DWELLER: 'Blue-Blue-Orange-Orange.'
TICKER: 'Great. That's the queen.'
LADDER DWELLER: 'Yellow-White – no, hang on, it's Yellow-Yellow-Blue-Pink.'

Maybe? The pink has some muck stuck to it, and the yellow paint spot is hanging off. Ladder dweller now can't see the target wasp as it's wandered round the back of the nest.

TICKER: 'Erm, there isn't a wasp with the marks Yellow-Yellow-Blue-Pink on this nest. Do you mean Yellow-Yellow-Blue-Red?'
LADDER DWELLER: 'Hmm … maybe. Dunno. It's gone now.'

Ticker pauses before writing down Yellow-Yellow-Blue-Pink. Flicking through the census sheets, she spots that a wasp with the markings Yellow-Yellow-Blue-Pink is usually on nest 32, which is on the wall with the obscene graffiti, about three metres away.

You can see how little things *can* go quite wrong. Especially when you're hot and sweaty, balanced on a ladder with a nest full of wasps in your face.

From our censuses it quickly became apparent that sometimes the wrong wasps were on the wrong nests. This is a bit naughty: in order to maximise indirect fitness, workers should be faithful to their family group and focus their efforts entirely on promoting the welfare of those who transport their gene variants to future generations. The most probable explanation was that we were being a bit sloppy: we are human after all. Perhaps it was the tropical heat, or too many sundowner gins the night before. Nonetheless, these misnomers were certainly there: around 10 per cent of wasps were recorded as being on the wrong nests.

Troubled by this, I returned a few months later to Panama, armed with a high-tech solution: I planned to stick radio frequency identification tags onto the backs of individual wasps and let the technology tell me whether nest infidelity was a real phenomenon or just human error. Equipped with electronic backpacks, my wasps were now swiping in and out of every nest in the vicinity. What a thrill. Near-complete, automated records of who went where, when and for how long confirmed that human error was not to blame: the wasps were *definitely* getting it wrong – around 40 per cent of workers were disobeying the rules and spending time on nests other than their home one.

Moreover, they appeared to be helping on the nests they visited, by bringing in forage and tending brood. Hamilton himself had spotted wasps of *Polistes canadensis* 'drifting' between nests and worried about the implications of this for his theory. With the benefits of genetic markers, we were able to show that these so-called 'drifters' appeared to be visiting nests to which they were related and ignoring those of non-relatives. Recall that in these tropical species, new nests are formed by groups of sisters setting up a home quite close to the mother nest. The resulting aggregations of extended family groups may in fact provide the right conditions for wasps to share their help across several related nests. But still, why share your altruistic efforts with distant relatives when you could just invest in the family group? This did not sit comfortably with Hamilton's theory at all.

We had a few ideas about why this might be. Perhaps wasps were playing the games of investment bankers. Any good stock-broker knows that investing all your assets in a single portfolio is a high-risk strategy. Spreading assets across several portfolios is a much safer idea, as it buffers the failure of any single fund. Perhaps *Polistes* workers were investing their assets (foraging effort) in several nests because the risks of investing in a single nest were too great.

By not putting all their indirect reproduction in one nest, altruists may end up passing on more of their gene variants to the next generation, even if those nests are merely distantly related. This could only be an evolutionarily stable strategy if there is a high risk of nest failure for any one nest in an aggregation. In the tropics, nest failure and brood death are common. In my first field season in Panama, I watched with tears of despair as birds made a meal of nests I'd been monitoring for three months. A few years later, I stood in solidarity with a PhD student as we watched army ants strip the brood from nests in an entire aggregation, his experiment reduced to a fraction of its intended sample size with military precision. A year later, a cock-tail of flesh flies, carnivorous caterpillars and parasitic wasps ravaged their way silently through another experiment, eating our precious data from the inside out. I am immune to doom now; I expect it and plan for it by hedging my experimental bets across several sites. Maybe the wasps are doing the same?

Or perhaps drifters were simply helping where help was most needed. We saw this happening across the globe in 2020 when the coronavirus pandemic first shook our societies. We looked locally to see how we could help, by sharing precious toilet rolls with neighbours* or delivering food to those who couldn't get groceries. We distributed our help according to need. Perhaps drifters are doing the same: if their home nest is replete with foragers and nest carers, they may do better to take their help elsewhere where it can make a worthwhile contribution.

The idea that the marginal benefit provided by a worker diminishes as the number of them in a colony increases was first suggested in the 1960s by Charles Michener, an American entomologist whose work on halictid bees shaped early thinking in sociobiology. So long as drifters share more gene variants with the nests they help than they do with the population at large, drifting behaviour could be explained by the diminishing returns in the value of a worker's help in large colonies.

Ten years after the first *Polistes* wasp was tagged, we have some answers, thanks to the valiant efforts of two determined PhD students. Thibault Lengronne is the student with whom I witnessed the army ant massacre. In his experiment, Thibault had attached radio tags to over 1,000 wasps across 93 colonies. He had monitored their movements (a mere 30,000) in and out of nests for weeks; he'd then carefully manipulated their brood and worker numbers to test the diminishing returns hypothesis for drifting.

And then came the army ants. He lost almost a third of his nests. Army ants were not after the adult wasps, just the brood. But in an experiment such as this, in which the ratio of workers to brood had been carefully calculated, and some nests had been

---

* In the first UK coronavirus lockdown (March 2020) one of the first commodities to be panic-bought from the supermarket shelves was toilet roll. Nobody really knows why toilet roll was so coveted. I for one could live without toilet roll, but not without pasta and wine.

manipulated to increase or decrease the need for help, having an army of stampeding ants eat all the brood was, quite frankly, inconsiderate. We arrived at this particular aggregation mid-raid and watched, helpless. Nothing comes between a battalion of raiding army ants and their prey. We were not the only observers: all of Thibault's adult wasps were sitting just off their nests, watching as their babies were taken away to be slaughtered. The balance of power had shifted: evolution had equipped these wasps with poison-tainted swords for a battle against larger predators and yet they were helpless against these tiny agents of war.

Wasps, student and supervisor were united in helpless bafflement. Thibault smoked a lot of cigarettes that day.

Despite the army ants and a string of other field-related mishaps, Thibault's experiment worked: wasps drifted more to nests where their help was most needed. Sadly, it took another six years, five journal rejections and many rounds of revision before this study was accepted for publication. Peer reviewers questioned its novelty or didn't understand the social network analyses we had conducted on the data, so we re-analysed data in every way they asked, and defended our modest sample size (damn those army ants). Yet the publication gods still refused to smile upon us. The study was finally published in 2021, 12 years after the army ants had marched on Thibault's experiments. By this time he had moved on to more profitable ways to spend his life than as a wasp researcher in academia. The sluggishness of the scientific publications process means rewards come too late for many a young researcher; the system fails them too often.

Meanwhile, Patrick Kennedy knocked on my door. A true disciple of Hamilton, he had just completed his undergraduate degree at Oxford University and was transfixed by drifting in *Polistes canadensis*. Could workers be treating a cluster of neighbouring nests like a banker's portfolio? Or was it the balance of need for help that explained drifting? While Thibault's experiments were sinking deep in the sticky soup of interminable peer review, Patrick attacked the problem of drifting with a cocktail of maths, modelling and gruelling field seasons in Panama. There was no way that he could repeat the punishing fieldwork that Thibault had endured: achieving the sample size that he had managed in the face of flesh-fly parasites, army-ant predators and the sheer expense in time and money of radio-tagging 1,000 wasps made a rerun unimaginable. We needed another way to tackle the question of diminishing returns.

Patrick decided to go to Panama to count wasps and monitor brood development in *Polistes* across several months. After a quarter of a million brood-cell observations (no reviewer could argue with *that* for a sample size), an unmentionable number of stings, and a lot of complicated modelling, the results were in: as the number of wasps on a colony increases, their usefulness diminishes. In evolutionary terms, there appears to be selection favouring wasps helping their neighbours when their help at home diminishes in value, so long as the neighbours are some form of relative.

In the months that Patrick spent with his unwanted wasps in the forgotten lavatories of Panama, he had another brilliant idea. Bet-hedging might not explain the specific case of extended altruism among drifting wasps in Panama, but perhaps it could explain altruism *in general*? Fifty-four years after William Hamilton's breakthrough, and after a long and hard battle with maths and modelling, Patrick realised that Hamilton's Rule was indeed missing a key component: environmental volatility.

Hamilton's Rule focuses on measuring the *average* reproductive success of actors (the altruist) and recipients. What if helping didn't actually change the *average*, it merely reduced the *variance* – the degree to which the values around the mean differed? This is exactly the reason why investment bankers spread assets across several portfolios – it might not increase the amount of money they make, but it certainly reduces the chance that they make a loss, or worse still lose all their investments. Bingo – by introducing a parameter to Hamilton's Rule that reflected environmental fluctuations, Patrick's models revealed that altruism was easier to evolve in volatile environments. This meant that altruism could evolve when the mean genetic benefits were unchanged, and paradoxically even when relatedness was very low.

One hundred years of painstaking research has revealed how wasps alter their behaviour when conditions at home and around them change: altruism is affected by how many workers there are, how many brood, how spritely the queen is, how ravaged with parasites the nest is. These wasp societies represent the first stages in the evolution of altruism and reveal how the flexibility in their behaviour allows them to exploit different strategies for gene propagation, depending on what volatile parameters ecology and evolution throw at them. You are not a wasp, but you do play out similar games to them, every day, games that determine how generous you are, whom you bestow your help on, and when to act selfishly.

Tell me now that you are *not* affected by what you can see, from just one hour in front of a nest of *Polistes* wasps.

# Part Five

# *Dinner with Aristotle*

Hornets and wasps … are devoid of the
extraordinary features which characterise bees;
this we should expect, for they have nothing
divine about them as the bees have.

Aristotle, 384–322 BC

# Prelude

Aristotle was the first published entomologist and was famously obsessed with honeybees. He extolled their organisational and behavioural virtues and devoted more pages to them in his opus *Historia Animalium* than to any other non-human organism. Less well known was his fascination with vespine wasps. With the help of his students at the Lyceum in Athens, Aristotle provided an impressive account of their natural history and behaviour across four books of *Historia Animalium* (Books 4, 5 and 9), describing the life cycle and colony development of yellowjackets ('*sphex*') and hornets ('*anthrene*') with remarkable accuracy and contrasting them with honeybees.

He understood their caste system, relating how their societies were made up of leaders or '*metrae*' ('wombs' – meaning the queens) and workers. He reported that the queens were 'bigger and gentler' and lived longer than the workers. He also observed that queens hibernated over the winter while the workers died, and that workers were produced earlier in the colony cycle and the sexuals (that is, males and next season's virgin queens) later. He understood more about their mating behaviour than did other classical writers, such as Ovid (50 BC), Virgil (30 BC) and

Pliny the Elder (AD 60), who all believed that wasps were created from the decomposing carcasses of horses.

Aristotle noticed that wasps were unlike honeybees in that they didn't swarm but instead formed new colonies alone as single foundresses. Similarly, unlike bees, they didn't store food. He acknowledged that although they did visit flowers, wasps were primarily hunters of other insects like flies, which they often beheaded before carrying back to their nest. He was a little confused about which sorts of wasps had stings, but apart from that his observations were remarkably perceptive. Aristotle was clearly intrigued by wasps.

Despite this appreciation, Aristotle described wasps as being 'devoid of the extraordinary features which characterise bees'. Honeybees and humankind were already good friends in his day and so he came to the topic with considerable background knowledge. Yet Aristotle got bee biology quite muddled, especially with regard to their castes and mode of reproduction. He talked of honeybees having three 'castes': kings, workers and drones, and saw no discernible anatomical sex differences between the three. Being a man of his times, he deduced that worker bees couldn't be female because they had stingers, and 'nature does not give weapons for defence to any females'. But neither could workers be males, since 'no males habitually care for their young', which is of course what he'd observed them doing. What, then, were workers? And how could offspring be generated, since, he pronounced, kings and drones were male?

Aristotle was, in general, quite obsessed with sex and modes of reproduction, and the bees flummoxed him. He reasoned that the three castes formed a hierarchy: kings at the top, then workers, and drones at the bottom. Kings reproduced their own kind and also workers. Workers reproduced drones, and drones reproduced nothing. This two-one-zero reproductive progression pleased Aristotle greatly. Its mathematical beauty delighted him (he was partial to the number three) and philosophers think that this is why he talked about bees having something 'divine' about them. It added to his thesis on how order, proportion and rationality pervaded the natural world, to even the 'lowest' (simplest) of animals.

Aristotle was, of course, mistaken with his three-casted bees. But he wasn't wrong about there being something peculiar with bee reproduction. As we learned in Part 4, the haplodiploid sex determination system of the Hymenoptera is pretty crazy. This craziness applies equally to bees, wasps and ants. Social bees, like ants and social wasps, have queens but no need for kings, as all the male genetic material a queen needs for egg fertilising is stored in her abdomen after mating.* Queens produce workers and virgin queens from fertilised eggs, and males from unfertilised eggs. We still call male bees drones, but they are most certainly not barren in terms of reproduction. It is Aristotle's fictional idea about how bees reproduce that caused him to pronounce that wasps were 'devoid' of the 'extraordinary features' found in bees, and that they had 'nothing divine about them as the bees have'.

If I could invite one person back from the grave to have dinner with me, it would be Aristotle. I'd do my best to throw together some of his favourite dishes from ancient Greece, emulating banquets that bore nostalgic witness to the heated arguments he would have had with his teacher Plato, and with his students at the Lyceum, about the natural world. Over a glass of Aristotle's favourite Limnio wine (watered down to his taste, of course, so as not to fog our discussions), we would swap tales about the world, about the science that his work inspired and the discoveries that were beyond his wildest imag-

---

* The termites (which are just social cockroaches) are quite different to bees, wasps and ants. They have kings and queens which remain together their whole reproductive life, and mate as needed to produce entirely diploid male and female offspring.

ination.* I'd do my best to fill him in on how the last two millennia of science had helped answer many of the questions he posed, but also how so much of his wisdom remains relevant today.

I would probably blush a lot and I'd certainly drink too much Limnio before the coriander-cabbage starter was done with – he being the greatest philosopher who ever lived. Over a main course of roasted lamb (or a flank of kid goat if I could get hold of any) served with Alexandria-style marrow, we'd get to the meat of the matter, and share our thoughts on our shared passion – that of watching insects. I would gently dismantle the beauty of his two-one-zero solution to bee generation, and hope that he didn't spill too much wine when he learned about haplodiploidy. I reckon he'd take the news that females *are* defenders and *can* bear stings OK, as he'd have seen how the role of females in human societies has changed since his day.

I'd love to talk more to him about the implicit gender biases that remain ingrained in our society today, but it's important I move onto wasps before he's too full of kid, marrow and wine to care. I would start by thanking him for his careful descriptions of the life cycles of *sphex* (yellowjackets) and *anthrene* (hornets), and congratulate him heartily on how much he got right. He might chuckle with pleasure to hear how his records on wasps remained the most accurate and complete for over 2,000 years. It might soften the news about bees not being so divine, after all. He would probably be a little surprised that I was so keen to discuss wasps rather than bees, but I think he'd have a healthy interest in learning about the science and secrets of vespine wasps that we've uncovered over the last couple of millennia.

---

* Wine historians believe Limnio to be the grape variety Lemnia that Aristotle and other writers from ancient Greece described as producing the famous red wine from the Greek island of Lemnos.

In this chapter, you are invited to eavesdrop on my dinner-party conversations with Aristotle about wasps.* Perhaps by the end, both Aris (he's OK with me calling him Aris so long as we occasionally include honeybees in the conversation) and you might be convinced that wasps are in fact worthy of the word 'divine'; not due to any incomprehensible spontaneous mode of reproduction, nor any godly creativity, but because of their sophisticated societies produced by evolution. Draw up a chair, pour yourself a glass of Aris's finest Limnio and let's see if I can persuade you both why vespine wasps really are worthy of the same veneration that honeybees enjoy.

# I

I take measure of my dinner guest.† He's a willowy, good-looking man despite being more than 2,400 years old. His clothes are a little drab by today's standards but no doubt would have been flamboyant in ancient Greece, ensuring that he stood out from the crowd. I had heard that Aristotle might have been a little vain, that he was always on-trend with his hairstyle. On another day, he might have sported clusters of well-ordered curls around his temple. But for dinner tonight he wears it long, in cascades of blond curls. He narrows his eyes as he peers at

---

* A word about our dinner party. Women would never have been permitted to dine with men in ancient Greece, except possibly in Sparta. Moreover, women would not be permitted to drink wine, except for therapeutic purposes. But Aristotle is a progressive philosopher and he understands that times change. He is happy to accept the customs of a Western twenty-first-century world. I'm relieved to get this awkward point out of the way from the outset. We can sit back and enjoy dinner with Aristotle.

† I am not a scholar of Aristotle. Please be forgiving of any historical errors and my artistic licence.

me over sharp cheekbones: he is perplexed. Why am I so interested in wasps? Do I not mind their stings? After all, wasps are 'all with stings and stronger [than bees] and their wound is more painful ... and proportionately bigger [than bees]'. It seems the reputation of wasps has changed little over the last millennia. Where to start?

Imagine a classroom for insects. Sitting next to the honeybee would feel a bit like being next to the class swot. I know all about this as at school I usually ended up beside the class swot. She was the teacher's favourite, had a perfectly ordered pencil case, always knew the answers, and (most annoying of all) she was a tiny bit smug about her overall brilliance. She also happened to be my best friend, and so I couldn't be too cross with her, and I guess I did quietly admire her brilliance.

In our insect classroom, honeybees are most definitely teacher's pet, described as 'humanity's greatest friend among the insects'. Their nests are the most ordered of any insect (at least they are when we put them in hives), their perfect rows of hexagonal cells, arranged with mathematical precision (Aris smiles), making even my friend's perfect pencil case look like the morning after a good night out. The honeybee pupil also rides on the tarsi of her sisters' industrious reputations as hard workers. Any beekeeper will tell you that honeybees don't only know the answers, they *are* the answer. To top it all, that monotonous, mindful buzz is the epitome of smugness. Definitely, the class swot.

Next to the honeybee sits an ordinary vespine wasp – the common yellowjacket *Vespula vulgaris* (*sphex*, I clarify, to Aris). She feels unfairly overlooked alongside the darling of the classroom. And she has good reason to feel this way. She too lives in a busy, highly organised nest full of committed, hard-working sisters and her mother is as magisterial in the family home as the honeybee's mother. Our *Vespula* pupil also performs her work to the highest standards. She knows the answers as well as her honeybee classmate does, but she is rarely asked questions by the teacher and so never gets the opportunity to prove her worth. The problem is that her reputation as a troublemaker precedes her, thanks to the end-of-term misdemeanours that she and her sisters are prone to.

Disruptive yet clever: that used to be a recipe for failure at school. Certainly, Aristotle would not have put up with this behaviour among his students at the Lyceum. But, I explain to him, thanks to progressive approaches in school education, we now value better the talents of those who don't easily conform to society's narrow expectations. The yellowjacket wasp deserves this same shift in our perceptions, so that she too can be championed. Society needs to be more accepting of her social idiosyncrasies and should focus on the extraordinary qualities she has to offer.

Where does one start in reforming the reputation of such a maligned creature? Luckily, the scientific roadmap has been laid out by that classroom darling, the honeybee. The evolved societies of honeybees and vespine wasps are remarkable examples of parallel evolution: both lineages have evolved the most complex form of sociality – superorganismality – independently from a solitary ancestral state.

There are eight species of honeybees, but the one we know best is the (semi-)domesticated species, *Apis mellifera*. Humans have harvested honey from wild *Apis* colonies for millennia, and some hunter-gatherer societies still do, but the bond between humans and bees underwent a step-change nearly 4,500 years ago – over two millennia before even Aris was born – a time when honey was a key ingredient in Egyptian cookery, and when beekeeping became an important industry. Remarkable archaeological relics of stone bas-relief carvings from 2400 BC (now displayed in the Neues Museum in Berlin) have shown how the Egyptians learned to keep bees in hives, and to use smoke to calm the insects, allowing them to extract honey. Even more remarkable are the 3,000-year-old hives that were excavated in 2007 by archaeologists in the Israeli city of Tel Rehov: radiocarbon dating of the spilled grain around the hives dated them to 970–840 BC.

Our long history of beekeeping as an industry laid the foundations for the scientific study of their colonies, behaviour and how they function. We know that bees are clever: individuals specialise in performing different tasks (brood care, hygiene, foraging) and yet they also respond to the needs of the colony, for example by shifting from brood care to foraging as needed. They have a waste-disposal system and keep their hives free of disease. They use an intricate dance-code to communicate the location and even the type of forage to their nestmates. The many books on bees attest to our fascination and wonder, as well as our scientific study of them and their behaviours.

My dinner guest nods with approval. He's warmed to hear that he started a two-millennia-long trend. After all, he was the first published bee biologist.

Vespine wasp colonies are just as large and impressive as those of honeybees, I tell Aris, and they have evolved many of the same amazing behaviours. For instance, they solve disagreements over reproduction in similar ways to honeybees: a single queen dominates reproduction, and workers are kept in line via a mechanism known as 'worker policing' (workers 'police' who lays eggs by going around eating those that have been laid by other workers). They have similar mating behaviours to honeybees: new queens mate with many males during a single mating flight.

Vespines are also very effective foragers: you and your al fresco banquet guests will know they are very efficient at finding food and they can also recruit nestmates (although we will learn shortly that they may not be as good as bees at this, and hear the reasons why). Vespine wasps also use pheromones to communicate, and they are equally (if not more) clever: they can learn landmarks and colours, and apply previous experiences to improve their decision-making. These are compelling parallels: vespine wasps have *probably* evolved many of the amazing phenomena that make us such big fans of honeybees. Even though vespine wasps are among the most universally recognised insects (I bet you can recognise a wasp, but you might struggle to identify a honeybee without the context of a hive), scientists still don't know the answers to many of the very basic questions about vespine biology: the depth of our understanding for the wasp is kindergarten-level, compared to the degree-level we have for bees.

Aristotle reaches for another juicy slice of kid. I top up his wine. After more than two millennia of fasting, he deserves a treat. And anyway, he's going to need some serious nourishment to help digest what I tell him next. I explain how the behaviours of honeybees and vespine wasps may be similar in their purpose, but the mechanisms by which they have achieved these complex traits may not be the same. Evolution is good at reinventing the same wheel, sometimes using the same machinery, but also via different machinery.

Evolution? Ah, I forgot. How could Aris have known about Darwin? I describe the way natural selection works, and how organisms are able to change over generations to best suit their environment. Aris furrows his brow as I tell him that evolution needs no help from an intelligent creator, such as a god. I unpack how Gregor Mendel's experiments with peas revealed to us that the unit of inheritance is something called a gene, that genes are like chapters in a big book called the genome which is an assembly and maintenance manual for the building blocks of life, and that each species has its own genome book. This instruction book can be edited and updated to suit different situations.

Aris is intrigued to hear that bees are an 'edited' version of a wasp-like ancestor and so share similarities in behaviour and life history due to evolution. Changes in life history can alter how natural selection acts. To persuade Aris that wasps are as divine as bees, however, I can see that I will need to present a logical, evidence-based comparison of these two impressive, flighted superorganisms. When conversing with the father of Western logic, your argument needs to be persuasive. Using Aristotle's famous three-phased recipe for persuasive rhetoric – *logos* (logical argument), *ethos* (credibility) and *pathos* (emotional impact) – I am hopeful that he (and you) will understand how vespines are just as much the darlings of the insect classroom as are honeybees.

# II

Dinner is going well, despite the unsettling news about divinity-free evolution. It turns out that Aristotle and I share a love of empirical observation and experimentation. We are soon swapping stories on how we handle wasp nests as study objects. He's astounded to hear how easy it is to use social media to solicit information from complete strangers about where wasp nests are. I show him how we can then use Google Earth to check how accessible a potential nest might be. He seems disturbed – perhaps a little seasick – by the street-view option. I ask how he sourced his nests; he has no idea. They just appeared when he asked for them. His students at the Lyceum were very resourceful and didn't bother him with practical details like this. But he had a lot to say about their nest structures:

'All their combs are six-sided, as are also those of the bees, and the comb is put together not of wax, but of rubbish and cobwebby stuff.'

I smile and tell him that there's a lot more than cobwebs and rubbish to a wasp nest, although they are very good at recycling.

'We've got a wasp nest in our loft!' My neighbour is breathless. 'Do you want it?' (Subtext: *please* rid me of this hell-ball of nature.) This is how I am greeted by many of my friends and neighbours of an autumn. I explain that the nest is now dead and so *you* – dear neighbour – can safely crawl among spider webs and forgotten memorabilia to remove it yourself. Confusion clouds their faces. It is a common misconception that nests of yellowjacket wasps (indeed, of any vespine) are there to stay for many years. After all, this is what honeybees do.

A second misconception is that their nest remnant will be a slumbering bomb of sleeping wasps who would make their feelings quite clear if disturbed. After all, this is what honeybees do. Honeybee colonies are perennial: they persist for years, sometimes decades. (Indeed, the fact that a highly fecund honeybee queen can live for up to 20 years is a perplexing and remarkable feat of evolution, as usually there is a price to pay for prolific reproduction: a shorter lifespan. Yet honeybee queens pump out millions of eggs in a lifetime and are among the longest-lived of insects. They appear to defy the so-called 'longevity-fecundity trade-off' rule.)

Vespine colonies, by contrast, usually have an annual nesting cycle: new nests are built each year by a young, mated queen, who, in temperate regions, has overwintered. This lone queen builds the first cells, lays some eggs and provisions them with prey that she hunts herself. (Note that a honeybee queen would never *dream* of foraging herself: she always has a band of diligent workers at her side to do that, even when founding a new colony.) These brood will be the first wasp workers and once they hatch, the wasp queen will never leave the nest again: she becomes an egg-laying matriarch, just like a honeybee queen.

Then the nest grows exponentially in size as worker offspring raise more worker siblings. Once it is big enough (a mere few thousand workers), the queen switches to laying sexual brood: these are the males and next season's virgin queens. At the end of the cycle – early autumn in temperate areas – the mother queen, her workers and her male offspring will all die. Newly mated sexual female offspring are her sole survivors and they will be the founders of the next season's colonies. This is why that wasp nest in your loft or shed will be entirely deserted by the start of winter, leaving only a papery shell as a memory of its former societal glory.

Sometimes vespine colonies will persist for more than a year: these are most commonly found in regions where *Vespula* are an invasive species; the warmer climate and absence of predators in New Zealand and Australia are good examples of this. There are rare occasions in native zones when nests inside especially cosy houses will persist for several years: a photo of a yellowjacket nest engulfing a bed in an old lady's overheated spare bedroom in England does the rounds on social media every year or so. But, as a rule, if you have a yellowjacket wasp nest on your premises, it'll only be there for a season and you yourself (my dear neighbour) can safely remove it from your loft come the end of autumn.

By this point Aris is standing up, waving his glass of finest Limnio dangerously. He cannot believe his ears: how can these people be so ignorant! Have they not read his *Historia Animalium*, in which he explained that, unlike bees, social wasps have an annual cycle? He spelled this out very clearly, more than 2,400 years ago:

'The workers do not live the whole year through, but they all die when winter sets in,' he says, 'but the leaders, which are called *metrae*, are seen through the whole winter and lurk in holes in the ground. For many ploughing and digging in the winter have seen *metrae*, but no one workers.'

I settle Aris back down in his seat (I hate seeing wine go to waste) and explain that despite his legacy, there are few translations of his words on wasps. Not many people in the twenty-first century can read ancient Greek, I say, but I will do my best to help set the record straight on his behalf.

Back to my neighbour and his loft. Before he unleashes the Hoover on that old nest, I beg him to take a moment to admire its structure, for it is one of evolution's engineering miracles, even more so than the honeybee nest. For thousands of years, beekeepers, philosophers (including Aristotle) and scientists have marvelled at the regular order of the honeybee's comb: perfectly aligned hexagons placed with mathematical precision to optimise cell strength and minimise building effort.

A classic school maths experiment is working out why honeybees make hexagonal cells and not circular or octagonal ones: it's all down to efficiency of cell-building, optimal reuse of cell walls and minimising wasted space. Hexagons are the most-sided shape that tessellates without having to add a second shape between them. Try the same trick with octagons or circles, and you soon find you need additional shapes to mortar up the gaps. In nature, bee nests are not square or rectangular – they are round or oval. They must, then, be comprised of cells with as many sides as possible. In theory, bees could make square cells, which would result in square combs – but the proportional increase in effort needed to complete a cell would be greater than for hexagons. And anyway, the brood they will contain are roundish in shape – and so more like a hexagon than a square. Clever bees? Maybe.

It turns out that bees are not the mathematicians we credit them with being (at least not in cell-building) – but wasps may well be. That perfect hexagonal bee cell starts off life as a rather mundane circular structure made of molten wax, which the bees knead, heat and mould. The clever hexagonal perfection kicks in when a 'triple junction' is formed – that is, when three circular pots fuse together. Bees make this happen by heating the wax in the right place, not through complex algebra and trigonometry. The perfect hexagonal cells of a honeybee nest, therefore, are the products of cookery by the workers, and not the mathematical genius attributed to them by early philosophers. The hexagons are an emergent property of this process. Intriguingly, only honeybees and some stingless bees make nice, neat combs. Bumblebees are incredibly messy – just like the university fresher embarking on their first foray into independent living, bumblebees pile up their brood pots in a jumble alongside pollen and honeypots. It's a mess.

Vespine wasps build their papery nests out of plant material and so they cannot use the same emergent potting and cooking methods as bees to construct perfect hexagonal cells. In fact, all of the 74 species of vespine wasps (that includes all the hornets and yellowjackets), almost all of the 1,100 Polistinae (paper wasps) and some of the 50 Stenogastrinae (hover wasps) construct paper variations on the hexagonal theme. Nest-building is costly for wasps – workers have to gather wood pulp, which is a risky activity. Just watch an industrious wasp working away on your garden fence – she's oblivious to your proximity, so intent is she on her work.

Nature breeds efficiency. And nature also breeds inventions: wasps were the first paper-makers – we stole both the idea and the method from them. An old Chinese story about the origins of paper made by humans goes that around 2,000 years ago (coincidentally the time when humans started making paper), a eunuch called Cai Lun was lounging under a tree, lazily watching a wasp scraping away at the tree trunk. He watched the wasp gather a bundle of bark pulp and transport it to her nest: she massaged the bark in her mandibles until it was moist and malleable, and then chewed at a cell in her nest, smoothing the newly pulped bark into a wafer-thin sheet and elongating the cell. That is how she made her nest: strong, light, pliable and insulated. The perfect place for her brood to develop. Cai Lun watched, amazed. And then made his own. Therein lay the birth of human-made paper, around 2,000 years ago.

My dinner guest's fork is placed with disturbing calmness back on its plate. Paper – this is big news. Aristotle had sweated blood etching his words onto hundreds of papyrus scrolls, catalogued carefully in his library at the Lyceum. Papyrus is constructed from strips cut from the stem of the papyrus plant *Cyperus papyrus*. Thin overlapping strips of pith are lined up; a similar sheet is laid on top, perpendicular to the first and the two layers are mashed together. It's not a million miles away from being paper, but it does lack the pliability and thinness of paper, and it does not last long.

Only 31 of Aristotle's 200-odd treaties survived him, the bulk of which were thought to have been lost after the fall of Rome. I express my sympathies, but he brushes it off saying that many of these documents were just lecture notes or draft manuscripts for reading aloud – he'd never intended them to be read or published. I pretend not to notice the mist of bewildered regret that clouds his face. If he'd had paper, so much more of his legacy might have survived, with an even wider influence on civilisation. The notion that only a few hundred years after he'd been scratching away on ephemeral plant pith, Cai Lun invented paper some 4,000 miles away in China: that was just too much salt in the wound.

Paper is incredibly versatile, I say cheerily, hoping to distract Aris. Human civilisation would not have advanced so much without it. We don't only use it for books, we make it into cardboard, and even use it to make furniture. But wasps have taken the versatility of paper to a whole new level. You can find paper nests that resemble string, footballs, tennis rackets, trifles, chamberpots, cradles, tree stumps and even designer dresses. Some are cryptic, underground or inside trees; others stand proud on branches, buildings and bridges. Some are enveloped inside a protective paper cover; others are exposed and easy-access. Endlessly diverse in form, they are uniform in function: just like your own house, the wasp nest functions to protect the family – the queen, adult workers and developing brood. But this diversity arises from the same basic structural design of hexagonal cells, just like honey-bees, but made of paper, not wax. If wasps can't simply heat up wax pots to make hexagons, how do they do it?

As with any construction project, economics matter. The cost to a wasp of building a new cell can be minimised by utilising existing cell walls. The first cell is the costliest as the wasp has to build all six of its sides, but even at this early stage the cell resembles a hexagon, not an amorphous bee-like pot. This suggests that the wasps are precise architects from the outset and that the hexagons are not an emergent property of a collection of cells. The second cell needs only five walls. Cell number three needs only four, if placed up against cells one and two. All subsequent cells require only three walls, if optimally positioned to exploit the existing walls of three other cells. That's half the cost of building a six-walled cell. Indeed, the wasps preferentially choose to add new cells in a corner where three adjacent walls are already in place. Simple algebra explains optimal nest growth and most species of wasps stick to this, forming circular combs of cells. In the case of the vespines, the combs are multi-layered, like a high-rise apartment block. The wasps even measure the size of the cells as they build; they use their antennae to keep track of the cell width.

Aristotle has perked up at the mention of mathematics. His scholarship under Plato was rooted in mathematics and he was interested in how nature might be explained by simple maths, especially if the number three was involved. Six-sided cells are a multiple of three. This pleased him greatly, and of course he was the first person to describe the hexagonal-shaped cells of a wasp nest. We raise a glass together as we wash down the last of our marrow and kid roast. Then I break the news to him: wasps are no more worthy of being labelled mathematical geniuses than honeybees are.

The apparent genius of nest construction is much simpler, but this simplicity makes it all the more impressive. The nest structures of social insects have attracted the attention of theoreticians, architects and evolutionary biologists for decades. But just over 50 years ago came a landmark, when (in 1959) French biologist Pierre-Paul Grassé introduced the concept of 'stigmergy' to explain insect nest construction. Stigmergy describes a mechanism of spontaneous coordination among biological agents that leaves traces – in this case, insect nest constructions – in the environment.

It's a rather ugly term to describe the beauty and spectacle of nature's constructions, from termite mounds and honeybee combs to ant and wasp nests above and below ground. They are often spectacular in appearance, and they are *always* breathtaking in their functionality. Social insect nests are veritable citadels, bastions, condominiums, complete with air-conditioning units and thermoregulatory systems, made of disease-, predator- and weather-resistant materials: these are all sources of inspiration and solutions for engineers and architects in our human world.

As Aris well knows, the term stigmergy comes from the Greek words *stigma* meaning 'sting' or 'puncture' and *ergon* meaning 'work'. Grassé used the compound term to describe the *indirect* communication that takes place among the insect architects. In fact, the communication is so indirect that it is not really communication at all. There is no master architect, building manager or even a blueprint for building these nests. Instead, Grassé realised that it is the previous action of an insect that guides their next move.

It's not just insects that 'stigmergise'; we do it too. A good example is the building of a wall: the position of each new brick will depend on what's there already. Placing the brick to overlap two other bricks makes for a stronger structure: a robot can build this wall just as effectively as a human by following these very simple instructions. Another human or robot can add to the wall without any direct form of communication, because they simply respond to the position of the existing bricks. So long as they know the rule.

Back in the wasp nest, each existing segment, cell wall, envelope or flap of nest provides a new cue with instructions to the worker on what they should do next. Sometimes the cue is just the physical structure itself (like the bricks in our robot's wall); sometimes the construction is also peppered with a pheromone, or chemical signal. So long as each individual follows their local instructions, there is no need for a 'grand plan': complexity emerges via simple mechanisms of self-organisation. This was an important step towards viewing the social insect colony as a 'superorganism'. Grassé's insights helped link the actions of the individual with the colony as another level of emergent individuality.

The legacy of Grassé's work on stigmergy is a small but exceedingly exciting area of biomimetic research. In the last decade or so, the mathematics of collective behaviour has benefited tremendously from advances in robotics and computer modelling, unravelling the secrets of group living in fish, cockroaches, ants, humans and even wasps. Using computer-bot 'wasps', which follow a set of simple computational rules, researchers have been able to recreate a variety of nest structures that closely resemble those of different wasp species. The wasp-bots follow a basic set of rules that tell them how to respond to a particular configuration of the emerging structure around them. Each performs random walks in a hexagonal 3D space, and acts purely on a stimulus-response basis, across a network of crossing paths known as a 'lattice swarm'. The bots could only detect the first 26 cells adjacent to their point of building, they could not remove any cell, and none of them had instructions on the nest structure as a whole.

These rules resulted in the building of complex nest structures resembling those in nature. There is no grand design; wasps act in response to their immediate environment following some very simple rules. Under certain conditions, like crowds, humans follow similar rules. Emergent self-organisation patterns in insects are often used in our own societies, for things like urban planning and crowd control at festivals. We move in similar ways to ants when we're in a crowd: we try to find the most efficient routes, by following the simplest rules which are sensitive to what others do around us.

Aristotle and I are hoping that my neighbour and you, dear reader, may now be a little more curious to take a closer look at the wasp nest in your loft. But be careful – the paper becomes very fragile and brittle once it is no longer kept moist by the constant tending of the wasps. Before you get to study the emergent mathematical wonders of the cells, you'll need to plough your way through several layers of cladding – the paper envelope.

Look closely at it: the envelope is constructed from tiny papery strips arranged into shell-like scallops that nestle together to form a nurturing cloak. Papery smiles within the shells can be rainbow-coloured, thanks to the materials used by the worker wasps to construct it. In the early spring you may have had your garden peace disturbed by the scraping of wasp mandibles on your fence posts or shed as they gathered materials. In a nest I collected recently from a neighbour's garden, I could see stripes of blue, green and grey – matching the paint on fences of the surrounding gardens. If you are an especially keen, interactive reader, you might try painting your fences different colours this spring, in the hope of helping your local vespines create cheery, multicoloured, beach hut-style nest decor.

Much like the cladding on the outside of a high-rise apartment block, the nest envelope functions to insulate, defend and weatherproof the interior. The multiple layers trap air and insulate the combs, ensuring that the brood they contain are maintained at the optimal temperature for development. In fact the envelope is so effective as a thermoregulator that even a thermal-imaging camera cannot detect a *Vespula* nest through the soil. You'll find that a nest in your lovely warm loft probably has fewer layers of insulating envelope than one in your garden shed. In honeybees, the hive structure serves this function for semi-domesticated colonies, but wild bee colonies do build a kind of envelope made of a resin (called propolis), which they use to fill any gaps in their tree-trunk nesting holes to keep their colony optimally thermoregulated.

Not all wasps build envelopes around their nests. In fact, the envelope has evolved in only the most complex of social wasp species, where colony sizes are large. All vespines have them. The envelope may help defend the colony from predators, parasites and pathogens, by providing a papery forcefield. The main predators of vespines are badgers, weasels, bears and large predatory birds like hawks, kites and eagles: a vespine nest full of protein-rich larvae is too much to resist, and these raiders are all very capable of tearing the papery forcefield aside in their ravishing hunger for some juicy wasp larvae. The adult wasps try to defend by stinging, of course, but predators appear undeterred by these attacks. Their leathery skin, thick fur or feathers may be effective in protecting them.

The envelope is more effective against smaller unwanted visitors. As Thibault found out in Part 4, ants are keen predators of wasp nests; but the *Polistes* nests that Thibault was studying don't have a nest envelope; this makes their brood easy prey. Having an envelope affords the vespine wasps some protection against tiny predators like ants and other small brood parasites like hoverfly larvae *Volucella* and other parasitoids. These tiny predators and parasites cannot penetrate the envelope, and so they need to access the nest through the sole entrance. Having a single, narrow entry point reduces the chances of these interlopers finding a way in, and it is also easier for the wasps to defend and to detect intruders.

These are compelling just-so stories. Unfortunately (and perplexingly), comparative studies across many species of wasps, exhibiting a plethora of evolutionary, ecological and social life histories, have been unable to find evidence for the idea that the envelope has evolved as a defence against predators and parasites.

An intriguing alternative explanation for the evolution of nest envelopes takes us back to Grassé's concept of stigmergy. The envelope may provide the instructions for efficient comb-building: by providing a clear termination point, wasps 'know' when and where to keep building cells and when and where to stop building them. The envelope is a dynamic structure, being expanded by the wasps as the colony grows. Using the envelope as a cue for when to build and when to stop could result in faster construction of the nest as it might prevent cells being built in the wrong place at the wrong time and ensure that combs are neither too big nor too small for the overall size of the nest.

Imagine building a house with multiple floors, but not having any instructions for how big each floor should be. No guidance on when to stop building could risk the floors being either too large for the footprint of the house, making it unstable, or too small, making it a poor use of the available space. This theoretical idea needs testing on real wasp nests; if envelopes do provide instructions on when to stop building, then these rules must be flexible enough to be updated as the nest grows.

What would be equally interesting is to find out whether the construction of the envelope is regulated by the immediate external environment. For example, air temperature appears to affect the way ants construct their nests. This works because temperature alters evaporation rates, which could then change the amount of airborne pheromone signals received by the workers which carry out the instructions on when and where to build. Simulations of nest-building behaviour by ant-bots have shown that changes in the levels of these pheromones resulted in the ant-bots building nests with different roof shapes. These different roof shapes would give nests different thermal properties, ensuring that the brood inside was kept at the right temperature, depending on the ambient conditions outside the nest. If ants can do this, wasps probably can too. There may, therefore, be further biological secrets lying within that papery envelope of your loft's wasp nest.

Peeling back the envelope, you will be greeted by a stack of brood combs. Unlike a honeybee hive, these combs will typically be arranged horizontally, with cells opening to the ground. Any comb can consist of hundreds of cells, each of which will have been the nursery to a developing wasp baby. The combs are stacked like 'floors' in a high-rise block of flats, held apart by pillars made of reinforced paper. They need to be strong, as they are the only links between combs, and a comb full of brood can weigh several hundred grams. There is about a 1-centimetre gap between combs, which happens to be just enough for wasps to move between them freely. Just like a honeybee nest, the inside of a vespine nest is a busy place, with workers tending brood, arriving back with forage and exchanging their secret 'social fluid'. The combs of honeybees function as a dancefloor for communication: if there is a wasp dance, or something similar, it must happen here.

A good engineer chooses her building materials carefully to suit the demands of the different parts of the construction. Honeybees produce only one kind of wax for their nest engineering, although they will also use resin they have collected from trees as extra insulation. Vespine wasps have one up on bees here, as they make different types of paper, depending on its intended use in the home. This makes sense when you consider the contrasting functions and mechanical loads of the structures within the wasp nest.

The comb's job is to house the brood, but by being arranged like the floors of a tower block, connected via pillars, combs also act as beams or cantilevers for the entire nest, and are subject to forces of both compression and tension. They also have to cope with the tension of the brood pushing against the cell walls from within. As a result, comb paper needs to be very refined and of high tensile strength.

Pillars, on the other hand, are made of much stronger, harder material, as the paper is more compacted, containing fewer air gaps. Sometimes the wasps upcycle the paper of pupal caps and add them to pillars, which appears to add extra strength.

Envelope paper is more rustic: being less dense but thicker than comb or pillar paper, it is good at trapping air and insulating the nest. The composition of envelope paper varies among species, depending on nesting locations. Wasps that nest in tree cavities or in the ground, like the common yellowjacket *Vespula vulgaris*, tend to have less robust envelope paper than species that are often aerial and exposed to predators and the elements (such as *Dolichovespula*).

How do wasps make paper to meet such different mechanical needs? Their secrets lie in their choice of raw materials and methods of processing. The rougher, less robust envelope paper is thought to be made mostly from rotting wood. Stronger paper must be made from fibres collected from more sound or well-weathered sources, like your shed. If you've ever tried making your own paper, you'll know that it needs a lot of water and mashing. Wasps make it in much the same way as we do (actually we should rephrase that: we make paper in the same way as wasps, as we copied them, thanks to our observant 2,000-year-old friend Cai Lun).

The mashed wood fibres stick together due to a process called hydrogen bonding, and luckily wasps have strong chewing mandibles to achieve this. They caress the wood and mix it with saliva, which influences the mechanical properties of the end product. There may also be extra-special ingredients in wasp saliva that help make it even stronger. To make paper for books like this one, we refine the paper, improving the flexibility of the fibres such that they entwine with each other into a complex interwoven mat. This increases the surface area of fibres that are in contact, permitting more bonds to form between them which are pulled together by capillary action. Wasps 'refine' their paper through mastication: the more they chew, the better bonded the plant fibres should be, and so the stronger and more robust the paper.

Evolution has taught wasps how to be structural engineers, architects and material scientists. Next time you come across a yellowjacket wasp nest, indulge yourself with the knowledge that it is a remarkable feat of engineering, built by a skilled and discerning workforce.

Aris shifts in his seat, and fiddles with his rings, pensively. Perhaps I've given him too much *logos* too quickly. It's a lot to take in. I'm dying to know what his great brain makes of it all. What have we missed, Aris? What would your next experiment be? He shoots a wistful gaze out of the window, purses his thin lips. But only a moment and then he's back with me. He drains his glass and, with a glint in his eye, he waves it at me, asking what the next course might be.

# III

I'm now serving Aris a small bowl of fassolatha – a modest white bean soup that is much enjoyed by Greeks today and is thought to have changed little over the last two millennia. I've had to open another bottle of Limnio too, which surprises me as Aristotle had a reputation for being very critical of drunkenness. I guess having been teetotal for over 2,400 years, he's letting his hair down. He is now telling me about his philosophy of animal biology. 'The beauty of an animal,' he explains, 'lies in the orderly arrangement of parts, and these parts must be of a definite magnitude.'

He believes there must be a mechanical, step-wise and logical explanation for animal behaviour. I am delighted that he's brought this up, as it gives me a chance to fill him in on what we now know about the mechanics of social life inside an insect nest, and to discuss with him some perplexing differences between vespine wasps and his beloved honeybees. I know he'll be enthralled to hear what slickly organised societies bees have, but he may be a little disappointed to hear about the wasps. I'm hoping he might have an explanation.

In 1776, the philosopher and economist Adam Smith revolutionised economics by introducing the idea of division of labour
to our factories – the production line was invented. By dividing
tasks into their component parts, Smith proposed that factories
could be more productive: specialists learn their jobs more efficiently and don't waste time switching between tasks, and this
could lead to the invention of machines. Smith was right: we are
very familiar with division of labour and the benefits it brings in
all aspects of our social lives.

Whether it's positional roles allocated to players in a football
team, specialist jobs of employees on a factory line, or the
responsibilities of government ministers for particular facets of
running the country, division of labour delivers results because
individuals can focus on specific tasks and get really good at
them. Performing one task over and over again results in efficient
workers who make fewer mistakes, before their product is passed
on to the next set of specialists. Being a cog in a machine may be
tedious, but if each specialist is committed and follows protocol,
the rewards can be significant. Adam Smith's introduction of
division of labour to industrial Britain marked the birth of
modern capitalism, nearly 250 years ago.

Aris nods. He knows all about the division of labour in
wasp nests. The *metrae* (queens) are the leaders: 'When the
worker wasps are born in the combs, the leaders no longer
work but the workers bring them in their food.' Exactly, I
reply, and I fill him in on how this same reproductive
division of labour is displayed by all social insects,
including many other types of wasps, like the open-nested
*Polistes* (of our Part 3), which he must surely have seen in
his time in Athens, perhaps nesting in the very eaves of his
Lyceum. But the insect factory I'm referring to here, I tell
him, concerns how the non-reproductive tasks are
organised. This is a division of labour among the

proletariat class and concerns our understanding of how the worker caste apportion tasks among themselves.

Let's start with honeybee workers. They have babysitters (the nurses), provisioners who go out shopping for food (the foragers), the house-maintenance team (comb builders), those who go out prospecting for new houses (scouts), hygiene-specialists, undertakers, a burglar defence team (guards) and law-enforcers (police). Each worker specialises in her allocated task, 'knows' her place and sticks (largely) to her task. It is hardly surprising that life-lesson similes for industrious, workaholic behaviours such as 'busy as a bee' have infiltrated our everyday language. Honeybee workers are the epitome of an Adam Smith kingdom, except they got there 100 *million* years before Adam did.

Is the wasp factory organised with the same orderly, salami-sliced precision as a honeybee society?

Apparently not.

Yellowjacket workers seem to be Jaquelines-of-all-trades. In a 2007 study of around 800 workers from two *Vespula germanica* colonies, only 10 per cent of workers specialised in a single out-of-nest task, while 61 per cent of workers performed more than two of these tasks during their life. In another study, scientists attached radio tags to 1,000 newly emerging workers and followed their comings and goings over a month or so. They found only very loose division of labour within colonies: individuals tended not to specialise in what jobs they did and they didn't show any consistent shifts in jobs through their lifetime.

The only sign of clear task specialisation in yellowjackets comes in the first week of life, when they invariably remain in the nest, carrying out brood care and nest-building. After a week, they start to forage. Such age polyethism is typical in most social insects. Recall that even the simple societies of *Polistes* show this sort of division of labour among workers, so it's hardly a hallmark of social sophistication.

Why does the vespine society not run in the same way as an Adam Smith factory, whereas those of honeybees do? One idea is that the benefits of specialisation for vespines do not outweigh the costs. Remember Smith's secret: specialised workers made factories more productive than did generalist workers. For decades, scientists assumed that the efficiency argument also explained worker division of labour in social insects: specialist worker insects must be better at their jobs than a generalist Jacqueline-of-all-trades worker. It wasn't until 2008 that someone actually bothered to test this.

The rock ant *Temnothorax albipennis* can be found in almost any European forest, nesting inside decaying logs. They are tiny and so are easily overlooked. In 2008, the German scientist Anna Dornhaus painted 1,142 of these ants and filmed them to determine how long each worker took to start and complete a task such as moving brood, or transporting a drop of honey or a piece of fly to the brood. Some workers specialised in specific tasks, while others didn't, giving Anna a nice mix of specialists and generalists.

Contrary to Smith's factories, the specialist ants were no better at their task than the generalists. In fact, sometimes the specialists were *less* efficient, meaning that they were neither learning to be better at their job nor naturally suited to the particular task that they had become a specialist in. Anna's results were profound: we had all assumed that task specialisation would benefit insects in the same way that it does humans. This same experiment has since been replicated in bumblebees and yellowjackets and the same patterns hold: specialist workers do not appear to be any more efficient at their job than are generalist workers. In fact, in yellowjackets, specialism seems to be an encumbrance! Specialist wasps tend to perform more trips and take longer trips than their generalist counterparts, and moreover specialist wasp foragers have a 6 per cent shorter lifespan than their generalist counterparts, suggesting that being a specialist incurs a longevity cost.

Diet might explain why it's worthwhile for bees but not wasps to evolve a clear division of labour among workers. If you go shopping intending to buy a specific style or make of jeans, you'll be at the shops longer than if you were content with any kind of trouser-type apparel. Because you're out for longer and because you're being so picky, you're also more likely to be victim to some unfortunate event (like having your wallet stolen, missing the last bus home or getting too hungry to make a good shopping choice). Given that prey type can be very patchy for these wasps, it may pay (in fitness terms) for the predatory forager to be a generalist rather than a specialist: just take what you can find rather than searching for a specific prey type.

Another explanation may come from the lifespan of a vespine colony and its workers. As Aristotle told us, vespines are annual species: a colony starts from scratch each year and it needs to grow rapidly from a small number of workers to a number large enough to support the production of sexual brood within a matter of months. Life in an insect colony has to be dynamic to cope with sudden crises outside the nest: foragers get swept away in rainstorms, sprayed with insecticide, snared by a predator or caught inside vehicles and transported miles from their colony.

Extreme levels of task specialisation might mean the colony is not able to respond to immediate and rapidly changing needs. Although honeybee workers tend to specialise in a specific task, as a colony they are very good at adjusting who does what in a crisis, shifting nurses to foraging and vice versa as needed. No one has tested how the workloads in a *Vespula* colony respond to some catastrophic loss of a bunch of workers. But given that most workers appear to be generalists, it probably doesn't matter: everyone just carries on with their many jobs as before (albeit with a reduced worker force). However, honeybee colonies always have a reliable source of workers, as they are perennial. Even when the mother queen decides to leave and set up a new nest, she is accompanied by a swarm of workers to help her. As vespine nests are mostly annual and don't typically swarm, they spend a considerable period of the colony cycle as a small society and yet they still need to respond to change dynamically.

*Vespula* workers themselves are also short-lived – an average of 14½ days – which amounts to about one week's life in the nest and one week's life outside, before they move on to wasp heaven. Perhaps there just isn't time to specialise. A better strategy for dealing with a crisis may be to invest in rapid production of short-lived generalist workers rather than longer-lived specialists. Selection for a 'Jacqueline-of-all-trades-mistress-of-all' strategy could be the trade secret of vespines: perhaps this is how their society can respond dynamically to the demands of building a superorganism made of several thousand parts within a few short months.

All this time, I've been pacing around our dining terrace, lost in a fury at the frustrating lack of answers. I sit down and look Aris squarely in the face. I am a guilty criminal ready to face my judge. I say: we simply do not know how vespines manage to maintain their large, complex and coordinated superorganismal societies, as they seem to lack the much-acclaimed task specialisation seen in bees. Scientists have probed vespine nests with technology that you, in ancient Greece, couldn't have fathomed would ever exist, and yet we've still failed to explain how wasps manage to coordinate their complex societies. I am embarrassed not to have the empirical pillar of persuasion that Aristotelian rhetoric expects. After over 2,400 years we should have done better.

Aris senses my angst. He tells me that noticing 'differences and similarities in life is part of what separates those who are living the good life from those who are merely living'. The parallel social worlds of honeybees and vespine wasps are beautiful (he wants to say 'divine' but doesn't want to trigger another lecture from me on evolution). That they have arrived at the same solution via a different means is also beautiful and interesting. He reminds me that we do have ideas as to why the social order of bee and wasp societies are not the same. It could be their contrasting ecologies: protein-hunters versus pollen-collectors. It might also be demography: colony and worker lifespan.

'Keep looking, keep studying, keeping questioning,' he says. There: that's a glimpse of what an inspirational, encouraging teacher he would have been to his students at the Lyceum. There is a lot we don't know about vespine wasps, but perhaps that's why I am so entranced by them. They are as much an enigma to us now as honeybee reproduction was to Aristotle more than 2,400 years ago. We figured the honeybees out; the vespines will follow.

# IV

Both Aris and I need a comfort break. When he finally returns to the dining terrace, he is full of excitement. About the toilet. I am worried that this excitement over modern sanitation might preclude further conversations about vespine wasps. Aris's toilet, around 300 BC, would have been state-of-the-art for the era, him being a gentleman of high social standing. He probably didn't have to place his behind on a dinner-plate-sized hole carved into an exceedingly smelly stone bench, straining away alongside 40 odd other people. He would have had a private loo, possibly with some primitive form of flush. He might even have adopted wiping techniques, using wool and rosewater to improve his own personal hygiene.

Ancient Greeks were among the first people to live in dense urban environments and they had learned through experience that poor sanitation and unmanaged sewage were connected with poor human health and mortality. Given the amount of time Aris spent in my loo, I am pretty sure he is more impressed with the progress we've made regarding toilet sanitation than with any improvement in our understanding of wasp life cycles over the last 2,400 years. I spot an opportunity to divert the conversation away from twenty-first-century toilets to vespine wasps: I dive in.

Good house hygiene is critical for a social insect. Disease control is paramount for protecting their colony, and so it's no surprise that many have evolved incredible defence and management systems designed to keep disease at bay. An important part of hygienic behaviour is detecting dead or parasitised brood and removing them safely. Honeybees are really clean: they bring out their dead, clean out hatched cells and generally do what they need to do to minimise diseases and pathogens in the hive.

As with husbandry of any domesticated animal, it is imperative that the honeybee farmer has a good understanding of diseases and their management. Pathogens like the spore-forming fungus *Nosema* that attacks adult bees, and parasites like *Varroa destructor* mites that feed and reproduce on the brood, are the biggest threat to the beekeeping industry. Beekeepers and bee scientists have made it a high priority to learn about honeybee hygienic behaviour, in order to help support and maintain healthy colonies. Honeybees have two types of specialist hygienists: those who detect and uncap 'bad brood' and those who remove them. This fine-scale division of labour results in uber-hygienists: bees that specialise in uncapping do it much faster than bees that specialise in cell-clearing, and vice versa.

Honeybee babies pupate inside a cell capped with wax. Once a pupa, the baby doesn't need feeding and workers can no longer see inside to check all is well. If it dies and is left undetected it will attract pathogens, putting neighbouring brood at risk. Luckily, honeybees have a system to clean up these unseen dead: smell. Dead pupae emit a volatile chemical – beta-ocimene. A worker gifted in undertaking will respond to this chemical and uncap the offending cell so that the cell-cleaners can come along and remove the dead pupa.

This might sound incredibly clever, but beta-ocimene is in fact the same chemical that bee larvae emit to signal to workers that they need feeding. All evolution is doing here is redeploying existing signal-response machinery for a different purpose. Producing this same cue at a different point in development (namely, the terminal point, death) snaps undertaker bees into action, activating molecular pathways in their brains.

'Death cues' are not just the forte of honeybees – they've been found in bumblebees and various ant species. Ants release fatty acids as they start to decompose, beckoning the undertakers to do some cleaning up. Some insects, like the imported fire ant *Solenopsis invicta*, don't wait until they are properly dead before summoning the cleaners. The dying send out warning signals so that they can be quickly detected and dispatched before they become sources for contamination.

For species that live in the ground – like many ants – there are specialist gravediggers who spend their time at a 'death dump' outside the colony. This is a mix of dead bodies and excrement. Once a worker becomes a gravedigger, there's no going back. And for good reason. Managing the dead comes with an occupational hazard – disease. To avoid the colony being infected with any diseases that might be lurking in the dump, the undertakers will carry their dead sisters out and deposit them beside (but not on) the graveyard. A gravedigger then takes over. The undertakers and the gravediggers never touch. In fact, if an undertaker accidentally enters the graveyard, she's doomed to join the gravediggers for life.

Unfortunately, we know little about how wasps deal with their dead. Brood cannibalism and brood removal have been frequently reported in nests of the 'easy to watch', envelope-free wasp species, like *Polistes*. Workers pluck brood from cells and drop them to the ground, but sometimes they chew up the extracted baby and feed it to a sibling brood. It's not clear why sibling cannibalism happens: it could be a way of recycling less impressive offspring to boost the growth of other brood. We simply don't know.

Other wasps adopt a more wholescale form of hygienic behaviour: they abandon or cut down the infested comb, complete with brood, and start again. Such drastic measures must be the only effective way to eradicate infestations of brood parasites like phorid flies. En masse genocide of your diseased offspring is a rather extreme form of spring cleaning, which highlights the costs of parasitism and disease to these insects.

It would be surprising if species like the yellowjackets and hornets didn't have an equally impressive set of chemical and behavioural tools up their tarsi as do honeybees. Societies are breeding grounds for diseases, and wasps are no strangers to parasites, pathogens and unwanted nest guests. Anecdotally, *Vespula* appear to keep their nests largely free of debris such as paper waste, discarded prey, faecal material, dead brood and adults, although housekeeping may break down when the nest has a poor workforce or is close to collapse. They certainly have the ability to control disease. One of the few examples of this comes from a study of *Vespula vulgaris* in which colonies that lost their queen were more likely to die from fungal infections than brood in colonies with a queen. The study's authors suggested this was because workers devoted less time to brood care and nest maintenance once the queen had died.

Brood are readily removed by workers who 'police' the reproduction by other workers. Some scientists thought that egg removal was perhaps a form of hygienic behaviour, getting rid of unviable worker-laid eggs, but so far no evidence has been found to support this.

Another tantalising morsel is hidden in the 1900 book *Wasps and their Ways* by the American biologist and educator Margaret Warner Morley (1858–1923). Well educated, with a postgraduate qualification in biology, Morley became a teacher, but is best known for her books on nature and biology. These were largely written for children and played an important role in school curricula at a time when the study of nature was just beginning. She writes in a chatty, personable way, and it's easy to see how children would find her books engaging and fun. At one point she even says, 'The wasp is a philosopher.' (This makes Aristotle chuckle.)

In her book about wasps, Margaret suggests that the drones (males) 'keep the vespiary clean, clearing away all rubbish and carrying out dead bodies'. But males only appear towards the end of the colony life: who cleans up before then? I like the idea of a female-only factory that reaches a point at which the mess gets too much, and so they raise some males to tidy up after them. But the reality is likely to be more complex. Perhaps males do help (if only to keep from being bullied by workers), but whether house hygiene is simply a task for a generalist workforce or part of a cleaning system akin to that of their socially complex vegetarian cousins remains an outstanding question.

I can see Aris's marvellous brain going into overdrive. He is astounded at the hygienic behaviour of honeybees and other social insects. He doesn't share my disappointment about our incomplete knowledge of hygiene in wasps. He tells me that we just need to look harder: they clearly have mechanisms to control disease. But given the weak level of division of labour among vespine workers, he agrees that they are unlikely to have dedicated hygienists, as the honeybees and ants do. He is energised by these known unknowns. If he weren't over two millennia old, I think he'd be leaping off to explore this himself.

# V

Aris and I are standing on the terrace now, enjoying the view from the top of Lycabettus Hill, the highest point in the centre of Athens. Aris is enthralled. In his day, only the quarry folk braved this hill. Where it was not bare from quarrying, it was forest ruled by hungry wolves. Or so he was told. Although his beloved Lyceum was little more than a mile from the hill, he has never climbed it. He tells me how the hill was created by Athena – goddess of wisdom and war and patroness of Athens – when she threw down a rock she was carrying. She had intended to use the rock to build the Acropolis, but dropped it because of some bad news that a raven brought her.

I catch Aris's eye: surely he knows that he no longer needs to be careful to observe the sanctity of the Olympian gods. He knew well that his predecessor Socrates had been to put death for disrespecting the gods. Aris and other philosophers, like Plato, trod a more diplomatic path, being careful not to raise doubts about the gods. A twitch of his chiselled chin tells me that he'd rather not discuss this further. We turn our attention to the marvellous panorama below.

It took little to persuade the priest of the beautiful church of Agios Georgios on Lycabettus Hill to host my private dinner party with Aristotle. (The priest has spent the last few hours inside the church, hovering like a teenager backstage at their favourite pop music gig, hoping to eavesdrop on our conversation.) A lot has changed in Athens since Aris last saw it. It's much bigger and noisier than he remembered. I point out his Lyceum to the south; he squints with confusion. Only ruins remain, nestled in a bit of park, overlooked by the squat, cubic-looking Athens Conservatoire. The Lyceum's ruins were only discovered in 1996. I won't take him any closer – the excavated remnants resemble an abandoned wasteland and bear little likeness to the intellectual hub that he founded well over 2,000 years ago.

A jingle of his rings and Aris is now pointing with great excitement, tracing the lines of the roads to one a few streets away from the ruins. 'Look! There! That's where it was,' he cries. I am confused. Did the archaeologists get the location of the Lyceum wrong? The Lyceum we know is due south, but Aris is pointing to a junction half a mile to the east.

Aris is oblivious to the fact that he may have exposed a serious flaw in modern archaeology.

'That was my favourite place to buy gastrin,' he shouts. 'It was the best in town. An old man, Spiro was his name, he made it and sold it from his front door. I only learned about it from my students – they always knew the best places to eat. I got all my best gastronomy tips from them.'

'I don't suppose you have any gastrin?' (He's looking a bit peckish again.)

Indeed I do. You can't serve a Greek meal without offering gastrin. Today, it is better known as baklava. And on the reliable authority of my friend the priest, I'm about to serve Aris the best baklava that modern Athenians can buy.

As I serve up the baklava, I reflect on how both Aris and I had gathered information from the people around us: Aris from his students, and me from the priest. This reminded me that I should tell Aris about how insects use social information. He's going to love this.

Social information is essentially a form of gossip. It allows the rapid dissemination of new information among individuals and is thought to be a particular benefit of group living. It's the opposite of private (or personal) information. Social insects are renowned for their use of social information. A good example of an evolved signal that communicates social information is the honeybee waggle dance that they use to recruit fellow nestmates to a place where work is required. When a foraging bee discovers a new patch of delicious flowers, she will return to the hive and 'dance' to a 'court' of her nestmates. This dance tells an attentive audience the distance and direction of the flowers.

If you know what to look for, anyone (even a human) can decode the dance and work out exactly where the bees are foraging. It's quite simple: the dance consists of runs and loops, during which time the dancer shakes her derrière from side to side and buzzes her wings. The duration of the waggle run tells us how far away the flowers are: on average a second of waggling represents around one kilometre (honeybees are clearly disciples of the metric system). The comb forms the stage for this performance and encodes important information about the direction of the flowers: if the waggler dances directly upwards on the comb, this means the flowers are in the same direction as the sun. If she dances at 30 degrees to the left of this vertical, the receiver bees should fly 30 degrees to the left of the sun.

Do wasps use social information in their foraging behaviour? Is there a wasp waggle-dance equivalent? There are clear benefits to recruitment via social information: your colony can exploit short-lived resources quickly. But something as sophisticated as the honeybee's waggle dance is costly to evolve. Recruitment may also only be adaptive (that is, propagating more copies of your gene variants) under particular social or ecological conditions.

Darwin's neighbour, Sir John Lubbock, 1st Baron Avebury, performed some of the earliest studies on recruitment in *Vespula*. This Victorian gentleman born into privilege was a banker as well as a baron, and the President of the Linnean Society between 1881 and 1886. Lubbock made important contributions as a biologist and archaeologist. We have him to thank for the terms 'Paleolithic' and 'Neolithic', and for his efforts as a Member of Parliament in promoting the study of science in English schools.

In 1888 he published a delightfully indulgent book, *Ants, Bees, and Wasps*, a collection of ten years' work, much of which he had published in the *Journal of the Linnean Society*. The book focused on exploring the 'mental condition and powers of sense' in these insects and it was pioneering, not only because of the questions he asked of his insects, but also because he individually marked them, allowing him to observe how they learned from previous encounters. He'd planned to conduct his experiments on bees but found ants were much easier to handle. As a result, ants dominate 9 of the 11 chapters of *Ants, Bees, and Wasps*. We are lucky there is a chapter on wasps, as Lubbock includes some real gems about the cognitive nature of wasps and the games he played with them at his home in Kent.

Lubbock's laboratory was his sitting room. He would hand-feed honey to individual wasps and sit in his room for hours recording the time it took for each wasp to return for more. Several pages of his notebook give blow-by-blow accounts of the comings and goings of an individual wasp: one account starts at 4.15 a.m. and runs *continuously* to almost 8 p.m. that same day, recording the exact arrival and departure times of his (solo) subject, without a single recruit to her secret honey stash. Not encouraging for a scientist looking for a glimmer of social information use.

But perhaps Lubbock used the wrong cue. Bees share information about the location of flower patches with their nestmates in order to recruit more 'shoppers' to deliver more food back to the nest to feed the brood. Wasps don't need to share information about sugar: it is a selfish commodity, needed only for the individual, not for the common work of rearing the colony's brood. If wasps recruit nestmates to food sources, it will most likely be to a patch of meat.

There are two ways that *Vespula* may use social information to find meat. One is via information at the food source. Humans use this sort of data all the time: a crowd gathers around a particular stall at the market, which must be a sign that the food there is good (or good value). The crowd acts as a 'local enhancement' cue. Wasps do this to some degree, but only if the conditions are right. When there are too many other wasps at a food source they give it a wide berth, if other sources are available. They actively avoid competitive interactions with members of the same species – wasps invented social distancing at the shops before we did.

Use of local enhancement cues also depends on the type of food: some species will only be attracted to a food by the presence of other wasps if it is sugar, while others only if it is protein. To complicate things even more, wasps respond differently to enhancement cues when there are different species involved: for example, if there's a bigger species of wasp at the feeding station, a scouting forager might think twice about butting in. Local enhancement cues flip, suddenly, to being local inhibition cues.

We have a lot to learn about how wasps perceive these cues and how context influences their use of them. We can't even be sure whether local enhancement communicates the *presence* of good food (like our street market stall) or the *absence* of a predator. But wasps' use of local enhancement information doesn't require a sophisticated communication mechanism like the waggle dance; it simply necessitates the ability to recognise the cue, and in this case the cue is that a food source is occupied.

The second way that *Vespula* use social information when foraging is from information at the nest. Experiments on *Vespula pensylvanica* in Hawaii showed that more workers were recruited to a plate of tasty chicken from colonies where the foragers had been permitted to return to the nest than from colonies where they were prevented from returning. This suggests that somehow information about the prey had been transmitted to naive nest-mates inside the home.

The cue that holds the information is not the vision of a wasp returning with a mouthful of chicken, it's the odour of the food. Scientists have found that workers inside a nest can be recruited to forage by exposing them to food odours as basic as scented sugar water in the absence of the forager herself. This tells us that foragers can be recruited without any behavioural stimulation and without any information that might communicate direction or distance. This is not so surprising. The smell of forage is important for recruitment in bees too: honeybees sample the scent of the pollen or nectar on the body of the dancer, as well as digesting information on the direction and distance of the forage patch. Bumblebees also sample the smells of the nectar deposited in honeypots by returning foragers and use that smell to help them locate the forage patch.

Aris has stopped stuffing baklava into his mouth. He is astounded. 'Dancing?' he questions. 'Do bees really dance for their dinner?' Well, for their baby sibling's dinner, yes, I say. Aris cannot believe that a dance, least of all a mathematically coded one, can tell other bees so precisely where to find food. I lick my honey-coated fingers and explain that the honeybee waggle dance was only discovered in 1945, and that the scientist behind the decoding, Karl von Frisch, was awarded a Nobel Prize for this breakthrough.

Ah, of course, Aris doesn't know about these prizes. They are awarded for outstanding discoveries or actions in science, literature, economics and peace, I tell him. The discoveries need to in some way confer enormous benefits to humankind. The first was awarded in 1901, and six are given out every year. You, Aris, would surely have been a recipient, if they'd existed in ancient Greece, I assure him. And Aris grins at me with the gratitude of a child who's just won first prize in an egg-and-spoon race. I wonder if anyone ever gave him a prize, or whether the world's greatest philosopher could ever have suffered from impostor syndrome.

'But what about the wasps? Do they have anything as impressive as this bee dance?' Aris is tucking back into his honey-drenched dessert, full of optimism.

The nearest thing social wasps have to a sort of waggle dance is gastral drumming, whereby adult wasps use their derrières as sticks to hit the surface of the comb.* The discovery of the percussional properties of vespine nests dates back to 1895 when French engineer and biologist Charles Janet† noted how the larvae of the European hornet *Vespa crabro* produced distinct noises – vibrations – while wriggling in their cells.

The middle of the twentieth century saw a smattering of reports on how larvae scraped their mandibles against the cell wall in a synchronous manner across the nest. Putting the nests in soundproofed boxes provided definitive evidence that vespine

---

* Gaster is the term used to describe the bulbous part of the abdomen in Hymenoptera. It is more accurate than just plain 'abdomen', which includes the first segment that is the thin waist constriction joining the abdomen to the thorax.

† Janet is better known for his contributions to the periodic table. But, topically, he also invented the formicarium – which allowed the observation of ants inside their nest, made visible between two planes of glass.

nests are veritable sound chambers: each comb acts as an amphi-theatre for a symphony of sounds, the connecting pillars allowing the required amount of movement to amplify vibrations while also dampening distortion. Confident that these sounds were real, scientists began to ask what they were for, the obvious question being: do wasps communicate through vibrational sounds? Scraping mandibles are thought to be a 'hunger call', made by larvae to signal to workers that they need feeding.

Gastral drumming itself wasn't discovered until the 1960s, when Japanese scientists used soundproofed wasp boxes to record the vibrations of the comb and discovered that the sounds were produced by workers striking the comb with their gaster through rapid thumps or drumming action. The drumming appeared to be contagious: once one worker started pumping her booty, others would join in, putatively 'amplifying' any signal it may encode. The drumming resulted in an increase in general nest activity.

No doubt eager to find a wasp waggle-dance equivalent, the scientists called this an 'awakening dance' because it mostly occurred in the early morning and it increased at night when they shined a light on the nest. The researchers speculated that the collective drumming served to 'wake up' the larvae as well as instigate workers to up their foraging activities.

Fifty years later, American scientists Bob Jeanne and Benjamin Taylor finally tested these ideas using the audio technology brought by the twenty-first century. They recorded the vibrations inside *Vespula germanica* nests with an accelerometer, and used playback experiments (playing sounds recorded from the nest *back* to the nest) to see how the colony responded. They found no support for the idea that gastral drumming signalled hungry brood. In fact, when brood were starved, drumming dropped to near zero. But they did find some evidence that gastral drumming appeared to recruit foragers: more wasps started foraging when the drumming sounds were played to them, suggesting the behaviour evolved to signal 'time to forage, ladies'.*

It's worth clarifying the difference between a cue and a signal here. As layman's terms we tend to use them interchangeably, but in evolutionary biology they mean quite different things. Cues are constructs or actions (for example, chemical products, behaviours) that occur for other reasons and relay information incidentally. Things used as cues have not been shaped by natural selection for this purpose but have been co-opted as sources of information: the presence of wasps at a food source is a cue.

Signals are constructs produced by natural selection to convey information between a sender and recipient: the honeybee's waggle dance is a signal. According to Bob Jeanne and Benjamin Taylor's experiments, gastral drumming by *Vespula* *might* be a signal. Increased drumming instigates workers to run around the nest, bumping into other workers. When they meet another worker, they engage in a form of fluid exchange in which they join their mandibles (think of it as an insect version of French kissing), but this is a cue, not a signal. We know that odours alone can instigate foraging in *Vespula*, so it may be the cues from the French kissing that promote foraging, and the gastral drumming signal might form only an indirect part of the recruitment process. By this definition, direct recruitment of foragers in social wasps recorded to date appears to be facilitated largely via cues, not signals, suggesting that vespines may not have evolved a signal as impressive as the honeybee's waggle dance.†

---

* Don't get too excited: playbacks of gastral drumming resulted in only an 11 per cent increase in foraging.

† It is worth noting that in their experiment, Bob Jeanne and Ben Taylor observed huge variation in drumming bouts, ranging from 4–137 seconds in duration. They postulate that perhaps the duration of a drumming bout carries information about the nature, distance or quantity of the forage, in a similar way to the duration of the honeybee's waggle dance.

There is one exception to this, which is as gruesome as the waggle dance is elegant. Honeybee and bumblebee workers leave scent marks at their food source to alert nestmates to its presence. These markings are thought to be inadvertent chemical 'footprints' left by foragers rather than an evolved mechanism of social information, suggesting they are cues not signals. So far there has been little evidence that vespines leave any such chemical footprint to indicate forage to nestmates, inadvertent or evolved; except, that is, for *Vespa mandarinia*, the giant Asian hornet. Foragers of this hornet raid honeybee hives, killing the worker bees and brood and carrying them back to their nest to feed to their own wasp brood.

To recruit nestmates, foraging wasps smear secretions produced by their glands, via their abdomen, onto the bee hive, which attracts more nestmates to assist in the slaughter. Why, then, have foraging signals evolved in *Vespa mandarinia* and in the social bees, but not in the rest of the social wasps? Most likely, it's a bit of evolutionary book-balancing: the benefits of evolving the signal must outweigh the costs. The giant Asian hornet is unusual in its raiding of whole honeybee colonies. Although other vespines hunt honeybees, and will even pick them off at the entrance of the hive, few will attempt to raid an entire colony. Many foragers are needed for a successful raid and so the benefits of evolving an effective way to recruit fellow raiders will be high. This hornet is a rare example in wasps of a shift from an independent hunter, like a tiger, to a social hunter – like a pack of wolves – where cooperation among many individuals is needed for a successful feast.

Aris is stroking his chin. 'Tell me,' he says, 'why is it that most of these magnificent societies of wasps, so grand as the honeybee, don't use social information about food like bees?'
The most likely explanation lies in the differences in their ecology, I muse. Unlike bees, the food resources of

social wasps tend to be ephemeral, patchy or local. This means there's little benefit to recruiting fellow foragers as the resources of many small patches of prey will be quickly exhausted. The pay-offs of being able to exploit a rare large patch are insufficient to drive the evolution of sophisticated recruitment mechanisms. The best strategy for social wasps is to distribute their foragers throughout the environment and be opportunistic hunters.

'Ah yes!' Aris's marvellous brain is whirring dangerously fast now. 'In Book 9, Chapter 42, of my *Historia Animalium,* do you recall that I described the hunting behaviour of vespines?' he says. 'That they "live not gathering flowers like the bees but eating many different forms of flesh … For they hunt the big flies and when they have caught [one], having taken off the head, they fly off bearing the rest of the body."

'I can see how these differences in ecology between the bees and wasps could be really important in – what was Mr Darwin's word – evolution. I recall seeing wasps hunt on dung, for that is where the flies are. The wasps are opportunistic hunters – they surely must have splendid sensing abilities to find new food patches quickly. I saw this: they search dung pats, catching flies, but move on when the flies are all beheaded, and before competition with other predators becomes too great. I remember this now. But this is exciting, as you've not yet solved the full story of how wasps hunt, have you?'

Aris is now leaping around the terrace. I wonder if he's about to act out his own waggle dance.

'The situation is not so bleak,' he shouts earnestly. 'You already have evidence that vespines *can* use social information to recruit nestmates to a food source – you've told me about the odours, the sight of other wasps and those vibrations of their American bottoms. It may not match the grand scale of honeybees and their dances with numbers, but there are golden threads here that need weaving together.

'Remember, "Nature does nothing in vain." You have work to do yet, to figure out the mechanisms of how wasps share information and why nature has made it so. The secret to success as a society of hunting wasps might involve active signals like gaster drumming interwound with the passive olfactory cues of a returning forager. Perhaps there's a Nobel Prize lurking in a nearby vespine nest, waiting to be discovered,' chuckles Aris to himself, with sparkling eyes.

There's something a little bit cheeky about this ancient philosopher that I rather like.

# VI

That sickly-sweet baklava has finished me off, but it seems that Aris's 2,400-year-long fast has left him with an insatiable appetite. I begin to wonder whether he has a digestive system at all; it seems to pass through him like water. Lucky I made that cheesecake. I used a recipe from Roman times, a few hundred years after Aristotle died, but he doesn't seem to notice. He's soon tucking into his cake and on to his next question.

'You've told me a lot about how bees and wasps tell others about food,' he says, 'but you've not told me anything about how they manage to find food in the first place. How do bees find the first flower, before telling their nestmates? And how do wasps find their first fly or worm?'

Wasps certainly need some pretty sophisticated cognitive abilities to learn how to hunt, updating their search image or cues depending on conditions. Bees have it easy: their 'prey' (flowers) don't move around or run away. By contrast, hunting hidden or moving protein is cognitively challenging and harder on the senses than foraging for 'static' quarry like the pollen-foraging bees. Aris hasn't read the earlier chapters of my book, so I fill him in on the incredible hunting prowess of the solitary wasps from Part 2,* on how they tend to be picky predators, with different families or genera of wasps specialising in hunting a specific type of prey.

A key life-history transition in the evolution from solitary to social living for wasps appears to have been the shift from being a specialist to a generalist predator. The foraging machinery of a generalist vespine may therefore be quite different from that of a spider-hunting or caterpillar-hunting specialist. And unlike a bee, the vespine needs to be skilled in hunting different types of food: carbohydrates (sugars from flowers) and live prey, but also carrion. Sometimes they are on the lookout for a personal treat – some nice carbohydrate or sugars from a plant or rotting fruit. Other times they are on social business, searching for protein to feed the larvae.

This means they need an eclectic sensory toolbox to help them find their food source, enabling them to respond to a mix of tactile, visual and olfactory cues, depending on the food and the context. Their sensory mechanisms have been selected by evolution to be flexible, depending on their mission and the type of resources available. When looking for carbohydrates (sugars),

---

* Aristotle did write a little about the spider-hunters in Book V of his *Historia Animalium*. 'The wasps that are nicknamed "the ichneumons" (or hunters), less in size, by the way, than the ordinary wasp, kill spiders and carry off the dead bodies to a wall or some such place with a hole in it; this hole they smear over with mud and lay their grubs inside it, and from the grubs come the hunter-wasps.'

foragers tend to use close-up visual cues to locate their food. This makes sense as flowers or fallen fruit (or your al frèsco dining spot) tend to be patchily distributed and so the precise location is not important to learn. When foraging for static protein sources like carrion, foragers rely more on visual landmarks to relocate their prey. This is logical as carrion rarely moves (at least not intentionally).

But having the right sensory toolkit is only part of being able to exploit resources effectively. Foragers need to be able to process and act on information received by the machinery, and to be able to modify and adapt so that they can respond to their constantly changing environment. This requires cognitive processes like learning – the ability to update information and respond through experience.

I stop in order to serve Aris another slice of cheesecake. He will need it. I'm going to start by telling him about the cognitive power of bees, as the scientific progress made since his day is even more astonishing than dancing by numbers.

Honeybees can be trained to solve difficult visual tasks such as learning to associate specific visual cues (for example, the colour green or a round shape) with something nice (for example, sugar) and other cues with something nasty (scientists tend to use quinine, which insects find as distasteful as we do, in the absence of gin). Bees can also recognise complex visual cues like a human face or even painting styles; for instance, bumblebees prefer Van Gogh's sunflowers to Gauguin's pastel-shaded vase of flowers.

Don't be too surprised: bees have evolved to be able to recognise (and update information on) complex visual signals of flowers to avoid deceptive flowers that don't reward the bee's pollination services. They use flower shape, structure, colour and they even detect iridescence. It's easy to take these abilities for granted – after all, our pet dogs and cats can recognise their owners, and crows and even fish have been trained to identify faces. These animals have dedicated neural circuitry in their brains for facial recognition, which required the evolution of specific brain structures. Insect brains are much simpler (a mere 1 million neurones compared to around 86 billion in a human brain) and smaller (around 1 cubic millimetre compared to 1.1–1.2 cubic metres in humans), and yet they too have specific regions that are activated for specific cognitive processes.

In recent years, the honeybee has become an important model for visual cognitive processing in insects, and a lot of the credit for this must go to Martin Giurfa, an Argentinian honeybee biologist who has pushed the boundaries of insect cognitive research. His seminal breakthrough came in 2001 when he showed that bees can learn relational concepts, using abstract interrelationships of cues, for example using information learned from one physical situation and applying it to another.

He found that bees could distinguish between the concepts of 'same as' and 'different from' in unconnected and contrasting objects. What does this mean? Well, it's a concept that you use every day without even thinking about it, for it is exactly this: AA = BB and CD = EF. Martin tested whether bees could make such a connection by using a Y maze with a choice of colours (yellow and blue) and horizontal or vertical stripes. Y mazes test whether what you see at the entrance to the maze (the bottom arm of the Y) influences which branch (the top two arms of the Y) you choose.

He was able to show that bees could be trained to choose a match – if a bee encountered yellow at the entrance to the Y maze and then had a choice between yellow and blue 'branches', it would choose the yellow branch (that is, following a 'sameness' rule) if it had learned that *colour-matching* produced a *positive* reward (such as sugar). You can equally well train the bee to colour-match blue – it's nothing to do with the colour per se. Similarly, a bee could learn to match specific line orientations (for example, vertical lines over horizontal ones) through sameness-matching: I saw vertical lines at the entrance and I've learned that the thing I see there is an indication of a reward, so if given the choice of a path with vertical lines on it and one with horizontal lines, I'll choose the path with vertical lines. Using a similar approach, bees could be trained to follow a 'difference' rule: if they saw yellow at the entrance, they *didn't* choose a yellow branch but something different (in this case, blue).

This is moderately impressive, but that was just the training phase. In the next experiment, the type of cue was switched. If a bee had been trained for sameness using colour cues, it was this time presented with a maze of line orientations. The bees chose correctly: in other words, if they had learned that *sameness* yielded rewards in colours (yellow + yellow = reward, or indeed blue + blue = reward), they would choose sameness in line orientations (that is, horizontal + horizontal, or indeed vertical + vertical) depending on which was presented, even though they'd had no previous experience of line orientations as cues.

Likewise, if they had learned that *difference* in colours yielded rewards, they would choose a combination of different line orientations (horizontal + vertical, or indeed vertical + horizontal). What was even more amazing is that these visual cues could also be replaced with odours, and the bees were able to apply the sameness or difference rules they had learned. Astonishingly, these experiments show that after learning an outcome from sameness or difference encounters, bees can transfer their abstract relational learning to different visual and olfactory cues.

Since then, Martin and his team have shown how bees can learn other types of relational concepts: they can tell whether there is 'more or less' of something, and whether something is above or below another thing. He's shown that bees count, and that they also have a concept of what zero means. They can learn to respond additively – that is, if trained that blue is good *and* yellow is good, when presented with blue and yellow they respond with twice the enthusiasm. This form of learning, in which ambiguous links between two or more stimuli are acted on, rather than individual experience of any of those stimuli alone, is known as configural learning. It is truly remarkable to find this in an insect since such relational learning was thought to require the neural complexity of a vertebrate brain.

Aris has stopped eating, and is watching my lips as I speak.
'How can this be?' He is barely audible.

Good thing you asked, Aris. We do actually know how bees manage this. We've long known that a part of the insect brain called the mushroom body (so named because it's shaped like a mushroom) is the region involved in higher-order cognitive function – that's things like storage and retrieval of memory. Martin Giurfa and his collaborators identified which *neurones* – these nerve cells communicate via electrical signals and are found in the bodies of almost all animals – within the mushroom body are responsible for learning responses.

To do these experiments, they trimmed back the cuticle (the hard covering) of the bee's head, opened it up and injected a neurotransmitter blocker in order to disrupt neural activity. The bees were then tested on complex pattern-learning tasks, which reveal the bee's abilities in configural learning. This is functional neurobiology and is a bit gruesome, but there's no better way to work out if a neurone is important or not. Using this approach, the team proved that neurones in a specific part of the brain are essential for the bee to be able to learn to respond to several stimuli on the basis of their combination. It was the first evidence that insects, like mammals, have specific parts of the brain that are needed for complex learning.

Martin Giurfa's lab is one of several around the world that have provided conclusive evidence that the bee brain is neither primitive nor rudimentary. Bees are not just associative-learning machines, they are reasoning, numerate, perceptive, complex cognitive organisms just like us. Despite their small brains and limited number of neurones, they have conceptual cognition. Just like you, they can link past experiences together for a future interaction with the world. This body of work has made scientists question what the minimal neural circuitry is for 'higher-level' cognitive function.

> Aris is ashen. 'Bees are like us,' he whispers. 'They share our politics and our intelligence? Socrates was right. We are not so special.'
> Privately, we permit a pensive pause.
> Then …
> 'What of the wasps?' he breathes.

Understanding how complex cognition is achieved by tiny, simple brains like those of insects can provide valuable insights into the development of artificial intelligence. (I mentioned this last morsel for you, reader, in case you're wondering what the wider significance of insect cognition might be to you, but I must confess that I whispered it a little, hoping Aris didn't hear as I don't think he could cope with learning about AI, computers and robots at the moment.)

But we need to broaden the net beyond the honeybee, in order to steal the best ideas from evolution's repeated experiments across different lineages. And this is where vespine wasps may have something to offer. Naturalists of the late nineteenth and early twentieth centuries were obsessed with the intelligence of insects, perhaps because of the apparent cleverness of honeybees, which humans had learned so much about during our millennia of semi-domesticating them.

The first person to write about the cleverness of yellowjacket wasps was our old friend Sir John Lubbock, Charles Darwin's neighbour and chum, in 1888. Lubbock's sitting-room laboratory had windows on two sides: he would open different ones alternately in order to test how well bees and wasps could adjust to changing entrance and exit routes. He noted how yellowjacket wasps were able to complete tasks that honeybees were unable to do.

One of his favourite experiments was to put an insect into a conical flask and position the opening away from a window: bees stupidly buzzed at the no-exit 'sunny side', while wasps quickly discovered the shady route out. Did this make wasps cleverer than bees? Of course not: it just tells us that they respond to different cues. Bees move instinctively towards light – after all, there are more likely to be pollen-laden rewards in sunny spots than shady ones. The prey of wasps, however, are often hiding in dark places like the undersides of rocks or holes in the ground: Lubbock's first experiments showed us that wasps are no strangers to dark, uninviting crevices and that visual cues are likely to be extremely important in hunting.

A few years later in 1900, our American naturalist Margaret Morley mused on the natural aptitude of vespines in her book *Wasps and Their Ways*. She tells us of experiments with coloured paper and wasps. It's not clear whether she performed these herself, but they must surely be some of the first experiments to demonstrate the learning abilities of yellowjacket wasps, and evidence that they can distinguish colours. If a piece of red paper was placed at the entrance to a yellowjacket nest, it would create great excitement among the returning foragers, causing them to fly around in a confused manner rather than entering the nest with clear intent and purpose.

After three hours the wasps became accustomed to their decorated doorway, and went in and out as if nothing had changed. If the red decor was then replaced with blue, the wasps once again became excited, but they adjusted to the change more quickly than they did the first time. Remove the paper altogether, and returning wasps were once again confused. Margaret reported an even cheekier experiment, in which the red decor was moved almost a metre away. The wasps chose the nestless red entrance instead of their undecorated real nest entrance. If you kept changing the colours, the wasps became desensitised over time and, like a child tiring of a game, ended up ignoring any decor change.

This account demonstrates that wasps perceive differences in red and blue colours, that they can learn to associate colours and use visual landmarks, and can easily update information as it changes. But if the information in that cue becomes unreliable they will learn to ignore it, and presumably use another cue that was not measured or manipulated. Margaret concluded that 'Wasps are capable of being educated' and that they 'possess a more versatile, if lower, intelligence than bees'. She recommended the study of learning in wasps as a 'new field of experiment'.

That was 120 years ago. She would be a little disappointed with the modest progress we've made since then. Scientists have shown that wasps have good spatial and olfactory memories. They can retain spatial maps in their heads for at least 24 hours without reinforcement, and they retain memories of smells for up to 30 days. It is likely, therefore, that wasps can learn using information from various pathways – visual and olfactory – in order to navigate and exploit their environment. But there is so much more to discover about their cognition and learning; we are far behind the honeybee researchers.

Aris sighs, nostalgic, perhaps, for the day when he would have suggested such experiments to his students. Once his mentor Plato died, Aristotle really embraced empirical study. He valued evidence, believing it the cornerstone to logic and persuasive argument.

I fill Aris in on what we discovered in Part 4 about how *Polistes* wasps learn to distinguish between individual nestmates based on their facial markings. Vespines are not so great at individual-level facial recognition: the more complex the society, the less need there is for individual recognition. A bit of role play helps explain this. Imagine you work in a giant telesales call centre alongside thousands of co-workers, where there's no chance of promotion. It's a hot-desking system and so you just grab the first available desk. You rarely end up sitting beside someone you know as there are too many of you and you're all wearing the same uniform, so it's hard to recognise individuals anyway.

Even if you could recognise your co-worker, there is no point in trying to impress anyone as there's no better (or worse) job in this call centre than the one you've got. You happily make small talk with someone new every day with no agenda of friendship, expectation of reciprocation or competition: you all have a job to do and it's the same as that of the person next to you, no matter who they are.

Just as there's no benefit to you in recognising your co-workers, there are no benefits to a honeybee or yellowjacket worker in recognising individuals, since there are no opportunities for promotion (once a worker, always a worker) nor are there any benefits from being especially nice to anyone as it's unlikely that you'll bump into the same individual again, so there's little opportunity for reciprocation. It's not surprising, therefore, that vespines (and honeybees for that matter) are equally hopeless at distinguishing one nestmate from another, unless of course it's the queen.

I am one of those people who sometimes find it hard to recognise human faces. It's called face blindness. I'm only a mild sufferer. I have no problem recognising friends and family, but I struggle with meeting people in large crowds, like at parties or conferences, especially if they've changed their appearance (hair, clothes, glasses) since I first saw them. It can be embarrassing;

people probably think I'm rude. Being aware of my handicap, I sometimes overcompensate and end up chatting animatedly to someone I think I've met before like a long-lost friend. It's also a handicap when watching films: I can't always work out who the characters are if they've changed their clothing.

Face blindness has a clinical name: prosopagnosia. Around 2.5 per cent of the population suffer from it, and by comparing the brains of face-blind people with those who have no trouble recognising and remembering faces, scientists have been able to identify the specific part of the brain involved in facial recognition – it's the fusiform gyrus. It allows people to identify faces better than similarly complex inanimate objects. Apparently there are people who are 'super-recognisers' too, who have superior facial recognition abilities.

Honeybees and vespines appear to be better at recognising human faces than I am. Early naturalists remarked on these abilities. Margaret Morley talked about how one wasp nest persistently attacked a young man, making the (unfounded) suggestion that 'Perhaps he smelt of deceit.' Scientists have recently found that honeybees and yellowjacket wasps use similar visual processing mechanisms to us, and this is why they can distinguish between us – yes, you've not misunderstood: wasps and bees recognise human faces.

We recognise faces by piecing together different landmarks – the nose, mouth, ears, eyes – to create a whole face; it's called 'holistic processing'. We get better at it through experience. Scientists presented images of human faces to honeybees and yellowjacket wasps, using similar methods to those used to assess humans for face blindness. They trained the insects to associate a target face (a white adult male) with a rewarding sugar solution, while a different face (the 'distractor' – which was a very similar-looking face in the grand scheme of things: another white adult male) would provide them with a 'punishment' solution containing quinine. The trained bees were then tested without the reward or punishment to see which face they would choose.

Between 80 and 90 per cent of trained bees chose the correct (target) face over the distractor, but if the faces were turned upside down, the bees chose a face randomly. This suggests that they can discriminate between similar-looking human faces, that they can learn to do this through conditioning and that they use physical landmarks on the face to recognise them, just like we do. The same experiment was repeated on yellowjacket wasps, with similar results.

This is pretty amazing, especially when you consider that there is no evolutionary reason for these insects to have developed the ability to recognise human faces. Perhaps it's not so surprising that honeybees have sophisticated learning abilities, since recognising and memorising flowers is a critical part of their foraging ecology. It is less obvious why yellowjacket wasps would have this ability, as they are generalist hunters who will catch almost any invertebrate they come across and so would not need the level of visual processing and learning seen in bees. Perhaps facial features are just physical landmarks to them: some people just happen to have better rock-mimicking noses or bush-like hair than others.

Aris is looking a little cross-eyed. I'm not sure if it's the wine, being over 2,400 years old, or the shocking realisation that insects can recognise people. To lighten the mood, I tell him about some of the messages I've received from members of the public who (as reported by Margaret Morley) complain to me about yellowjacket wasps from specific colonies that have chased them on multiple occasions, in preference to their friend.

Understandably, these people feel personally victimised by wasps. They are convinced the wasps were 'out to get them'. Perhaps there is something about their face that these specific wasps have learned to associate with a threat, or it could be the cologne they were wearing. The important point is that these experiments tell us that the hymenopteran brain, despite having less than a million neurones, can perform remarkably complex tasks, ones that we previously thought were limited to humans, or at least vertebrates. Large brains are clearly not necessary for processing complex stimuli. Ecology can drive the development of tiny brains to carry out complex cognitive tasks.

# VII

The night is drawing in, and Aristotle is finally looking sated. We have switched to drinking Athens's finest tap water. In Aristotle's day, there was of course no running water. Women would fetch it daily from nearby springs. Water was precious, and revered as a quality drink in Aris's time, and the philosophers were especially fond of it, often adding it to their wine to avoid drunkenness.

Indeed, we do not want any drunkenness for the final topic I am going to discuss with Aris: that of law and order.

Ancient Greece had a very bottom-up approach to law and order. Perhaps it had something to do with being the birthplace of democracy. Justice and social cohesion were largely enforced by the citizenry – which excluded slaves, foreigners, women and children. If an offence did come to court, a bunch of laymen would be assembled without any kind of court official, lawyer or official judge. Two 'litigants' (elite men of standing) would argue about whether the act was in fact unlawful, and a jury of 500 citizens would decide if the offender was guilty.

The jury would be committed to their service for an
entire year, and during that time they would be
responsible for making new laws as well as controlling all
aspects of the political system. If you had a reputation as a
tyrant, you risked being ostracised: a mere 6,000
signatures could place you in exile for ten years. In Aris's
time, Athens was a little different to the rest of Greece:
Athenian courts would have an orator who would deliver
a speech written by a speechwriter. These writers are
thought to have been the closest thing Athens had to a
modern-day lawyer.

Certainly, Aristotle's triad for persuasive oratory – *logos*,
*ethos* and *pathos* – must have come in handy here, as did
storytelling. Trials essentially became rhetorical battles,
and had little to do with law. Mixed into this first
democracy were spates of civil war, known as 'stasis',
which broke out among groups of citizens who disagreed
over social, economic or political issues.

Law and order are paramount in any well-functioning society,
whether it's ancient Athens, a honeybee hive or a wasp colony.
Worker wasps do not reproduce; instead, as we've seen, they pass
on their genes by helping raise close relatives – their siblings. But
this is not perfect as they are not raising clones. Moreover,
although yellowjacket workers can't mate – they lack the
sperm-storage sac that their mother queen has in her abdomen
– they can lay unfertilised (male) eggs. (I remind Aris how
haplodiploidy works.) So every female in the colony has the
capacity to lay male eggs. This creates conflict over reproduction:
queens against workers, and workers against workers. Yet workers rarely reproduce when the queen is alive. How is law and
order maintained?

The best way to minimise conflict is to remove the commodity under contest. My children fight over access to the Xbox (I

explain to Aris that this is like a very popular board game): I can achieve zero conflict by simply unplugging it. (Confiscation, Aris.) Nothing to fight over: they sulk away, silent. Job done. If I were a yellowjacket queen, therefore, my preferred line of attack in controlling wayward worker reproduction would be to stop them being able to develop their ovaries. Then no one else could lay eggs and so there would be no conflict.

Indeed, this is exactly what some of the most complex ant societies have done: workers of the *Atta* leafcutter ants have no ovaries – there is nothing to develop. Complete worker sterility in insects is rare, though, and workers in both honeybee and *Vespula* yellowjacket colonies can develop ovaries and cause conflict. This is because workers can still gain a slim but important slice of the reproductive pie if they manage to lay eggs themselves.

The next-best thing that a *Vespula* queen can wish for is some way of suppressing ovarian development by her workers through an honest signal of her own fertility. Queens produce a chemical that signals their fertility and yields them control over worker reproduction. These long-chain cuticular hydrocarbons (we met them in Part 4) act as a mother-made ovicide, stopping workers developing ovaries and regressing any development they have had. Even more remarkably, this same set of saturated hydrocarbons also controls worker reproduction in a range of other ants and social bees and wasps. It is likely, therefore, that the same chemical truncheon gives queens the iron hand of suppression over her potentially rebellious subjects across societies of bees, wasps and ants. It sounds more like the plaything of a Greek god than evolution.

No matter what form of societal rule you impose, there will always be evaders. In a vespine nest, a small portion of workers will escape the allure of the suppressive royal perfume, develop their ovaries and pump out some male-destined eggs. Why should they bother doing this? After all, workers do pretty well (in genetic terms) by helping their mum pump out more sisters and brothers.

This is where the sex life of complex social insects starts to make things a bit more lively: just like honeybees, a yellowjacket queen mates with lots of males. She stores the sperms from all her suitors (usually around 7–10 males) in her sperm-storage sac and uses them to fertilise the eggs she lays. This means that her daughters have 7–10 different fathers among them. While this could be good for her (genetic diversity affords all sorts of benefits, like disease defence or improved division of labour), it's not great news if that happens to be you – a proletarian daughter (that is, a worker) – rather than royal daughter (that is, next season's queen). The reason is that as a worker of a queen who's mated seven times, only one in seven of the sisters you help rear are in fact *full* sisters. The other six are your half-sisters, which in genetic terms are worth a fraction of a full sister.

Herein are sown the seeds of conflict, rebellion and retaliation among workers. If you can get away with secretly laying your own (male) eggs, alongside appearing to be a committed worker, your genetic return increases dramatically. How is it that the colony does not descend into proletarian egg-laying chaos? Evolution has an Athenian solution for this: let your citizens be the law-enforcers. The other workers are avid policers of discontent – they move in and gobble up most of the proletarian offspring before they get anywhere near maturity. While this ensures that most (or all) of the male brood are the offspring of the queen, it does come with a cost to the colony: workers spend a lot of time sniffing and chomping eggs when they should be tending to their mother's brood.

Gobbling up the eggs of your sisters is called worker policing, and it is one of the many mechanisms with which evolution has equipped complex insect societies to keep the peace and reduce conflict in the family. Laying an egg might not sound an especially aggressive act, but it is the epitome of proletarian revolt if you're a worker in a super-society, if you have the physiological ability to develop your ovaries, *and* can get away with it. Worker policing was first discovered in honeybees, but it has since been found in all sorts of social insects, including wasps but especially ants, in whose colonies multiple mating is commonplace. While the phenomenon of policing is in itself astounding, the fact that it has evolved multiple times independently in each of these insect lineages suggests that evolution is onto a good thing here, reinforcing the idea that policing is an important mechanism that regulates conflicts over reproduction in the more complex societies where workers can still lay eggs.

Worker policing has been discovered in the vespine wasps. Not only do they police, they can adjust their policing behaviour in response to their mother's mating behaviour. Mating behaviour matters because the number of males that the queen has mated with affects the relatedness equation for workers.

It might be too late in the evening for even Aristotle to keep up with this. I decide to take him through how mating behaviour affects the relatedness of workers to male brood, given the complications of haplodiploidy. Sketching out on a napkin, I explain how, when a queen is singly mated, workers are more closely related to their nephews than they are to their brothers (the queen's sons).

However, I continue, if a queen is multiply mated …

Aris whips the pencil from my hand with great gusto. 'Oh yes, let me do this one!' he squeals with delight. He sketches as he speaks: 'When the queen has mated with many males, the workers are more closely related to the queen's sons than they are to their nephews. And this is because the nephews are the sons of their half-sisters, with whom they may share as little as 12 per cent of their gene variants.'\*

---

\* The exact relatedness depends on the paternity skew; that is, how even (or skewed) is the share of eggs that each father's sperm gets to fertilise.

Between you (dear reader) and me, I am starting to feel the quirky mix of unease and delight that I experience when I realise my students are cleverer than me (which is quite often). Aris is now explaining to me the science of wasps; I am no longer the teacher.

'Ah, and now I see that it is simple: we expect colonies with singly mated queens to have no worker policing, but colonies with multiply mated queens to have lots of worker policing. Correct?'

Correct. Of course. I don't know why I am surprised, him being a genius and all.

The cousins to the *Vespula* yellowjackets are the darker *Dolichovespula*. All 18 species of this wasp genus share the same 'long face' (due to an extra-big space between their 'cheek' and mouth parts, compared to *Vespula*) that their name suggests. The Saxon wasp *Dolichovespula saxonica* is the perfect species in which to look for worker policing because its queens are sometimes singly mated and at other times mate multiply. Scientists used genetic markers to estimate relatedness among workers (which tells them how many times the queen has mated) and the maternity of males (which tells them whether males are queen- or worker-offspring). They found that workers in both types of colonies laid lots of eggs, but the workers treated worker-laid eggs differently depending on the number of times their mum (the queen) had mated. As predicted, worker policing was detected in the nests with multiply mated queens, but less so in the nests with singly mated queens.

Aris grins with delight. I am not sure whether this is because he is impressed with the experiment or that he's pleased with himself for guessing so quickly what the result would be. He's beginning to remind me of my best friend, the classroom swot I sat next to at school.

Worker policing by egg-eating is apparent in other vespine species, but the deeper we look, the more things crop up that are inconsistent with the theory of such policing. For example, in the multiply mated *Vespula vulgaris* we would expect worker policing: less than 0.5 per cent of workers in an average colony have activated ovaries, and their eggs are removed efficiently once laid. In fact, when given a choice, workers are able to selectively remove worker-laid eggs over queen-laid eggs. However, genetic analyses have indicated that workers were no more closely related to queen-laid eggs than to worker-laid eggs. Relatedness differences could not explain the selective removal of worker-laid eggs.

The hornet *Vespa crabro* provides another example. It has a singly mated queen and yet (contrary to the predictions of worker policing) workers eat worker-laid eggs. In other words, these insects are not responding to the relatedness pay-offs delivered by male maternity, as implied so perfectly in the honeybee and the Saxon wasp. The explanation may be that policing helps reduce colony-level conflict, and guarantees that workers work, rather than getting distracted by egg-laying; this results in more efficient and productive societies. Effective policing means fewer individuals act selfishly, and so it may help resolve the conflicts caused in the evolution of societies. Policing is not exclusive to social insects: in primate groups policing helps control group conflict; in bacteria, cells that don't cooperate are policed; and of course in human societies policing suppresses law-breakers. No matter what type of organism or society you are, without policing, cooperation breaks down. Maybe ancient Greece would have had fewer civil wars if they'd had police.

Aris appears refreshed by his switch to water.

'OK!' His voice is excited again. 'Now we understand why worker policing happens, can you also tell me how it happens? What is the secret used by workers to know their

relatedness to the queen or the eggs? Indeed, how do
workers tell a worker egg from a queen egg?'

Indeed, we do have answers Aris! Scientists have discovered that
queens produce perfumes – pheromones – that indicate their
fertility. But they also use pheromones to mark their eggs, like a
royal seal. *Vespula* queens, for example, mark their eggs with a
long-chained hydrocarbon, which gives eggs a royal perfume,
indicating to workers that they shouldn't destroy them.
Normally, workers can't produce this pheromone and so their
eggs smell different, allowing the wasp police to selectively eat
worker-laid eggs.

To test experimentally whether this really is the magic chemical that orchestrates worker policing, scientists artificially induced
workers to produce it. Like all social insects, *Vespula* queens have
high levels of juvenile hormone relative to workers and this is an
honest signal of their fertility. The level of juvenile hormone in
the body influences the cuticular hydrocarbon profile of an individual, including the production of this particular royal perfume.
If you apply a synthetic version of juvenile hormone to *Vespula*
workers, you can induce them to smell more like a queen and lay
eggs that look (in chemical terms) like queen-laid eggs. One of
the compounds that these workers overproduced was the magic
long-chained hydrocarbon, the royal perfume used by queens to
mark her own eggs. The eggs laid by the manipulated workers
were less likely to be policed than eggs laid by untreated workers:
the scientists had created workers that could cheat the system
and revealed the secret to worker policing.

Aris claps his hands and swivels a double pirouette in his
chair. He's tickled pink by this. 'I knew it,' he cries as he
jumps to his feet and proceeds to leap around the terrace,
flinging off his sandals as he frolics. 'Wasps are clever
indeed! Fancy using perfumes to police a city of proles.

Ha! But scientists can create workers that cheat their queen? Some would say this is the trickery of gods.' I am unsure which direction Aristotle is going with this. For a moment he looks a little scared.

'But I am no fool like them! There is no trickery here, or divine intervention: it is merely the power of the scientific method that reveals to us the wonders of nature. Ha!' Aris has the right to feel vindicated, famous as he is for being the 'father of the scientific method'. His lolloping has gained new vigour.

'You have told me marvellous things, my dear; your scientist friends have unearthed secrets that my friends and I could never have imagined. The bees certainly deserve to be revered, for they are clever, ingenious, resourceful and resilient. They count, they learn, they communicate – I won't forget those waggles!' He shrieks with glee as he waggles his own derrière, a mock mimic of a bee.

'And how incredible that they measure their lives in the threads of their beings – genes, you called them – and they change their behaviour to reproduce copies of their own gene variants through the bodies of relatives. They can even create male offspring without sex! And such impeccable methods to maintain law and order – that's why their societies are so successful, surely? How improved Athenian life would be if we listened to the bees and their ways.' Arms are flailing now. Fingers are fiddling with his trademark jewellery at tremendous velocity. Rings cling precipitously to bony fingers, desperate to belong as he throws his arms my way in an extravagant gesture.

'But to the wasps – I have to admit that it is a persuasive rhetoric. To compare the ways of wasps to those of the bees – that is good *logos*.' A pause. 'Why did I not think of that?' Beads of sweat blossom on his forehead, with a fleeting moment of regret for a missed opportunity, perhaps.

'It is remarkable how the bee and the wasp form parallel worlds of insect wonder. What astonishing architects wasps are, perhaps even more so than the bee. I had suspected that the organisation of their societies would share elements with the bee. But you and your scientist friends have such clarity in this: how "super-teams" of experts share tasks among themselves, but can adjust jobs as demand changes.

'Why, such organisation is far superior to Spiro's gastrin workers, who argue over who does what, and waste so much time complaining and being always late. Spiro should look to the wasps to learn how to manage his workers! Hey Spiro, did you hear that?' Aris runs to the edge of the terrace, shouting this in the direction of his favourite gastrin shop. He wipes his eyes. Are these tears of laughter, for his spirits are high? Or are they of nostalgia for the friends of a bygone world?

'And such tiny brains, with their neurones (is that the word you used?), allow these little animals to learn so well! My students would be amazed to hear how wasps can learn to recognise landmarks, changing colours and even human faces. Indeed, *my students* could learn a thing or two from those tiny brains.' He chuckles to himself, leaning jauntily against the terrace balustrade, taking a rest from his exertions. And then he's off again, skipping across the flagstones.

'Bees and wasps are so clever, but in different ways. Isn't that what makes them so intriguing and important? Wasps comprehend the world around them, but they are sensitive to different aspects of it compared to the bees. Sometimes the tools they use to understand the world are the same as the bees', but sometimes they are different. Of course, this makes perfect sense: bees and wasps fill different places in nature. Bees seek flowers, while wasps

Inside the nest of the European hornet, *Vespa crabro*.

Collecting hornet nests for diet analysis. The contents of larvae guts can be sequenced to reveal what they have been fed.

A nest of the African paper wasp, *Belonogaster juncea*. These elegant wasps are common across the African continent where they hunt caterpillars, making them possible agents of sustainable pest control for local farmers.

The heath potter wasp, *Eumenes coarctatus*, with a horse chestnut moth caterpillar.

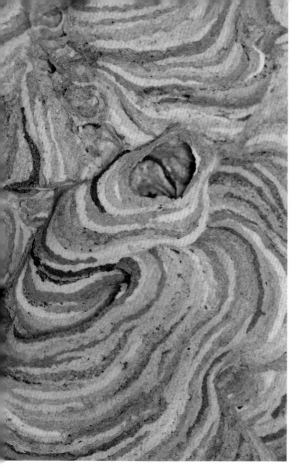

Yellowjacket wasp nests are architectural marvels. Varied plant materials are used to build them – garden fences, sheds, rotting wood, fresh stems – resulting in a colourful nest envelope. Inside are the brood combs, layered like a high-rise block of flats. Each cell contains a baby wasp.

The yellow-legged Asian hornet, *Vespa velutina*, preys on a wide diversity of insects, including foraging honeybee workers as they arrive back at their hive.

The solitary digger wasp, *Ammophila*, on the hunt for a caterpillar for her offspring to feed on.

Social wasps are generalist hunters – they hunt any insect prey that is in abundance. Their hunting habits mean they are valuable in both natural and farmed ecosystems as nature's pest controllers.

The oldest account of wasp pollination was communicated by Charles Darwin in 1870; tarantula hawk wasps, *Hemipepsis*, were observed sucking nectar from plants in South Africa.

22 genera of orchid rely on thynnid wasps for pollination. These plants have evolved to smell, feel and look like a female thynnid wasp. Male wasps can't resist attempting to copulate with the flowers, and in doing so they collect pollen which they transfer to the next flower.

Fig wasps have evolved a mutualistic relationship with figs. The fig serves as a safe nursery for the developing wasp brood. The fig benefits from the wasp carrying its pollen to another flower.

Larvae of social wasps provide adult workers with nutrition. But at the end of the season, when most larvae have pupated, social wasps need other sources of nutrition. They visit flowers for nectar and, inadvertently, help pollinate. Two hornets pollinating: *Vespa velutina* (above) and *Vespa crabro* (below).

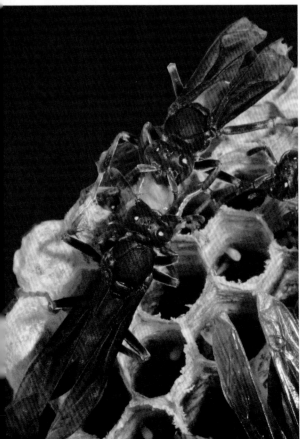

The 'night hornets' (*Apoica*) are an astonishing sight in neotropical forests. They spend the day on their nest, with their bright yellow abdomens warning off any predators. At night they go hunting!

Workers of the tropical paper wasp *Polistes canadensis* sharing prey to feed to their sibling brood.

seek meat. Each has *evolved* the right tools to ensure they excel in their work.'

The old philosopher spins round to face me, eyes rolling and bony gums flashing at me, as he says the word '*evolved*'; clearly pleased to have learned a new word, and a concept that helps explain so much of the natural world that was unexplained in his time. He swings onto the chair beside me, close enough for me to smell his cologne – a musk that would have covered a multitude of personal hygiene sins in his day.

Unexpectedly, he clasps my hands in his, a delicate assemblage of bones shrouded in rough, papery skin. I am staring into the hollows of the greatest philosopher of all time, wondering how it could be that millennia-old eyes sparkle so brightly. Behind the sparkle, I sense a shift in mood. The time has come for Aristotle to pass judgement on the progress science has made in revealing the secrets of wasps since his day: are wasps worthy of the same veneration as bees?

'My dear, the *ethos* presented by your scientist friends is compelling.'

I feel a 'but' coming. I am wondering if Aristotle knows about the 'feedback sandwich'. I use it all the time with my own students – squeeze the bad-news-tuna-mayo between two positive slices of supportive wholemeal bread.

'The ingenious experiments provide multitudes of evidence that is, to me, credible and compelling; even those American beating bottoms!' He adds this with a cheeky smile. 'What your scientists have achieved is incredible: how it is that they can fiddle with the brain machinery of insects, or train wasps to reveal what they can learn, is astonishing. That scientists are now able to read secrets in the fabric of their bodies – their DNA – to explain when and why they break the rules, is unfathomable to anyone except the gods. But this is no celestial mystery; it is the science of your times. And I am humbled by it.'

An earnest squeeze of my hands assures me he is being genuine in his admiration of the science of wasps. But anxiety lingers in his grip and the pupils of his ancient, clever eyes grow ever wider as he fixes me. I dare not blink.

'Now. To the *pathos*. Your emotional rhetoric is moving, my dear. I feel your frustrations and your delights – for this is the emotional turmoil I see churning inside you. I see how it consumes you in your quest to unfurl the secrets held inside the world of wasps. I see how anxious you are in your persuasion, as if it is your last chance. You feel you must impress me, perhaps others. You offer personal apologies for the holes in the science of wasps, shouldering a responsibility that is not yours to bear. You must direct this passion to persuade others to help bear the torch that has been lit by the science of wasps.'

No one has ever explained to me so clearly how I feel. Aristotle is right. I am on a constant high-octane mission to defend wasps, challenge perceptions of wasps, and especially to balance the scientific scales for the wasp against the bounty of scientific belovedness bestowed upon the bee.

I am not sure whether it is the remarkable empathy of my 2,400-year-old dinner guest or because I've not blinked for several minutes, but my eyes are certainly stinging with tears.

'My dear, this has been the most fascinating dinner I have had for a very long time.' I try not to take the context into account here, this being the first dinner he's had for over 2,400 years. 'The world of the wasp is most certainly wonderful. If I had my time again, it would be wasps that occupied my studies, alongside bees and humans. Please congratulate your scientist friends for me on the progress you have all made.

'Most importantly, do not give up. The world deserves to learn more about these creatures that hide behind their stings and difficult reputations. They are indeed one of nature's wonders and they must inspire future generations of scientists. The age of the wasp is surely upon you all.' I nod with childlike hope into Aris's sparkling eyes, and squeeze his hands more tightly. I don't want to let go of this wonderful, bony bundle of energy, wisdom and charisma, who fills me with such optimism and thirst to know more.

'I have one final word, my dear, that is missing from your rhetoric on wasps …'

The old philosopher leaps from his chair, dragging me to my feet, and spins me around the terrace with the carefree glee of a toddler on a bouncy castle, shrieking at the top of his ancient lungs …

'EUREKAAAA!'*

---

* A 'eureka moment' is used to describe the time when something wonderful, surprising or profound is discovered: Einstein's theory of relativity; Newton's apple and discovery of gravity; Californian gold prospectors; Fabre's 'mental revelation' on wasps; Hamilton's solution to altruism; a PhD student completing a late-night experiment in the lab. The word 'eureka' can be translated as 'I've found it'. It was in fact not Aristotle who coined the phrase, but another Greek scholar, Archimedes, who famously leaped out of the bath tub and ran down the streets stark naked yelling 'Eureka! Eureka!', after discovering how the displacement of water could allow the volume of irregular objects to be measured with precision. Despite being a great story, this is unlikely to be true. First, Archimedes never actually wrote this account; it was first written down 200 years after he died, and so is likely to have been embellished and 'improved' through many oral retellings. Second, a scientist of Archimedes' stature was unlikely to have arrived at such an important insight in the bath. He is more likely to have come to the discovery while exploring his laws of buoyancy, and by using precise measuring scales. It's just as likely that 'eureka' was used by all the great Greek scholars. Although Archimedes was born nearly a century after Aristotle, for the Aristotle at my dinner table, this word certainly feels right.

# Part Six

# *Nature's Pest Controllers*

If the benefits of nature are assigned no value,
then they are treated as having no value.

Dame Professor Georgina Mace, FRS (2014)

# Prelude

I fell in love with wasps because of their endless forms and fascinating behaviours. I got hooked on the complex drama of their soap operas, on how they provide glimpses into the evolution of social behaviour. I've spent the last 20 years telling people about this. They nod politely but still ask: 'Yes, but what is the *point* of wasps?' What they really mean is: 'What can wasps do for me? Why should I value them?'

For me, the enigmatic lives of these insects were enough: I didn't need another reason to value them. I shied away from the idea that we might have to attach a human-centric value to them. Twenty years on, I get that not everyone shares my fascination. We have an obligation to give people a reason to value wasps.

The concept of putting a value on nature was popularised at the start of this century, when conservationists shifted their efforts from measuring and managing threats, and limiting overexploitation of threatened species, to working out what ecosystems (interconnected communities of organisms and their physical environment) have to offer people. This approach focuses on the functions of these ecosystems, the value of the environmental 'goods' that they provide, and how ecosystems ultimately support and contribute to the quality of our lives. By emphasising such value, nature becomes an asset for us and that means we have a reason to care for it.

There are some sobering statistics on the state of nature and humanity's impact upon it. Up to a million plant and animal species are expected to face extinction within the next few decades due to human activities. Vertebrate populations have declined by 58 per cent since 1970; 322 species of terrestrial vertebrates have gone extinct since 1500 and the remaining species show on average a 25 per cent decline in abundance. Insects are doing equally badly: 33 per cent of species are declining overall. In the UK (which has some of the best records of insect populations), insects have declined by 30–60 per cent over the last four decades.

Species extinctions are not a new phenomenon: they have occurred throughout the history of life on earth, but current rates are 100 to 1,000 times higher than the background rate. This is especially concerning for insects, a group that has historically been remarkably resistant to extinction. It is the perfect storm of climate change, the loss of natural habitats, the spread of invasive species and an increase in intensive land-use by agriculture, including pesticides, which are to blame.

Why should we care if some species are declining or go extinct? Each species has a place in the fabric of natural communities; each species helps knit together the complex network of the ecosystem. Changes in the abundance of key species can trigger domino effects in others, cascading across whole ecosystems and sometimes driving them to the brink of collapse. The implications of declining biodiversity are much more severe than lamenting the loss of a wildflower meadow you remember walking through as a child, or the coral reef you visited on an exotic holiday. Natural ecosystems have a critical role to play in mitigating climate change, in maintaining air, soil and water quality, and supporting food production. Responsible stewardship of our ecosystems and the services they provide is paramount.

In the early 2000s the study of ecosystem services gave conservation biologists a new target for their endeavours: beyond protecting habitats and managing declining populations, they began scrambling to assign a value to nature in terms of what it does for us. What is the role of a particular organism in an ecosystem? Perhaps it's a pollinator or predator; or perhaps it recycles nutrients, tills soil or disperses seeds? What products does it provide us with? Is its 'value' to us as food, fuel or medicine? Or perhaps it plays an integral part in our culture and wellbeing by enriching where we live or recreate.

One way to value nature is in economic (monetary) terms. Pricing up nature's services can, however, open a can of worms. If the market value changes, does this alter how much we care for or protect nature? The answer is undoubtedly yes. A classic example is the value of pest control provided by Mexican free-tailed bats in American cotton plantations. Before 1990, free-tailed bats were regarded as very important because they were a key predator of moth pests in the cotton fields. However, in the 1990s cotton genetically modified with the bacterium *Bacillus thuringiensis* was introduced, which made the plants toxic to insects and the pest-controlling services of the bats obsolete. Over the next two decades, the economic value of the bats plummeted by 78 per cent. The moths have since begun evolving resistance to the genetically modified cotton, and so the economic value of the bats will rise again. But how can you justify a conservation programme on the basis of an ecosystem service that fluctuates so much in value?

Recently, there has been a shift in emphasis away from putting a price on nature and more towards recognising its broader benefits to people. This approach still considers the economic and ecological 'value', but crucially it also acknowledges how central and pervasive human culture is to valuations of nature and it elevates the importance of local and indigenous knowledge in understanding nature's contributions. The need to assess and promote knowledge of biodiversity and its role in human societies has been formally recognised in a global effort by governments, academic and civil society in the Intergovernmental Science-Policy Platform on Biodiversity and Ecosystem Services (IPBES). This work is essential to inform policy on responsible stewardship of the planet and its ecosystems.

We don't only count the good things that nature has to offer us; it's important to consider the bad things too, such as disease transmission and predation. But context is everything: a carnivorous animal might be viewed as beneficial under some circumstances – perhaps in helping control populations of wild deer – but detrimental under others because it might attack livestock. Cultural context is also critical: during my work in Malaysia, for instance, macaques were a real menace at the Hindu temples near our wasp field sites. I saw them destroy vegetation, rip up rubbish bins, intimidate passers-by and even steal people's belongings. Yet to the local people the monkeys have spiritual value because they are sacred to Hindus. Also, the animals had become so habituated to temple life that they behaved in a peaceful and compliant manner during rituals and ceremonies, reinforcing the positive emotions of worshippers towards the monkeys. Putting a value on nature, therefore, is complex. The interplay of economics, culture, context and ecology is critically important.

How exactly do wasps contribute? From economic and ecological perspectives, insects are well known for the beneficial contributions they make to people. For example, 88 per cent of flowering plants are pollinated by insects like bees, butterflies and flies. Such pollination is thought to be worth more than $250 billion a year worldwide, contributing to almost 10 per cent of the value of the world's agricultural production. Predatory insects are valued as biocontrol agents used to curb insect pests of agricultural crops, with an estimated worth of at least $417 billion per year. These figures are based on contributions to farmed crops, and so are very much the minimum wage for nature's services because they overlook the value of pollination and predation that these insects perform in natural ecosystems. Unfortunately, such estimates also overlook the role of many insect groups, including the hunting wasps.

Insects have important cultural roles too: our millennia-long relationship with bees, for instance, has strongly influenced the high value we give them, above and beyond their economic and ecological contributions. The less cheerful side of insects' contributions to people include their role as vectors of disease. Aside from the death toll, the annual economic costs of mosquito-borne diseases to humans is thought to be in excess of $12 billion. Many insects are considered to be pests, and culturally we are primed to fear such 'creepy-crawlies'.

Wasps are not known as vectors of human diseases, and they are only technically worthy of the term 'pests' when we end up transporting them to places where they don't belong, However, as we learned in Part 1, our cultural relationship with wasps is rocky. Would a better appreciation of their ecological and economic value help counter the sticky cultural relationship we have with them? Could we use a measure of their usefulness to influence this relationship, to see how wasps' contributions to people might match that of bees, say? At a time of heightened concern about the status of insect populations globally, turning our attention to the more enigmatic fauna – like wasps – has never been more important in our quest to understand how nature contributes to humankind.

In 1900, the schoolteacher and natural history writer Margaret Morley cautioned us to think about what a world without wasps might look like: 'The world could not afford to lose its wasps,' she wrote. 'How do we know but that the sudden extermination of the wasp kind might unbalance the whole solar system, and disorganise the universe generally?'

A world without wasps may not destabilise the solar system, but we can at least be sure that we would suffer without them. In the latter parts of this book, I'll explain why this is so. You may be surprised by the many positive ways in which wasps contribute to human life. They are predators, pollinators, decomposers and seed-dispersers. They are providers of nutrition and medicines. They are indicators of environmental health. The closer you look, the more you'll realise that wasps are an invaluable natural commodity. They deserve a better place in the blended world of humans and nature.

# I

'This is a good one – lots of brood, and not too many males!' Ruben shouted down the ladder from under his sweaty wasp-hat. It was 2019. Ruben was a master's student working with me. We were in Zambia, collecting nests of the social wasp *Belonogaster*. We were not sure what species we were working with – African wasps are practically unstudied, especially these elegant social wasps whose elongated bodies take the concept of the wasp waist to extremes. We had chosen them primarily because they are found in abundance nesting under the eaves of rural farm buildings and outhouses, and we'd seen them bring home big fat caterpillars to feed to their brood. Could this be where we'd find one of the secrets of how these wasps contribute to people?

Around 70 per cent of Zambian agriculture is family-scale production: grow your patch of maize or sorghum, treat it well, keep it safe and it will get you through the year. It's a hand-to-mouth existence in a country where the price of food in the shops is similar to that in the UK but the average daily salary is less than a dollar. A bad crop year poses a serious problem for a family. The challenges facing subsistence farmers in Zambia have just got worse. In 2016 the fall armyworm arrived in Africa. The name 'worm' is misleading: it is a lepidopteran caterpillar and a major global pest of agricultural crops, including maize and sorghum.

These caterpillars can cause complete crop failure. Farmers in the Americas have been tackling them for decades: they have created resistant strains of crops, a sophisticated factory industry for biocontrol agents, and have access to all the latest pesticides. Zambians don't. Genetically modified crops are banned in much of Africa; the continent lacks American-style industrial-scale agriculture; and the available (and affordable) pesticides are old, ineffective against armyworms and sprayed by hand rather than systemically, meaning that farmers are exposed to a nasty cock-tail of chemicals. The Zambian government has been heavily subsidising the use of these pesticides in an attempt to stave off famine in a nation already living on the edge of existence. There is an urgent need for a more sustainable solution to food security here, one that is kind to both people and nature.

Biological control (or biocontrol) is a method of pest eradication that exploits pre-existing predator-prey relationships. It is a key ecosystem service, alongside pollination, and has an estimated value of well over $400 billion a year. In the US alone, the value of natural biocontrol provided by insects annually is estimated to be $4.5 billion.

Parasitoid wasps – the ones that rarely sting – account for almost 50 per cent of the 230 invertebrate species that are commercially used as biocontrol agents. These tiny pest control-lers are like house elves – you never see them, only evidence of their work. We met them briefly in Part 1 as ways to eradicate clothes moths. For the price of a good bottle of wine, you can be the proud owner of enough *Trichogramma* wasps to strip your house clean of clothes moth eggs. Let them run free – don't worry, you won't even see them, their wing span is about 0.5 millimetres

– and within a few weeks, you'll be moth- (and wasp-) free. The wasps lay their eggs inside moth eggs, which then hatch and feed off the moth egg, killing it. The wasps can't survive without the moths and so as soon as the moths have been properly eradicated, the wasps will slip away as quietly as they appeared.

If you don't fancy having your home overrun by tiny wasps that you can't see, perhaps you might settle for using them outdoors to control caterpillar populations in your garden. Like a pick-n-mix, you can choose the species of *Trichogramma* you need for your personal pest problems.

Biocontrol by parasitoid wasps has proved revolutionary in agriculture. Take the mealybug – a type of scale insect – from South America. Mealybugs adore cassava, a cash crop that is nutritionally sustaining and grows well in the tropics, so long as the mealybugs stay away. In their homeland, mealybug populations are kept at bay by the 1-millimetre-long parasitoid wasp *Anagyrus lopezi*, which lays its eggs in mealybugs and nothing else. When cassava was first introduced to Africa and Asia to help feed hungry humans, everything went swimmingly, with both small-scale farmers and larger-scale industrial farms reaping the nutritional or financial benefits of this life-giving crop. That is, until the mealybug arrived.

It snuck in unnoticed by hiding in produce from its native South America and spread unchecked from one cassava farm to the next, causing 60–80 per cent reduction in crop yields. Asia's and Africa's cassava was only saved by a rapid introduction of *Anagyrus lopezi*, which within a year was being mass-reared and released over farm fields by planes to splendid effect. The economic value of this tiny parasitoid wasp to farmers across the Asia-Pacific has been calculated at $14.6–$19.5 billion per year.

Solitary hunting wasps (the ones that paralyse prey with their sting and carry it to a burrow to lay an egg on) are similar to parasitoids in that they tend to be prey specialists. In the late

1800s Jean-Henri Fabre (our star Wasp Whisperer) noted that all the caterpillars being hunted by the digger wasp *Ammophila* in his garden were of a single species: *Noctua segetum*, the common cutworm or turnip moth, a pest of root vegetables. Do you remember in Part 2 how an *Ammophila* wasp taught Fabre to find caterpillars hidden underground? The wasp would drum her antennae on the earth and he would dig for her. From this Fabre made the connection to suggest that agriculturalists could exploit the services of these wasps in pest control. By 'assisting her to multiply', we might benefit from these natural enemies.

Fabre was certainly onto something here. As specialist predators (just like parasitoid wasps), solitary hunting wasps offer great potential as biocontrol agents if they happen to be fond of the crop pest that needs controlling. Surprisingly, only four species of solitary hunting wasps have been adopted for commercial biocontrol today. The best known is the Emerald jewel wasp, *Ampulex compressa*, the ever-famous cockroach zombifier that we also met in Part 2. Less well known are two species of Bethylid wasps (*Cephalonomia stephanoderis* and *Prorops nasuta*) that are natural enemies of the coffee berry borer beetle, and another Bethylid wasp (*Goniozus legneri*) that is used to control lower navel orangeworm.

Unlike the parasitoid wasps, the use of solitary hunting wasps for biocontrol in non-native regions has not been very successful. The number of failed introductions of these species outnumber those that have been successful. This is probably due to a poor understanding of their life histories and behaviour; for example, it turns out that these wasps adapt rapidly to new conditions, such that when they are introduced to a new environment they often shift their prey preference away from the intended pest. If the contributions of solitary hunting wasps to people as biocontrol agents are to be harnessed, the best approach seems to be to adopt a local, native species. But for a group of such understudied insects of such endless diversity, we simply don't have the knowledge base to roll this idea out on a country-by-country basis at a commercially viable scale.

Using natural enemies to control insect crop pests began to fall out of favour in the 1930s when synthetic chemicals were developed to kill common agricultural pests. The bitter irony is that pesticides don't just kill the target pests, they also affect other wildlife that comes into contact with them, either directly (such as bees visiting crops that have been treated) or indirectly (like the bird that eats the bee that has foraged on treated crops).

Rachel Carson's 1962 book *Silent Spring* drew the attention of the American public to the hazards of pesticides. The impact of this book was (and still is) momentous, and instigated a movement calling for strict regulation of the use of these chemicals, influencing pesticide policies around the globe. And yet here we are today, still using pesticides, and still arguing over how damaging they are, despite the mountainous backdrop of scientific evidence. It's hard to understand why anyone would choose a chemical over a biological agent, especially one with such widespread success as that enjoyed by parasitoid wasps.

Yet there is a dark side to parasitoid wasps and their contributions as biocontrol agents. Parasitoids work best when used to tackle a specific host (pest) that they have evolved to exploit. Indeed, they are often rather fussy in their choice of host. Take the case of Africa's and Asia's mealybug-infested cassava: there was no native species of parasitoid wasp in those regions that was adapted to lay eggs in this alien pest, and so a non-native species of parasitoid wasp had to be introduced to do the job. Things can go wrong when you introduce an alien species. Aliens can behave unpredictably in novel environments because there are different selection pressures and opportunities to their native realm. The result is that they don't always stick to the job they were employed to do, and they can become invasive, an out-of-control population that is problematic for native biodiversity and humans.

Parasitoid wasps also require infrastructure and money to be produced and distributed. In São Paulo State in Brazil, for example, parasitoids are produced on an industrial scale in order to keep fall armyworm populations in check. Dedicated factories work year-round rearing tiny wasps so that they are available in their millions to be released into plantation deserts of maize monocultures at precisely the right time. These factories are owned by rich, multinational agri-businesses which can afford the considerable year-round investment that is needed to guarantee that there will be armies of parasitoids ready to disembark as soon as pest season kicks off.

It's both fabulous and terrible: fabulous because this is mass production of a natural biological enemy of the pest, and so reduces the likelihood that chemicals will be used in crop production; terrible in that it is only the large agricultural industries that can afford to factory-farm these miniature agents of control. For the small-scale subsistence farmers I met in Zambia, this is just a fairy tale.

The social wasps have enormous capacity to impact on local insect populations, if only because of the tens to hundreds or even thousands of committed hunters (the foragers) that head out to local fields, parks and gardens in search of prey every day. So it is not surprising that the idea of them being effective pest controllers has been around for over 150 years.

In 1868 the British physician Edward Latham Ormerod wrote the book *British Social Wasps*, the first monograph of its kind, which won him the accolade of being elected as a Fellow of the Royal Society.* It is a book written from the heart, for Ormerod, who wrote extensively on medicine and natural history, clearly

---

* To be an elected Fellow of the Royal Society is the scientific equivalent to an Oscar – a lifetime achievement award. Fellows include luminaries like Isaac Newton, Charles Darwin, Albert Einstein, Dorothy Hodgkin, David Attenborough and Georgina Mace.

had a soft spot for these insects. He broke with fashion to write passionately and excitedly about a facet of nature that even then was despised. He opens the book with a statement that remains relevant today: 'It is only those who have learned to love wasps as some naturalists love bees who will be at pains to understand them.'

Woven among Ormerod's meticulous descriptions of vespine anatomy, his wonder at the cathedral architecture of their nests, his musings over their social economy and how wasps sleep, he reiterates the notion that we are missing a trick by ignoring the pest-controlling prowess of social wasps: 'The practical result of destroying all the wasps on Sir T. Brisbane's estate was [that] in two years [time] the place was infested, like Egypt, with a plague of flies.'

This might well be the first reported experiment to demonstrate how social wasps contribute to people through their pest-control services. Ormerod goes on to describe how you could gather up 'handfuls of wings of insects' at every wasps' nest: 'If the benefit of insects to man is to be measured by the number of other insects that they destroy, wasps must be our benefactors indeed.'

Following Ormerod's line of reasoning, Margaret Morley in 1900 berated her readers for not giving wasps the credit they deserve for their services as fly-catchers: 'The butcher ought to welcome her [the wasp] as the small amount of meat she consumes is more than paid for in the large number of flies she catches, thus protecting him from one of the greatest nuisances he has to contend with.'

In the early twentieth century some dabbled with the notion of exploiting social wasps in agriculture. On colonial plantations in India and the West Indies, the idea of using social wasps as a natural way to control pests became rather popular. On St Vincent and St Kitts in 1913, colonialists reported anecdotally that when wasp populations were encouraged, cotton crops appeared less plagued by the lesser cotton leafworm *Anomis argillacae* and they saw less need for pesticides. Ten successful crop years of pesticide- and pest-free cotton production on St Vincent were attributed to the paper wasp *Polistes annularis*, whose colonies had been moved into purpose-made wasp sheds erected in the fields by the planters in 1900.

In the 1950s and 1960s agriculturists used this same idea, constructing wooden huts on the margins of crop fields and moving wasp nests in in an attempt to establish their populations as natural enemies of pests. In Japan, such relocation of *Polistes* nests into sheds on crop fields appeared to be associated with a reduction in populations of the cabbage butterfly *Pieris rapae*, with as little as a single colony of *Polistes chinensis antennalis* being recommended for controlling a starting population of five caterpillars among 100 cabbages in a season. In 1950s America, tobacco-growers under pressure to reduce pesticide residues in their plants spotted that *Polistes* was a dominant natural enemy of the tobacco hornworm (*Protoparce sexta*).* When they relocated wasp nests to shelters constructed on the edges of fields, hornworm populations were reduced by 60 per cent and crop damage by 74 per cent.

In all these examples, native wasps – species that were already in abundance locally – were encouraged. Using resident species as pest controllers meant that the predator and prey relationships were already in existence, and so there were none of the concerns that apply to introduced species in upsetting the delicate balance of the local ecosystem or hunting the wrong thing. These accounts suggest that nurturing populations of local, native social wasps can help reduce pest populations in crop fields.

---

* It's worth noting that this was not a sign of mid-twentieth-century environmentalism by tobacco companies, more that they wanted to reduce the costs of production and minimise residual chemicals that might affect the aroma for American smokers.

Encouraging though these descriptions are, the scientific effort in assessing the impact and value of predation by social wasps has been lamentable. At the time of writing I estimate that there have been 40 times more research papers on the ecosystem services provided by bees than social wasps.*

The focus on bees is understandable given their proven importance to both farmed and natural ecosystems. But this does not excuse the fact that compelling anecdotes from over a century ago on the predatory services of social wasps have gone almost unnoticed. If the same amount of research had gone into studying wasps as it has for bees, we'd have an idea of how much their services are worth to us and how much more potential they hold if we can learn to better harness their assets. In a world without wasps, how much would we have to invest to keep ecosystems balanced and healthy? How much would we be spending on pest-control infrastructure?

This information is *useful* if we want people to value the wasps living in their backyard, and it is *essential* if we want hunting wasps to be valued as an economic and environmental win in agricultural and natural ecosystems. At a time when our planet's biodiversity is screaming silently for a more compassionate relationship with people, it has never been more important to explore and embrace ways for us to work with the assets of nature rather than against them.

Could harnessing social wasps as natural pest controllers be a step towards a more sustainable, natural way of taming the relationship between nature and people? To answer this question, we need to know what social wasps eat, how much they eat and whether people are open to working with wasps.

---

* Note that this figure is specific to *social* wasps, and excludes the huge literature on biocontrol by parasitoid wasps and the small literature on biocontrol by solitary hunting wasps.

# II

'Look! It pulls out very nicely, just like a sock!' I was brimming with pleasure as I whipped out the gut from within a mound of voluptuous tissue.

Georgia looked at me, horrified.

She had just started her master's degree project in my lab at University College London, where she would spend the next eight months examining the gut contents of vespine wasp larvae. The day before, she had been trussed up in a bee-suit, reinforced with gaffer tape (wasps get in places that would never occur to a bee), digging up yellowjacket wasp nests in a London park. Today she was learning how to extract the guts from the larvae of the nests she had dug, and next she'd be preparing guts for DNA sequencing in order to find out what these wasps actually ate.

I think she might have been having second thoughts – the sock-like gut analogy was a step too far. But I have to say, it is so *very* satisfying to find the gut slides out so smoothly from a larva's inner sanctum. When it comes out cleanly, you are left with a thin tube of wasp gut, binding a Pandora's box of partially digested prey. These guts provide clues to the identities of the wasp's dinner.

We cannot put a value on social wasps as nature's pest control-lers, whether as biocontrol agents in agricultural fields or as population regulators in natural ecosystems, unless we know what they hunt. Recall that adult social wasps don't actually consume the prey themselves. They kill it before transporting it back to their nest as food for the brood.

The most obvious source of victims' DNA is from the dead bodies being dragged through the front door. Wasps are not the most subtle slaughterers, and they certainly don't try to cover their tracks. But their prey may have been brutally disfigured, so much so that you cannot use any distinguishing features to identify it. Often prey is too big to carry back in one piece. Ants solve this problem by teaming up to carry an oversized prize back to the nest. Wasps haven't mastered the art of formation flying, so transporting the quarry is a one-wasp job.

Smallish prey may be carried whole, but even these will have been munched a bit by the hunter in preparation to feed to hungry baby siblings. For bigger victims, bits will have to be chewed off; their disembodied portions may still be heavier than the wasp, though, and the hunter may need to make several trips to transport the whole prey item, limb by limb if necessary. An added incentive to chop up the kill before delivery is the juicy haemolymph (aka insect blood) that the hunter might snack on before serving it to the baby diners back at the nest.

Until recently, the only way to identify the victims was to dissect the chewed-up remains. Food balls of prey would have to be collected from foragers, intercepted as they arrived at the nest entrance, their stolen booty then cut up under a microscope. This method is tedious but it has gone some way to helping scientists pick out the prey types of social wasps. Remnants of flies, butterflies, moths, spiders, bees and ants have all been found, suggesting that social wasps have broad, eclectic tastes on the hunt. The fleshier and larger victims (like plump caterpillars or leggy spiders) are more likely to have been dismembered and filleted before arriving at the nest, making them harder to identify, and so these methods have probably favoured the identification of smaller prey (like flies, small bees and ants) that more often arrive in one piece.

Scientists are now able to interrogate the nature of wasp prey more deeply by looking at the DNA. Just as you'd sweep a crime scene for traces of the criminal's DNA, you can probe a mashed-up prey ball for DNA signatures of the unfortunate victim. This method is called 'e-DNA' – short for 'environmental DNA' – and it is used routinely by forensic scientists to pick up trace evidence at crime scenes. It has detected genetic material shed from saliva, skin, urine, poo (basically anything that might be left behind by a visitor) in soil, water, blood, snow or even air.

Using DNA barcoding – in which fragments of DNA ('barcodes') are sequenced – scientists can quickly work out who was present at a specific location. eDNA methods scale up this approach in 'metabarcoding', by which barcodes for a range of different organisms can be detected and sequenced. This approach has been incredibly successful. For example, sequencing river water uncovers the community of fish, bacteria, birds and crustacea that pass through; sequencing the blood sucked by leeches or mosquitoes reveals which mammal species are present in an area; and now scientists are sequencing dust (Philip Pullman should be pleased) and even air to identify which animals have passed through.

One of the first studies to use DNA barcoding of wasp prey explored the contents of the food balls brought back to the nest by foragers of a paper wasp (*Polistes humilis*) and a vespine wasp (*Vespula germanica*) that nest in the same areas in southern Australia. The scientists compared examination under a microscope with DNA identification of prey and found that the DNA methods added an important layer of information about the prey. The food balls of the paper wasps were comprised exclusively of Lepidoptera (butterflies and moths). This wasn't that surprising, as fragments of moth wings and caterpillars had been easy to spot under a microscope. But the DNA analysis confirmed that nothing had been missed by the morphological methods: there was nothing but butterflies and moths in their diet. The food balls of the vespines, however, were much more diverse: half of the prey were flies, and only 5–10 per cent were Lepidoptera. The prey also included bees, wasps, ants, spiders, grasshoppers, crickets and dragonflies. Flies and Lepidoptera turned out to be the prey types that were most missed by morphological identification, along with a cheeky bit of chicken and kangaroo, which would never have been identified under a microscope!

The mention of cheeky kangaroos highlights a messier side to the prey of social wasps. As well as catching live prey, they scavenge from decaying bodies. Carcasses are a brilliant source of amino acids, lipids, proteins, carbohydrates, vitamins and minerals, although you need to know your carcass well if you're after a specific nutrient, as the quality of these resources depends on who the deceased is and how long they've been rotting for.

Social wasps are so effective at harvesting delicious meals from rotting flesh that the local name for the swarm-founding paper wasp *Agelaia* – a common species in South America – is 'carniceras', which is Spanish for 'butchers'. Mammalian DNA has been detected from molecular analyses of adult wasp guts; wasps have also been spotted harvesting protein from reptiles, pigs and rats, and bird carcasses can be stripped to the bone within hours by the actions of social wasps. There is a bright side to this dirty secret: scavenging on carcasses makes social wasps useful decomposers and nutrient-recyclers. They also prey on the eggs and larvae of flesh flies, which colonise carcasses, and so are doing an extra bit in regulating fly populations where there is an abundance of rotting flesh.

Sequencing the contents of food balls is a fantastic idea, but it's still quite labour-intensive and open to sampling bias. You have to sit at the nest and manually catch foragers as they arrive, steal their prey and hope they don't take it personally. The food balls collected will depend on the time of day and weather conditions when the scientists were out collecting. But there are other ways of collecting prey DNA.

The wonderful thing about a wasp larva is that it doesn't poo until it begins its metamorphosis, via a pupa, into an adult wasp. This means a larva's guts contain remnants of everything it has eaten in its short life. The nest of a social wasp, therefore, is packed with hundreds to thousands of busily digesting guts, housed conveniently in individual larvae, that can reveal the secrets of what these insects hunt, especially if we throw some state-of-the-art molecular technology at it.

And this is why Georgia and I were pulling guts from vespine larvae.

Invertebrate guts have been the curios of many DNA sequencing projects over recent years: the hosts of parasitoid wasps and the tick's last supper have been uncovered by sequencing their guts. But the guts of those invertebrates contained only a single species. The guts of vespine wasps will be a part-digested cocktail of species from a broad mix of groups. The more complex the mix of groups in the sequencing pool, the harder it is to make sense of the data.

Metabarcoding methods have been used successfully on spider guts, which are generalist predators by virtue of their webs catching anything that flies by. Fourteen nests, 500 guts and a few stings later, we found out what the common yellowjacket wasp hunts (in the south of England, at least). As expected, *Vespula* wasps are most certainly generalists: we detected DNA from spiders, beetles, flies, butterflies, moths, bugs, bees, other wasps, ants, grasshoppers, lice, lacewings, dragonflies, caddisflies, harvestmen. All the usual suspects, and more: caddisflies and harvestmen had never been identified as wasp prey before. We were left thinking: Is there anything these wasps *don't* hunt?

While we were busy whipping out wasp guts in southern England, an intriguing method for analysing wasp diets was being cooked up on the other side of the world, where social wasps are, quite deservedly, unwanted. It is worth a small detour here to share a thought for New Zealand, where the diets of *Vespula* wasps have been causing some trouble.

New Zealand is a land of extreme natural beauty and home to many species that are found nowhere else in the world, but sadly it has been besieged by many alien species including wasps. Ordinarily, I would be deeply jealous of anyone who lives in an area that has such an abundance of social wasps: the UK offers comparatively little. But our Antipodean friends have had a rough ride due to the accidental introduction of *Vespula* wasps from the UK. Wasps in the wrong place can be ecologically (and socially) catastrophic, and the reason for this lies in their hunting behaviour. The case of New Zealand is a prime example.

The first *Vespula vulgaris* was spotted in New Zealand in 1921. In fact, this was the first record of the species outside its European native range. But it wasn't until the late 1970s that populations became properly established. Within 30 years, these invaders had completely altered the ecological balance of one of New Zealand's most precious native habitats: the beech forests. Before the wasps arrived, the forests were rich with an entwined cocktail of biodiversity – invertebrates, microbes, plant, soil and vertebrates all interconnected and protected by grandfatherly beech trees and a tiny, grubby-looking endemic insect with a messy habit.

The sooty beech scale insect (*Ultracoelostoma assimile*) is a true bug – a hemipteran. These bugs excrete a sugar-rich honeydew from their behind which attracts an eclectic mix of invertebrates and vertebrates who feast on the sugary droplets; in return, they defend the sugar bugs from predators.* The sugar actually comes from the plant, not the insect: the bug plunges its mouth parts into the tree, tapping into the sugar-rich plant juices.

This sugar solution bursts into the insect at such high pressure that the excess (of which there is lots) explodes from the bug's anus to hang from its behind as tantalising jewel-like droplets at the end of long waxy tubes. The beech trunks are covered in

---

* Bug-farming by other insects is a beautiful relationship, which evolution has repeated time and time again. You may have seen this in your garden: ants supping from the anuses of aphids. The presence of the ants deters predators who would eat the aphids and/or the plant.

white tubes, which droop ethereally from the tree: each one is an exceedingly long anus belonging to a single bug. Beautiful, sugar-drenched anuses. By being very long, the anus serves to keep the sugar-hunters – bats, birds, ants, bees – a safe distance away from the actual insect.

Any honeydew that isn't slurped up by a sugar-craved diner drops onto the bark of the beech tree, providing the perfect breeding ground for a black sooty fungus – hence the name given to the bug: the sooty beech scale insect. This fungus supports another chain of beautiful biota: beetles and moths feast on the fungus and its own secret microbiome of microorganisms. Along come the birds and lizards, many of which are found only in these beech forests, who munch on the moths and beetles. It's a beautifully balanced food web that revolves around an endemic bug with one long, sweet butthole.

Then along came the alien *Vespula* wasp: sugar-crazed and opportunistic, she feasts like a hungry teenager at a sushi bar who knows they're not picking up the bill. She slurps up the honeydew but also picks off the protein feasts – the other insects, the ones who (unlike her) have an evolutionary right to feed at the sugar-stranded tree. This precious, unique ecosystem has not evolved to accommodate such a greedy intruder. Wasp populations here can reach densities of around 10,000 workers per hectare, which is a biomass of around 3.8 kilograms of wasps! They reduce the standing crop of honeydew by more than 90 per cent during the main 'wasp season', which lasts for five months of the year.

Their ecological dominance has had cascading effects across the food web: they exclude other insects like honeybees that feed on the honeydew; they prey on the other invertebrates so voraciously that the chance of them surviving the wasp season is practically nil; they remove so much honeydew that there is little left for the native birds, making honeydew such an unprofitable resource for the birds that the wasps have effectively induced a change in the birds' foraging behaviour, or in some cases have driven the birds from the forest altogether.*

I mentioned at the start of this chapter that when putting a value on nature it is important to consider the dark side, as well as the bright side in their contributions to people. Aside from being a minor menace at picnic time in the summer, the only significant way in which wasps have a detrimental impact on people and ecosystems is when they become invasive, like they have in New Zealand's beech forests. In their defence, this is not just a wasp thing. Globally, invasive insects cost a minimum of $70 billion per year. There is even an official list of the 'World's 100 Worst Invasive Species', collated and maintained by the International Union for Conservation of Nature. Creatures on that list include European rabbits, cane toads, mosquitoes, water hyacinth, domestic cats, giant African land snails, common starlings and the fire ant. There are only two wasps on it (that's just 2 per cent of the world's worst invasive species) and they are the two that cost New Zealand in excess of $90 million per year. But in the grand scheme of things, wasps are not as detrimental to humans as you might think.

\*   \*   \*

* One small redeeming feature for the wasp here is that they may be inadvertently (and indirectly) sequestering carbon. In a well-balanced New Zealand beech forest without wasps, a lot of honeydew ends up on the forest floor, where it fuels a rich fungal community and associated fungus-feeders. The wasps' foraging means less honeydew reaches the forest floor. This results in a bacteria-rich community with an associated complement of bacteria-feeders replacing the fungal one. Rates of decomposition are slower in fungi-rich environments than bacteria-rich ones because fungal communities are more conservative in recycling carbon and nutrients than are bacterial ones. And so, these wasps are not only altering the above-ground biodiversity, they are also altering the below-ground biodiversity and associated nutrient cycle, sequestering more carbon in the ground than a forest without wasps. It seems that wasps invented carbon-offsetting long before we thought of it, not that this can in any way redeem the huge ecosystem imbalance these invaders are causing in New Zealand's beech forests.

The silver lining of having an invasive wasp problem is that New Zealand has become a hotbed of wasp research. Nestled in that silver lining are some secrets about what wasps eat.

The onset of wasp pupation is celebrated with an almighty big poo. The poo solidifies at the bottom of the nest cell into a hard black mat called the meconium. Social wasps usually reuse cells, and so it's no private latrine: the meconium constitutes layers of poo from several different larvae. Just as rock strata tell stories of the geological past, layers of meconium at the bottom of a wasp brood cell could provide an historical record of what larvae have been fed over a season. However, sequencing layers of excreted digested gut contents that have been decaying on a wasp nest over many weeks is no mean feat. The DNA is degraded, even more so than that of the larval guts that Georgia and I sequenced. Sequencing 'ancient' DNA (known as 'aDNA'), which is highly degraded and often in low quantities, is now pretty mainstream: if scientists can sequence the DNA from 450,000-year-old hominid remains, then month-old wasp poo should be trivial.

Researchers in New Zealand sequenced wasp poo from the nest cells of four species, all of which are invasive – two vespines (*Vespula vulgaris* and *Vespula germanica*) and two paper wasps (*Polistes chinensis* and *Polistes humilis*) – in order to explore how social wasps share resources. The hypothesis they wanted to test was first posed by none other than Charles Darwin. Using the logic that close relatives are likely to be ecologically similar, sharing habitat and food preferences, unlike more distant relatives, Darwin reasoned that close relatives should compete more intensely with each other than do more distant relatives. Among related species, therefore, you would expect one species to be displaced spatially (a nice way of saying 'physically pushed out') or to adapt their diets so that they occupy different ecological niches. Knowing how wasps share resources is really important in determining their role in regulating insect populations, and especially in working out how effective they might be as pest controllers in the company of close (and distant) relatives.

No one would wish for the invasion of four alien species, but New Zealand's unfortunate situation did provide a rare natural experiment to test Darwin's longstanding hypothesis. If food niches of relatives overlapped, there should either be competitive spatial displacement of one species in each congeneric pair – that is, only one species of *Vespula* and one species of *Polistes* nesting in any given spot – or, if you found species of the same genus sharing the same habitat, they must be pursuing different menus. Inside 148 old samples of poo, DNA from 105 prey species was detected across the four wasp species sampled on an island off the north-east coast of New Zealand.

The two species of *Polistes* appeared to be sharing the same hunting grounds but (at least partially) selecting different prey types: hurrah, Darwin was right (of course)! However, the two *Vespula* species appeared to be hunting very similar things. They managed to coexist by nesting in different places, with areas of the island that were mostly *Vespula vulgaris* and other areas with mostly *Vespula germanica*. Bravo to Darwin again: as predicted, these wasps were avoiding competition with each other by forming loose species ghettos across the island.

Wasps are eclectic hunters, but they are discerning enough to modify their use of resources in order to minimise competition with others who may share the same tastes. Some wasps (like the *Polistes* in the New Zealand study) do this by hunting different types of prey; other wasps (like the *Vespula* in the study) do this by hunting the same thing but in different areas. Being able to adapt and alter prey choice in response to their surroundings makes social wasps especially valuable as predators in natural environments, and suggests that they are unlikely to outcompete other organisms, at least in their native zones.

But this flexibility is also really useful if social wasps are to be harnessed by farmers for biocontrol. If a farmer knows how different species of wasps partition resources, they could manage the composition of the wasp community so as to maximise the wasps' pest-controlling potential. For example, based on this one study, if I had a farm, I would be happy to encourage native populations of both species of *Polistes*, because they will sort out among themselves how to share the prey types, but I would rather encourage just one species of *Vespula*, because if the two are mixed in close proximity they would be likely to compete.

What have we learned about the prey of social wasps? The bottom line is that they are largely generalist hunters, unfussy about what they catch and opportunistically catching whatever they come across. This may be a very good trait to have in natural ecosystems in which you would want to avoid having a dominant predator that might decimate local populations of a particular species. But do generalist hunters make promising pest controllers?

To find a good pest controller you'd typically choose a predator that specialises in your pest species, like the parasitoids or solitary hunting wasps. However, it may very well be their generalist nature that makes social wasps good pest controllers. In a meta-analysis of generalist arthropod predators (admittedly, none of which were wasps), 75 per cent of studies showed a significant reduction in pest numbers. In other words, generalist predators *can* have a surprisingly significant impact on pest populations.

Moreover, despite being generalists, social wasps still appear to favour a diet of caterpillars and flies, which also happen to be the most common group of insect pests. The very fact that social wasps are opportunistic generalists is a bonus: if there's a caterpillar plague in your field, you can be pretty certain that the local social wasps will be checking out that pop-up restaurant in town. Also, because social wasps are ubiquitous around the globe, you can be confident of finding a native species that is locally adapted to hunting pests. This means there is no need to import an alien species, and that there will be no unexpected inter-specific interactions or wider disruption of ecological food webs. You simply exploit the eclectic diets of the social wasps on your doorstep.

# III

Knowledge about *what* wasps eat is edging us towards being able to put a value on their contributions as natural pest controllers. But the critical missing link here is knowing *how much* they eat. Because of their large colony sizes, with hundreds to thousands of hunters and hungry brood in a single colony, social wasps have the potential to remove large biomasses of prey from ecosystems. Exactly how much prey does a social wasp nest consume?

Quantifying this is not easy. Almost all efforts to do so have been for invasive populations of social wasps, which (as we will learn) are not representative of the same species in their native zones. One place to start is to weigh the prey they come home with: prey biomass brought home by colonies of *Vespula germanica* in New Zealand has been estimated at around 1.8 kilograms per nest for annual colonies. Yet if these invasive wasps overwinter, as they occasionally do in New Zealand, nests become a lot larger. Biomass estimates from two such nests that overwintered were 26.6 kilograms and 99 kilograms of prey over their two-year life cycles.

Based on the diet composition for this species and the typical mass for the different arthropod orders, this would mean a single annual *Vespula germanica* colony in New Zealand removes around 18,000 caterpillars, 2,340 Hymenoptera, 3,300 flies and 18,000 spiders – a total of around 41,640 individual insects, for just one colony. For mid-sized overwintering colonies, the figures exceed this by an order of magnitude, with 630,000 caterpillars, 82,000 Hymenoptera, 115,500 flies and 630,000 spiders, amounting to almost 1.5 million individual arthropods being removed from the ecosystem by a single nest.

To understand the impact on habitats, however, we also need to consider how many nests there are. In these invasive populations, there can be up to 40 nests per hectare: scale these numbers up for even the most modest population densities and several million individual insects are being removed from each hectare every year.

On the other side of the world in Hawaii,* the experimental removal of wasp nests of another invasive species of *Vespula* (*Vespula pensylvanica*) resulted in a rapid increase in densities of spider and caterpillar populations, suggesting that these wasps were responsible for reducing spider populations by 36 per cent and caterpillars by 86 per cent. Such numbers are quite shocking, but they shouldn't surprise us too much: we already know that invasive species, including social wasps, have unprecedented impacts on the ecosystems they invade.

In a quest to understand the beneficial contributions of social wasps via predation, we need to focus our attention on the more typical situation of wasps in their native zones. Less is known about the biomass of prey that is consumed by social wasps on their home patch, but the numbers of insects and overall biomass consumed is most certainly much smaller than by invasive populations. Native homelands for *Vespula* are temperate, with short summers and cold winters, which means colonies grow more

* Hawaii is one of the only places on earth which was not naturally colonised by social insects – not a single termite, ant, social bee or wasp species was found there before we started introducing them. The absence of predators like ants and social wasps has been suggested as an explanation for the high proportion of flightless endemic insect species that persist in dense and largely unprotected populations. The godfather of 'sociobiology', Edward O. Wilson, called Hawaii a natural controlled experiment for the ecological and evolutionary effects of social insects.

slowly than in invasive zones and they rarely persist over the winter.

Without overwintering, colony size is reset to one (the new queen) every spring,* making the predatory impact of native populations somewhat more modest. We lack direct measures of biomass consumed by social wasps in their native regions, but we have some data on their colony demographics, which permits some back-of-the-envelope calculations about the contributions of social wasps as population regulators in their native biomes.

Here's what we know so far.

If there is one clear message to start with, it is that wasp populations, nest densities, nest sizes and sexual production in native zones vary hugely from year to year, making it difficult to put a figure on how much wasps consume. At the end of the UK summer, I am often asked by friends, family and journalists why there are so many wasps around this year. I am never asked this in a bad wasp year because no one is concerned if they haven't seen a wasp that summer. But it does not take a wasp expert to notice that there are good and bad years for wasps.

In 1789, the naturalist Gilbert White mused over the idea that there are abundant and scarce 'wasp years' in the UK. Other naturalists have noted similar possible cycles of couplets of years when *Vespula* wasps were abundant, and couplets when they

---

* A little recap on the life cycle of vespines. It takes a few weeks for a newly founding queen to ramp up her colony size, as she has to rear the first workers herself. Once worker production is in full swing, she stays home as a professional egg-layer, and leaves the dirty outdoor and grindstone child-rearing work to her daughter workers. The colony grows exponentially until late summer, at which point the males and sexual females (virgin queens) are produced. Around this time there are fewer larvae to feed, as most have pupated and don't need feeding. Workers have less protein-hunting to do, and they have to look a bit harder to satisfy their own nutritional needs as there is less of that yummy sugary fluid from the larvae. This is why in temperate regions you rarely notice social wasps until late summer, when furloughed workers start to get a little unruly at your picnic.

were scarce. Is there a two-year cycle in wasp populations? The plot thickened after some long-term wasp records from the UK suggested that it wasn't a two-year but a *seven*-year cycle of abundance and scarcity of wasp populations. Do wasp numbers follow seven-year (or maybe two-year) cycles of plenty and poverty?

Unfortunately, most of these reports were as statistically robust as the musing of an English village cricket team arguing over wickets at the pub in the height of summer. A twin set of long-term wasp data collected over 23 years in the UK and New Zealand tested these claims with some proper statistics, and relegated the two- (or is it seven-?) year cycle of wasp demography to the realms of wasp mythology. Certainly, wasp populations vary year on year, but this is due to the weather, and not a cicada-style multi-year cycle. *Vespula* wasps do well when there's a warm and dry spring and a not-so-wet winter, and if the previous year saw an abundance of wasps, this will have an impact too.

Estimating the densities at which *Vespula* nests occur in native regions is surprisingly challenging as they are hidden and cryptic, rather smaller and more spread out than in invasive zones, making them harder to spot. The best estimate we have is from a 32-year-long dataset on wasp nests destroyed at the Royal Horticultural Society's Wisley Gardens in Surrey, in the south of England.

Wisley is a fabulous spot for wasps, as well as plants. At this gardeners' dreamland, wasps have been aggressively managed for years in order to avoid them damaging crops of grapes, or the National Collection of apples, pears and plums (woe betide the wasp that gets between the English and a good Rosemary Russet). A total of 587 *Vespula vulgaris* nests were removed between 1977 and 2008 across the site of 97 hectares, with an average of 0.2 nests per hectare, ranging from barely 0.15 nests per hectare in bad wasp years to 0.74 nests per hectare in good wasp years: this is around 200 times fewer nests per hectare than found in New Zealand. We need to be cautious with these data as they are from only one site, and only based on nests that were destroyed, but it's the best we have for *Vespula* densities for native zones at the moment.

The next part of the equation concerns the size of nests: the number of brood produced and the amount of prey needed to sustain them. Over the course of the colony cycle in the UK, nests of the common yellowjacket (*Vespula vulgaris*) produce an average of 9,600 adult wasps: this includes 7,274 workers, 1,438 males and 890 virgin queens.* Because larvae don't poo, we can make the assumption that whatever a mature larva weighs is roughly equal to what it was fed. However, as a general rule, only 10 per cent of energy stored as biomass makes it to the next trophic level. So for every 10 grams of prey, only 1 gram is converted into wasp. Therefore, let's assume that a larva requires roughly ten times its equivalent adult weight in protein to complete development. The average worker, queen and male

---

* In 1973, biologist Philip Spradbery wrote the fantastic book *Wasps: An Account of the Biology and Natural History of Solitary and Social Wasps*. This monograph remains a rare and unparalleled resource on the nesting biology of European vespines. UK-born Philip removed his first wasp nest when he was 16. He moved to Australia in 1971, after his PhD on caste determination in British vespines at Queen Mary's University London. He spent the rest of his life working as a research entomologist, studying the threat of screw-worm flies to Australia's livestock industries and making award-winning marmalade. In between the orange peel and screw-worms, he remained a passionate advocate for European social wasps. His frequent media appearances earned him the nickname 'Dr Wasp', as he provided advice via a dedicated wasp hotline from his home laboratory. Philip understood the threats these invasive insects posed in Australia, not just to human health but also as predators of important pollinators of native plants. But he also appreciated the importance of wasps in their native regions. Philip's book remains an invaluable go-to source for vespine biology. Buried in his monograph on wasps is essential information on numbers of cells and wasps within colonies that I used here to estimate the amount of prey a native *Vespula* nest might remove in a season. Philip died in 2019; I am sad I never got to meet him.

weigh about 23 milligrams, 163 milligrams and 85 milligrams respectively. If we multiply these by the numbers of individuals produced, this tells us that the average yellowjacket nest needs a minimum of 4.3 kilograms of prey during its colony cycle. Using data from our UK gut-sequencing project, this is around 9,300 average-sized caterpillars, almost 20,000 Hymenoptera, 15,000 flies and 43,650 spiders (which generally weigh a lot less than other prey): a total of 87,950 arthropods per colony.

Even for the largest reported nests, the total estimated prey biomass needed is 6.5 kilograms, which comes in at just shy of 130,000 insects per colony. Based on the Wisley estimates of nest densities, *Vespula* wasps are likely to be removing over 30,000 arthropods per hectare and up to 234,000 per hectare in a good wasp year. These numbers are significant, but they are modest compared with the overwintering nests found in New Zealand.

In their native range, therefore, social wasps are important regulators of the wider invertebrate community and play a key role in balancing ecosystems. I am often asked whether wasps are contributing to the decline of other 'more useful' insects, such as bees and hoverflies. Based on these calculations, I think it's safe to say that social wasps are not contributing to the recent 'insectageddon', at least not native wasp species. They are unfussy, opportunistic predators who are likely to be creaming off the most abundant invertebrates they encounter. This makes them rather useful as general caretakers of ecosystems: they help keep a diverse community of arthropod populations in check, without hunting any to the brink of local existence. In natural ecosystems, this is an especially good thing. We can be pretty sure that a world without wasps would have a lot of tiny spiders and flies running around, whether you're in New Zealand or the UK.

# IV

It seems that Edward Ormerod was not being overly dramatic in 1868 when he described Sir T. Brisbane's estate as 'infested … with a plague of flies' after his local wasp nests were culled. There is no doubt that wasps play critical roles in regulating the populations of other insects. Despite this, we are today still failing to appreciate the wasp as part of nature's own army of pest controllers.

The case of the RHS Garden at Wisley is a fine example: the RHS spends time and money eradicating wasps from its gardens even today, although such management is largely limited to nests that may present a safety hazard to visitors and staff. But the gardens benefit from the natural pest-control services of foraging wasps to a minimum of 296,010 arthropods in a 'bad' wasp year, or a whopping 2,269,800 in a 'good' wasp year. These arthropods include many of the pests most feared by RHS gardeners – caterpillars, aphids, flies. There is a general awareness among RHS staff that wasps are a part of the biodiversity that healthy gardens support, but they admit that their management of wasps is not perfect. What a poster-child the RHS could be for the rising generation of biodiversity gardeners if they actively promoted local wasps as agents of biocontrol.

The situation at Wisley is far from unusual. Many farmers and gardeners are aware that wasps may be useful, as they hunt insect pests. But there's no handy pocket guidebook that explains how these wasps can be successfully managed as pest controllers, and where and when they are likely to have the most impact. I'd like to finish this part of the book, therefore, with a few words about this.

How effective are wasps at controlling pest populations? The anecdotes from the British colonies in the early 1900s were encouraging: they give us multiple reports of the presence of wasps on plantations being associated with lower levels of crop pest infestation. But it needed experiments that manipulate the exposure of pests to wasps to move these reports beyond correlations and anecdotes to scientifically robust evidence.

In 1980, American scientists relocated nests of *Polistes fuscatus* wasps into cabbage fields infested with caterpillars of the cabbage white butterfly, *Pieris rapae*. The average wasp nest consumed around 460–560 caterpillars within a season, and the presence of wasps resulted in a 62 per cent reduction in pest populations and produced heavier cabbages than in the absence of wasps. This proved to be the best evidence yet that wasps were effective biocontrol agents. It also transformed colonial anecdotes into concrete evidence on how wasp populations can be artificially inflated to access their predatory power as pest controllers in crop fields.

In 2019, we expanded on this experiment under more controlled conditions, meaning that we could be certain to exclude other potential predators of the pests. We relocated nests of the beautiful Brazilian paper wasp, *Polistes satan*, into a large screen house (like a big greenhouse, but with mesh insect netting as walls and ceilings instead of glass) and treated them to some maize and sugar cane plants infested with caterpillars of two lepidopterans – the fall armyworm and sugar-cane borer respectively.*

The wasps were able to detect the pests even when they were hidden inside the plants, suggesting they use odour to locate their prey. They chewed greedily into the plants to extract hidden quarry and would compete with each other for access to especially large, juicy caterpillars. Most importantly, the pest populations were significantly reduced and the plants sustained less damage compared with those from which wasps were

---

* The fall armyworm (*Spodoptera frugiperda*) and sugar-cane borer (*Diatraea saccharalis*) are two of the most economically damaging insect crop pests in the world, incurring several billion dollars of losses in crop yield annually.

excluded. This was the experimental evidence needed to prove that social wasps can be very effective as biocontrol agents of some of the world's most troublesome crop pests.

As discussed, one of the reasons why social wasps have been largely overlooked as effective pest controllers is because of their generalist diets. Typically, a crop will be ravaged by a single pest species, such as the fall armyworm in Zambia and Brazil. Does this make social wasps any use to farmers, who are only really interested in a biocontrol agent that will hunt their specific insect pest to extinction? How can they be sure the wasps will actually eat the intended prey? One aspect of social wasp biology suggests that this is not too much of a concern: wasps can fixate on an especially rewarding and abundant prey source to the exclusion of most other species.

Let's go back to that American cabbage field in the 1980s. The scientists repeated the same experiment with wasps the following year and the results were not so encouraging: they saw only a 27 per cent reduction in pest populations. However, while waiting for the cabbages to grow, the *Polistes* wasps discovered a rival 'supermarket' in an adjacent alfalfa field, where a smorgasbord of several different species of caterpillars lured them in. Even once the cabbages had grown and were bursting with their own healthy population of cabbage white caterpillars, three-quarters of wasp foraging trips were still to the alfalfa field. This highlights the importance of understanding the biology of a biocontrol agent and the context of its local environment: *Polistes* are opportunistic hunters who head for the highest prey densities and tend to fixate on previously rewarding foraging patches. Even if another prey pops up, it takes time for them to cotton on and switch type.

Natural biological systems are complex. It is important that we understand ecological interactions and behavioural plasticity in order to work effectively with social wasps as biocontrol agents. With an understanding of how they fixate on specific prey, wasps can be trained to favour pest types in particular areas. If the American scientists had known about this, they could have primed their wasps to fixate on cabbage white caterpillars in their experimental fields by providing them as a supplemental food while waiting for the cabbages to mature.

Exploiting social wasps in biocontrol has the potential to be useful to farmers and gardeners anywhere in the world where they occur naturally in abundance. But the people who might reap the most benefits are those living in areas where labour is cheap and chemical pesticides are relatively expensive, and especially in small-scale mixed-crop farming where pests may be more diverse. I'd like to take you back to Zambia, where we were exploring the potential for using local social wasps as pest controllers.

The vast majority of Zambian crop production is conducted on small-scale, family farms. It's a subsistence life with serious consequences for a family if their crop fails. Pesticides are applied regularly in order to minimise crop failures, and often these are old-fashioned, highly toxic chemicals that are sold in an unregulated manner. Many farmers lack a basic knowledge of the chemicals, the hazards and how to use them effectively and safely. Pesticide poisoning is a common occurrence, especially among women, who comprise 80 per cent of the agricultural labour force in sub-Saharan Africa. It is the women you will see in the fields, tilling the soil or spraying the crops with pesticides, often with a baby strapped to their backs. Reducing pesticide use here is not just of relevance to biodiversity; it is a humanitarian duty and one that goes to the heart of gender equality. Replacing pesticides in these farms with natural pest enemies deserves a lot more attention that it has received so far.

Social wasps are promising candidates for the sub-Saharan family farmer to reduce her reliance on toxic pesticides. Social wasps of the genera *Belonogaster*, *Ropalidia* and *Polistes* are abundant in sub-tropical/tropical Africa, and are ubiquitous in rural farming communities: a few nests will typically be seen on any one house, more if they've not been noticed and cleaned away. Their small paper-nest colonies lack the envelope of the vespine wasps, and are easily relocated into vespiaries – any form of basic open-sided shed would do. These vespiaries can be placed in a convenient location in crop fields, away from dwellings.

Because these wasps often nest in dense aggregations, you can establish a wasp hub consisting of several nests and many hundreds of foragers. Recall how a single nest of *Polistes* would hunt over 500 caterpillars in that American cabbage field. Scale this up and you'd soon have an army of elegant pest controllers working away in the fields. Little equipment or training would be needed: a pair of washing-up gloves, a home-made wasp hat and a long-sleeved shirt and trousers will protect from stings; a good strong zip-lock bag and some tape or glue is all that is needed to relocate the nests.

I won't pretend there wouldn't be teething problems: wasps in these parts of the world are especially understudied and we have already learned the importance of understanding the complex web of ecology. But the building blocks are there. Social wasps could be nature's gift to the subsistence farmer, especially if they were integrated into a wider programme of conservation agriculture with habitat restoration providing oases of biodiversity alongside crop fields.

The idea of taming the much larger yellowjacket or hornet nests for biocontrol might sound a little more challenging. Not so: in rural communities of Japan and India, such husbandry methods have already been honed to perfection, not for biocontrol but as sources of nutrition. To understand this better, you need to meet Ngalengshim, who lives in a tiny village in the hills of Manipur, in north-east India. He is part of a village cottage industry built on ancient traditions and practices. Here they capture colonies of the giant Asian hornet, *Vespa mandarinia*, and farm them for their brood.

Wasp larvae are rich in protein and low in fat.* Insect protein is a viable healthy alternative to eating meat and insect-farming a realistic solution to global food security concerns. Ngalengshim's community have perfected the art of rearing these wasps safely and effectively. Similar approaches are practised with yellowjacket wasps in rural communities in Japan, where wild *Vespula* colonies are collected from the forest each spring, set up in a type of wasp hive, and nurtured until the end of the season whereupon the sexual brood (which are much larger than the worker brood) are harvested for a tasty meal. In some parts of Japan, these wasp brood sell for $100 per kilogram. It is a small step to adopt these same husbandry methods to harness the immense predatory power of these wasp colonies in the crop fields.

---

* A word about farming insects for food. Per unit of consumable protein, insect-farming is twice as efficient as rearing chicken, at least four times as efficient as pig meat and 12 times as efficient as cattle meat. For every gram of protein, insect-farming uses 17 times less water than cattle, and five times less than pig- or chicken-farming. Compared to traditional livestock, insects emit fewer greenhouse gases and ammonia, consume less water, take up less space and have fewer welfare issues. At least 2 billion people across the globe consume insect protein as part of their diet – it's called entomophagy. Over 2,000 insect species are eaten, with beetles (31.1 per cent), butterflies and moths (17.6 per cent) and wasps, bees and ants (14.8 per cent) being the most prominent. Wasps account for 4.8 per cent of the insect species consumed, with 98 wasp species reported being eaten across 19 countries (but the number is probably a lot more as they are often not identified). Wasps are usually eaten as larvae or pupae, and social species, like the Asian giant hornet, are especially popular because of the bonanza prize of thousands of brood from a single nest. They are a popular street food in East Asia, Africa and South America, and in rural China wasps are the most common edible insects for sale. Amino acids extracted from hornets have long been used as a nutritional supplement, with reported benefits for endurance during exercise. Asia, Africa and South America have long traditions of wasp-based entomophagy; demand is so high that the wasp-food market has to be supplemented from other countries such as China, New Zealand and the Republic of Korea. Furtive prospectors from Japan make regular trips to New Zealand to harvest the super-sized invasive yellowjacket wasp nests.

Social wasps as biocontrol have a lot going for them. But there is quite a large elephant in the room that I've been ignoring. It doesn't matter how good these insects are as biocontrol agents if people are not prepared to work with them. Will the knowledge that social wasps can be of use to people through biocontrol be enough to persuade us to tolerate them, and to invest in learning how to work with them safely?

If we can overcome our fears of honeybees and their stings, we can surely do the same for wasps. There may be additional unexpected bumps along the way – in some cultures wasps are tied up with witchcraft or religious beliefs, for example. A successful relationship with wasps will need to surmount cultural mountains as well as the biological ones. Only then can social wasps be universally welcomed as the farmer's friend.

There is now no doubt that the chemicals we use to keep our crops free of insect pests are detrimental to wildlife, ecosystems and human health. We need to be looking for more sustainable approaches to agriculture, and to at least minimise our reliance on harmful chemicals. If you're one of the industrial-scale agricultural giants, you can afford to mass-produce parasitic wasps in factories and deploy them in their millions into your green seas of agricultural monoculture.

But if you're a subsistence-level farmer, and especially if you're in a developing country, it's worth considering the local social wasps as your doorstep pest-controlling friends. Their biology, behaviour and life cycles suggest that they have tremendous untapped potential as an environmentally friendly, low-cost, low-tech solution to pest control. There is still a lot to learn, but I hope I've made a case for exploring the role of social wasps as the future farmer's best friend.

This is why a few of us, at least, are still up ladders in the agricultural homelands of Zambia (and Brazil, Nigeria and Cameroon), playing with wasps.

# Part Seven

# *The Secret Pollinators*

There are certain flowers that may be justly
called wasp-flowers, because the head of the
wasp and the cup of the flower fit each
other so prettily.

Margaret Morley,
*Wasps and Their Ways* (1900)

# Prelude

To many people the term 'insect' is synonymous with 'pollinator'. This implicit link is driven by the wide research and public focus on the importance of insects such as bees as pollinators, their contributions to the pollination of human-cultivated crops, and the recent concerns about how global declines in insect populations might affect these services. Over 75 per cent of crops worldwide directly depend on insects as pollinators, making insect pollination worth over $250 billion per year globally.

Without insect pollinators we would lose between 5 and 8 per cent of all crop production. This might not sound huge, but in the last five decades our pollinator-dependent global agriculture has grown twice as quickly as agriculture that does not depend on pollinators. To people like me in a country like the UK, loss of pollinators would present some annoying first-world sacrifices, like no morning coffee or chocolate treats, no rapeseed oil with which to cook my kids an evening meal and no comforting bedtime hot cocoa.

On a more serious level, without insect pollination the economic and health costs would be catastrophic. Pollinator-dependent crops are sources of important micronutrients including vitamins A and C, folic acid, calcium and fluoride. Without these nutrients there would be surges in global levels of preventable diseases. For example, scientists estimate that pollinator losses could result in around 1.4 million additional deaths due to heart disease.

The effects of pollinator losses would be felt most acutely by people living in poorer regions and who are already challenged by malnutrition. Areas like western, northern and central Africa have been identified as especially vulnerable, because millions of people there rely on effective pollinator networks to sustain family-scale smallholdings. Beyond food, we also have insect pollinators to thank for the production of biofuels (from things like sunflowers, soybeans and oilseed rape), food for livestock, construction materials, medicines and culturally important materials for musical instruments, arts and recreational activities, including the flower-rich green spaces that we enjoy. Pitched alongside malnutrition and starvation, these latter commodities might seem trivial, but there is growing evidence for the positive direct effects that pollinators have on things that influence our wider wellbeing, mental health and happiness.

The importance of pollinators to wild ecosystems is even harder to quantify: more than 90 per cent of tropical flowering plant species and around 78 per cent of temperate plant species rely at least in part on animal pollination. Scientists are still struggling to work out how to factor these commodities into estimates for the value of insect pollinators because the economic value of natural ecosystems is less tangible. Even more elusive are the contributions made by pollinating insects that are not bees, hoverflies or butterflies. Let's look at the relationship between wasps and plants, and how their contributions to pollination are missing from current valuations of insects in ecosystems.

# I

If I asked you to name a pollinating insect, my hunch is that it wouldn't be a wasp. It would most likely be a bee. Bees certainly deserve a good share of the pollinator footlights fame-list: more than 90 per cent of the leading 107 global crop types are pollinated by bees. The reason why bees are so great at pollinating is because, unlike *almost* any other insect, bees go out of their way to collect pollen: some (the corbiculate bees) have evolved specialist pollen-collecting, big fat rear legs ('pollen baskets') and they also often have hairy bodies which become easily coated in pollen dust.

The western honeybee *Apis mellifera* is the most versatile of the pollinators and it is the species that we have our longest cultural relationship with. Although originally native to Eurasia and Africa, *Apis mellifera* now has a cosmopolitan distribution, having been introduced almost worldwide. In the last five decades the number of honeybee hives has increased globally by 45 per cent. The honeybee's popularity should come as no surprise: they are easily managed, relatively unfussy about the flowers they visit, and have the double benefit of being a producer (of honey and wax) as well as a servicer (as pollinator).

For rural communities in at least 50 countries around the world, beekeeping has deep cultural roots, with honey products providing livelihood security and helping alleviate poverty. In parts of Europe and the USA, bee-farming is industrial in scale: famously, thousands of honeybee hives are trucked tens of thousands of kilometres across continents to follow seasonal changes in pollination of crops, from almonds and alfalfa to broccoli and squash. Similarly, hives are shipped between countries to exploit peak bloom periods and maximise honey yields. In other words, honeybees are worked hard for their honey and their pollinating services. And they are exemplary employees.

But there's a cost to this. Such intensive honeybee management is threatening native pollinator-plant networks. A recent study compared wild pollinator communities with and without honeybees in Teide National Park in Tenerife, one of the Canary Islands. Up to 2,700 beehives are moved to the park every year to take advantage of spring blooms for prime honey production. In a year when the beehives were not introduced to the park, scientists conducted an experiment to compare spring pollinator-plant communities with and without honeybees.

They found that native pollinators (insects like beetles, solitary bees and hoverflies) visited flowers less often in the presence of honeybees. This is because honeybees visit flowers frequently, making them collectively efficient at draining flowers of nectar, leaving little for other insects. To make matters worse, honeybees are generalist foragers and so it's not just a small selection of plants that they drain dry: in this particular study, honeybees visited more plant species (13 of the 17) than any of the other insects recorded. This means the whole pollinator-plant network shifts when the honeybees arrive, with fewer interactions between insects and plants, and an overall simplification of the pollination network. The effect on native pollinators was a devastating hit on their diversity, which in turn saw lower reproductive success, and hence diversity, of the plant community. In short, habitats dominated by honeybees show a much-depleted ecosystem function.

This study is just one of dozens that are documenting how our obsession with managing honeybees (for their services) may be having serious long-term negative impacts on natural ecosystems. This isn't too much of a surprise if we remind ourselves that honeybee-farming is like any other large-scale agricultural product. The honeybee is the cow of the insect agricultural world: we select the breeds that produce the most honey, with the most prolific and efficient worker forces, along with docile, non-swarming queens.

But times are changing. The western honeybee is one species of around 22,000 species of bees, all of which visit flowers and pollinate. In fact, around 50 bee species are already managed for their pollination services, with 12 being used on a regular basis. Bumblebees, for example, are popular choices for greenhouse pollination. Anyone can easily purchase colonies online or even at garden centres and they require much less skill and management than does a honeybee colony. Over a million commercial bumblebee colonies are shipped around the world today to pollinate a wide range of crops, but especially those belonging to the solanum family (which includes tomatoes, potatoes and aubergines) and capsicums (peppers and chillies).

These plants cannot be pollinated by honeybees because the pollen can only be dislodged if the flowers are vibrated vigorously. Bumblebees and some solitary bees do this by buzzing their flight muscles rapidly, causing the flower to shake, in a process called sonication or buzz pollination.

Solitary bees are not thought to be as useful as social species for commercial-scale pollination because their populations tend to be less dense and more prone to local fluctuations in nesting success. Despite this, a few species are marketed as farmer's friends, including the leafcutter bee (*Megachile rotundata*) and Alkali bees (*Nomia melanderi*), which are both excellent pollinators of alfalfa, and *Osmia* bees, which are useful pollinators of fruits such as apples and nuts such as almonds. Another 700 species of wild solitary bees have been recognised for their contributions to crop pollination. You may even be encouraging some of these species in your own backyard: a sprinkle of special bee-friendly flower seed mixes promises to attract native bees to your garden, or perhaps you've installed a luxury solitary bee hotel.

But the pollinators that contribute to people reach far beyond honeybees and fancy bee hotels. Flies, beetles, moths and butterflies are all renowned for their pollination contributions to both crop flowers and wildflowers. Non-bee pollinators have been poorly studied relative to bees, but change is afoot.

Flies were recently identified as the most abundant crop pollinator, after bees, and they visit a wider range of crops than other groups like butterflies and moths. A variety of flies, such as hoverflies or drone flies, are now commercially reared and managed for crop pollination, and you can purchase your own culture. They are sold primarily to the European fruit and vegetable industry as a nature-inspired pollination solution that is 'economically viable and environmentally sustainable'. Hoverflies have many generations per year, producing many thousands of eggs per female. They also pollinate more than 500 different plant species. Taken together, hoverflies undoubtedly provide a credible alternative to honeybees and bumblebees. An added bonus is that the larvae of some hoverflies are also biocontrol agents, effective in controlling pests such as aphids, whitefly, thrips and spider mites.

After bees and flies, butterflies are the next most regular visitors of flowers. But how effective are they in transferring pollen? Their spindle-thin legs and exuberant tongues prevent close contact with the flower, and so little pollen collects on their bodies. But pollen clings to those long legs, and butterflies tend to fly further and carry pollen further away from the parent plant than other insects, so that saplings aren't competing to grow under the shadow of their parent plant.

Despite their beauty and their long-legged flights, butterflies are not greatly valued as commercial crop pollinators, but this may be about to change. Cotton can (and does) self-pollinate, yet cotton plants can also mate through the transfer of pollen from one plant to the stigma of another – a process known as cross-pollination, mixing up gene pools across plants. Genetic diversity is good for farmers: cross-pollinated plants produce cotton 'bolls' that are 20 per cent heavier. In 2021 scientists found that cross-pollination mediated by butterflies was contributing $120 million per year to cotton crop harvests in Texas alone.

Bees and hoverflies also contribute to cotton pollination, but they visit the flowers at different times of day to the butterflies. Cotton flowers remain viable for only a few hours, and so every pollinator-minute matters for the plant's success. A tripartite pollination network of hoverflies, butterflies and bees is segregated politely in time and space. Flies take the early-morning shift, then come the butterflies who take up the same locations on the outer parts of the plant as their early-morning counterparts. Bees don't arrive until the sun is properly up, and when they do they tend to visit flowers near the centre of the plant. Altogether, these insects straddle the full flowering time and the distribution of flowers on the plant.

It's not just the cotton farmers who are rubbing their hands in delight at this orderly use of time and space: ecologists are also pleased because it is an excellent example of functional complementarity, a term they use to describe how insects divide their services (in this case pollination) across multiple functional axes (in this case time and space). The diverse traits of the different pollinators mean that collectively they are likely to be providing a more consistent and robust service under variable environmental conditions. With the effects of climate change, robustness of pollination services to environmental variation is becoming ever more important. In an industry that generates over $7 billion per year, it's astonishing that it took until 2021 for someone to bother to work out which insects are responsible for the cross-pollination of cotton.

# II

Bees do it; hoverflies do it; even butterflies and beetles do it. It should be no surprise that wasps do it too. In fact, some of the most enchanting and incredible evolutionary stories about pollination involve wasps. Let's open the storybook of wasps and their extreme relationships with plants.

Fig wasps are a group of tiny, non-stinging parasitoid wasps whose entire life cycle revolves around (you guessed) figs. It's a two-way mutualism, a co-evolved dependence by both wasps and figs: without these minuscule insects there would be no figs but, equally, without the figs the wasps cannot complete their life cycle. Figs are quite marvellous. They are to ecosystems as Gandalf is to hobbits: a vital guardian. With their sumptuous fruits they sustain thousands of species of frugivorous mammals, birds and insects, and in return they benefit from having their seeds scattered widely.

Fig trees can help us curb our destruction of the natural world, because they are brilliant pioneers for reforestation efforts and are important in supporting urban wildlife. The fig itself is actually an enclosed flower head, an urn-shaped structure that contains thousands of very simplified flowers. The fleshy urn walls mean the precious reproductive structures of the fig are well protected from predators and parasites since the only entrance is narrow and encrusted with scales, making it almost impossible for anything to reach the fig's inner sanctum. Luckily, a family of specialist pollinators have bounced along hand in hand with this peculiar plant through its evolutionary journey: these are the aganoid wasps, or fig wasps.

When a female wasp infiltrates a fig fruit, she scatters hundreds of eggs. Inadvertently she also carries on her body pollen from her own fig nursery, which gets wiped onto the stamens (reproductive parts) of the fruit. After egg-laying, the female wasp dies and is absorbed by the fig.* Baby wasps grow up inside the fig, alongside the fig seeds that develop in the pollinated flowers. Male fig wasps hatch first. They are wingless and have a single function: to mate with their sisters. If insect incest wasn't enough, it is also sex without consent because males mate with their sisters who lie captive in their figgy nursery.

In a last-ditch attempt to redeem their gallantry, males then carve exit tunnels through the flower head. The exit tunnels are not for the males: these boys never see daylight – they live their entire lives in the maternity ward of the fig, and die once the tunnels have been completed. The tunnels are for their mated sisters to escape the chamber of infant incest. Freshly mated females romp deliciously around the fruit, coating themselves in pollen before exiting via the tunnels in search of their own fig maternity ward to pollinate.

The fig-wasp story is 75 million years old, making it one of the most ancient of evolutionary friendships as well as one of the most extreme. Within its story are coordinated patterns of genomic evolution in the genes responsible for morphological development in the plant, and those that control organ development and body size in the wasp. Until recently, the fig-wasp evolution story was thought to be a perfect friendship of fidelity, with each fig having its very own devoted wasp genus, committed to a marriage of single-partner pollination and unwavering loyalty. Genomic analyses, however, have revealed that this flawless fairy tale of co-evolution is not so perfect: there's been a lot of host-switching and fig hybridisation in its evolution. Infidelity has driven the evolution of the

* So, contrary to much media hype, you are not likely to be munching dead wasps when you eat a fig. The fig produces an enzyme called 'ficin' that digests the wasps completely. Ficin is so effective at digesting animal proteins that people from native tribes in Central America eat fig sap to treat intestinal worm infections. Perhaps this means figs are vegan-friendly after all.

enormous diversity in both figs and wasps. Indeed, the fig genus *Ficus* is one of the most diverse of the woody plant genera, with over 800 species described and as many species of pollinating wasps.

Where would we be without fig wasps? Superficially, there would be no figgy pudding, no fig bruschetta, no fig-infused tagines. Economically, the hit would be a bit more painful, especially for countries like Turkey, whose fig exports are worth almost $300 million per annum. In 2019, the world fig trade was valued at almost $600 million (that's around 162,000 tonnes of figs), making them the world's 2,551st most-traded product (out of 4,648).

Because of their tiny size (1–2 millimetres) and short adult life (one to two days), fig wasps are thought to be especially vulnerable to global warming. Experimental rearing of tropical fig wasps at a range of global warming scenarios has suggested that an increase of 3°C or more would reduce the active lifespans of adults: with every 2°C increase in temperature, fig wasps were between 1.4 and 2.6 times more likely to die. Shortened lifespans mean they would have less time to locate a receptive host, pollinate and lay eggs. The knock-on effect to fig plants could be devastating. Given the importance of fig plants in natural and human-modified environments, the health of these tiny pollinators should be of great concern to us.

In truth, the damage to the fig industry is the least of our concerns, as growers can still trick figs to ripen in the absence of wasps by spraying them with plant hormones. But the most lamentable loss would be the hard work of 75 million years of evolutionary history and the incredible biodiversity it has produced: remember it's not just the fig plants (around 800 species) and the wasps (around 800 species), it's the Gandalfian guardianship that fig trees provide to whole ecosystems. The lost ecosystems supported by figs would have knock-on effects across multiple trophic levels, disrupting wider bionetworks. Let's hope the short generation time of fig wasps provides them with the evolutionary advantage they need to adapt.

You will have remembered, I hope, that bees are just wasps that have forgotten how to hunt. Just to confuse you, I'm now going to tell you that there are also wasps that have forgotten how to hunt. The Masarinae are vespid wasps that look deceptively similar to their flesh-hungry relatives, but in fact they are gentle vegetarians who wouldn't know what to do with a juicy caterpillar or voluptuous fly if you served it up to them on a plate. All 350 species have lost the ability to hunt and instead collect pollen and nectar from plants, using their long bee-like proboscis (tongue). It is no surprise that they are known as 'pollen wasps'.

Why are these wasps and not bees? They don't have the bees' pollen baskets on their hind legs. Instead, they store pollen inside their bodies in a special gut cavity called the crop.* Back at the nest, the pollen wasp regurgitates the pollen, mixes it with a little nectar and places it in a pre-prepared cell with a freshly laid egg. Retaining the vespine-like appearance of their close relatives probably helps ward off predators. Pollen wasps are patchily distributed in parts of Africa, western USA, Central and South America, Australia, parts of southern Europe and the Far East including China. In fact, the only continent they're not found on is Antarctica. With such a cosmopolitan reputation you'd think we know a fair bit about them, yet unfortunately they are among the least well-studied wasps. They were once thought to be quite rare, but the reality is that if you look, you'll find them in abundance. A hotspot for pollen wasp research (and, as it turns out, the wasps themselves) is South Africa, and

---

* Bees can also store pollen in their crops. These are the colletid bees of the subfamilies Euryglossinae and Hylaeinae. Most other bees store pollen on their bodies, in their pollen baskets.

it is from here that we can learn more about these wasps and their contributions to pollination.

Are pollen wasps any good at pollinating? There are several reasons to think they are. First, the brood of pollen wasps are reared exclusively on a pollen-nectar mix of food. This means that provisioning mothers make more visits to flowers than do carnivorous wasps, who only sip nectar for their own personal pleasure. Second, pollen wasps appear to be rather particular in their choice of flowers, more so than other pollinating insects. Ninety per cent of the plants they visit belong to just two families: Aizoaceae (fig-marigolds) and Asteraceae (which include asters, daisies and sunflowers). For some species, pollen wasps are the only (or the most abundant) flower-visiting insect, which suggests that they are important pollinators for those plants at least.

However, because pollen wasps store collected pollen inside their bodies in their crops, it's not entirely clear that they transfer pollen between flowers effectively. To pollinate, pollen needs to be free and easily rubbed off onto the flower. Pollen that adheres accidentally to the body of the pollinator is the best sort, and this means that a nectar-collector (like a non-Masarinae wasp) could be just as effective as a dedicated pollen-collector (like a bee or Masarinae). Pollen wasps have a suite of pollen-collecting behaviours that might help assure the plant of its side of the pollination pledge. Sometimes the wasps simply nibble the pollen directly from the plant using their mandibles and ingest it. Pollen that collects on their body is brushed towards their mouth using pollen brushes ('scopa') on their forelegs. Bees have these too, of course – they are usually called pollen baskets – but they are normally on their hind legs. The evolution of scopa in both bees and pollen wasps is an example of parallel evolution, where the same solution to a similar problem has appeared independently in different lineages – evolution is not remotely embarrassed about reinventing the same wheel multiple times over, as we know. Why not, if it works!

Any wasp that is not a pollen wasp has rather short, stubby mouth parts that are good enough to satisfy personal desires for sugar and water. But to collect food for brood the basic wasp nectar-sucking kit needs improving. Pollen wasps have solved this problem in the same way as bees, butterflies and other nectar-probing insects, by evolving a long suctorial proboscis. This permits pollen wasps to access deep parts of flowers that ordinary wasps can't reach. Unlike butterflies, pollen wasps can retract their long tongues inside their body, which avoids the inconvenience of having to fly along with long curled tongues hanging out.

As well as mixing nectar into the pollen loaf for the brood to feed off, the proboscis is used to collect water to moisten soil during nest construction. Elongated proboscii have evolved at least twice in the Masarinae, and among the 350 species they show how evolution has accessorised variations on the basic drinking-straw design, depending on their ecology and evolutionary history. Pollen wasps have discovered one trick that bees have overlooked: the ability to extend their proboscis into the flower's corolla tube *after* landing on the flower. They can do this because their tongue can be propelled forward from its looped resting position in the mouth space. Long-tongued bees can't do this: they need more room to swivel and unfold their proboscii, meaning that many must undergo a rather ungainly manoeuvre before slurping up nectar.

Pollen wasps are really interesting from an evolutionary perspective. Why did they become pollinivorous? We can look to the bees for answers here. We learned in Part 1 that the ancestors to the bees were small Ammoplanidae wasps that hunted tiny pollen-eating insects, and how a few stray pollen grains may have helped trigger the switch from meat to pollen. Something similar probably happened in the pollen wasps. They are about the same age as the original bee, dating from around 100 million years ago, which was when species of flowering plants underwent a huge diversification event. To exploit this new range of plant products, some wasps became pollen wasps and others became bees.

The story of bee evolution also explains why there are so few species of pollen wasps. Switches in diet alone are not enough for diversification of species to occur. The first bees to evolve from wasps were the Melittidae, specialist pollen-feeders that visit only a few species of host plants: there are only 203 bee species in this family. When bees evolved the ability to exploit a wider range of pollen, they saw a huge explosion in speciation, giving rise to the 22,000 other species of bees. Of course, this doesn't mean that all bees today are generalists – far from it; some species became specialists 'again', as they evolved to occupy new unexploited food niches.

Pollen wasps have all the required trademarks of being an effective pollinator. They are fussy foragers and appear to have a monopoly on a large number of plants from only a couple of families. They have evolved fantastic foraging equipment to ensure they can reach the best nectar. They have tools of morphology and behaviour that serve to move pollen around, and their evolutionary journey appears to be one that mimics their cousins the bees. Those who know them best suggest that pollen wasps are likely to be as important as bees in pollination. But observations of insects on flowers is not proof of pollination; experimental evidence is lacking. And this is still where we're at with pollen wasps.

Orchids are renowned for their beauty. But lift the veil and you'll find Shakespearian levels of sexual deceit. The primary victims are male solitary wasps, mostly from the family Thynnidae. The orchids have evolved to mimic a rather sexy-looking female wasp: the flower doesn't only *look* like a sexy female, it *smells* like one. Males can't help themselves. Giddy with excitement, they grip the flower, preparing to deliver their seed. Some realise they've been duped and quit before letting rip, while others are so carried away by the flower's impeccable mimicry that they copulate and even ejaculate. In most cases the plant's deception is tuned to deceive a single wasp species, ensuring the orchid doesn't accidentally hybridise with another orchid species. And so male wasps swoon helplessly from one flower to another, casually spreading orchid pollen from flower to flower, along with their own, hopelessly spent seeds.

How on earth do orchids evolve to mimic female wasps? Evolution is clever but lazy, and so the best way to evolve effective deception is to exploit existing traits and behaviours of the victim. The first challenge is to lure the victim in, and the plant does this by using the smell of sex: female wasps produce a volatile sex pheromone – an airborne chemical signal – which allows males to find them. These orchids have evolved to mimic this smell, making them stink of female wasps eager to attract a mate and so able to entice lust-crazed males from long distances away.

Smell is just the orchid's first weapon of sexual deception. To avoid the male wasp aborting once he gets a good look, orchids tantalise the full spectrum of the male wasp's senses. To the human eye an orchid might look like a poor physical mimic of a female wasp, but put on your wasp-spectral visuals and you'll find that the colours of orchids are perceptually identical to their pollinator's potential mates. Now the orchid smells and looks like a sexy female wasp, but does it *feel* like one? The orchid needs to have curves in all the right places to persuade a male to copulate. There is evidence that orchids do this: some have appendages, described rather hopefully as an 'insectiform' lip, that appear to mimic the female. But the jury is still out on how effective orchid lips are in sexual deceit.

Once you've lured a male into your floral lair, you need to make sure you deposit pollen on him quickly and effectively before he sees through your disguise and aborts. Typically, female solitary wasps (and bees) mate with just one male, but males will attempt to mate with as many females as they can get their tarsi on, so there has been strong selection in the evolution of male mating behaviour for them to mate with females quickly and vigorously, before she can get away or before another male tries to get in his way. Enthusiastic insect sex is certainly good for the orchid, which needs the male visitor to jiggle around enough to ensure the pollen is transferred onto its body.

The third essential requirement of floral deception is that pollen is transferred to another flower of the same species. Solitary male wasps are perfect for this, as they have no sooner mated with one female than they're off looking for the next, carrying pollen from one desperate copulation attempt to another. Position is also important: you want to guide your victim such that their pollen load is delivered to the right place – your stigma. Some orchids have long hair-like structures that point towards the stigma, perhaps guiding the pollinator's genital claspers and pollen load to the bullseye. After the orchid has successfully deceived its male, some species can alter their smell to be repellent rather than attractive to ensure it doesn't get self-pollinated. Clever.

It's clear that orchids benefit from the male wasps' visitations: they get pollinated. What do the wasps get out of visiting orchids? Nothing! This is pure exploitation on the part of the plant. It is surprising that the Thynnidae wasps have not evolved to escape this usury. There is some suggestion that they may not always be completely deceived. Male wasps collected from populations where orchids are present release less sperm when deceived into ejaculation than those that have not experienced orchids. Perhaps males get wise to deception after a few encounters, or perhaps they perceive more 'females' (either orchids or real females) in their environment and so choose to spread less sperm across more potential mates.

The wasp side of the story is still unwritten. What is clear is that the orchids rely on these wasps for pollination. If the Thynnidae wasps disappeared, so would the 22 genera of orchids that depend on these wasps, unless, that is, the orchids evolved to exploit another unsuspecting quarry of orchid sex.

# III

Fig wasps, pollen wasps, orchid wasps and the flowers that nurture, reward or torment them are unusually clear examples of wasp–plant evolved interactions, where plants depend, to greater or lesser extent, on specific wasps for pollination with varying degrees of benefits to the wasps. Apart from these rather special wasps, the idea that wasps pollinate is one largely based on unsubstantiated anecdotes of unproven potential. That doesn't sound very encouraging, but stick with me while we walk through what we *do* know.

Let's start with motives. While the brood crave protein, adult wasp diets consist of mostly carbohydrates, which they get in part from feeding on nectar from flowers. Parasitoid wasps (the non-stinging, ovipositor-clad ones) don't get intimate enough with their victims to steal any juicy haemolymph and so flowers are likely to be an essential fuel-stop for them. Solitary hunting wasps (the stinging ones we met in Part 2) do sometimes slurp a cheeky bit of haemolymph from their prey, but supplementing with sugar from elsewhere is a nutritional must.

Social wasps have reasons to sup nectar at the two ends of their colony cycle. Recall that adult wasps feed off the sugary liquid secreted by the larvae. At the start of the season, spring queens are rearing their first brood, so resources from larvae will be minimal as there are too few larvae in her small nest to keep her carb-cravings satiated. Once the colony is in full swing, foragers' nutritional needs will be at least partly sated by the sugary treats dispensed by the larvae, in return for the prey they are fed. But by the end of the summer, when most of the brood have spun pupal caps, workers miss out on this nutritional supplement. This is when you start to see them scouting around at your picnic (in temperate regions). Your ice-cream, juice and beer are, in evolutionary terms, very new sugar-shops for wasps. They exploit these opportunistically alongside their evolutionary staple carb: nectar. Hogweed, goldenrods, ivy and heather all compete with your picnic (plant them close by and they might lure your unwanted picnic guests away).

It is this catholic taste for sugar that means most wasps will snack on any old flower. In a survey of wasp–plant interactions in the literature, we identified records of solitary and social hunting wasps on almost 800 different species of plants from 106 families.* The relationships between social wasps and plants are especially intriguing. Overall, these wasps seem to be remarkably unfussy about the type of plant they visit. Workers are likely to be utilising the nectar supplies from the most abundant species of plants within the foraging range of their nests. The bigger the nest, the more workers and the more wasp–plant connections that are being wound into the network.

If the wasps are indeed pollinating, this is likely to be a very robust plant-pollinator network from both the plants' and the wasps' perspectives as neither plant nor wasp is critically dependent on the other's presence, so if one goes locally extinct, it won't upset the community too much. Because they lack a preference for any specific plant, social wasps may be better able to persist in degraded or fragmented habitats. For this reason, it has been suggested that social wasps could be important as 'back-up' pollinators: when conditions become too unbearable for bees, wasp pollination may help sustain remnants of an ecosystem.

* These numbers excluded the parasitoid (non-stinging) wasps which are likely to rely on flowers for carbohydrates more than hunting wasps.

Wasps also disperse the products of pollination: seeds. We shouldn't be too surprised by this. After all, flightless wasps (ants) are championed for their services as seed-dispersers. They are responsible for the dispersal of over 11,000 species of flowering plants, and seeds have evolved a lipid-rich appendage that ants use to carry the seed back to their nest, where the seed is discarded (and so 'dispersed') while the delicious appendage is fed to the brood. Seed dispersal by wasps has only been reported for 10 plant species involving 12 species of wasp, all of which are social. In some cases, wasps appear to be the primary dispersers, such as the yellow-legged Asian hornet (*Vespa velutina*) that spreads the seeds of wild asparagus, *Stemona tuberosa*. In other cases, wasps merely augment seed dispersal, along with wind, gravity and/or ants.

In a few cheeky cases, wasps will steal seeds from their industrious ant relatives, carrying them further afield. Some wasps may even be more effective in seed dispersal than ants, or at least they may improve the dispersal services of ants by their presence, suggesting an indirect impact on seed dispersal. This subject is so poorly studied that we have little idea of how important the seed-dispersal services of wasps really are.

Visitations by wasps to flowers only really matter to the plant if the wasps are effective at collecting and transferring pollen. Nectar is there to reward insects that pollinate. Do these sugar-crazed wasps just grab their nectar loot and run, without fulfilling their side of the insect–plant pollinator pact?

An obvious first question is whether wasps do in fact transport pollen. Most of them lack the pollen-carrying tools and the overly hairy bodies of bees. Unless pollen can stick to their bodies and be transported from one flower to another, wasps may be pretty hopeless as pollinators. Recent research has shown that the hairs on bees are positively charged and attract negatively charged pollen from the flowers they visit. These electric interactions are thought to have evolved to enhance pollination. Although wasps are not as hairy as bees, it is possible they too have electric interactions that might aid pollination; so far, no one has thought to look at the electrical properties of wasps.

One study attempted to quantify pollination efficiency of a diverse array of insects visiting buckwheat plants. Five different species of wasps (four being social) were observed visiting the flowers, along with some hoverflies, honeybees, other flies and ants. By counting the number of compatible pollen grains deposited per minute, the researchers were able to assemble a kind of pollinator league table.

The honeybee outperformed all the other insects – no surprises there. But the wasps didn't do too badly: they certainly carried pollen and were middle-ranked in their efficiency, beating some hoverflies, but they appeared to be quite lazy and clumsy pollinators, with some of the lowest rates of flower visitation and not being especially quick in their 'flower-handling time'. Perhaps generalist flower-visiting wasps are pollinating, but just in a more laidback manner than the pollinator supremes.

One of the earliest scientific papers to report the pollinating potential of wasps was presented to the community of the Linnean Society in London by none other than Charles Darwin. In 1870 Darwin read a paper by the naturalist James Mansel Weale on the visitations of 'a large black and yellow wasp' to a range of plants in South Africa's Eastern Cape. Weale had observed these wasps (which we know now to be *Hemipepsis* – a relative of the spider-hunting *Pepsis* that we met in Part 2) 'busily sucking the drops of nectar ... pushing their proboscides eagerly into the flower', but most importantly he also observed 'pollen-masses attached to their tarsi, to the long hairs of the sternum and coxae, and to the spines of the leg'.

Despite these detailed descriptions, the idea that Weale's wasps could be pollinating went largely ignored for over 100 years. It was briefly revisited in the 1970s, only to be dismissed because the wasps were perceived as 'unreliable and unsteady pollinators'. However, the last decade has brought new research indicating that four species of *Hemipepsis* wasps are specialised pollinators of a guild* of South African plants, which includes 23 species from across the dogbane, orchid and asparagus families, 18 of which are pollinated *exclusively* by wasps. Apart from one sexually deceptive orchid species (such as we met earlier), all these plants reward their wasp visitors with nectar, and pollination is successful in around 40 per cent of those visited by the wasps.

Bizarrely, Weale's wasps are often injured by the flowers in their enthusiasm to access the nectar. Typically, foraging females lose parts of their palps; these mouth parts serve as organs of touch and taste, and are important in inspecting potential food and prey. Pollination is usually mutualistic, not antagonistic. Considering how much wasps rely on their senses to catch the right prey, it's hard to believe that the costs to the wasp in being so battered are outweighed by the nectar treats they receive. Perhaps the plants have been selected to manipulate the sensory organs of these insects to keep them as loyal pollinators, a strategy to minimise interspecific cheating.

That plants can manipulate the behaviour of wasps should no longer surprise you; recall the sexually deceptive orchids that lure in male Thynnidae wasps by mimicking a mate. Plants do make decisions, just like animals, and orchid trickery extends far beyond Thynnid wasps: of the 30,000 species, about a third have evolved to recruit animal pollinators via deception rather than reward. *Dendrobium sinense* is an orchid that is endemic to the

---

* A guild is a collection of species that are ecologically similar. In this case a 'pollination guild' is a group of plants that are reliant on a common pollinator.

Chinese island Hainan. It lures the hornet *Vespa bicolor* to the centre of its flower, in exactly the spot needed for it to secure its pollen onto the back of the wasp. The orchid does this by smelling like a honeybee nest under attack. When threatened by a predator (like the hornet), honeybees release a chemical that warns nestmates that they're under attack, and, incredibly, these orchids have evolved to synthesise this exact volatile compound. Hornets respond to the deception by aggressively pouncing on the flower, just as they would when hunting a honeybee. It's no surprise that hornets appear to be this orchid's only effective pollinator.

Other orchids have cast their pollinator net a little wider, using another form of chemical deception. At least two species (*Epipactis helleborine* and *Epipactis purpurata*) are known to emit green-leaf volatiles which lure in wasps. In their original form, these chemicals are a kind of distress call sent out by plants when they are under attack from insects like caterpillars: life-saving predators (like wasps) rush to the rescue and remove the caterpillars. The orchids have 'learned' (through natural selection) to cheat this mutualism by synthesising these chemical signals in the absence of any predators.

*Vespula vulgaris* and *Vespula germanica* workers respond to this evolved signal, flocking to the plant in anticipation of an easy protein meal, only to be disappointed and inadvertently smothered with pollen. Chemical signals alone are enough for the wasps to find the plant: the orchids tend to grow on the floor of dark coniferous forests where visual cues are hopeless. Few other pollinators are found on these forest floors, which may explain why there has been strong selection for the orchids to evolve effective mechanisms to exploit pollinators that don't mind the dark, like wasps.

\*    \*    \*

These incredible stories of co-evolution, mimicry and deceit provide solid evidence of how plants have been under strong selection to evolve weird and wonderful ways of enticing wasps in; and these would only have evolved if the enticed wasps actually boosted the reproductive success of the plants through pollination. Apart from the pollen wasps, few wasps have evolved special pollen-collecting accessories, and most are sorely lacking in body hair, to which pollen could otherwise cling.

If plants benefit from wasp visits, we'd expect to see signs of adaptative trait evolution to help them attract wasps and exploit their nectar-loving habits. Collections of such traits can be used to predict the most effective pollinators; these traits are traditionally to do with flowers and include things like the time of day that flowers are open, type of reward, flower colour, scent, orientation, size, symmetry and so on. The main assumption is that flowers adapt to attract best the insect that is most efficient in removing, transferring and depositing pollen.

For example, plants that are best pollinated by bees are day-flowering, with petals that are blue, pink, purple, white or yellow, orientated horizontally, upright or as pendants, with weak odour and strong ridges that act as nectar guides: we might call flowers that fit this description 'bee flowers'. They offer a wealth of rewards to their pollinators: nectar, pollen, resins, oils or fragrances. Conversely, flowers pollinated by long-tongued flies are limited to pink or purple and are tubular, with no perceptible odour; they offer only nectar rewards.

'Wasp flowers' tend to be brown, green or purple (note there is little overlap with bee flowers here), have a strong odour (again, unlike bee flowers), are bell-, dish- or gullet-shaped, and have no nectar guides. Wasps are rewarded solely with nectar. The predictive power of the 'wasp flower' concept is not huge but it is significant, meaning that flowers with these traits are predicted to be visited by wasps more than any other insect. If this pollinator concept is to be trusted, it suggests that there has been selection for plants to evolve sets of traits that are especially attractive to wasps, and for this reason wasps must be the most effective pollinators for at least some plants.

Wasps visit a diverse array of flowers, and they carry pollen and even seeds. But the critical experiment is one that can test whether wasps can fill the shoes of the pollinator supreme: the bee. One study has done just this, using the perennial herb whorled milkweed, which is used medicinally by Indigenous Americans. This plant has clusters of flowers that ordinarily are pollinated by honeybees and bumblebees, but when bees were excluded experimentally from a field of these plants, guess which insects moved in? *Polistes* paper wasps.

In the absence of bees, the rate at which the wasps visited the milkweed flowers increased by 100–300 per cent. Critically, the paper wasps were just as efficient as the bees at pollen transfer, so much so that the lack of bee pollination was entirely compensated for (in terms of pollen transfer) by the wasps. Vindication! Wasps do pollinate. And their contributions to pollination can match that of bees!

The relationship between wasps and plants is a beautiful and bizarre one. Occasionally it is a pact of fidelity, but mostly wasps and plants agree on a hedonistic contract with little commitment. And yet plants have gone out of their way to evolve the means to attract, manipulate and respond to wasps. We have a long way to go before we will know exactly where wasps sit in the pollinator league tables. But as it stands, we can be sure that wasps' relationships with plants are important to people, to ecosystems and to the planet.

# Last Word

# *A Future with Wasps*

If the bee disappears from the surface of the
earth, man would have no more than four
years left to live.

Anon.

Despite popular belief, Albert Einstein almost certainly didn't say this. But it doesn't take a genius (or even a physicist) to appreciate that the health and survival of our own species depends on that of other species. Bees are a good choice to help communicate this message; everyone has a place in their heart for bees and the good services they provide us with. But the same mantra should apply to all of nature, including the parts that are a little harder to understand, like wasps. I hope this book has given you reasons to appreciate how much poorer the world would be without wasps.

Wasps are one of nature's most secret and neglected gems. Their endless forms showcase some of evolution's wildest and most impressive work; they are diverse and beautiful, strange and shocking. Their ways are intimately entangled with those of other insects, but also with fungi, bacteria, plants, soil, ecosystems and even us. In the last 500 years, we have changed the fabric of this planet faster than at any other time in its 4.5-billion-year history. Our actions have triggered extinctions and declines in biodiversity that may be comparable in extent and rapidity to the five previous mass-extinction events of the earth's history.

We may be responsible for our planet's sixth mass extinction. Insects are one of the canaries in the mine for planet earth's warning system: two-thirds of global insect populations have almost halved in abundance. These losses have cascading impacts on the functioning of ecosystems and our own health and well-being. Not all organisms are doing badly, though. Some insects, in particular, are thriving in the new habitats we are creating. They are hitching a lift on our rapid global transport system to pastures new, adapting their lifestyles to fit better with the changing world we've given them.

How are wasps doing in the human-modified epoch of the Anthropocene?

The truth is that we don't really know.

There are some heartbreaking anecdotes of maladaptation. Take the elegant mud-daubing wasp *Sceliphron jamaicense*, for example (we met her relatives in Part 2). This slender super-model wasp builds her nests out of mud and so she is actually an urban enthusiast: all those concrete buildings provide her with endless nesting sites to position her tubular pots. Windowsills, eaves of buildings, doorways – they all make safe, sturdy nurseries to entrust her babies to. If her pots manage to escape the attention of the fastidious human, urban life can prove to be a better place for a growing family of wasps than can the secret depths of forests or undiscovered riverbanks.

One day out in the city, our chic *Sceliphron* mama finds an especially pliable source of mud, so moist and yet so strong. This feels good! She weaves it into her pot with a curious sense of pride, then pops in a few tasty spiders, squeezes out a precious egg and seals the pot. She can't resist casting a last admiring glance at her pot – there is something of a modern twist to it, she can't quite put her tarsi on why. A few weeks later, the egg has hatched and the baby *Sceliphron* has feasted greedily on the spider bounty left by her mother. Fully pupated, she is ready to break out into the world. She has a good pair of mandibles on her and starts work chipping away at the crumbly clay of her nursery pot.

Except this pot doesn't crumble. It is rock-hard. Impenetrable. She tries again and again until her mandibles finally snap. That mud-pot-with-a-modern-twist, so admired by her mother, was concrete. She dies, imprisoned in her urban nursery.

Many organisms adapt well to urban life. But sometimes they are victims of their own adaptive success. This mud-daubing wasp responded to the same cues that had served her ancestors so well for millions of years. But in an urban environment, these can sometimes be a trap – an ecological trap. Her kind will have to wait for evolution to mould a mutant wasp that chooses not to build her nest out of concrete.

Such stories are rare. Not many people have bothered to look at how human-modified environments are affecting wasp behaviour and their populations. Anecdotally, many wasps, not just mud-daubers, appear to like human constructions, especially the abandoned ones, as they make rather secure and undisturbed nesting sites. Indeed, wasp-strewn urban jungles have been common themes at almost every step of my journey with the wasps. The undersides of concrete bridges in Malaysia sheltered the shy hover wasps that ignited my fascination with these creatures. A bullet-scarred building on the outskirts of Panama City was my first introduction to *Polistes*.

After that followed the concrete frame of the sewerage works in the otherwise Panamanian tropical paradise of Barro Colorado Island, and then there was a crumbling American army base near the notorious slums of Colón. The best wasp populations in Trinidad were strewn across the eaves of abandoned houses, with only rabid dogs for company. The walls of the house I stayed at in Zambia accommodated more wasp nests than the nearby forest. Closer to home, what better place to find a *Vespula* nest than your very own loft (or your neighbour's!). Wasps certainly seem to like some of what we create, especially when we neglect it a little.

But these are all anecdotes. The state of wasp populations in the world is poorly documented. Evidence that some are declining, with species even going extinct, is apparent, though. In the UK, 10 species of hunting wasps have been listed as extinct since the mid-nineteenth century. Another study found that populations of 98 species of the UK's hunting wasps declined by 38 per cent between 1970 and 2011. The richness of wasp species declined in three-quarters of sites sampled over an 80-year period in England, with the greatest declines in areas surrounded by arable farmland.

In other countries, the pattern is no less concerning. The abundance and species richness of social wasp species has declined in urbanised parts of Brazil. Although the data are scarce, the overall picture suggests that hunting wasp populations are declining worldwide. The state of parasitoid wasps is even less well known. These insects may be especially sensitive to extinction events, given that they are specialists that rely entirely on carefully evolved relationships with host species. Worryingly, because parasitoid wasps are such an integral part of many food webs, their extinction could have catastrophic knock-on effects in ecosystems beyond the wasps themselves.

It's not all bad news, though: another study found that *Vespula* populations in the UK had remained relatively stable over the last 100 years, and the European hornet populations were actually expanding, suggesting that the vespine wasps may have some level of resilience to human-modified landscapes. We already know that these insects are good at adapting to new geographical regions as invasive species, and so perhaps it is not surprising that they are faring better than other insects as their native environment becomes more and more modified by us.

The future looks especially bright for species of wasps that manage to establish populations in new countries. Climate change is likely to open doors across the globe to these opportunistic settlers. Already milder winters have seen *Vespula* populations expand northwards in Finland, and perennial nests grow larger and more prevalent at lower latitudes. In Poland the earlier onset of spring is opening opportunities for queens to get started with nest-building ahead of time. The UK's Rothamsted suction traps that have sampled wasps for 39 years have shown us how warmer, drier years can result in a boost in wasp populations by two orders of magnitude. As we warm our planet, *Vespula* and *Vespa* wasps will certainly benefit: wider geographic ranges, larger colonies, possibly interconnected colonies. All this suggests our lives and our native ecosystems will be touched by a little more unrequited vespine love.

As with other insect groups, it is clear there are wasps that are likely to be winners and others that will be losers in the Anthropocene. But we have little idea why. The anthropogenic causes of bee declines include loss of forage patches, habitat fragmentation and use of pesticides. These are equally likely to be affecting wasps. There is some evidence that insecticides may interfere with the hunting efficiency of wasps, which is hardly surprising since these chemicals are generally designed to mess with the functioning of insects, and there is plenty of evidence that the chemicals' effects reach non-target species.

The ecological and economic impact of declining wasp populations is likely to be significant: we may yet see that 'plague of flies' that Edward Ormerod warned us about over 150 years ago, and the role of wasps as our 'back-up' pollinators may be lost before we can quantify it. We don't yet know what the costs of declining wasp populations will be, but it is likely to be similar to that of bees. Think of the millions it would cost the global farming economy if parasitoid wasps became a rarity.

Understanding the effects of declining wasp populations is therefore just as important, timely and urgent as it is for bees and other insects. Shockingly, only one wasp is listed on the

International Union for Conservation of Nature's Red List (*Tachysphex pechumani*), only nine species of wasps are listed on the UK Priority Species list, and, of all the social wasp species found in Europe, *Vespa crabro* is the only one protected by law (in Germany). There are no conservation programmes with a wasp as their poster-child.

We're not entirely sure what a world without wasps would look like or how long humans would have left to live if wasps 'disappear from the surface of the earth'. But we can take a guess. Without the endless forms of wasps as hunters, parasites, pharmacists, chemists, toolmakers, negotiators, superorganisms, architects and defectors, we would wrongly believe humans to be the most complex and intriguing organisms on the planet. Without the services of wasps as pest controllers, pollinators, seed-dispersers and decomposers, our forests, grasslands, parks, gardens, deserts, highlands, moorlands and heathlands could not support planetary health in the way they currently (just about) do. Without wasps, there would have been no bees to pollinate the planet, ants to clear up the debris and sculpt the earth, or geniuses to misquote.

So. What next?

Over the last decade we have started to move beyond the perspective of valuing nature through the blinkered spectacles of economics. Our relationship with it has become a two-way, dynamic process: we've moved from 'Nature *for* people' to 'People *and* nature'. The people and nature view takes the emphasis away from a focus on a select set of 'showcase' species or coveting a few protected areas. It makes us consider how we share our lives with nature every day, all day, not just on odd trips to a park or forest.

It's this environmental cohabitation that we need to focus on. Form and function still matter, and the value of nature's services are by no means diminished, but we are starting to value nature for its adaptability and resilience because this is what nature needs in order to cope with the speed and extent of change we are causing to the planet we cohabit. Applying the ethos of people and nature to every facet of biodiversity is the bold action that is needed for rapid recovery of the natural world.

Where do wasps fit into this vision of the future?

Maybe we can make wasps work better for us. The remarkable array of services they provide could be harnessed. We could manage wasps more successfully to maximise their assets for the benefit of our health, wealth, welfare and happiness. We have an ancient history of making honeybees work for us, to the extent that they are now semi-domesticated. We've exploited the 'Bees and people' mantra magnificently. Why not 'Wasps and people'?

Promoting sustainable use of native wasps in farming, as pollinators and predators, as food sources and decomposers, could have wide-reaching benefits to our planet. Integrating the management of wasp populations (with *people*) alongside natural ecosystems (with *nature*) would be a win-win for farmers, the wasps and the wider biodiversity of the human/nature blended ecosystems of the future.

Wasp researchers are late to the party: we've not given the endless forms of wasps the attention they deserve. We are only just starting to work out *what* wasps do for us, and *how* we can better value them. Wasps are the challenging child of the insect world. They are an enigma to us – misunderstood, neglected, maligned, deranged, pointless. Because we've not taken the time to become properly acquainted with their challenging ways, we are only at the beginning of our journey in appreciating them for being different.

Time is not on our side: we need a rapid catch-up in the science of wasps to oil the gear-shift required for us to live with them. I don't mean just tolerating them; I mean living *well* with wasps so that it is normal to value them as pest controllers, pollinators and nutrition-suppliers; so that it is normal to admire them for their enigmatic beauty, their curious life stories and as marvellous playthings of evolution; so that when we see a wasp, we pause, smile and give it an appreciative nod, thanking it for reminding us of the many hidden charms and wonders on this planet; so that we wander more curiously among the endless forms of wasps.

And other organisms, of course.

Even slugs.

# NOTES

**Part One: The Problem with Wasps**

9. *Young Mr. Sorley* E.M. Forster, *A Passage to India* (Edward Arnold Publishers Ltd, London, 1924)

12. *What he had been asking for wasn't science fiction – it was evolution* Dhand, A.A., *City of Sinners* (Bantam Press, 2018)

17. *With two fellow wasp-fanatics, Alessandro Cini and Georgia Law* Sumner, S. et al. (2018) Why we love bees and hate wasps. *Ecological Entomology* 43 (6), 836–45

19. *people have searched for 'bees' on the internet six times more often than they have for 'wasps'* Google Trends data

22. *'they terrorize housewives, ruin picnics, and build large aerial nests'* Evans, H.E. and West Eberhard, M.J., *The Wasps* (University of Michigan Press, 1970)

22. *'Social wasps are amongst the least loved insects'* Hamilton, W.D., 'Foreword'. In *Natural History and Evolution of Paper-Wasps*, edited by Stefano Turillazzi and Mary Jane West-Eberhard, v–vi (Oxford University Press, 1996)

22. *Phil Lester ... called his book on them* The Vulgar Wasp Lester, Philip J., *The Vulgar Wasp: The Story of a Ruthless Invader and Ingenious Predator* (Victoria University Press, 2018)

24. *There are around 150,000 described species of Hymenoptera* Stork, N.E. (2018) How many species of insects and other terrestrial arthropods are there on earth? *Annual Review of Entomology* 63, 31–45

24. *scientists estimate that there are likely to be 5.5 million species of insects on the planet* Ibid.

25. *estimates suggest that there are between 600,000 and 2.5 million species of Hymenoptera* Ibid.

25. *They can be inserted through tiny crevices into tree trunks* Zhu, F. et al. (2018) Symbiotic polydnavirus and venom reveal parasitoid to its

hyperparasitoids. *Proceedings of the National Academy of Sciences of the United States of America* 115, 5205–5210

26. *mean body size of newly described British beetles decreased significantly* Gaston, K.J. (1991) Body size and probability of description: the beetle fauna of Britain. *Ecological Entomology* 16, 505–508

27. *Over the last 34 years, scientists have reared* Fernandez-Triana, J.L. et al. (2014) Review of *Apanteles sensu stricto* (Hymenoptera, Braconidae, Microgastrinae) from Area de Conservación Guanacaste, northwestern Costa Rica, with keys to all described species from Mesoamerica. *ZooKeys* 383, 1–565

28. *there are likely to be between two and three times more parasitoid wasp species than there are beetles* Forbes, A.A. et al. (2018) Quantifying the unquantifiable: why Hymenoptera, not Coleoptera, is the most speciose animal order. *BMC Ecology* 18, 21

31. *When the first hymenopteran came along a mere 280 million years ago* Misof, B. et al. (2014) Phylogenomics resolves the timing and pattern of insect evolution. *Science* 346, 763–767

32. *boasts the oldest hymenopteran fossil dating back to the era of the dinosaurs, around 245 million years ago* Ibid.

33. *Scientists think that the diverse diets of* adult *vegetarian sawflies* Oeyen, J.P. et al. (2020) Sawfly genomes reveal evolutionary acquisitions that fostered the mega-radiation of parasitoid and eusocial Hymenoptera. *Genome Biology and Evolution* 12, 1099–1188

35. *the virus alters the composition of the caterpillar's saliva* Tan, C.W. et al. (2018) Symbiotic polydnavirus of a parasite manipulates caterpillar and plant immunity. *Proceedings of the National Academy of Sciences of the United States of America* 115, 5199–5204

35. *stimulated to release airborne chemicals that hyperparasitoid wasps use to find parasitoid wasp larvae* Zhu, F. et al. (2018) Symbiotic polydnavirus and venom reveal parasitoid to its hyperparasitoids. *Proceedings of the National Academy of Sciences of the United States of America* 115, 5205–5210

36. *the figs have hybridised extensively* Wang, G. et al. (2021) Genomic evidence of prevalent hybridization throughout the evolutionary history of the fig-wasp pollination mutualism. *Nature Communications* 12, 1–14

36. *These parasites have evolved as a lineage embedded within the honest gallers* Blaimer, B.B. et al. (2020) Comprehensive phylogenomic analyses re-write the evolution of parasitism within cynipoid wasps. *BMC Evolutionary Biology* 20, 1–22

39. *They are the Vespinae* Huang, P. et al. (2019) The first divergence time estimation of the subfamily Stenogastrinae (Hymenoptera: Vespidae) based on mitochondrial phylogenomics. *International Journal of Biological Macromolecules* 137, 767–773

41. *the combined biomass of ants on the planet exceeds that of humans* Hölldobler, B. and Wilson, E.O., *The Ants* (Springer Verlag, 1990)

42. *over 750 described species of preserved ants have been found from at least 70 locations across the planet* Barden, P. (2017) Fossil ants (Hymenoptera: Formicidae): ancient diversity and the rise of modern lineages. *Myrmecological News* 24, 1–30; Barden, P. and Engel, M.S. (2020) Fossil social insects. *Encyclopedia of Social Insects* DOI: 10.1007/978-3-319-90306-4-45-1

42. *all of these fearsome creatures went extinct in the late Cretaceous mass-extinction event* Boudinot, B.E. et al. (2020) *Camelosphecia* gen. nov., lost ant-wasp intermediates from the mid-cretaceous (Hymenoptera, Formicoidea). *ZooKeys* 1005, 21–55

44. *the crabronids* Branstetter, M.G. et al. (2017) Phylogenomic insights into the evolution of stinging wasps and the origins of ants and bees. *Current Biology* 27, 1019–1025

44. Melittosphex burmensis Danforth, B.N. and Poinar Jr., G.O. (2011) Morphology, classification, and antiquity of *Melittosphex burmensis* (Apoidea: Melittosphecidae) and implications for early bee evolution. *Journal of Paleontology* 85, 882–891

44. Discoscapa apicula Poinar, G. (2020) Discoscapidae fam. nov. (Hymenoptera: Apoidea), a new family of stem lineage bees with associated beetle triungulins in mid-Cretaceous Burmese amber. *Palaeodiversity* 13, 1

44. Psenulus Peters, R.S. et al. (2017) Evolutionary history of the Hymenoptera. *Current Biology* 27, 1–6

45. *his theory finally appears to have received some evidence* Sann, M. et al. (2018) Phylogenomic analysis of Apoidea sheds new light on the sister group of bees. *BMC Evolutionary Biology* 18, 1–15

45. *another piece of 100-million-year-old Burmese amber provided definitive evidence of a pollinating wasp* Grimaldi, D.A. et al. (2019) Direct evidence for eudicot pollen-feeding in a Cretaceous stinging wasp (Angiospermae; Hymenoptera, Aculeata) preserved in Burmese amber. *Communications Biology* 2, 1–10

**Part Two: The Obsessions of Wasp Whisperers**

47. *This is to be* E.G. Reinhard, *The Witchery of Wasps* (The Century Co. New York, 1929), p. 291

51. *they don't intend to imply any logical thinking on the part of the insects* Rau, P. and Rau, N., *Wasp Studies Afield* (Princeton University Press, 1918)

52. *these only really made it into the public eye* Fabre, J.H., *The Hunting Wasps* (Hodder & Stoughton, 1915) and Fabre, J.H., *More Hunting Wasps* (Hodder & Stoughton, 1920)

56. *an area of wasp biology waiting to be noticed* Kumpanenko, A., Gladun, D. and Vilhelmsen, L. (2019) Functional morphology and

evolution of the sting sheaths in Aculeata (Hymenoptera). *Arthropod Systematics and Phylogeny* 77, 325–338

56. *another biomechanical solution provided by wasps* Stetsun, H., Rajabi, H., Matushkina, N. and Gorb, S. N. (2019) Functional morphology of the sting in two digger wasps (Hymenoptera: Crabronidae) with different types of prey transport. *Arthropod Structure and Development* 52, 100882

58. *'The Spider-Hunters'* From Peckham, G. and Peckham, E., *Wasps: Solitary and Social* (Archibald Constable & Co., 1905)

58. *'The Bug-Hunters'* From Peckham, G. and Peckham, E., *The Instincts and Habits of the Solitary Wasps* 2 (Wisconsin Geological and Natural History Survey, 1899)

58. *'Thirteen Ways to Carry a Dead Fly'* From Evans, H., *Wasp Farm: A Scientist's Vivid Account of the Remarkable Lives of Wasps* (George G. Harrap & Co., 1963)

59. *scour the literature to identify the prey for as many solitary wasp species as we could find* Brock, R. et al. (2021) Ecosystem services provided by aculeate wasps. *Biological Reviews* 96, 1645–1675

61. *solitary wasp venom, and how it influences behaviour and ecology, remains poorly studied* Schmidt, J.O. (1982) Biochemistry of insect venoms. *Annual Review of Entomology* 27, 339–368

62. *Rocha e Silva named the factor responsible for this activity 'bradykinin'* Hawgood, B.J. (1997) Mauricio Rocha E. Silva MD: Snake venom, bradykinin and the rise of autopharmacology. *Toxicon* 35, 1569–1580

63. *They concluded that it was a bradykinin-like chemical* Jaques, R. and Schachter, M. (1954) The presence of histamine, 5-hydroxytryptamine and a potent, slow contracting substance in wasp venom. *British Journal of Pharmacology and Chemotherapy* 9, 53–58

63. *The result is an effective numbing of the victim's nerve activity* Piek, T. (1991) Neurotoxic kinins from wasp and ant venoms. *Toxicon* 29, 139–149

65. *may explain why COVID-19 patients struggle to breathe* Garvin, M.R. et al. (2020) A mechanistic model and therapeutic interventions for covid-19 involving a ras-mediated bradykinin storm. *Elife* 9, 1–16

65. *infiltrating cell walls and causing tumour cells to die* Moreno, M., Zurita, E. and Giralt, E. (2014) Delivering wasp venom for cancer therapy. *Journal of Controlled Release* 182, 13–21

74. *the cleanest nursery nature can buy* Strohm, E. et al. (2019) Nitric oxide radicals are emitted by wasp eggs to kill mold fungi. *Elife* 8, 1–35

81. *wasp species that are a little more eclectic in prey choice tend to be a bit more slapdash* Budrys, E. and Budriene, A. (2012) Adaptability of prey handling effort in relation to prey size in predatory wasps (Hymenoptera: Eumeninae). *Annales Zoologici Fennici* 49, 58–68

87. *Anything beyond will likely be too deep to pinpoint* Obeysekara, P.T. et al. (2014) Use of herbivore-induced plant volatiles as search cues by *Tiphia vernalis* and *Tiphia popilliavora* to locate their below-ground scarabaeid hosts. *Entomologia Experimentalis et Applicata* 150, 74–85

87. *to indicate the presence of explosive materials like TNT, Semtex and gunpowder, or illicit substances like cocaine* Olson, D. and Rains, G. (2014) Use of a parasitic wasp as a biosensor. *Biosensors* 4, 150–160

87. *scientists discovered that females of this wasp could be taught to associate a specific type of molecule with a reward through associative learning* Lewis, W. J. and Tumlinson, J.H. (1988) Host detection by chemically mediated associative learning in a parasitic wasp. *Nature* 331, 257–259

89. *Other, closely related wasps are deterred by the same cue* Kruidhof, H.M. et al. (2013) Effect of belowground herbivory on parasitoid associative learning of plant odours. *Oikos* 122, 1094–1100

91. *in 1949 wrote with endearment of hand-rearing these wasps* Shafer, G.D. *The Ways of a Mud Dauber* (Stanford University Press, 1949)

94. *the wasps use spider smell, not web design, to choose their prey* Polidori, C. et al. (2007) Factors affecting spider prey selection by *Sceliphron* mud-dauber wasps (Hymenoptera: Sphecidae) in northern Italy. *Animal Biology* 57, 11–28

96. *The success rate of the pompilid wasp's spider-hunt can be as low as zero per cent* Rayor, L.S. (2014) Attack strategies of predatory wasps (Hymenoptera: Pompilidae; Sphecidae) on colonial orb web-building spiders (Araneidae: *Metepeira incrassata*). *Journal of the Kansas Entomological Society* 69, 67–75

97. *exploit the spiders' web-fleeing anti-predator behaviour to get them away from the sticky webs for an easier hunt* Ibid.

101. *Petrunkevitch's 1926 30-page account of his experiments* Petrunkevitch, A. (1926) Tarantula versus tarantula-hawk: A study in instinct. *Journal of Experimental Zoology* 45, 367–397

**Part Three: How to Have a Social Life**

105. *Evidently the higher* Evans, H.E. and West-Eberhard, M.J., *The Wasps* (University of Michigan Press, Ann Arbor, 1970), p. 265

108. *solitary wasps transitioned to wasp societies* Szathmary, E. and Maynard Smith, J. (1995) The major evolutionary transitions. *Nature* 374, 227–31

109. *at least 25 times in multicellular organisms* Grosberg, R.K. and Strathmann R.R. (2007) The evolution of multicellularity: a minor major transition? *Annual Review of Ecology, Evolution, and Systematics* 38 (1), 621–54

109. *at least six times among the social insects as sociality* Boomsma, J.J. and Gawne, R. (2018) Superorganismality and caste differentiation as points of no return: how the major evolutionary transitions were lost in translation. *Biological Reviews* 93 (1), 28–54

110. *the social insects account for 75 per cent of the world's insect biomass* Hölldobler, B. and Wilson, E.O., *The Ants* (Springer Verlag, 1990)

115. *scientists had been able to trace the different foraging strategies of fruit flies* Osborne, K. et al. (1997) Natural behavior polymorphism due to a cGMP-dependent protein kinase of *Drosophila*. *Science* 277, 834–836

117. *found to involve an interaction between epigenetic marks* Anreiter, I. et al. (2017) Epigenetic mechanisms modulate differences in *Drosophila* foraging behavior. *Proceedings of the National Academy of Sciences of the United States of America* 114, 12518–12523

117. *she used her observations on the natural history of this little-known Neotropical wasp* West-Eberhard, M. (1987) 'Flexible strategy and social evolution'. In *Animal Societies: Theories and Facts*, 35–51; West-Eberhard, M.J., 'Wasp societies as microcosms for the study of development and evolution'. In Turillazzi, S. and West-Eberhard, M.J. (eds), *Natural History and Evolution of Paper Wasps* (Oxford University Press, 1996), 290–317

117. *her landmark book* West-Eberhard, M.J., *Developmental Plasticity and Evolution* (Oxford University Press, 2003)

121. *the very machinery of conditional expression that evolution needed* Sumner, S. et al. (2006) Differential gene expression and phenotypic plasticity in behavioural castes of the primitively eusocial wasp, *Polistes canadensis*. *Proceedings of the Royal Society B: Biological Sciences* 273, 19–26

124. *Pollen-foragers tend to switch from nursing to foraging at a younger age than nectar-foraging workers* Amdam, G.V. et al. (2004) Reproductive ground plan may mediate colony-level selection effects on individual foraging behavior in honey bees. *Proceedings of the National Academy of Sciences of the United States of America* 101, 11350–11355

125. *An up-flick of vitellogenin's baton* Ibid.

126. *demonstrating its role as the mechanistic monarch of reproductive regulation* Giray, T. et al. (2005) Juvenile hormone, reproduction, and worker behavior in the neotropical social wasp *Polistes canadensis*. *Proceedings of the National Academy of Sciences of the United States of America* 102, 3330–3335

130. *Fairhead admitted he had overlooked the holes in the interior walls of their houses as wear and tear* Fairhead, J.R. (2016) Termites, mud daubers and their earths: a multispecies approach to fertility and power in West Africa. *Conservation and Society* 14, 359–367

136. *diapause … a state of seasonal dormancy that insects use to sit out unfavourable environmental conditions* Hunt, J.H. and Amdam, G.V. (2005) Bivoltinism as an antecedent to eusociality in the paper wasp genus Polistes. *Science* 308, 264–267

138. *environmental cues* Reynolds, J.A. (2017) Epigenetic influences on diapause. *Advances in Insect Physiology* 53, 115–144

138. *Feed your brood highly nutritious food* Hunt, J.H. et al. (2007) A diapause pathway underlies the gyne phenotype in *Polistes* wasps, revealing an evolutionary route to caste-containing insect societies. *Proceedings of the National Academy of Sciences of the United States of America* 104, 14020–14025

138. *they are expressed differently* Hunt, J.H. et al. (2010) Differential gene expression and protein abundance evince ontogenetic bias toward castes in a primitively eusocial wasp. *PLoS One* 5, e10674

139. *similarities extend to changes in physiology, gene transcription, and protein production related to nutrient storage, stress resistance and metabolism* Amsalem, E. et al. (2015) Conservation and modification of genetic and physiological toolkits underpinning diapause in bumble bee queens. *Molecular Ecology* 24, 5596–5615

139. *This could be more evidence for a diapause toolkit being co-opted for the evolution of castes* Ibid.

140. *The shift from larval diapause to adult-stage diapause appears to have coincided with some sort of caste evolution* Santos, P.K.F. et al. (2019) Loss of developmental diapause as prerequisite for social evolution in bees. *Biology Letters* 15, 8

141. *if these same bees are nesting in colder latitudes, they have only one brood in a season and so remain solitary* Field, J. et al. (2010) Cryptic plasticity underlies a major evolutionary transition. *Current Biology* 20, 2028–2031

**Part Four: Playing the Game**

145. *I had devoured a 316-page thesis on* Polistes canadensis *studied in Panama by John Pickering* Pickering, J. (1980) Sex ratio, social behaviour, and ecology in *Polistes* (Hymenoptera, Vespidae), *Pachysomoides* (Hymenoptera, Ichneumonidae) and *Plasmodium* (Protozoa, Haemosporida). PhD Thesis: Harvard University, Cambridge, Massachusetts

151. *you've read William Hamilton's 1964 paper on his theory of kin selection explaining why altruism can evolve* Hamilton, W.D. (1964) The genetical evolution of social behaviour. II. *Journal of Theoretical Biology* 7, 17–52

153. *whose societies are likely to represent the first stages in the evolution of one of the longest-standing puzzles in the natural sciences* Bourke, A.F.G. (2021) The role and rule of relatedness in altruism. *Nature* 590, 392–394

157. *a brilliant solution to the perfect flaw of the haplodiploid hypothesis* Trivers, R.L. and Hare, H. (1976) Haplodiploidy and the evolution of the social insects. *Science* 191, 249–263

160. *As Hamilton predicted* Southon, R. et al. (2019) High indirect fitness benefits for helpers throughout the nesting cycle in tropical paper wasps. *Molecular Ecology* 28, 3271–3284

160. *The so-called 'monogamy hypothesis'* Boomsma, J.J. (2009) Lifetime monogamy and the evolution of eusociality. *Philosophical Transactions of the Royal Society B: Biological Sciences* 364, 3191–3207

165. *these wasps seem to be especially good at learning* faces Tibbetts, E.A. (2002) Visual signals of individual identity in the wasp *Polistes fuscatus*. *Proceedings of the Royal Society B: Biological Sciences* 269, 1423–1428; Sheehan, M.J. and Tibbetts, E.A. (2011) Specialized face learning is associated with individual recognition in paper wasps. *Science* 334, 1272–1275

166. *the genetic basis of their cognitive superpowers* Miller, S.E. et al. (2020) Evolutionary dynamics of recent selection on cognitive abilities. *Proceedings of the National Academy of Sciences of the United States of America* 117, 3045–3052

167. *therein lies the evolutionary fodder to be co-opted into an honest signal* Tibbetts, E.A. and Dale, J. (2004) A socially enforced signal of quality in a paper wasp. *Nature* 432, 218–222

168. *nests in these sorts of aggregations are often related* Southon, R. et al. (2019) High indirect fitness benefits for helpers throughout the nesting cycle in tropical paper wasps. *Molecular Ecology* 28, 3271–3284; Lengronne, T. et al. (2012) Little effect of seasonal constraints on population genetic structure in eusocial paper wasps. *Ecology and Evolution* 2, 2610–2619

169. *researchers worked out that* Polistes *look for a specific part of this chemical cue* Turillazzi, S. et al. (2006) Habitually used hibernation sites of paper wasps are marked with venom and cuticular peptides. *Current Biology* 16, R530–1

170. *wasps will form aggregations of loosely related nests in the same area* Lengronne, T. et al. (2012) Little effect of seasonal constraints on population genetic structure in eusocial paper wasps. *Ecology and Evolution* 2, 2610–2619

176. *The results are, as a whole, a bit of a muddle* Nonacs, P. and Hager, R. (2011) The past, present and future of reproductive skew theory and experiments. *Biological Reviews of the Cambridge Philosophical Society* 86, 271–298

177. *none of the current reproductive skew models has explained* Ibid.

178. *A canny subordinate will tout her commodity around* Grinsted, L. and Field, J. (2017) Market forces influence helping behaviour in cooperatively breeding paper wasps. *Nature Communications* 8, 13750

181. *a wasp that is soon to inherit the throne should be less inclined to engage with such danger* Field, J. et al. (2006) Future fitness and helping in social queues. *Nature* 441, 214–217

182. *instead they duel each other using their antennae* Taylor, B.A. et al. (2020) Queen succession conflict in the paper wasp Polistes dominula is mitigated by age-based convention. *Behavioral Ecology* 31, 992–1002

183. *fights that resulted in successors to the throne who were not the oldest wasp* West-Eberhard, M. (1969) The social biology of Polistine wasps. *Miscellaneous Publications, University of Michigan Ann Arbor* 15, 1–101

185. *Even when an old wasp is experimentally gifted queenhood on a nest* Sumner, S. et al. (2010) Reproductive constraints, direct fitness and indirect fitness benefits explain helping behaviour in the primitively eusocial wasp, *Polistes canadensis*. *Proceedings of the Royal Society B: Biological Sciences* 277, 1721–1728

186. *With or without a period of conflict* Field, J. et al. (2000) Insurance-based advantage to helpers in a tropical hover wasp. *Nature* 404, 869–871

188. *we were able to show that these so-called 'drifters'* Sumner, S. et al. (2007) Radio-tagging technology reveals extreme nest-drifting behavior in a eusocial insect. *Current Biology* 17, 140–145

189. *The resulting aggregations of extended family groups may in fact provide the right conditions* Lengronne, T. et al. (2021) Multi-level social organisation and nest-drifting behaviour in a eusocial insect. *Proceedings of the Royal Society B: Biological Sciences.* 288: 20210275

**Part Five: Dinner with Aristotle**

197. *an impressive account of their natural history and behaviour across four books of* Historia Animalium Translation Spradbery, J.P., *Wasps: An Account of the Biology and Natural History of Social and Solitary Wasps* (University of Washington Press, 1973a)

199. *It added to his thesis on how order, proportion and rationality pervaded the natural world* Lehoux, D. (2019) Why does Aristotle think bees are divine? Proportion, triplicity and order in the natural world. *British Journal for the History of Science* 52, 383–403

201. *you are invited to eavesdrop on my dinner-party conversations with Aristotle about wasps* A lot of what I learned about Aristotle's appearance, teachings and history has come from this respected source: J. Humphreys (2021) Aristotle (384–322 BC), *Internet Encyclopedia of Philosophy*

202. *'all with stings and stronger [than bees] and their wound is more painful … and proportionately bigger [than bees]'* Aristotle, *Historia Animalium*. Book 9, Chapter 41

202. *'humanity's greatest friend among the insects'* Edward O. Wilson uses the phrase in his endorsement of Thomas Seeley's 2010 book *Honeybee Democracy* (Princeton University Press)

204. *the 3,000-year-old hives that were excavated in 2007 by archaeologists in the Israeli city of Tel Rehov* Seeley, T.D., *The Lives of Bees: The Untold Story of the Honey Bee in the Wild* (Princeton University Press, 2019)

207. *'All their combs are six-sided'* Historia Animalium. Book 5, Chapter 23

210. *The hexagons are an emergent property of this process* Karihaloo, B.L. et al. (2013) Honeybee combs: How the circular cells transform into rounded hexagons. *Journal of the Royal Society Interface* 10, 2–5

214. *another level of emergent individuality* Theraulaz, G. (2014) Embracing the creativity of stigmergy in social insects. *Architectural Design* 84, 54–59; Theraulaz, G. and Bonabeau, E. (1999) A brief history of stigmergy. *Artificial Life* 5, 97–116

216. *the envelope is so effective as a thermoregulator* Personal communication from Dr Jenny Jandt, University of Otago, New Zealand

217. *these raiders are all very capable of tearing the papery forcefield aside* Detoni, M. et al. (2021) Evolutionary and ecological pressures shaping social wasps collective defenses. *Annals of the Entomological Society of America* 114, 581–595

217. *Using the envelope as a cue for when to build and when to stop* Rahmani, M. et al. (2019) An improved approach for the collective construction of architectures inspired by wasp nests. *Insectes Sociaux* 66, 73–80

219. *Wasps that nest in tree cavities or in the ground* Spradbery, J.P., *Wasps: An Account of the Biology and Natural History of Social and Solitary Wasps* (University of Washington Press, 1973)

220. *Wasps 'refine' their paper through mastication* Cole, M.R. et al. (2001) A quantitative study of the physical properties of nest paper in three species of Vespine wasps (Hymenoptera, Vespidae). *Insectes Sociaux* 48, 33–39

222. *the production line was invented* Smith, A., *The Wealth of Nations* (Strahan & Cadell, 1776)

223. *In a 2007 study of around 800 workers from two* Vespula germanica *colonies* Hurd, C.R. et al. (2007) Temporal polyethism and worker specialization in the wasp, *Vespula germanica. Journal of Insect Science* 7, 43

223. *In another study, scientists attached radio tags to 1,000 newly emerging workers* Santoro, D. et al. (2019) Behaviourally specialized foragers are less efficient and live shorter lives than generalists in wasp colonies. *Scientific Reports* 9, 1–10

224. *In 2008, the German scientist Anna Dornhaus painted 1,142 of these ants* Dornhaus, A. (2008) Specialization does not predict individual efficiency in an ant. *PLoS Biology* 6, 2368–2375

225. *being a specialist incurs a longevity cost* Santoro, D. et al. (2019) Behaviourally specialized foragers are less efficient and live shorter lives than generalists in wasp colonies. *Scientific Reports* 9, 1–10

226. *part of what separates those who are living the good life from those who are merely living* Humphreys, J. (2021), Aristotle (384–322 BCE), *Internet Encyclopedia of Philosophy*

228. *This fine-scale division of labour results in uber-hygienists* Barrs, K.R. et al. (2021) Time-accuracy trade-off and task partitioning of hygienic

behavior among honey bee (*Apis mellifera*) workers. *Behavioral Ecology and Sociobiology* 75, 1

231. *but so far no evidence has been found to support this* Helanterä, H. et al. (2006) Worker policing in the common wasp *Vespula vulgaris* is not aimed at improving colony hygiene. *Insectes Sociaux* 53, 399–402

231. '*The wasp is a philosopher*' Margaret Morley, *Wasps and Their Ways* (Dodd, Mead, 1900), p. 13

231. '*keep the vespiary clean*' Ibid., p. 56

235. *In 1888 he published* Lubbock, J., *Ants, Bees and Wasps: A Record of Observations on the Habits of the Social Hymenoptera*, 9th edition (Kegan Paul, Tench & Co., 1888)

237. *somehow information about the prey had been transmitted to naive nestmates inside the home* Wilson-Rankin, E.E. (2014) Social context influences cue-mediated recruitment in an invasive social wasp. *Behavioral Ecology and Sociobiology* 68, 1151–1161

237. *foragers can be recruited without any behavioural stimulation and without any information that might communicate direction or distance* Jandt, J.M. and Jeanne, R.L. (2005) German yellowjacket (*Vespula germanica*) foragers use odors inside the nest to find carbohydrate food sources. *Ethology* 111, 641–651

238. *noted how the larvae of the European hornet* Vespa crabro *produced distinct noises* Janet, C. (1895) Etudes sur les fourmis, les guêpes et les abeilles. *Mémoires de la Société zoologique de France* 8, 1–140

239. *The drumming resulted in an increase in general nest activity* Schaudinischky, L. and Ishay, J. (1968) On the nature of the sounds produced within the nest of the Oriental hornet *Vespa orientalis* F. (Hymenoptera). *Journal of the Acoustic Society of America* 44, 1290–1301

239. *more wasps started foraging when the drumming sounds were played to them* Taylor, B.J. and Jeanne, R.L. (2018) Gastral drumming: a nest-based food-recruitment signal in a social wasp. *Science of Nature* 105, 1–9

241. *few will attempt to raid an entire colony* Matsuura, M. (1984) Comparative biology of the five Japanese species of the genus *Vespa* (Hymenoptera, Vespidae). *Bulletin of the Faculty of Agriculture, Mie University* 69, 1–131

242. *The best strategy for social wasps is to distribute their foragers throughout the environment and be opportunistic hunters* Jeanne, R.L. and Taylor, B.J., Individual and social foraging in social wasps. In Jarau, S. and Hrncir, M. (eds), *Food Exploitation by Social Insects: Ecological, Behavioral and Theoretical Approaches* (Taylor & Francis Group, 2009), pp. 53–78

243. '*Nature does nothing in vain*' From Aristotle's *Generation of Animals*. GA 741b5. J. Humphreys (2021) Aristotle (384–322 BC), *Internet Encyclopedia of Philosophy*

245. *Bees can also recognise complex visual cues like a human face or even painting styles* Chittka, L. and Walker, J. (2006) Do bees like Van Gogh's Sunflowers? *Optics and Laser Technology* 38, 323–328

247. *bees can transfer their abstract relational learning to different visual and olfactory cues* Giurfa, M. et al. (2001) The concepts of 'sameness' and 'difference' in an insect. *Nature* 410, 2–5

248. *there's no better way to work out if a neurone is important or not* Devaud, J.M. et al. (2015) Neural substrate for higher-order learning in an insect: Mushroom bodies are necessary for configural discriminations. *Proceedings of the National Academy of Sciences of the United States of America* 112, E5854–E5862

251. *They can retain spatial maps in their heads for at least 24 hours without reinforcement* Moreyra, S. et al. (2017) Long-term spatial memory in *Vespula germanica* social wasps: the influence of past experience on foraging behavior. *Insect Science* 24, 853–858

251. *they retain memories of smells for up to 30 days* Gong, Z. et al. (2019) Hornets possess long-lasting olfactory memories. *Journal of Experimental Biology* 222, 1–8

253. *The trained bees were then tested* Dyer, A.G. et al. (2005) Honeybee (*Apis mellifera*) vision can discriminate between and recognise images of human faces. *Journal of Experimental Biology* 208, 4709–14

254. *The same experiment was repeated on yellowjacket wasps* Avarguès-Weber, A. et al. (2017) Recognition of human face images by the free flying wasp *Vespula vulgaris*. *Animal Behavior and Cognition* 4, 314–323; Avarguès-Weber, A. et al. (2018) Does holistic processing require a large brain? Insights from honeybees and wasps in fine visual recognition tasks. *Frontiers in Psychology* 9, 1–9

257. *a range of other ants and social bees and wasps* Holman, L. (2018) *Behavioral Ecology* 29 (6), 1199–1209

260. *They found that workers in both types of colonies laid lots of eggs* Foster, K.R. and Ratnieks, F.L.W. (2000) Facultative worker policing in a wasp. *Nature* 407, 692–693

260. *As predicted, worker policing was detected in the nests* Bonckaert, W. et al. (2011) Colony stage and not facultative policing explains pattern of worker reproduction in the Saxon wasp. *Molecular Ecology* 20, 3455–3468

261. *when given a choice, workers are able to selectively remove worker-laid eggs over queen-laid eggs* Foster, K.R. and Ratnieks, F.L.W. (2001) Convergent evolution of worker policing by egg eating in the honeybee and common wasp. *Proceedings of the Royal Society B: Biological Sciences* 268, 169–174

262. *Scientists have discovered that … Vespula queens, for example, mark their eggs with a long-chained hydrocarbon* Oi, C.A. et al. (2015) Dual effect of wasp queen pheromone in regulating insect sociality. *Current Biology* 25, 1638–1640

262. *If you apply a synthetic version of juvenile hormone to* Vespula *workers* Oliveira, R.C. et al. (2017) Hormonal pleiotropy helps maintain queen signal honesty in a highly eusocial wasp. *Scientific Reports* 7, 1–12

262. *eggs laid by the manipulated workers were less likely to be policed than eggs laid by untreated workers* Oi, C.A. et al. (2020) Reproduction and signals regulating worker policing under identical hormonal control in social wasps. *Scientific Reports* 10, 1–10

**Part Six: Nature's Pest Controllers**

269. *If the benefits of nature* Mace, G.M. (2014) Whose conservation? *Science* 345, 1558–1561

271. *We have an obligation to give people a reason to value wasps* Dirzo, R. et al. (2014) Defaunation in the Anthropocene. *Science* 345, 401–406

272. *Up to a million plant and animal species are expected to face extinction* IPBES report, 2019

272. *322 species of terrestrial vertebrates* Ibid.

272. *in the UK … insects have declined by 30–60 per cent over the last four decades* Ibid.

273. *how can you justify a conservation programme on the basis of an ecosystem service that fluctuates so much in value* Adams, W.M. (2014) The value of valuing nature. *Science* 346, 549–551

273. *there has been a shift in emphasis away from putting a price on nature* Díaz, S. et al. (2018) Assessing nature's contributions to people: Recognizing culture, and diverse sources of knowledge, can improve assessments. *Science* 359, 270–272

274. *contributing to almost 10 per cent of the value of the world's agricultural production.* IPBES (2016) *The assessment report of the Intergovernmental Science-Policy Platform on Biodiversity and Ecosystem Services on pollinators, pollination and food production,* Secretariat of the Intergovernmental Science-Policy Platform on Biodiversity and Ecosystem Services

275. *annual economic costs of mosquito-borne diseases to humans* https://www.cdc.gov/malaria/malaria_worldwide/impact.html

275. *'The world could not afford to lose its wasps'* Morley (1900), p. 81

278. *The economic value of this tiny parasitoid wasp to farmers across the Asia-Pacific has been calculated at $14.6–$19.5 billion per year.* Wyckhuys, K.A.G. et al. (2020) Ecological pest control fortifies agricultural growth in Asia-Pacific economies. *Nature Ecology and Evolution* 4, 1522–1530

279. *'assisting her to multiply'* Henri Fabre, *The Hunting Wasps* (Hodder & Stoughton, 1915), p. 382

281. *In 1868 the British physician Edward Latham Ormerod produced the book* British Social Wasps Ormerod, E.L., *British Social Wasps:*

*An Introduction to their Anatomy and Physiology, Architecture and General Natural History* (Longmans, Green, Reader and Dyer, 1868)

282. *'It is only those who have learned to love wasps as some naturalists love bees who will be at pains to understand them.'* Ibid., p. 1

282. *'The practical result of destroying all the wasps on Sir T. Brisbane's estate'* Ibid., p. 22

282. *'If the benefit of insects to man is to be measured'* Ibid., p. 228

282. *'The butcher ought to welcome her'* Morley (1900), p. 20

282. *On St Vincent and St Kitts in 1913, colonialists reported* Ballou, H.A. (1915) West Indian wasps. *Agricultural News* 14, 298

283. *Ten successful crop years of pesticide- and pest-free cotton production on St Vincent* Ballou, H.A. (1909) Treatment of cotton pests in the West Indies in 1907. *West Indian Bulletin* 9, 235–241

283. *In Japan, such relocation of* Polistes *nests* Morimoto, R. (1960) *Polistes* wasps as natural enemies of agricultural and forest pests. II (Studies on the social Hymenoptera of Japan. XI). *Scientific Bulletin for the Faculty of Agriculture, Kyushu University* 18, 117–132

283. *controlling a starting population of five caterpillars among 100 cabbages in a season* Morimoto, R. (1961) *Polistes* wasps as natural enemies of agricultural and forest pests. III (Studies on the social Hymenoptera of Japan. XII). *Scientific Bulletin for the Faculty of Agriculture, Kyushu University* 18, 243–252

283. *When they relocated wasp nests to shelters constructed on the edges of fields, hornworm populations were reduced* Rabb, R.L. and Lawson, F.R. (1957) Some factors influencing the predation of *Polistes* wasps on the tobacco hornworm. *Journal of Economic Entomology* 50, 778–784; Lawson, F.R. et al. (1961) Studies of an integrated control system for hornworms on tobacco. *Journal of Economic Entomology* 54, 93–97

287. *scientists are sequencing dust* Clare, E.L. et al. (2021) eDNAir: Proof of concept that animal DNA can be collected from air sampling. *PeerJ* 9:e11030

287. *One of the first studies to use DNA barcoding of wasp prey explored the contents of the food balls … in southern Australia* Kasper, M.L. et al. (2004) Assessment of prey overlap between a native (*Polistes humilis*) and an introduced (*Vespula germanica*) social wasp using morphology and phylogenetic analyses of 16S rDNA. *Molecular Ecology* 13, 2037–48

290. *invaders had completely altered the ecological balance of one of New Zealand's most precious native habitats* Lester, P.J. and Beggs, J.R. (2019) Invasion success and management strategies for social *Vespula* wasps. *Annual Review of Entomology* 64, 1–21

292. *in some cases have driven the birds from the forest altogether* Beggs, J. (2001) The ecological consequences of social wasps (*Vespula* spp.) invading an ecosystem that has an abundant carbohydrate resource. *Biological Conservation* 99, 17–28

292. *Globally, invasive insects cost a minimum of $70 billion per year* Bradshaw, C.J.A. et al. (2016) Massive yet grossly underestimated global costs of invasive insects. *Nature Communications* DOI: 10.1038/ncomms12986

293. *if scientists can sequence the DNA from 450,000-year-old hominid remains* Meyer, M. et al. (2016) Nuclear DNA sequences from the Middle Pleistocene Sima de los Huesos hominins. *Nature* 531, 504–507

295. *In a meta-analysis of generalist arthropod predators* Symondson, W.O.C. et al. (2002) Can generalist predators be effective biocontrol agents? *Annual Review of Entomology* 47, 561–594

296. *Biomass estimates from two such nests that overwintered* Harris, R.J. (1996) Frequency of overwintered *Vespula germanica* (Hymenoptera: Vespidae) colonies in scrubland-pasture habitat and their impact on prey. *New Zealand Journal of Zoology* 23, 11–17

297. *these wasps were responsible for reducing spider populations by 36 per cent and caterpillars by 86 per cent.* Wilson, E.E. et al. (2009) Life history plasticity magnifies the ecological effects of a social wasp invasion. *Proceedings of the National Academy of Sciences of the United States of America* 106, 12809–12813

299. *A twin set of long-term wasp data collected over 23 years in the UK and New Zealand* Lester, P.J. et al. (2017) The long-term population dynamics of common wasps in their native and invaded range. *Journal of Animal Ecology* 86, 337–347

299. *the previous year saw an abundance of wasps, this will have an impact too* Ibid.

299. *A total of 587* Vespula vulgaris *nests were removed between 1977 and 2008* The figures are based on data presented in Table 1 of Archer, B.Y.M. and Halstead, A. (2014) Population dynamics of social wasps (Hymenoptera: Vespidae) in the Royal Horticultural Society's garden at Wisley, Surrey. *Entomologist's Monthly Magazine* 150, 19–26. The area of the Wisley site monitored between 1977 and 2008 was further clarified by Dr Andrew Sailsbury, principle entomologist at Wisley RHS, to be 97 hectares, not the 41 hectares referred to in the paper. The mean number of nests per year was 18.34, and the range per year was 14–72. Estimates of nests per hectare were rounded up from calculations using these figures.

300. *this includes 7,274 workers, 1,438 males and 890 virgin queens* Spradbery, J.P., *Wasps: An Account of the Biology and Natural History of Social and Solitary Wasps* (University of Washington Press, 1973a)

301. *Even for the largest reported nests* Reported in ibid.

302. *but they admit that their management of wasps is not perfect* Personal communication with Dr Andrew Sailsbury, principle entomologist at Wisley Gardens, RHS

303. *the presence of wasps resulted in a 62 per cent reduction in pest populations and produced heavier cabbages* Gould, W.P. and Jeanne, R.L. (1984) *Polistes* wasps (Hymenoptera: Vespidae) as control agents for lepidopterous cabbage pests. *Environmental Entomology* 13, 150–156

303. *pest populations were significantly reduced and the plants sustained less damage compared with those from which wasps were excluded* Southon, R.J. et al. (2019) Social wasps are effective biocontrol agents of key lepidopteran crop-pests. *Proceedings of the Royal Society B: Biological Sciences* 286, 20191676

304. *Even if another prey pops up, it takes time for them to cotton on and switch type* Gould, W.P. and Jeanne, R.L. (1984) *Polistes* wasps (Hymenoptera: Vespidae) as control agents for lepidopterous cabbage pests. *Environmental Entomology* 13, 150–156

305. *farmers lack a basic knowledge of the chemicals, the hazards and how to use them effectively and safely* Ngowi, A.V.F. et al. (2007) Smallholder vegetable farmers in Northern Tanzania: Pesticides use practices, perceptions, cost and health effects. *Crop Protection* 26, 1617–1624

305. *Pesticide poisoning is a common occurrence, especially among women* Lekei, E. et al. (2020) Acute pesticide poisoning amongst adolescent girls and women in northern Tanzania. *BMC Public Health* 20, 1–8

305. *comprise 80 per cent of the agricultural labour force in sub-Saharan Africa* Country Gender Assessment Series (2019) *National gender profile of agriculture and rural livelihoods.* Food and Agriculture Organisation of the United Nations

307. *Insect protein is a viable healthy alternative to eating meat and insect-farming a realistic solution to global food security concerns* Ghosh, S. et al. (2021) Chemical composition and nutritional value of different species of *Vespa* hornets. *Foods* 10, 1–15

307. *Similar approaches are practised with yellowjacket wasps in rural communities in Japan* Nonaka, K. (2010) Cultural and commercial roles of edible wasps in Japan. In *Forest Insects as Food: Humans Bite Back* pp. 123–130

**Part Seven: The Secret Pollinators**

311. *Over 75 per cent of crops worldwide directly depend on insects as pollinators* Klein, A. et al. (2007) Importance of pollinators in changing landscapes for world crops. *Proceedings of the Royal Society B: Biological Sciences* 274, 303–313

311. *making insect pollination worth over $250 billion per year globally* Bauer, D.M. and Sue Wing, I. (2016) The macroeconomic cost of catastrophic pollinator declines. *Ecological Economics* 126, 1–13

311. *Without insect pollinators we would lose between 5 and 8 per cent of all crop production* IPBES (2016) *The assessment report of the Intergovernmental Science-Policy Platform on Biodiversity and*

*Ecosystem Services on pollinators, pollination and food production,*
Secretariat of the Intergovernmental Science-Policy Platform on
Biodiversity and Ecosystem Services; Gallai, N. et al. (2009)
Economic valuation of the vulnerability of world agriculture
confronted with pollinator decline. *Ecological Economics* 68, 810–821

311. *pollinator-dependent global agriculture has grown twice as quickly* Potts,
S.G. et al. (2016) Safeguarding pollinators and their values to human
well-being. *Nature* 540, 220–229

313. *In the last five decades the number of honeybee hives has increased
globally by 45 per cent* Ibid.

314. *habitats dominated by honeybees show a much-depleted ecosystem
function* Valido, A. et al. (2019) Honeybees disrupt the structure
and functionality of plant-pollinator networks. *Scientific Reports* 9,
1–11

316. *After bees and flies, butterflies are the next most regular visitors of flowers*
Rader, R. et al. (2020) Non-bee insects as visitors and pollinators of
crops: biology, ecology and management. *Annual Review of
Entomology* 65, 1–20

317. *it took until 2021 for someone to bother to work out which insects are
responsible for the cross-pollination of cotton* Cusser, S. et al. (2021)
Unexpected functional complementarity from non-bee pollinators
enhances cotton yield. *Agriculture, Ecosystems and Environment* 314,
107415

319. *Within its story are coordinated patterns of genomic evolution* Zhang, X.
et al. (2020) Genomes of the Banya tree and pollinator wasp provide
insights into fig-wasp coevolution. *Cell* 183, 875–889

319. *Infidelity has driven the evolution of the enormous diversity in both figs
and wasps* Wang, G. et al. (2021) Genomic evidence of prevalent
hybridization throughout the evolutionary history of the fig-wasp
pollination mutualism. *Nature Communications* 12, 1–14

320. *In 2019, the world fig trade was valued at almost $600 million* https://
oec.world/en/profile/hs92/figs-fresh-or-dried

320. *an increase of 3°C or more would reduce the active lifespans of adults*
Jevanandam, N. et al. (2013) Climate warming and the potential
extinction of fig wasps, the obligate pollinators of figs. *Biology Letters*
9, 3

322. *pollen wasps appear to be rather particular in their choice of flowers*
Gess, S.K. and Gess, F.W., *Wasps and Bees in Southern Africa*, 24
(SANBI Biodiversity Series, 2014)

324. *a huge explosion in speciation, giving rise to the 22,000 other species of
bees* Murray, E.A. et al. (2018) Pollinivory and the diversification
dynamics of bees. *Biology Letters* 14, 20180530

326. *perhaps guiding the pollinator's genital claspers and pollen load to the
bullseye* Gaskett, A.C. (2011) Orchid pollination by sexual
deception: Pollinator perspectives. *Biological Reviews* 86, 33–75

327. *choose to spread less sperm across more potential mates* Brunton Martin, A.L. et al. (2020) Orchid sexual deceit affects pollinator sperm transfer. *Functional Ecology* 34, 1336–1344

328. *we identified records of solitary and social hunting wasps on almost 800 different species of plants from 106 families* Brock, R.E. et al. (2021) Ecosystem services provided by aculeate wasps. *Biological Reviews* 96, 1645–1675

329. *wasp pollination may help sustain remnants of an ecosystem* Mello, M.A.R. et al. (2011) High generalization in flower-visiting networks of social wasps. *Acta Oecologica* 37, 37–42

330. *observed 'pollen-masses attached to their tarsi, to the long hairs of the sternum and coxae, and to the spines of the leg'* Weale, J.P.M. (1871) Observations on the mode in which certain species of Asclepiadeae are fertilized. *Botanical Journal of the Linnean Society* 13, 48–58

331. *research indicating that four species of* Hemipepsis *wasps* Shuttleworth, A. and Johnson, S.D. (2012) The *Hemipepsis* wasp-pollination system in South Africa: A comparative analysis of trait convergence in a highly specialized plant guild. *Botanical Journal of the Linnean Society* 168, 278–299

331. *pollination is successful in around 40 per cent of those visited by the wasps* Shuttleworth, A. and Johnson, S.D. (2009) Palp-faction: an African milkweed dismembers its wasp pollinators. *Environmental Entomology* 38, 741–7

331. *mouth parts serve as organs of touch and taste* Ibid.

332. *in exactly the spot needed for it to secure its pollen onto the back of the wasp* Brodmann, J. et al. (2009) Orchid mimics honey bee alarm pheromone in order to attract hornets for pollination. *Current Biology* 19, 1368–1372

333. *Collections of such traits can be used to predict the most effective pollinators* Dellinger, A.S. (2020) Pollination syndromes in the 21st century: where do we stand and where may we go? *New Phytologist* 228, 1193–1213

**Last Word: A Future with Wasps**

338. *two-thirds of global insect populations have almost halved in abundance* Dirzo, R. et al. (2014) Defaunation in the Anthropocene. *Science* 345, 401–406

339. *She dies, imprisoned in her urban nursery* Falcón-Brindis, A. et al. (2018). A fatal nest construction: man-mixed cement used by mud-daubing wasps. *Sociobiology* 65: 524–526

340. *In the UK, 10 species of hunting wasps have been listed as extinct since the mid-nineteenth century* Ollerton, J. et al. (2014). Pollinator declines. Extinctions of Aculeate pollinators in Britain and the role of large-scale agricultural changes. *Science* 346, 1360–1362

340. *Another study found that populations of 98 species of the UK's hunting wasps declined by 38 per cent between 1970 and 2011* Outhwaite, C.L. et al. (2020). Complex long-term biodiversity change among invertebrates, bryophytes and lichens. *Nature Ecology & Evolution,* 1–9

340. *The richness of wasp species declined in three-quarters of sites sampled over an 80-year period in England* Senapathi, D. et al. (2015). The impact of over 80 years of land cover changes on bee and wasp pollinator communities in England. *Proceedings of the Royal Society B: Biological Sciences* 282: 8

340. *The abundance and species richness of social wasp species has declined in urbanised parts of Brazil.* Zanette, L.R.S. (2005). Effects of urbanization on neotropical wasp and bee assemblages in a Brazilian metropolis. *Landscape and Urban Planning* 71 (2–4), 105–121

340. *vespine wasps may have some level of resilience to human-modified landscapes.* Jonsson, G.M. et al. (2021). A century of social wasp occupancy trends from natural history collections: spatiotemporal resolutions have little effect on model performance. *Insect Conservation and Diversity* 14 (5), 543–555

341. *drier years can result in a boost in wasp populations by two orders of magnitude.* Lester, P.J. et al. (2017). The long-term population dynamics of common wasps in their native and invaded range. *Journal of Animal Ecology* 86 (2), 337–347

341. *There is some evidence that insecticides may interfere with the hunting efficiency of wasps* Bommarco, R. et al. (2011). Insecticides suppress natural enemies and increase pest damage in cabbage. *Journal of Economic Entomology* 104 (3), 782–791

# ACKNOWLEDGEMENTS

In January 2020, I opened my laptop and tapped out the first words of this book. About the same time, on the other side of the world – in Wuhan, China – life as we knew it quietly took a dark turn. A global pandemic is an inconvenient time to write a book: lockdowns, home-schooling, isolation, loneliness, fear of an unknown disease, hospitals pushed to breaking point, friends losing loved ones, and a national shortage of toilet paper. There were certainly more important things to think about and deal with than words about wasps. But thanks to so many fabulous people (and a fair amount of experimental sourdough baking), here it is.

First and foremost, I thank my wonderful husband, Nick, without whom this book would never have been finished. Thank you for keeping the troops entertained, (mostly) clean and fed on my weekend writing binges; thank you for taking an avid interest in my word-count spreadsheets, for humouring my bursts of excitement on learning new things about wasps, for your home-made gin and tonics, and most importantly for always loving and believing in me. You're allowed to read it, now it's finished.

Ruben, Roselle and Theo – thank you for quietly getting on with growing up while your mother was possessed by this book. Actually, you weren't so quiet, but that's fine too: your fabulous jazz piano playing (Ruben), your singing, dancing and general love of life (Roselle) and your wiser-than-your-years narration on everything (Theo) have been the soundtrack to my book writing. It must be peculiar having a mother who is constantly thinking about wasps, hunting for wasps or talking about wasps; thank you for humouring my eccentricity and obsession. I never intended to be like this.

I have dedicated this book to my parents, Frances and Graham. I can't remember a time when you have not loved, encouraged and supported me. Thank you for inspiring me to always try harder, aim higher, think bigger and embrace every opportunity that life throws my way. Thank you also for being the brave, patient, kind souls who read the first drafts of this book, in its most scraggy and indulgent form, when I didn't dare ask anyone else to read it. You said all the right things to spur me on to the next phase. I hope you like the final version, dedicated to you, for the endless love, support and encouragement you have given me. Oh, and for slugs.

A very special thanks also to my mother-in-law, Rosemary, who turns out to be an amazing proofreader (future authors – snap her up!). Thank you for ploughing so heroically through my entire book proofs in under a week: you corrected more typos and grammatical errors than wasps I have painted; and I cannot tell you how reassuring it was to hear that (despite the typos) my book is indeed quite readable and interesting! If I could read half as fast as you and spot half the typos you spotted, I'd have written this book a lot more quickly. Let's just agree not to mention the Oxford comma at the next family reunion.

The content of this book has been bubbling away for quite some years, and all because of the many, many talks I had been invited to give by local natural history societies, beekeeper societies, Women's Institute meetings, festivals, schools and student groups. There are too many to name, but thank you to you all for your kind invitations, friendly audiences and enthusiastic questions on aspects of wasps that I'd never thought about before. Little did I realise how these talks would form the foundations of a book – this book.

From village hall rants about wasps, a book proposal was born, and it developed into something coherent under the careful guidance of my fabulous agent, Will Francis. Will – thank you for believing in me from the word go, for skilfully shaping my overly enthusiastic musings about wasps into something that publishers would be interested in. Your expert eye, careful word-crafting and re-weaving of narrative was magic to behold.

While bouncing along the writing rollercoaster of excitement, horror, thrills, frustration, wonder, annoyance and liberation, I reached several points where I convinced myself 'this is it: I'm done!' My wiser self now knows that finishing the first, second or even third draft of a book is not the end. But at each of these stop-off points, my astute editor – Arabella Pike at HarperCollins – was there to greet me with a plethora of frank feedback and encouragement. Thank you, Arabella, for steering my writing style away from 'chattiness' into something that others might like to read, for our late-night brainstorms, and for believing in me despite my tardy respect for deadlines. Interlaced with Arabella's brilliance was the equally awesome Iain Hunt, who must be the best copy-editor a new author could wish for. Iain, your eagle-eye for phrasing, grammar, structure and relevance smoothed out the ruggedness of my writing, making it decidedly more digestible and sensible. Thank you for your long hard hours with my tousled words. And to Jo Thompson for your help with photos: oddly this was one of the hardest bits about the book, and I couldn't have pulled this together without your calm patience and your keen eye for a cute lookin' wasp!

In the troughs of my writing rollercoaster I peered over the edges of frustration, obsession and sometimes wondered if I glimpsed a little madness; I tasted some of the euphoria and horror that I had heard was the life of a writer. I loved it more than I hated it, but it was not without challenge. Along the road were some patient friends who I tried not to bore too much with my latest troubles with wasps and words on lockdown walks, paddle-board evenings or a much-needed glass of wine – you know who you are. I apologise to the many friends who politely asked 'Is it finished yet?' only to be greeted with an unwanted outpouring of unnecessary detail on some book issue of the moment. A special thanks to Adam Rutherford for his pep-talks, and to Nichola Raihani who had traversed her own journey into the book world a year before me and who has been a kind of 'first-book mentor' to me. Thank you, Nichola, for introducing me to all the right people, advising me on what to do and when. If my book is half as brilliant as yours, I'll be very happy.

While I lost myself in the endless forms of wasps, my research group at UCL endured a long period of neglectful leadership. Thank you for putting up with my incoherent rants about wasp-ish details that were of little relevance to you, and for discussing my book chapters when you'd have much preferred that we were discussing your latest results. I promise I'm back now (at least until the next book!). Special thanks to long-suffering lab members past and present, who took the time to read and critique drafts of my chapters, especially Owen Corbett, Robin Southon, Emeline Favreau, Patrick Kennedy, Chris Wyatt, Ben Taylor, Alessandro Cini, Iona Cunningham-Eurich, Cinita Oi, Ryan Brock. And to my colleagues near and far – for your insights, corrections, sanity-checks and encouraging words, especially Sylvia Ceausu, Michael Ohl, Gavin Broad, Liam Crowley, Stuart Roberts and Jenny Jandt – so grateful for your time and expertise. These clever people give me hope that I may have

avoided *substantial* egregious errors. No doubt errors remain –
but those are entirely mine.

To the hundreds of scientists without whom there would be
nothing about wasps (or indeed bees) to write: thank you. If
you're not named in the text, you're named with your publications in the endnotes. I hope that I have not misrepresented you
or your science, or deviated too far from the page in my more
indulgent moments of florid writing. Many of the stories in the
book were inspired (directly or otherwise) by my own wasping
travels and experiences: such adventures were only made possible
by the generosity and kindness of so many people across the
world. Special thanks to John Walters for introducing me to the
world of potter wasps; to Adam Hart, my partner-in-crime for
wasp evangelism; to Bob Brown for teaching me how to dig a
vespine nest and Filipe Salbany (aka our local bee whisperer) for
your ever willingness to dig wasp nests at short notice; to the
Tidmarsh family for inexplicably humouring me by hosting a
wasp nest in their garden shed. And to the many people in
far-flung places: Trinidad (Andrew Stevenson, Baldeo and family,
Chris Starr), Brazil (especially Fabio Nascimento and his lab),
Malaysia (especially Durai, Tina and the people of Bukit Fraser,
who remembered me after 20 years), and especially Panama –
special thanks to Bill Wcislo, the Gamboa community and staff
at 'Tupper', Galeta field station and Barro Colorado Island for
your support, help and patience (especially with my very bad
Spanish).

My journey into the world of wasps would never have come
about without some special modern-day Wasp Whisperers, who
have taught, mentored and inspired me over the years. Jeremy
Field – for teaching me how to use an insect nest, hold a pipette,
write a sentence and other waspish life-skills; I am so glad you
tricked me into the world of wasps in the first place with the ruse
that 'these wasps don't sting' (not true!). Mary Jane West-
Eberhard – for your great ideas, but also being so down to earth,

welcoming and teaching me to 'just *watch* the wasps'. Joan Strassmann – who remains an inspiration to me even though she no longer studies wasps. Thank you also to those who prefer the vegetarian and flightless wasps but who've contributed enormously to my growth as a scientist, especially Koos Boomsma and Andrew Bourke. And of course the Wasp Whisperers of the past, who feel like old friends but will never know what a huge influence they've had on me and this book – especially Margaret Morley, Elizabeth and George Peckham, Howard Evans, Edward Ormerod and Jean-Henri Fabre.

Finally, thanks to J. S. Bach, who probably didn't like wasps at all, but whose music has played a big part in getting me through this book. His music took me to a place where I could focus amid the chaos and stress of the last two years. A particular thanks for that bottom G in the opening of his Cello Suite No. 1 in G major, which casts a spell of calm creativity on me and has become the starting prelude to my every day of writing. If he'd written more than six cello suites I might have finished sooner.

Seirian Sumner
March 2022

# ILLUSTRATIONS

Jean-Henri Fabre (*Granger/Alamy Stock Photo*)

Collected wasp nests (*Natural History Museum*)
A parasitoid wasp (*John Tomsett*)
A sawfly (*David Fotheringham*)
The giant Asian hornet (*John Horstman*)
Gall wasp eggs (*Sandra Standbridge/Getty*)
The beewolf, carrying a hunted honeybee (*Steve Everett*)
A solitary wasp impaling its prey (*blickwinkel/Alamy*)
A jewel wasp using venom on a cockroach (*ZUMA Press, Inc./ Alamy*)
A sand wasp paralysing a caterpillar (*Paul Starosta/Getty*)
A spider-hunting pompilid wasp attacking a wandering spider (*Ray Hamilton*)
A mud nest (*Denis Crawford/Alamy*)
The mud-daubing wasp (*Rolf Nussbaumer Photography/Alamy*)
The mammoth wasp (*Nick Brischuk*)
Hover wasps nesting in a tunnel (*Seirian Sumner*)
*Polistes canadensis* wasps building a nest (*Patrick Kennedy*)
A wasp with a radio frequency identification tag (*Aidan Weatherill*)

*Polistes* paper wasp facial patterns (*Michael Sheehan*)

Inside the nest of the European hornet (*Westend61/Getty*)

Collecting hornet nests for diet analysis (*Seirian Sumner*)

A nest of the African paper wasp (*Patrick Kennedy*)

The heath potter wasp (*John Walters*)

Yellowjacket wasp nests (*Seirian Sumner*)

The yellow-legged Asian hornet (*Lessy Sebastian/EyeEm/Getty*)

*Polybia* (*Vinícius Souza/Alamy*)

*Ropalidia* (*yod67/Getty*)

*Ammophila* (*imageBROKER/Alamy*)

A wasp pollinating (*Eric Lowenbach/Getty*)

A wasp attempting to mate with an orchid (*Tim Gainey/Alamy*)

Fig wasps (*Danita Delimont/Alamy*)

The Asian hornet (*David Element*)

The native European hornet (*Steven Falk*)

Night hornets in Nicaragua (*Rob Francis/Alamy*)

The tropical paper wasp (*Kathryn Booth*)

# INDEX

ACE/ACE 2 enzymes 64
Aculeata 37
adaptive trait evolution 333
aDNA ('ancient' DNA) sequencing 293
African killer bees (Africanised bees) 21
*Agelaia* (paper wasp) 288
age polyethism 123–4, 223–4
Aizoaceae 322
Alkali bees (*Nomia melanderi*) 315
allele 115, 149, 151, 152, 153, 154, 156, 158, 159, 162, 172$n$
altruism 150–63, 161$n$, 170, 176, 179, 186–90, 267$n$; 'drifters' and 187–92; family group and 160–3; Haldane and 149–51; Hamilton's Rule and 151–63, 167, 168, 171–2, 192–3, 267$n$; haplodiploidy and 155–8; microsatellites, discovery of and 158–9; monogamy as condition for 160–1; *Polistes* societies and 150–63, 161$n$, 170, 176, 179, 186–90; relatedness and 154–63, 172$n$, 174, 176, 177
American cockroach (*Periplaneta americana*) 65–6

*Ammophila* 76–84, 86, 90, 91, 279
Ammoplanidae 44, 323
*Anagyrus lopezi* (parasitoid wasp) 278
*Anomala orientalis* (beetle) 86
antennae 43, 66, 73, 75, 83, 84–5, 96, 99, 182–3, 213, 279
Anthropocene 338, 341
antibiotics 38, 43, 69, 71–4, 75, 128
antiseptic 69–70, 75
ants 24, 31; death cues 229; haplodiploidy and 155, 157, 199; nests 218; predators of wasp nests 189, 190–1, 217; seed-dispersal 329; sex ratio 157–8; superorganisms 39, 110; wasps as ancestors of 5, 30, 40–3, 46, 63, 105, 111, 113; 'wasp kinins' 63; worker 224, 257. *See also individual species name*
*Apanteles* (braconid micro-wasp) 27
*Apis mellifera*. See western honeybee
*Apis mellifera scutellata*. See East African lowland honeybee
apitherapy 60
Apoid wasps 63

Área de Conservación de Guanacaste, Costa Rica 27–8

Aristophanes: *The Wasps* 13

Aristotle 3, 150, 195–207, 200*n*; bees and 159, 195, 197, 198–9, 200, 201, 202, 205–7, 221, 231–2, 241–3, 244, 263, 264–5, 266; dinner-party conversation with 201–67, 201*n*, 240*n*, 244*n*, 267*n*; *Historia Animalium* 197, 208, 242, 244*n*

Asteraceae 322

*Atta* leafcutter ants 257

'awakening dance' 239

*Bacillus thuringiensis* (bacterium) 273

bacteria, insect relationships with 70–5

Banks, Iain: *Wasp Factory, The* 16–17

'beast ants' 42, 43

bees 3–4; altruism and 153, 160, 162–3; Aristotle and 159, 195, 197, 198–9, 200, 201, 202, 205–7, 221, 231–2, 241–3, 244, 263, 264–5, 266; 'bee flowers' 333; beekeeping, history of 203–5; beewolf and 66–75; 209–10, 216, 219; diapause and 136, 139, 140, 141; extinction of 335, 341; haplodiploidy 155; hive structure 209–10, 216; hygiene practices 228–9, 231–2; Hymenoptera group and 24; learning/recognition 245–50, 251, 252, 253–4, 264–5; human fascination with 2–4, 7, 17, 18–19, 21, 202–5, 206, 207; pollination and 311, 312–17, 321, 322, 322*n*, 323, 324, 326, 329–30, 333, 334; social evolution 110–11, 122, 123–4, 125, 127, 153, 160, 162–3; sting 3*n*, 18, 22, 54, 54*n*, 306;

superorganisms 39; task specialisation among 225, 226, 227; venom 60–1; wasp ancestors of 4, 30, 43–6, 61, 105, 140, 323–4; wasp-bee (transitional state that links wasps to bees) 44–6; wasp, closest living relatives to 44–6; worker policing 259. *See also individual species name*

beetles 2, 26; diversity of 5, 23–4; Haldane and 27; parasitoid wasp brood host 28; pest control and 279, 289, 201; pollination and 314, 315, 318; prey of wasps 32–3, 58–9, 64, 69, 70–1, 85, 86, 87; number of species 5, 23–4. *See also individual species name*

beewolf (*Philanthus*) 58, 61, 66–75, 67*n*

behavioural flexibility 123–4

*Belonogaster* (paper wasp) 40, 276, 305–6

beta-ocimene 229

bethylid wasps 279

Bible 13

biological control (biocontrol) 6, 26, 27, 86, 274, 277–308, 316

blue tit 162

bombykol 84–5

braconid micro-wasp 27

bradykinins 62–5

Brisbane, Sir T. 282, 302

Brock, Ryan 59

brood: cannibalism 230; combs 148, 218–19; parasites 217, 230; removal 230, 231

bumblebees 110, 125, 139, 210, 224, 229, 237, 241, 245, 315, 316, 334

*Buprestis* jewel beetle 58–9

butterflies 2, 7; diapause and 169; holometabolous 31; pest control and 274, 283, 286, 287, 289,

303; pollination 274, 312, 315–17, 318, 323. *See also individual species name*

cabbage butterfly (*Pieris rapae*) 283, 303
Cai Lun 211–12, 220
Carson, Rachel: *Silent Spring* 280
cassava 278, 280
caterpillar 14, 22, 25;
    holometabolous 31; parasitoid wasps and 26, 27, 28, 31, 32, 34, 35; pest control and 277, 278, 279, 283, 286, 287, 295, 296–7, 301, 302, 303, 340, 305, 306; pollination and 332; solitary wasp prey 58, 61, 62, 76, 79, 80, 83–4, 85–6, 89, 90, 98, 112, 131, 137, 244. *See individual species name*
celibacy 39, 146, 150
*Cephalonomia stephanoderis* (Bethylid wasp) 279
*Cerceris* 59, 66, 69, 74
Chain, Ernst 72
Chalcidoidea 36
chemical cues 33, 35, 43, 84–90, 94–8, 163–4, 169, 172*n*, 205, 214, 218, 262, 325; 'cues', definition of 240
Christie, Agatha: 'Wasps' Nest' 13
Chrysidoidea 38
Cini, Alessandro 18, 59
classic market theory 177–8
Clever Hans (horse) 87–8
climate change 272, 317, 320, 340–1
co-evolution 4, 45, 61, 72–4, 93, 318, 319, 333
Coleoptera (beetles) 31
colony persistence 207–8
colour perception 205, 245–7, 250–1, 264
concession models 174–6
co-regulated traits 124

cotton 273–4, 282–3, 316–17
COVID-19 64–5, 111, 130, 135, 178, 190*n*
Crabronidae/crabronid wasps 44, 56, 58, 63, 81
Cretaceous period 42, 44, 95; mass extinction event 42
cross-pollination 316–17
cryptic species 23–4
'cues', definition of 240
cuticular hydraocarbons 94, 163–4

Darwin, Charles 3, 6, 22, 52, 68, 77, 79, 80, 205, 235, 242, 250, 281*n*, 293, 294, 330; *On the Origin of Species by Means of Natural Selection* 23, 57, 150
death cues 229
'death dump' 229–30
declines, wasp 340–2
*Dendrobium sinense* (orchid) 331–2
Dhand, Amit 11–13
diapause 136–41, 168, 169
diets 30, 44–5, 138–9, 225, 285–308, 324, 327; amounts of food consumed, measuring 296–308; food ball sequencing 285–8; meat, wasps first develop taste for 32–4; meconium sequencing 293–4; prey DNA, collecting 286–9; resource sharing 293–5; social wasps as opportunistic generalist hunters 295–6, 304–5; vegetarians 4, 16, 30, 31–2, 33, 36, 44, 61, 80, 231, 321. *See also* prey
digestive system 33, 243
diploid organism 149, 156, 199*n*
Diptera 31, 34
*Discoscapa apicula* (extinct species of crabronid wasp) 44
disease control/hygienic behaviour 223, 228–32

division of labour/task
  specialisation 161*n*, 222–9, 232,
  258
DNA 27, 30, 115, 116, 126, 149,
  155, 156, 158, 159, 265, 285–9,
  293, 294; aDNA 293; barcoding
  287; eDNA 286–7
*Dolichovespula* (social wasp) 219,
  260
*Dolichovespula saxonica*. See Saxon
  wasp
dominance interactions 164–5
Dornhaus, Anna 224
'drifters' 187–92
drone flies 316
Dufour, Léon 58–9, 58*n*, 66, 69,
  70, 75

East African lowland honeybee
  (*Apis mellifera scutellata*) 21
Ebola virus 129–30
economic value, nature and 6,
  273–8, 312
ecosystem services 273, 274, 284
ectoparasitoids 25
eDNA (environmental DNA)
  286–7
eggs 12, 15–16, 25, 26, 28, 30, 31,
  32, 33, 35, 36, 37*n*, 38, 54–5,
  71, 74, 75, 100, 101, 318–19;
  haplodiploid genetic system and
  155; queen and 171, 173, 179,
  180–1, 183, 186, 199, 207, 208,
  256, 257–61; social evolution of
  wasps and 108, 109, 112, 114,
  116, 118, 122, 125, 128, 131,
  137; worker policing and 204,
  231, 258–62
Einstein, Albert 337
Emerald jewel wasp (*Ampulex
  compressa*) 65–6, 279
endoparasitoids 25, 35
environmental cohabitation
  342–3
environmental volatility 192–3

epigenetics 116–17
*Epipactis helleborine* (orchid) 332
*Epipactis purpurata* (orchid) 332
eumenid 111, 113–14, 127–8, 135,
  138
Eumeninae 63, 81
European beewolf (*Philanthus
  Triangulum*) 66–75, 67*n*
European hornet (*Vespa crabro*) 19,
  238–9, 261, 340, 342
European paper wasp (*Polistes
  dominula*) 166–7, 169, 170,
  178, 179, 181, 182
Evans, Howard: *The Wasps* 105;
  'Thirteen Ways to Carry a Dead
  Fly' 58; *Wasp Farm* 91
extinctions 31, 39, 42, 43, 89, 272,
  304, 328, 337–8, 340

Fabre, Claire 78
Fabre, Jean-Henri 52–4, 53, 57,
  58–9, 63, 66–70, 75, 76, 77, 78,
  79, 80, 81–2, 83–4, 90, 98,
  101–2, 103, 103*n*, 113, 267*n*,
  279; *Souvenirs Entomologiques*
  52, 58–9
face blindness 252–3
facial markings 164, 165, 166–7,
  252
Fairhead, James 130
fairyflies 26
fall armyworm 277, 281, 303,
  303*n*, 304
family group, altruism and 160–3
fear of wasps 13, 14, 18, 19, 25,
  38
*Ficus* 320
fig wasps 7, 36, 318–21
fights, nest societies and 183–6
fire ant (*Solenopsis invicta*) 229,
  292
Fleming, Alexander 69, 71, 72
flies, pollination and 316
Florey, Howard 72, 72*n*
food ball sequencing 285–8

foraging: cognitive abilities/
recognition and 243–55;
optimal foraging theory 78–9;
social information and 234–43
fossil record 31, 32, 41–4, 95
foundresses (group of females who
found a new colony together)
159–60, 163, 164, 166, 168,
170, 171–2, 173, 174, 178–9,
181, 198
fruit fly 117
functional complementarity 317
fungi 41, 70–1, 72, 73, 74, 292*n*,
337

gall wasps (Cynipidae) 36–7
gastral drumming 238–40, 240*n*
gene expression 64–5, 115–16,
116*n*, 120, 131, 134
'gene of importance' 123
genetic mutation 45, 72, 95, 115,
119, 166
genetically modified crops 273, 277
gene variants 41, 149–53, 154,
157, 162, 172, 172*n*, 182, 186,
188, 189, 190, 235, 259, 263
German yellowjacket. See *Vespula
germanica*
germ theory 69
giant horntail 32
Gibbons, Dr Bob 133
Giurfa, Martin 246–9
Grassé, Pierre-Paul 213–15, 217
Gray, Asa 22
green-leaf volatiles 332
group living, altruism and 160–3

Haeckel, Ernst: *Generelle
Morphologie der Organismen* 57–8
Haldane, J.B.S. 23, 27, 149–51
halictid bees 190
Hamilton, William D. 22, 143,
167, 168, 174, 188–9, 191,
267*n*; Hamilton's Rule 151–63,
168, 171–2, 192–3, 267*n*

handler bias 87–8
haplodiploidy 155–8, 155*n*, 172*n*,
200, 256, 259
Hare, Hope 156–8
Hawaii 237, 297–8, 297*n*
heath potter wasp (*Eumenes
coarctatus*) 14, 63, 111–13,
128–41, 134*n*
Heatley, Norman 72
*Heliothis zea* (moth) 87
'hell ant' 42
*Hemipepsis* (spider wasps) 330–1
hexagonal cells 202, 209–10, 212
hexamerin 138
hibernacula 169–70
histamines 60–3
Hölldobler, Bert 41
holometabolous insects 31, 97
*Homonotus* (spider-hunting wasps)
61, 100, 100*n*
honeybee: African killer bees and
21; age polyethism 123–4;
altruism and 150; Aristotle and
159, 195, 197, 198–9, 200, 201,
202, 205–7, 221, 231–2, 241–3,
244, 263, 264–5, 266;
beekeeping and 203–4; beewolf
and *see* beewolf; behavioural
flexibility 123–4; co-regulated
traits 124; death cues 229;
disease control/hygienic
behaviour 228–9, 230, 231–2;
foragers 123, 237; hive structure
209–10, 216, 219; human
fascination with 2–4, 7, 17,
18–19, 21, 202–5, 206, 207;
juvenile hormone and 125–6;
learning 6, 164, 245–52, 253,
254; perennial colonies 207;
pollination 313–16, 330, 334;
royal jelly and 14–15; social
evolution 122–3, 124, 125, 146,
147, 150, 207–8; sting 3*n*, 18,
22, 54, 54*n*, 306;
superorganisms 39, 121; task

honeybee (*cont ...*)
specialisation 223–9; vespine
wasp parallels 204–5, 207–8,
209–10; Vitellogenin and
124–7, 124*n*; waggle dance
234–42, 240*n*, 263; worker
policing and 259
hornet 13, 19–20, 31, 38, 39, 49,
63–4, 150, 195, 197, 200, 210,
230, 238, 241, 261, 306, 307*n*,
329, 332, 340. *See also
individual species name*
hoverflies 15, 217, 301, 312, 314,
316, 317, 318, 330
human faces, recognition of 245,
252–4, 264
hunting: beewolf and 66–75;
hunting wasps 4, 6, 12, 15, 42,
54, 55–8, 56*n*, 66, 67, 70, 85*n*,
86–7, 90, 93, 99, 120, 243, 275,
278, 279, 284, 295, 327, 328,
328*n*, 340; olfactory skills and
87–90; prey fidelity 58–60; prey
profitability 75–6; processing
prey 75–82; solitary wasps and
50–103, 244, 278–80; spiders,
wasp-hunting 91–102; sting and
52–7; underground/chemical
detection and 83–7; venom and
60–6 *see also* venom
Hunt, Jim 136, 138
husbandry methods 306–8
hyaluronic acid 64–5
hydrogen bonding 220
Hymenoptera 24–5, 25*n*, 30, 31,
33, 37, 43, 57, 71, 74, 105, 156,
160, 199, 238*n*, 296–7, 301
hyperparasitoids 26, 35

ichneumonid wasps 22, 26
indirect fitness 151, 152, 179, 185,
188
intelligence, foraging/hunting and
243–55. *See also* recognition
skills

Intergovernmental Science-Policy
Platform on Biodiversity and
Ecosystem Services (IPBES)
274
International Union for
Conservation of Nature (IUCN)
292; Red List 342
invasive species 19, 22, 86, 166,
208, 272, 280, 292, 293, 296–9,
300*n*, 307*n*, 340
'iron-maiden ants' 42

Janet, Charles 238, 238*n*
Japan 283, 306, 307, 307*n*
Jeanne, Bob 239, 240, 240*n*
*Journal of the Linnean Society* 235
juvenile hormone 125–7, 262

kairomone 86
Kennedy, Patrick 191
Kerr, Warwick 21
kin recognition 163, 168–70,
178–9
kinins 60, 64

Law, Georgia 18, 285, 289
Leadbeater, Elli 179–80
leafcutter ants 74, 257
leafcutter bee (*Megachile rotundata*)
315
learning/cognitive abilities 87–90,
164, 165, 166, 245–55
Lengronne, Thibault 190, 191–2,
217
Lepidoptera 31, 34, 85, 277,
287–8, 303
lesser cotton leafworm (*Anomis
argillacae*) 283
Lester, Phil 22; *The Vulgar Wasp* 22
Linnean Society 235, 330
Lister, Joseph 69
literary references, wasp 12–17
Lubbock, 1st Baron Avebury, Sir
John 6, 250; *Ants, Bees, and
Wasps* 235–6

Mace, Dame Professor Georgina 269, 281*n*
maladaptation 338–40
Malaysia 2, 5, 180, 274, 339
Malyshev, Sergei Ivanovich 45
mammoth wasp 63–4
mandibles 12, 16, 38, 42, 56, 67, 76, 80, 92, 93, 98, 101, 183, 211, 216, 220, 238–9, 240, 322, 338–9
Manipur, India 306–7
Masarinae 321–3
mastoparan 65
Mattos, Alexander Teixeira de 52
mealybug 278, 280
meat, wasps first develop taste for 32–4
Melittidae 324
*Melittosphex burmensis* 44
metapleural gland 43
Mexican free-tailed bat 273
Michener, Charles 190
microarrays 121
*Microplitis croceipes* 87
microsatellite 158–9
micro-wasps 26
milkweed flowers 334
Miocene period 41
Mitoparan 65
molecular sequencing 30
monogamy hypothesis 160–1, 161, 162
Morley, Margaret Warner: *Wasps and Their Ways* 231, 250–1, 253, 254, 275, 282, 309
mud-dauber wasp (*Sceliphron*) 91–6, 338–9
mutualism 318, 331, 332

National Trust 134
native wasps 283–4, 301, 343
natural selection 23, 24, 50, 52, 79, 82, 93, 94, 99, 109, 140, 162, 205, 206, 240, 332
nectar foragers 124, 125

neonicotinoids 64
nests 208, 216, 219, 233–4; annual nesting cycle 207–9; brood combs 212–13, 218–19; densities 299–300; disease control/hygienic behaviour 228–32; division of labour/task specialisation in 222–7; drifters 187–92; paper envelope 215–18; recognition within 163–70; size of 300–1; social structure/ hierarchy within 108–11, 143–93; 'stigmergy' 213–15; structure 209–21; superorganism 108–9
New Zealand 22, 208, 289–94, 292*n*, 296–7, 299, 300, 301, 307*n*
nitric oxide 74
*Noctua segetum* (common cutworm or turnip moth) 279
non-native species 279–81, 290–4
Northern blotting 121
*Nosema* (fungus) 228
nurses 108, 123, 223, 225

odour detecting 86–90
optimal foraging theory 78–9
orange-legged furrow bee (*Halictus rubicundus*) 141
orchids 7, 324–7, 331–2
Ormerod, Edward Latham: *British Social Wasps* 281–2, 302, 341
Orussidae 33
*Osmia* bees 315
Osten, Wilhelm von 88
Ouamouno, Emole 129, 130
ovaries/ovarian development: queen suppressing worker 257–8; social evolution, ovarian blueprint for 113–28, 141; worker policing and 257–63
Ovid 197

ovipositor 25, 26, 31–2, 33, 34, 35, 37, 37*n*, 55, 85*n*, 327
*Oxybelus* 56

Panama 113, 120, 121, 122, 145–6, 183, 188, 189, 192, 339
paper envelope, wasp nest 210–18
paper wasps 39–40, 110, 113–14, 165, 166, 170, 283, 287, 288, 303
parasites 5, 25, 30, 35, 36, 38, 148, 149, 161, 161*n*, 162, 164, 174, 192, 216, 217, 228, 230, 318, 342
parasitoidism 34, 38
parasitoid wasps: biocontrol and 6, 277–81; chemical cues and 85–90; diet/prey 34–7; dispause and 138, 139; extinction and 340, 341; fig wasps 318, 318*n*; identifying 26–7; number of species 27–8; pollination 327, 328*n*; sting and 54–5
Pardi, Leo 148–9, 153, 165, 168–9
pasta 118–19, 127
Pasteur, Louis 69
Paul IV, Pope 13
Pavlovian (or classical) conditioning 88–9
Peckham, George and Elizabeth 58, 77–81, 91, 93, 95–6, 103*n*, 113
penicillin 71, 72, 72*n*, 73
*Pepsis heros* (tarantula hawk wasp) 101
pest control 2, 6, 7, 269–308, 342, 343; biological control (or biocontrol) 277–308; diets/prey, analysing 285–308; effectiveness of wasps at controlling pest populations 302–3; native species and 279–80, 283–4; non-native species and 279–81; parasitoid wasps and 6, 277–81; pesticides and 272, 277, 280, 283, 305; resource sharing of

wasp populations and 293–5; RHS Garden at Wisley 299–302; social wasps and 276, 281–4, 288–9, 295–6, 304–8; solitary hunting wasps and 278–80, 284*n*, 295; training wasps to favour pest types in particular areas 305; yellowjacket or hornet nests and 306–7; Zambian agriculture and 276–8, 281, 304, 305–6, 339
pesticides 61–2, 64, 272, 277, 280, 283, 305, 341
Petrunkevitch, Alexander 101–2, 102*n*
phenotypic flexibility 114
pheromones 54*n*, 84–5, 172*n*, 205, 214, 218, 262, 325
*Philanthus* (beewolf) 58, 61, 66–75, 67*n*
phorid flies 230
Phosphorus-32 (32P) 121
phylogenetic tree 29–46
Pickering, John 145–6
picnic wasp. *See* yellowjacket
pit viper 62
plasticity, behavioural 118, 120, 123–4, 304–5
Plato 199, 213, 232, 251
play, insects and 96–7
pleiotropy 126
Pliny the Elder 198
*Poecilpompilus mixtus* (spider wasp) 97
*Polistes* (paper wasp) 39–40, 113; altruism and 150–63, 161*n*, 167, 168, 170, 176, 179, 186–90, 192–3; diapause and 138–40, 169; drifters 187–92; Hamilton's Rule and 151–62, 168, 171–2, 192–3; nests 217, 222, 230; pest control 283, 287, 293–5, 303, 304, 305–6; pollination 334; queen selection 171–86; recognition skills

163–70, 178–9, 252; social behaviour/evolution of 110, 119, 120–2, 123, 126, 138–9, 143, 145–53, 159–93, 223–4, 252

*Polistes annularis* (paper wasp) 283

*Polistes canadensis* (paper wasp) 145, 146, 173*n*, 182–3, 186, 188, 191

*Polistes chinensis* (Asian paper wasp) 283, 293

*Polistes fuscatus* (American paper wasp) 165–6, 303

*Polistes humilis* (common paper wasp) 287, 293

*Polistes satan* (paper wasp) 303

pollination 6–7, 18, 30, 36, 274–5, 309–34; back-up pollinators, role of wasps as 328–9; 'bee flowers' 333; bumblebee and 315; butterflies and 316–17; cotton pollination 316–17; cross-pollinated plants 316–17; fig wasps and 318–21; flies and 316; honeybee and 313–16, 330, 334; insect pollinators, importance of 311–12; Masarinae and 321–2; orchids and 324–7, 331–2; parasitoid wasps and 327; plant manipulation of wasp behaviour 324–7, 331–4; pollen transportation 329–30, 333–4; pollen wasps and 321–4; seed dispersal 329; social wasps and 327–9; solitary bees and 315; solitary wasps and 326; 'wasp flowers' 333–4; wasps and 318–34

Pompilidae (spider-hunting wasps) 12, 63, 80–1, 96–101

*Popillia japonica* (beetle) 86

population cycle 298–9

potatoes 126–7

Potter Wasp Guild 135

prey: beewolf hunting and 66–75; olfactory skills and 87–90; prey fidelity 58–60; processing 75–82; profitability 75–6; solitary wasps and 50–103, 244, 278–80; spiders as 91–102; sting and 52–7; underground/ chemical detection 83–7; venom and 60–6 *see also* venom

proboscis 321, 323

propodeum 34

*Prorops nasuta* (Bethylid wasp) 279

prosopagnosia 252–3

*Prosphex* (fossil wasp genus) 45

*Prosphex anthophilos* (fossil wasp) 45

*Psenulus* 44

queen: annual nesting cycle and 207–8; Aristotle and 197–8, 199; death 230; evolution of role 112–13, 114, 117, 118, 119, 120–1, 123, 125–6, 127–8, 131, 136, 138–9, 140, 147; haplodiploidy and 155–6; honeybee 207–8; mating flight 204; nesting cycle and 207–8; recognition skills and 168; royal jelly and 14–15; selection of 171–86, 204; worker policing and 258–63

radio tags 190, 192, 223

Rau, Phil and Nellie 51*n*, 91, 92

Réaumur, René de 136

recognition skills: colour perception 205, 245–7, 250–1, 264; facial markings 164, 165, 166–7, 252; foraging and 243–55; human faces 245, 252–4, 264; individual 163–8; kin 168–70, 178–9; spatial maps 251; visual landmarks 245, 251

recruitment, social information and 234–42

Reinhard, Edward G.: *The Witchery of Wasps* 47
relatedness 154–61, 162, 172*n*, 174, 176, 177, 193, 259, 259*n*, 260–2
reproductive skew theory 173–7
RNA (ribonucleic acid) 116, 116*n*, 131, 134
Rocha e Silva, Maurício 62–3
rock ant (*Temnothorax albipennis*) 224
*Ropalidia* (paper wasp) 40, 305–6
Royal Horticultural Society: Wisley Gardens 299–302
rules of thumb 170, 178–9
Russell, Eric Frank: *Wasp* 13

SARS-CoV-2 64
sawflies 31–7
Saxon wasp (*Dolichovespula saxonica*) 260
scientific publications process 191
scoliid wasp 43, 63–4, 80
'scopa' (pollen brushes) 322
seed dispersal 329
*Segestria* (tube-dwelling) spider 98–9
selective sweep 166
Senegalese Creation story 13–14
sex ratio 157–8
Shafer, George D.: *Ways of a Mud Dauber* 91
Shakespeare, William 3, 13, 35; *The Taming of the Shrew* 9
'signals', definition of 240
silkworm moth (*Bombyx mori*) 85
sixth mass extinction 338
Smith, Adam 221, 222, 223, 224
Smithsonian Tropical Research Institute 113, 146, 148
social fluid 172–3, 219
social information 233–43
social insects 40, 58*n*; age polyethism and 123, 223–4; altruism and 151, 159, 161*n*; diapause and 136, 139; division of labour 222, 223–4; hygiene and 228, 231; juvenile hormone and 126; nest structures 213, 214; numbers of 110; ovarian development 127; recognition skills 163; social information and 234; solitary ancestors of 125; superorganisms among 109; trophallaxis and 172*n*
social life, evolution of 22, 39, 105–93; altruism and 150–63, 161*n*, 167, 168, 170, 176, 179, 186–90, 192–3, 267*n*; diapause blueprint for 136–41; drifters 187–90; Hamilton's Rule and 151–62, 168, 171–2, 192–3; nest and *see* nest; ovarian blueprint for 113–35, 141; potter wasps and 111–12, 113, 128–35, 134*n*, 136–7, 139; queen selection 170, 171–86; recognition skills *see* recognition skills; simple societies, *Polistes* 110, 119, 121–2, 123, 146–7; social insects, numbers of 110; superorganisms 108–19; unrelated subordinate wasps 178–9
social wasps: annual cycle 208; ants and 40–1; cuticular hydrocarbons and 94; declines 340, 342; gastral drumming 238–40, 241–2; nests 216–17; pest control 281–4, 284*n*, 285–90, 293, 294–8, 298*n*, 300*n*, 301, 304–8; pollination 327–8; popularity of 22; solitary wasp ancestor, evolution from 111, 113, 122, 127; societies 110, 113, 114, 122, 127, 149; species of 39–40; sting 38–9, 54, 54*n*, 56*n*, 60. *See also individual species name*
sociobiology 190, 297*n*

sociogenomics 120
solitary bees 75, 122, 314, 315
solitary digger wasps 76–84, 86, 90, 91, 279
solitary hunting wasp 4, 15–16, 56*n*, 90, 278–80, 284*n*, 295, 327
solitary potter wasps 14, 63, 111–13, 128–41, 134*n*
solitary wasps: biocontrol 278–80, 284*n*, 295; beewolf and 66–75; families of 59*n*; hunting/prey and 50–103, 244, 278–80; life cycle 14, 50–1; number of species 57; 'original bee' and 4; pollination and 324–6, 327, 328; social evolution 108, 110, 111–41, 134*n*; solitary digger wasps *see* solitary digger wasps; solitary hunting wasp *see* solitary hunting wasp; solitary potter wasps *see* solitary potter wasps; sting 38–9, 52–7, 80–1; writings of early naturalists/Wasp Whisperers and 49–103
sooty beech scale insect (*Ultracoelostoma assimile*) 290–1
spatial maps 251
species extinctions 272–3
species, number of wasp 2, 3, 4–5, 7, 24–8
sphecid wasps 63, 91, 95, 97
Sphecidae digger wasps 63
*Sphecomyrma freyi* (fossil ant) 43
Sphecomyrminae 43
spiders, hunting of 12, 58, 63, 91–102, 244, 244*n*
Stenogastrinae 15–16, 40, 180, 210
stigmergy 213–15, 217
sting: bee 3*n*, 22; evolution of 31–2, 37–9, 54–5, 54*n*, 85*n*; human hatred of 3, 18, 22, 25, 38–9; neurotoxins and 19;

pollination and 45–6; prey carrying and 56; protocols 80–1; removing 54; solitary wasp hunting and 52–7, 56*n*, 58*n*, 66, 67, 75, 76–8, 80–1, 85*n*, 91–2, 93, 96, 278–9; venom *see* venom
*Streptomyces* (bacteria) 73, 74
Streptomycin (antibiotic) 73
superorganisms 39, 40, 74, 108–19, 121, 161*n*, 203, 206, 214, 226, 342
symbiosis 35
Symphyta 31
*Synagris cornuta* (solitary eumenid wasp) 127–8

*Tachysphex pechumani* 342
tarantula 12, 97, 101, 102*n*
task specialisation 223–9
Taylor, Benjamin 182, 239, 240, 240*n*
Teide National Park, Tenerife 314
Thomas, Dylan 7–8
thrips 44, 45, 160, 316, 323
Thynnidae 59*n*, 324–7, 331–2
Tibbetts, Liz 165, 166, 167
*Trichogramma* 277–8
Trichoptera 31
Trivers, Robert 156–8
trophic chains 26
tug-of-war models 175–6
turnip sawfly (*Athalia rosae*) 32
Turrillazzi, Stefano 169

UK Priority Species 342

*Varroa destructor* (mite) 228
vegetarian diet 4, 16, 30, 31–2, 33, 36, 44, 61, 80, 231, 321
venom 12, 19, 25, 35, 35*n*, 37, 37*n*, 38–9, 50, 52, 53–4, 54*n*, 55, 60–6, 67, 69, 70, 76, 80, 96, 169
vertical transmission 73

*Vespa bicolor* (hornet) 332
*Vespa mandarinia* (giant Asian hornet) 19–20, 241, 306
Vespinae 39
vespine wasps 40, 101; annual nesting cycle 207–8; Aristotle and 197–8, 200–8, 210, 213, 216–17, 219, 221, 224–8, 232, 238–44, 249, 250, 252; cognitive abilities, foraging and 243–55; hygiene in nests of 227–32; law and order in nests of 255–63; nest building 210–21; pest control and 6, 253, 257, 259, 261, 282, 285, 287, 289, 290–5, 298*n*, 300*n*, 306, 307, 307*n*; pollination and 321, 340, 341; social information, use of 232–43; task specialisation 222–7; worker policing and 204, 253–4, 258–63. *See also individual species name*
*Vespula germanica* (German yellowjacket) 223, 239, 287, 293, 294, 296, 332
*Vespula pensylvanica* (western yellowjacket) 237, 297
*Vespula vulgaris* (common yellowjacket) see yellowjacket, common (*Vespula vulgaris*)
Virgil 197
viruses 25, 35, 64, 129–30
visual landmarks 245, 251
Vitellogenin 124–7, 124*n*

waggle dance 234–42, 240*n*, 263
waist, wasp 13–14, 15, 30, 31, 34, 37, 43, 64, 76–7, 91, 98, 101, 276
Walters, John 132–3, 135
wasp-bee (transitional state linking wasps to bees) 44–6
'wasp flowers' 333–4
Wasp Hound 87, 88, 90
Wasp Whisperers 47–103

*Wasp Woman, The* (film) 14–15, *15*
Wcislo, Dr Bill 146, 147, 168
Weale, James Mansel 330–1
West-Eberhard, Mary Jane 22, 113, 119–20, 131, 183; *Developmental Plasticity and Evolution* 117–18; *The Wasps* 105
western honeybee (*Apis mellifera*) 5, 21, 203, 313–15. *See also* honeybee
western yellowjacket. See *Vespula pensylvanica*
White, Gilbert 298–9
Wilson, Edward O. 41, 297*n*
Wisconsin Natural History Society 77
Wisley Gardens, Royal Horticultural Society 299–302
worker bee 14, 44, 54, 54*n*, 123, 124, 146, 150, 198, 241
worker wasp: altruism and 150–64, 193; Aristotle 197–9; determination of caste 15, 110, 114, 117, 118, 119, 120, 121, 136, 138–41, 181–2, 183–4, 185; diversity of behaviours within 122; drifters 188, 189, 190–2; gene expression in 120, 121, 125–6, 127–8; haplodiploidy and 155–6; nest and 204, 208–9, 210, 212, 214, 216, 218, 219, 222–7, 229, 230, 231–2; recognition skills *see* recognition skills; roles of 108, 112–13, 125, 126, 127–8, 221–32; worker policing 204, 253–4, 258–63

xyelid 32

yellowjacket, common (*Vespula vulgaris*): annual nesting cycle 207–8; Aristotle and 197–8, 200–8, 210, 213, 216–17, 219,

221, 224–8, 232, 238–44, 249, 250, 252; cognitive abilities 6, 203, 243–55; colony persistence 208; declines 340–1; diet 289–95; disease control/hygiene in nests of 227–32; eggs 16; human perception of 6, 24, 203; invasive species 208–9; law and order in nests of 255–63; life cycles 197, 200; nest densities 299–300; nest sizes 300, 301; nest structure 148, 207, 208, 216, 219–21, 233–4; pest control and 6, 253, 257, 259, 261, 282, 285, 287, 289, 290–5, 298n, 300n, 306, 307, 307n;

pollination and 6–7, 332; prey biomass 300–1; social evolution 6, 110, 146–7, 148, 150, 223–32; social information, use of 232–43; sting 38–9; task specification 223–7; venom 63; worker 223–5, 226, 230, 256–8, 261; worker policing and 204, 253–4, 258–63
yellow-legged Asian hornet (*Vespa velutina*) 19, 329

Zambia 276–8, 281, 304, 305–6, 339
*Zethus miniatus* 113–14, 115–16
zombification 65–6, 279